O9-CFT-889

"In this book, George and Bennett explain how research methods such as process tracing and comparative case studies are designed, carried out, and used as the basis for theory development in social science. They provide an invaluable research guide for any scholar interested in the case study approach. But the book is much more than an account of how to do case study research. The authors also offer a sophisticated discussion of the philosophy of science that will be useful to anyone interested in the place of case-study methods in broader debates about social science methodology, and they give a discerning analysis of policy-relevant theory that is sure to draw the attention of a research community increasingly concerned about the social and political relevance of modern social science. In scope, clarity, and erudition, this book sets a new standard not only in the analysis of case study methods, but also in the study of social science methods more broadly."

—*David Dessler, Associate Professor of Government,*
College of William & Mary

"This book combines clear and concise instructions on how to do qualitative research with sophisticated but accessible epistemological reasons for that advice. The volume provides step-by-step templates on ways to design research, compare across cases, congruence test and process trace, and use typological theories. This guidance is illustrated with dozens of concrete examples. Almost no other methodology text comes close to matching the authors' top-to-bottom synthesis of philosophy of science and practical advice."

—*Colin Elman, Executive Director,*
Consortium on Qualitative Research Methods,
Assistant Professor of Political Science, Arizona State University

"This landmark study offers to scholars of all methodological persuasions a philosophically informed, theoretically nuanced, and methodologically detailed treatment of case study analysis. With this book Alexander George and Andrew Bennett help all of us in improving our research, teaching, and disciplinary debates."

—*Peter J. Katzenstein, Walter S. Carpenter, Jr.,*
Professor of International Studies, Cornell University

"*Case Studies and Theory Development in the Social Sciences* makes an indispensable contribution to the growing literature on qualitative methods in the social sciences. It provides a definitive analysis of case study methods

and research designs, anchors those methods in contemporary philosophy of science, and argues that case study, statistical, and formal approaches can and should be mutually reinforcing in the development and testing of social theories."
—*Jack S. Levy, Board of Governors' Professor, Rutgers University*

"Today, more and more social scientists recognize the importance of cases in social and political research and are looking for new ways to make their research more case-oriented. George and Bennett show how in this important new work. The beauty of their approach is their careful integration of theory and method and their conviction that the pursuit of empirical knowledge is profoundly theory dependent."
—*Charles Ragin, Professor of Sociology, University of Arizona*

"This is an extraordinarily valuable book—a guide written with the practitioner in mind, very sophisticated in its approach to the subject, but loaded with practical advice. George and Bennett show how systematic, rigorous, and above all meaningful case study work is to be done. This is the sort of book scholars—and not just graduate students—will want to come back to over and over again."
—*Marc Trachtenberg, Professor of Political Science,*
University of California at Los Angeles

"Andy Bennett and Alex George have written an immensely helpful practical guide to the case method. It offers sharp insight on scientific inference and very useful how-to guidance on doing case studies. Graduate students in social science: don't leave home without it!"
—*Stephen Van Evera, Professor of Political Science,*
Massachusetts Institute of Technology

"The history of social science shows that well-designed case studies can be both a fertile source of new theories and a powerful tool for testing them. *Case Studies and Theory Development in the Social Sciences* raises our understanding of case study methodology to a new level of rigor and sophistication. George and Bennett provide a careful analysis of the virtues and pitfalls of comparative case study research and offer valuable advice for any scholar engaged in qualitative research. The more widely this book is read, the better future social science will be."
—*Stephen M. Walt, Robert and Renée Belfer Professor of International*
Affairs, John F. Kennedy School of Government, Harvard University

Case Studies and Theory Development
in the Social Sciences

The BCSIA Studies in International Security book series is edited at the Belfer Center for Science and International Affairs at Harvard University's John F. Kennedy School of Government and published by The MIT Press. The series publishes books on contemporary issues in international security policy, as well as their conceptual and historical foundations. Topics of particular interest to the series include the spread of weapons of mass destruction, internal conflict, the international effects of democracy and democratization, and U.S. defense policy.

A complete list of BCSIA Studies appears at the back of this volume.

Case Studies and Theory Development in the Social Sciences

Alexander L. George and Andrew Bennett

BCSIA Studies in International Security

MIT Press
Cambridge, Massachusetts
London, England

Copyright © 2005 by the Belfer Center for Science and
International Affairs
John F. Kennedy School of Government
Harvard University
Cambridge, Massachusetts 02138
(617) 495-1400

All rights reserved. No part of this book may be reproduced, stored in a retrieval system,
or transmitted in any form or by any means—electronic, electrostatic, magnetic tape,
mechanical, photocopying, recording, or otherwise—without permission in writing from
the Belfer Center for Science and International Affairs,
79 John F. Kennedy Street, Cambridge, MA 02138.

Library of Congress Cataloging-in-Publication Data

George, Alexander L.
Case studies and theory development in the social sciences / Alexander L. George and
Andrew Bennett.
p.   cm.—(BCSIA studies in international security)
Includes bibliographical references and index.
ISBN-13: 978-0-262-07257-1 (hc. : alk. paper)—978-0-262-57222-4 (pbk. : alk. paper)
ISBN-10: 0-262-07257-2 (hc. : alk. paper)—0-262-57222-2 (pbk. : alk. paper)
1. Social sciences—Methodology.   2. Social sciences—Case studies.
I. Bennett, Andrew.   II. Title.   III. Series.

H61.G46   2005
300.72.2—dc22   2004064985

10   9   8   7

For Gabriel Almond,
A dear friend and esteemed colleague whose support and
encouragement made a vast difference.

—ALG

and

For Sophie Ruina Bennett,
In hopes of an equally long and well-lived life.

—AB

Contents

Preface

An extended methodological dialogue is bringing the comparative advantages of case study methods for theory development into sharper focus. Our own personal dialogue began with intermittent conversations in the 1990s on our independent work on case study methods. We both felt that the time was ripe to draw on the lessons learned from the widespread use of sophisticated case study methods developed in recent decades. These include Alexander George's method of "structured, focused comparison of cases," which outlines process-tracing and other within-case modes of analysis as key complements or alternatives to controlled comparison of cases, Arend Lijphart and Harry Eckstein's extremely useful elaborations of different theory-building kinds of case studies, and Charles Ragin's analysis of interactions effects and comparative methods of studying them.

This book draws on the work of many scholars over the past thirty years to raise the standards and explicate the procedures of theory-oriented case study methods. Further experience with theory-oriented case study research will no doubt lead to further refinements. This book seeks to advance earlier discussions of case study methods in three particular areas. First, in contrast to earlier discussions that focus on case comparisons, we emphasize that qualitative research usually involves a combination of cross-case comparisons and within-case analysis using the methods of congruence testing and process-tracing. Within-case methods of analysis can greatly reduce the well-known risks of inferential errors that can arise from using comparative methods alone. Second, we elaborate on the methods of congruence testing and process-tracing, discussing them in detail and providing examples from recent research. Third, we develop the concept of typological theorizing, which resembles both Robert K. Merton's discussion of "middle-range theory" and Paul Lazarsfeld's notion of a "property space." We argue that typological theories involving several variables can better capture the complexity of social life than the two-variable typological theories that are common in the social sciences, and we offer methods for building typological theories in ways that keep this complexity manageable and clarify the task of selecting which cases to study.

In the process of writing this book, we have attempted through conferences, workshops, a web site, and other organized efforts to stimulate interest in improving and disseminating case study methods. In particular, together with Colin Elman of Arizona State University and David Collier of the University of California at Berkeley, we have established the Consortium on Qualitative Research Methods (CQRM), which sponsors an annual training institute in these methods for advanced graduate students and junior faculty. The institute convenes each January at Arizona State University, which generously funds the consortium with member departments and research institutes. In addition, we have assisted David Collier in the creation of a new Qualitative Methods section of the American Political Science Association. Information on both the Qualitative Methods Section and CQRM can be found on their shared web site (www.asu.edu/clas/polisci/cqrm/).

A note is in order regarding the development of our own interests in this subject and the division of labor in this book. Alexander George's interest in case study methodology developed in the 1960s while he was a researcher at the RAND Corporation working on generic problems of avoiding and managing interstate conflict during the Cold War. The first of these problems concerned extended deterrence on behalf of weaker U.S. allies; soon thereafter the research program extended to problems of using coercive diplomacy to reverse an adversary's action against an ally or friendly neutrals, and then to managing conflicts to avoid unwanted escalation.

George was interested in finding ways of studying historical instances of these generic problems that would permit valid, usable "lessons" to be drawn from case findings. These lessons should be formulated in ways that would help policy specialists diagnose accurately new cases of each of these phenomena so that informed judgments could be made in deciding whether and how to use one of these strategies in each new situation. George and his RAND colleagues found little in the academic literature that provided methods for studying historical experience from this perspective. Accordingly, it was necessary to devise a case study methodology to analyze past instances of each of these generic problems to identify conditions and procedures that were associated with successful or failed outcomes. The challenge was to find ways of doing comparative analysis of a number of instances of each generic problem in ways that would draw analytical explanations of each case into a broader, more complex theory, one that would discourage reliance on a single historical analogy.[1]

The aim was to identify more specific, differentiated causal patterns of successful and ineffective ways of employing each strategy. These patterns would initially consist of generalizations of quite limited scope. Such middle-range theories on deterrence, coercive diplomacy, and crisis management would consist of a variety of conditional, contingent generalizations (for a discussion of our use of middle-range theory, see Chapters 11 and 12).

For this purpose, George adapted methods of historical explanation to convert descriptive explanations of case outcomes into analytic explanations comprised of variables.[2] This procedure made use of an inductive approach for theory-building, but it was *analytic* induction, not raw empiricism. The black boxes of decision-making and strategic interaction were opened up and efforts were made to study actual processes of decision-making and of strategic interaction insofar as available data permitted.

In this research, George and his colleagues were not interested in— and indeed their methods did not permit—using the findings of a few cases that were not necessarily representative to project a probability distribution of different patterns discovered for the entire universe of instances of, for example, deterrence. Rather, contingent generalizations were intended to help policy specialists first to diagnose and then to prescribe for new situations, much as medical doctors do in clinical settings. This theme runs through all of the publications of George's research program over the years and finds its latest, most detailed statement in Chap-

---

1. The key objective of the important book by Richard E. Neustadt and Ernest R. May, *Thinking in Time: The Uses of History for Decision Making* (New York: Free Press, 1986), is to suggest various ways in which policymakers can avoid relying on a single historical analogy. However, these authors do not address the question of how the lessons of a number of cases of a given phenomenon can be cumulated to provide a differentiated theory. For a more recent statement on the need to derive "lessons" from historical experience, see William W. Jarosz with Joseph S. Nye, Jr., "The Shadow of the Past: Learning From History in National Security Decision Making," in Philip Tetlock et. al., *Behavior, Society, and International Conflict*, Volume 3 (New York: Oxford University Press, 1993), pp. 162–189.

2. In Harry Eckstein's terminology, an ideographic atheoretical explanation was converted into a "disciplined configurative" study. An early explicit example of this procedure was contained in Gabriel Almond, Scott Flanagan, and Robert Mundt, eds., *Crisis, Choice, and Change: Historical Studies in Political Development* (Boston: Little, Brown, 1973), pp. 22–28.

ter 12 of his 1993 book on *Bridging the Gap* between scholarly research and policymaking.

Another early step in George's development of what he later termed the method of "structured, focused comparison" was his codification of Nathan Leites' concept of "operational code beliefs." George converted Leites' analysis into a set of *general questions* that could be asked in studying the operational code beliefs of other elites and individual leaders. He called attention to the potential use of the set of philosophical and instrumental beliefs embraced by an operational code in comparative studies of leaders.[3] A large number of these types of studies were done after the publication of George's codification of operational code beliefs.

George's comparative work on deterrence led to the further development of the structured, focused method.[4] He published an early version of this method in 1979, greatly elaborating on the brief description of it in his 1974 book on deterrence.[5] Also in 1979, George published a companion piece that addressed more detailed aspects of the method.[6] This second article provided the first detailed statement about process-tracing in case studies and the congruence method, both of which receive detailed treatment in the present book.

George also introduced the structured, focused method into a course he team-taught with several historians. This collaboration resulted in a book co-authored with Gordon Craig, *Force and Statecraft*, which has been updated several times since first published by Oxford University Press in 1983. George also taught a Ph.D. level seminar on structured, focused

3. Alexander L. George, "The 'Operational Code': A Neglected Approach to the Study of Political Leaders and Decision-Making," *International Studies Quarterly*, Vol. 13, No. 2 (June 1969), pp. 190–222. Ole Holsti contributed to the refinement of operational code research, and Stephen Walker has developed a detailed research program and many publications on operational codes.

4. See Alexander L. George and Richard Smoke, *Deterrence in American Foreign Policy: Theory and Practice* (New York: Columbia University Press, 1974), pp. 95–103. The earlier book, *The Limits of Coercive Diplomacy*, edited by Alexander L. George, David K. Hall, and William E. Simons (Boston: Little, Brown, 1971), was a comparative study of three cases, but did not explicitly follow the rubrics of structured, focused comparison. However, this was the research design of *U.S.-Soviet Security Cooperation: Achievements, Failures, Lessons,* coedited with Philip T. Farley and Alexander Dallin (New York: Oxford University Press, 1988).

5. Alexander L. George, "Case Studies and Theory Development: The Method of Structured, Focused Comparison," in Paul Gordon Lauren, ed., *Diplomatic History: New Approaches* (New York: Free Press, 1979).

6. Alexander L. George, "The Causal Nexus Between Cognitive Beliefs and Decision-Making Behavior: The 'Operational Code' Belief System," in Lawrence S. Falkowski, ed., *Psychological Models in International Politics* (Boulder, Colo.: Westview Press, 1979), pp. 95–124.

comparison through the 1980s that became a required course at Stanford for graduate students in comparative politics. Many international relations students took it as well, and it led to the completion of many theses and to the publication of numerous books using the structured, focused method.

Andrew Bennett's interest and training in case study methods began when he was one of George's undergraduate students at Stanford University in the early 1980s. Bennett then used qualitative methods in books on Soviet and Russian military interventions and burden-sharing in the 1991 Persian Gulf War.[7] Bennett has taught a graduate seminar in case study methods at Georgetown since 1997.

This book is very much a product of close co-authorship, and each of us has contributed to every chapter, but it is worth noting which author is primarily responsible for each chapter. Alex George is the primary author of Chapters 3, 4, 5, 8, 9, 12, and the Appendix, while Andy Bennett is the primary author of Chapters 2, 6, and 11. Chapters 1, 7, and 10 were truly joint efforts with equal contributions by both authors.

Organization of the Book

It may be helpful to steer readers toward the chapters that are likely to meet their interests.

Chapter 1 surveys the developments over a period of years that have improved the direction and quality of case study research and its contributions to theory development. Readers will note that our objective in this book, as in our previous works, is to raise the standards for case studies and explicate procedures for improving their value.

Chapter 2 provides a concrete demonstration of how case studies combined with quantitative methods have contributed to the development of research on democratic peace theory. It illustrates of one of the major themes of the book, namely the purposes best served by different research methods, and how knowledge cumulates within a research agenda.

These two chapters should satisfy general readers who want to understand the role and contribution of case studies for the development of theories but have no plans for doing such research themselves.

For readers who are undertaking Ph.D. dissertations and for instructors who offer course work and guidance on case study methods, we

---

7. Andrew Bennett, *Condemned to Repetition? The Rise, Fall, and Reprise of Soviet-Russian Military Interventionism, 1973–1996* (Cambridge, Mass.: MIT Press, 1999); and Andrew Bennett, Joseph Lepgold, and Danny Unger, eds., *Friends in Need: Burden-Sharing in the Gulf War* (New York: St. Martin's Press, 1997).

present a manual in Part II and Part III of the book. A detailed Note to Parts Two and Three provides additional information on the development of the manual for doing case study research. We have also included an Appendix, "Studies That Illustrate Research Design," which briefly reviews the research designs of numerous books. We expect these ingenious and varied research designs to be helpful to Ph.D. students contemplating such research and to professors in designing instruction on case methods.

Acknowledgments

This book would not have been possible without the support of many programs and individuals. We wish to thank the MacArthur Foundation for funding a conference that helped launch the book project; the Carnegie Corporation of New York for additional research funding; and the Stanford University Center for International Security and Cooperation and Columbia University's History and Political Science Departments for sponsoring workshops on our book.

We want to give special thanks to David Dessler, Jack Levy, David Collier, Colin Elman, Miriam Fendius Elman, James Mahoney, Gary Goertz, and Bear Braumoeller for insightful suggestions on major portions of the manuscript. We want to thank many other colleagues as well for their useful suggestions on various chapters, including Hayward Alker, Robert Art, Pierre Atlas, Aaron Belkin, Aaron Boosehecker, Henry Brady, Lynn Eden, Leslie Eliason, Mary Jane Fox, David Friedman, John Lewis Gaddis, John Gerring, Emily Goldman, Jack Goldstone, Stuart Gottlieb, Thomas Homer-Dixon, Ronald Jepperson, Chaim Kaufmann, Jane Kellett-Cramer, Charles Kiami, Deborah Larson, Jeff Legro, Roy Licklider, Dan Lindley, Daniel Little, Andy Loomis, Timothy McKeown, Ron Mitchell, Andrew Moravcsik, Gerry Munck, Dan Nexon, Charles Ragin, Volker Rittberger, Scott Sagan, Steve Saideman, Daniel Schwartz, Jack Snyder, Detlef Sprinz, Brian Taylor, Charles Tilly, Stephen Van Evera, David Waldner, Steve Walt, and Yael Wolinsky.

Michael Boyle provided excellent suggestions for improving the entire manuscript to make it more accessible to Ph.D. students contemplating case study research. Eliana Vasquez provided much essential support in a cheerful and efficient manner.

We wish to thank Sean Lynn-Jones and the Belfer Center for Science and International Affairs and MIT Press for hosting a conference on our book and for outstanding help at every stage of the publishing process. Miriam Avins did an excellent job as copyeditor in streamlining and clarifying a complex manuscript. Alex George expresses deep appreciation to Belinda Yeomans for her years of invaluable research assistance and administrative services, and Andy Bennett thanks her for her exceptional work in organizing a manuscript written on two coasts by authors incompletely socialized to e-mail.

Finally, we want to express particular thanks to Bob Keohane and Gary King for insightful and very useful suggestions on an earlier draft of our manuscript. Their constructive approach to our work has been especially valuable in view of the fact that we express important disagreements with their book, *Designing Social Inquiry* (co-authored with Sidney Verba, who lacked time to give us comments). Our disagreements have been intellectual, not personal, and they stem from a shared interest in improving research methods of all kinds. One of our central themes is that statistical methods, case studies, and formal models should be regarded as complementary, rather than competitive. Research can progress more effectively through diverse methods than it can through any one method alone.

—Alexander L. George
Stanford, California

—Andrew Bennett
Washington, D.C.
September 2004

Part I
Case Studies and Social Science

Chapter 1

Case Studies and Theory Development

After decades of rapid and contentious change, social science research methods are entering a new phase of development conducive to cross-method collaboration and multi-method work. The changes in these methods over the past four decades have been truly revolutionary. With improvements in computing capabilities, databases, and software, statistical methods and formal models increased rapidly in their sophistication and their prevalence in published research in the 1960s and 1970s. While qualitative and case study methods have also become more sophisticated, the proportion of published research using these methods declined sharply in the 1960s and 1970s, as these methods had already been prominent or even dominant in the social sciences, and their share of the social science market naturally declined as the more novel statistical and formal methods of research grew. To take one example from a leading journal in our own field of political science, between 1965 and 1975, the proportion of articles in the *American Political Science Review* using statistics rose from 40 percent to over 70 percent; that using formal models rose from zero to over 40 percent; and the proportion using case studies plunged from 70 percent to under 10 percent, with about 20 percent of the articles using more than one method.[1] Other social science disciplines, including sociology, history, and economics, have undergone methodological changes as well, each in its own way and at its own pace.

These rapid and far-reaching shifts in research methods in earlier decades were naturally contentious, as they affected opportunities for re-

---

1. Andrew Bennett, Aharon Barth, and Ken Rutherford, "Do We Preach What We Practice? A Survey of Methods in Political Science Journals and Curricula," *P.S.: Political Science and Politics*, Vol. 36, No. 3 (July 2003), p. 375.

search funds, teaching positions, and publication outlets. Even scholars with similar substantive interests have formed into largely separate communities along methodological lines. To take another example from our field, of two journals that cover similar theoretical issues and policy concerns, *The Journal of Conflict Resolution* publishes almost no case studies, and *International Security* publishes almost no statistical or formal work. Such methodological specialization is not in itself counterproductive, as every journal needs to establish its own niche. In this instance, however, there is troubling evidence of a lack of cross-method communication, as each of these journals frequently cites its own articles and very rarely cites those published by the other.[2]

More recently, however, a variety of developments has made possible an increasingly sophisticated and collaborative discourse on research methods in the social sciences that focuses upon the essential complementarity of alternative methodological approaches.[3] Over the past few decades, proponents of case study methods, statistics, and formal modeling have each scaled back their most ambitious goals regarding the kinds of knowledge and theories that they aspire to produce. Practitioners of each approach have improved and codified their techniques, reducing some of the problems identified by their critics but also gaining renewed appreciation for the remaining limits of their methods. The mix of methods has become fairly stable, at least in our own field, with each method secure in its ability to contribute to theoretical progress. In contrast to the sharp changes in methods used in journal articles in the 1960s and 1970s, the mix of methods used in articles in the top political science journals has been fairly stable since the mid-1980s, and in recent years

---

2.   Ibid., p. 376.

3.   A useful commentary on developments in case study research is provided by Jack Levy, "Qualitative Methods in International Relations," in Michael Brecher and Frank P. Harvey, eds., *Millennial Reflections on International Studies* (Ann Arbor: University of Michigan Press, 2002), pp. 432–454. See also the excellent treatment of these issues in Stephen Van Evera, *Guide to Methods for Students of Political Science* (Ithaca, N.Y.: Cornell University Press, 1997). In their 1996 review of the state of political science, Robert Goodin and Hans-Dieter Klingemann argue that in the "Jacobin" behavioral revolution of the 1960s and the "Thermidorian" reaction that followed, contending factions "heaped Olympian scorn" on one another. This scenario was then replayed in the "Manichean" controversy over rational choice theory. More recently, they argue, there has been a "rapprochement," fostered by the rise of the "new institutionalism," and "political scientists no longer think in the either/or terms of agency or structure, interests or institutions . . . realism or idealism, interests or ideas . . . science or story-telling . . . mono-causality or hopeless complexity." They do not see this rapprochement as a sloppy "'live and let live' pluralism," but as a sign that the present generation of political scientists are "equipped with a richer toolkit than their predecessors." Robert Goodin and Hans-Dieter Klingemann, eds., *A New Handbook of Political Science* (New York: Oxford University Press, 1996), pp. 10–13.

roughly half of these articles used statistics, about the same proportion used case studies, slightly fewer than a quarter used formal models, and about one in five used more than one method.[4]

Moreover, a new generation of scholars has emerged with training in or at least exposure to more than one methodology, allowing easier translation among the different forms through which fundamental epistemological limits are embodied in different methods. Developments in the philosophy of science have also clarified the philosophical foundations of alternative approaches. Finally, the various fields in the social sciences have, at different speeds and to different degrees, addressed the historical, sociological, and postmodernist "turns" by focusing on norms, institutions, and actors' identities and preferences, but doing so through largely neopositivist means. As a result, scholars are increasingly working collaboratively across methodological divides to advance shared substantive research programs. Most of this cross-method collaboration has taken place sequentially, as different researchers have used the methods in which they are most adept but have also drawn on the findings of those using other methods. Because cross-method collaboration in the social sciences has until recently rarely involved one or more individuals working on the same publication with different methods, it has been underappreciated.

A prerequisite for this revitalized methodological dialogue is a clear understanding of the comparative strengths and limits of various methods, and how they complement each other. This book contributes to this dialogue by focusing on the comparative advantages of case study methods and on these methods' ability to contribute to the development of theories that can accommodate various forms of complex causality.

The case study approach—the detailed examination of an aspect of a historical episode to develop or test historical explanations that may be generalizable to other events—has come in and out of favor over the past five decades as researchers have explored the possibilities of statistical methods (which excel at estimating the generalized causal weight or causal effects of variables) and formal models (in which rigorous deductive logic is used to develop both intuitive and counterintuitive hypotheses about the dynamics of causal mechanisms). Perhaps because case study methods are somewhat intuitive—they have in some sense been around as long as recorded history—the systematic development of case study methods for the cumulative building of social science theories is a comparatively recent phenomenon (notwithstanding notable contributions to these methods by John Stuart Mill). Only in the past three de-

---

4. Bennett, Barth, and Rutherford, p. 374.

cades have scholars formalized case study methods more completely and linked them to underlying arguments in the philosophy of science.

Indeed, statistical methods have been so prominent in recent decades that scholars' understanding of case studies is often distorted by critiques based on the assumptions of statistical methods. We argue that while case studies share a similar epistemological logic with statistical methods and with formal modeling that is coupled with empirical research, these methods have different methodological logics. Epistemologically, all three approaches attempt to develop logically consistent models or theories, they derive observable implications from these theories, they test these implications against empirical observations or measurements, and they use the results of these tests to make inferences on how best to modify the theories tested.[5] Methodologically, these three methods use very different kinds of reasoning regarding fundamental issues such as case selection, operationalization of variables, and the use of inductive and deductive logic. These differences give the three methods complementary comparative advantages. Researchers should use each method for the research tasks for which it is best suited and use alternative methods to compensate for the limitations of each method.

In addition to clarifying the comparative advantages of case studies, this book codifies the best practices in the use of case studies; examines their relationship to debates in the philosophy of science; and refines the concept of middle-range or typological theories and the procedures through which case studies can contribute to them. Our focus extends to all aspects of theory development, including the generation of new hypotheses as well as the testing of existing ones.

Throughout the book, we have paid special attention to the method of process-tracing, which attempts to trace the links between possible causes and observed outcomes. In process- tracing, the researcher examines histories, archival documents, interview transcripts, and other sources to see whether the causal process a theory hypothesizes or implies in a case is in fact evident in the sequence and values of the intervening variables in that case. Process-tracing might be used to test

---

5.   While at this general level the epistemologies of alternative research methods are quite similar, significant differences remain, as these methods are optimized for different epistemic aims. These aims include the estimation of measures of correlation for populations of cases and the establishment of probabilistic levels of confidence that these correlations are not due to chance (tasks at which statistical methods are effective when the assumptions necessary for these methods are met), the development and testing of historical explanations and the detailed exploration of hypothesized causal mechanisms in the context of particular cases (where case studies have comparative advantages), and the deductive development of logically complete and consistent theories (the forte of formal modeling).

whether the residual differences between two similar cases were causal or spurious in producing a difference in these cases' outcomes. Or the intensive study of one deviant case, a case that fails to fit existing theories, may provide significant theoretical insights. Process-tracing can perform a heuristic function as well, generating new variables or hypotheses on the basis of sequences of events observed inductively in case studies.

Typological theories also receive more attention than their one-chapter allotment in the book would suggest. Such theories provide one way of modeling complex contingent generalizations. They frequently draw together in one framework the research of many social scientists, cumulating their individual efforts into a larger body of knowledge. The procedures we recommend for developing typological theories also foster the integration of within-case analyses and cross-case comparisons, and they help researchers opportunistically match up the types of case studies needed for alternative research designs and the extant cases that history provides. This helps to resolve the problem of case selection, one of the most challenging aspects of case study research designs. In addition, typological theories can guide researchers toward questions and research designs whose results will be pertinent to problems faced by policymakers. One of the chief goals of political science, as noted in Chapter 12, is to provide policymakers with "generic knowledge" that will help them form effective strategies.

Highly general and abstract theories ("covering laws," in Carl Hempel's term), which set aside intervening processes and focus on correlations between the "start" and "finish" of a phenomenon, are too general to make sharp theoretical predictions or to guide policy.[6] For example, Kenneth Waltz's structural-realist theory, which posits that the material structure of the international system—the number of great powers, the balance of material power among them, the nature of contemporary military and economic technologies, and the geography of the system—creates structural incentives (such as the incentive to balance against other powerful states) that states can defy only at their peril. Though this theory dominated the field of international relations for some time, it is not a theory of foreign policy, as Waltz himself emphasizes, but a theory of constraints on foreign policy and of the predicted price to be paid for ignoring them.[7]

Theories that describe independent, stable causal mechanisms that

---

6. Here and in the next few paragraphs we draw directly from distinctions among covering laws, causal mechanisms, and typological theories suggested by David Dessler (private communication, January 7, 1998).

7. Kenneth Waltz, *Theory of International Politics* (New York: McGraw-Hill, 1979). For additional discussion, see Chapter 12.

under certain conditions link causes to effects also fail to provide specific guidance to those in search of policy guidance. For example, a theory may address the contribution a specific democratic norm makes to the fact that democracies have rarely fought one another—but without contingent generalizations on the conditions under which the norm is actualized and those under which it is overridden by other mechanisms, such a theory cannot tell policymakers whether they should, say, promote the adoption of this norm in newly democratic states. In contrast, middle-range typological theories, which identify recurring conjunctions of mechanisms and provide hypotheses on the pathways through which they produce results, provide more contingent and specific generalizations for policymakers and allow researchers to contribute to more nuanced theories. For example, one typological theory identifies subtypes of ways in which deterrence might fail: through a *fait accompli* or series of limited probes by a challenger, through a misperception of the adversary's will or capabilities, through the intrusion of domestic politics into decision-making, and so on.

The next section of this introduction discusses six reasons why we have undertaken the task of codifying case study practices and theory. We then offer a definition of case studies, outline their advantages and limitations, and conclude with a short discussion of the plan of the book.

Advances in Case Study Methods

The time seemed ripe to offer a book that would allow readers to view and assimilate advances and debates in case study methods and that might help these methods find wider use and acceptance. First, interest in theory-oriented case studies has increased substantially in recent years, not only in political science and sociology, but even in economics—arguably the most ambitious social science in its epistemological aspirations. Scholars in these and other disciplines have called for a "return to history," arousing new interest in the methods of historical research and the logic of historical explanation, discussed in Chapter 10.[8]

Second, several developments in the philosophy of science in the past three decades, discussed in Chapter 7, have provided a firmer foundation for case study methods. In particular, the "scientific realist" school of thought has emphasized that causal mechanisms—independent stable factors that under certain conditions link causes to effects—are central to causal explanation. This has resonated with case study researchers' use of process-tracing either to uncover evidence of causal mechanisms at work

8. See, for example, Terrence J. McDonald, ed., *The Historic Turn in the Human Sciences* (Ann Arbor: University of Michigan Press, 1996).

or to explain outcomes. We also find Bayesian logic useful in assessing how "tough" a test a particular case poses to a theory, and how generalizable the results are from a given case. This logic helps to refine Harry Eckstein's discussion of using crucial, most-likely, and least-likely cases to test theories. A crucial case is one in which a theory that passes empirical testing is strongly supported and one that fails is strongly impugned. Since cases suitable for such doubly discriminating tests are rare, Eckstein emphasized the inferential value of instances where a theory fails to fit a case in which it is most likely to be true, and hence the theory is strongly undermined, or fits a case in which it is least likely to be true, and thus is convincingly supported.[9]

Third, we wished to engage contemporary debates among rational choice theorists, structuralists, historical institutionalists, social constructivists, cognitive theorists, postmodernists, and others, who at times may see themselves as having a stake in debates over case study or other methods. We argue that theoretical arguments are for the most part separable from methodological debates and that case study methods have wide applicability. For example, much of the early political science research on rational choice theories relied on formal models and statistical tests, but a growing number of rational choice theorists are realizing that case study methods can also be used in conjunction with or to test rational choice theories.[10] Social constructivists, cognitive theorists, and historical institutionalists may welcome the comparative advantages of case studies for addressing qualitative variables, individual actors, decision-making processes, historical and social contexts, and path dependencies. Meanwhile, structuralists may worry that case studies are more amenable to these social and institutional theories than to materialist theories. We maintain, however, that case studies (as well as statistical and formal methods) are useful for theory development across all these schools of thought and that they can incorporate both material and ideational variables. Postmodernists will be skeptical of our aspiration to cumulative theoretical knowledge, but even they may find our version of case study methods useful in studying discourses, identities, and interactions systematically.

Fourth, there is growing interest across the social and physical sciences in modeling and assessing complex causal relations, such as path dependence, tipping points, multiple interactions effects, selection ef-

---

9. Harry Eckstein, "Case Studies and Theory in Political Science," in Fred Greenstein and Nelson Polsby, eds., *Handbook of Political Science*, Vol. 7 (Reading, Mass.: Addison-Wesley, 1975), pp. 79–138. For further discussion, see Chapter 6.

10. An important example is Robert Bates et al., *Analytic Narratives* (Princeton, N.J.: Princeton University Press, 1998).

fects, disproportionate feedback loops, equifinality (many alternative causal paths to the same outcome), and multifinality (many outcomes consistent with a particular value of one variable). Case study methods, particularly when used in the development of typological theories, are good at exploring many of these aspects of complex causality.

Fifth, we found it necessary to address an imbalance in our field, and perhaps in others, between the mix of methods that we and our colleagues use in our own research and that which we teach to our students. Although almost half the articles published in the top political science journals in recent years used case studies, only about two-thirds of the thirty top-ranked graduate programs in political science offer a dedicated graduate course in qualitative or case study methods, and only two of these departments require such a course.[11] In contrast, all of the top thirty departments offer courses in statistics, and almost all of these departments require some training in statistics, often several courses. We believe that graduate students should be trained to produce cutting-edge research in their method of choice (which requires more courses for statistical methods than for qualitative methods) and to be critically aware consumers of research using the other two methods.[12] In this regard, this book is designed as a text for teaching students cutting-edge qualitative methods.

Finally, the publication of *Designing Social Inquiry: Scientific Inference in Qualitative Research (DSI)* by Gary King, Robert O. Keohane, and Sidney Verba has greatly influenced our field and usefully forced us to clarify our thinking on case study methods.[13] We find much to agree with in this important work.[14] At the same time, we find it necessary to qualify

---

11. Bennett, Barth, and Rutherford, "Do We Preach What We Practice?"

12. We do not necessarily expect individuals to do state-of-the-art work using more than one method in a single research project. There are examples in our field of exceptional and well-trained individuals doing excellent multi-method work, but while we want to encourage this practice, we do not want to set it as the standard expectation for Ph.D. theses, books, or articles. Since it is sufficiently difficult to do cutting-edge work with one method, we suspect most multi-method work will involve collaboration between researchers who are expert at different methods, a practice that deserves encouragement.

13. Gary King, Robert O. Keohane, and Sidney Verba, *Designing Social Inquiry: Scientific Inference in Qualitative Research* (Princeton, N.J.: Princeton University Press, 1994).

14. Some points of agreement involve fairly standard methodological admonitions: leave a clear and replicable record of your research methods, generate a list of observable implications for alternative hypotheses under consideration, specify what empirical findings would call into question each of these hypotheses, and keep in mind that

DSI's central argument that there is one "logic of inference." If this logic of inference refers in a broad sense to the epistemological logic of deriving testable implications from alternative theories, testing these implications against quantitative or case study data, and modifying theories or our confidence in them in accordance with the results, then perhaps on a very general level there is one logic that is the modern successor of the still-evolving positivist tradition, although many disagreements remain about particular aspects of this logic.[15]

If, however, the logic of inference refers to specific methodological injunctions on such issues as the value of single-case studies, the procedures for choosing which cases to study, the role of process-tracing, and the relative importance of causal effects (the expected change in the dependent variable given a unit change in an independent variable) and causal mechanisms as bases for inference and explanation, as *DSI* appears to argue, then we disagree with the overall argument as well as some of the methodological advice *DSI* provides to case study researchers on these issues. *DSI* risks conflating these epistemological and methodological logics by stating that "the same underlying logic provides the framework for each research approach. This logic tends to be explicated and formalized clearly in discussions of quantitative research methods."[16]

We take up our disagreements with *DSI* (in this chapter and in Chapter 8); here, for reference, we merely list them, starting with our epistemological differences and proceeding to our methodological ones. One critique is that although *DSI* disavows being "a work in the philosophy of the social sciences," it implicitly makes many important philosophical assumptions regarding highly contested issues in the philosophy of science.[17] For example, *DSI* suggests that causal mechanisms are in some sense less fundamental to causal explanation than what *DSI*

---

science is a social enterprise in which no research is perfect and diversity of belief serves as a useful check on individual misperceptions and biases. We also agree that counterfactual analysis can serve as a useful cross-check on theorizing, that reconfiguring one's theory after seeing some of the data is defensible as long as it leads to new predictions on other data that hold up to additional empirical tests, and that parsimonious theories are desirable but should not be pursued at the cost of oversimplifying a complex world and reducing our ability to produce rich explanations. Most of these points are raised in King, Keohane, and Verba, *Designing Social Inquiry*, pp. 7–33.

15. Postmodernists would of course disagree with us and with *Designing Social Inquiry* on the applicability of positivist logic, even broadly construed, to the social sciences.

16. King, Keohane, and Verba, *Designing Social Inquiry*, p. 3.

17. Ibid., p. 3.

defines as "causal effects."[18] This runs counter to our view that causal mechanisms and causal effects are equally important to causal explanation. More generally, in our view *DSI's* treatment of causal mechanisms is unsatisfactory, as we detail in Chapter 8. Robert Keohane has given a clearer exposition of the nature and importance of causal mechanisms for explanation in his later publications.[19]

We also critique *DSI* for emphasizing almost exclusively the epistemic goal of hypothesis testing (sometimes known as the "logic of confirmation"), neglecting other aspects of theory development, such as the formation of new hypotheses or the choice of new questions to study. *DSI* relegates these goals, the "logic of discovery," to a quotation from Karl Popper that "there is no such thing as a logical method of having new ideas. . . . Discovery contains 'an irrational element,' or a 'creative intuition.'"[20]

We agree that there is no linear logic of discovery, but we emphasize theory development, focusing on hypothesis formation and the historical explanation of individual cases, as well as the testing of general hypotheses. We outline procedures that are conducive to the generation of new hypotheses, such as the study of deviant or outlier cases.

Another concern is that *DSI* pays little attention to problems of causal complexity, particularly equifinality and multiple interactions effects. It addresses these subjects very briefly, discussing only the simple case of two-variable interactions, and it tends to be optimistic on how easily statistical models can address complex interactions within a realistic sample size.[21] We emphasize that various kinds of complex causal relations are central concerns of the social sciences, including not only equifinality and multiple interactions effects, but also disproportionate feedback loops, path dependencies, tipping points, selection effects, expectations effects,

---

18. Ibid., pp. 85–87.

19. Robert Keohane, "Problematic Lucidity: Stephen Krasner's 'State Power and the Structure of International Trade,'" *World Politics*, Vol. 50, No. 1 (October 1997), pp. 150–170; and his unpublished paper that focuses on the importance of causal mechanisms in efforts to explain the extinction of dinosaurs: "Dinosaurs, Detectives and Causal Mechanisms: Coping With Uniqueness in Social Science Research," paper presented at American Political Science Association Annual Meeting, September 4, 1999, Atlanta, Georgia. In the latter paper, Keohane also concedes that "[Ronald] Rogowski was right [in his *American Political Science Review* (June 1995) critique] to criticize *Designing Social Inquiry* for not emphasizing sufficiently the importance of elaboration of models and the deduction of implications from them." Keohane also notes that he and his co-authors of *Designing Social Inquiry* "implicitly recognized the importance of theory . . . but we certainly did not emphasize it enough."

20. King, Keohane, and Verba, *Designing Social Inquiry*, p. 14.

21. Ibid., pp. 85–87.

and sequential interactions between individual agents and social structures. Our approach to the problem of complexity is to recommend process-tracing as a means of examining complexity in detail and to suggest typological theorizing as a way to model complexity; *DSI* does not distinguish between typological theories, which model causal relations of equifinality, and mere taxonomical typologies.[22]

On the methodological level, we take issue with *DSI*'s arguments on case selection criteria, the value of single-case studies and "no variance" research designs, the costs and benefits of increasing the number of cases studied, and the role of process-tracing. On case selection criteria, *DSI* gives the standard statistical warnings about selection on the dependent variable and argues that single-case research designs are seldom valuable.[23] This advice overlooks the opportunities for studying deviant cases and the dangers of certain forms of selection bias in case studies that can be more severe than those in statistical studies.

DSI also argues for increasing the number of observable implications of a theory both within cases and across them. While we agree that increasing the number and diversity of observable implications of alternative theories is generally extremely useful, *DSI* tends to understate the dangers of "conceptual stretching" that can arise if the means of increasing observations include applying theories to new cases, changing the measures of variables, or both. *DSI* acknowledges, for example, that additional cases to be studied must be "units within which the process entailed by the hypothesis can take place," but it does not cite here or elsewhere Giovanni Sartori's well-known article on the subject of conceptual stretching.[24]

We also disagree with *DSI*'s treatment of process-tracing as simply another means of increasing the number of observable implications of a theory. In fact, process-tracing is fundamentally different from statistical analysis because it focuses on sequential processes within a particular historical case, not on correlations of data across cases. This has important implications for theory testing: a single unexpected piece of process-tracing evidence can require altering the historical interpretation and theoretical significance of a case, whereas several such cases may not greatly alter the findings concerning statistical estimates of parameters for a large population.

DSI's arguments on all these methodological issues may be appropri-

---

22. Ibid., p. 48.

23. Ibid., pp. 129–132, 210–211.

24. Ibid., p. 221; and Giovanni Sartori, "Concept Misformation in Comparative Politics," *American Political Science Review*, Vol. 64, No. 4 (December 1970), pp. 1033–1053.

ate to statistical methods, but in our view they are ill-suited or even counterproductive in case study research. We differ, finally, with *DSI* on a presentational issue that is primarily pedagogical but has important implications. This is the fact that there is an unresolved tension in *DSI* between the authors' emphasis on research objectives that address important theoretical and policy-relevant problems and the fact that many of the examples used to illustrate various points in *DSI* are either hypothetical or entail research objectives of a simple character not likely to be of interest to sophisticated research specialists.

This gap is aggravated by the fact that many of the hypothetical and actual examples are of quantitative, not qualitative research. *DSI* cites very few qualitative research studies that in its authors' view fully or largely meet the requirements of its methods or deserve emulation, nor do the authors cite their own works in this regard.[25] This is not surprising

---

25. Five earlier publications by Gary King are listed in the bibliographical references, but the single reference to "King" in the index refers to one of his large-N statistical studies, described on page 189. Only one article by Sidney Verba is listed in the bibliographical references ("Some Dilemmas of Political Research," *World Politics*, Vol. 20, No. 1 (October 1967), pp. 111–127), and the only references under "Verba" in the index refer to a large-N statistical study later published as Sidney Verba, Kay Lehman Schlozman, and Harry Brady, *Voices and Equality: Civic Voluntarism in American Politics* (Cambridge, Mass.: Harvard University Press, 1995). It is referred to briefly in the text to indicate that parsing an explanatory variable can avoid the problem of bias due to endogeneity (pp. 193–195), and later to provide "an example of seeking additional observable implications of one's hypotheses" by working with subunits of a national state (pp. 220–221).

Five earlier publications by Robert Keohane are listed in the bibliographical references at the end of the book, but there is no discussion of these works in the *DSI* text as examples of the methods recommended in the book. Keohane's detailed introductory essay for a subsequent collaborative small-n study he coedited (Robert O. Keohane and Marc A. Levy, eds., *Institutions for Environmental Aid: Pitfalls and Promise* (Cambridge, Mass.: MIT Press, 1996)), published two years after *Designing Social Inquiry*, makes no reference to identifying "observable implications" of the theories examined in the book. This small-n study employs procedures closely resembling those of the method of structured, focused comparison and process-tracing. Thus, Keohane writes, the case studies in the book "are written according to a common analytical format to ensure consistency and a comparability across cases. . . . We have insisted on such a systematic approach for two reasons: (1) to ensure that each chapter [reporting a case study] systematically considers the *sequence of action* relevant to the effectiveness of financial transfers, from explanatory and evaluative standpoints as well as descriptively, and (2) to facilitate a process of drawing out *generalizations across cases, about conditions for success and failure* of financial transfers and mechanisms" (pp. 16–17; emphasis added).

In correspondence with Alexander L. George (April 8, 2003), Robert Keohane acknowledged that two students whose dissertations he supervised, Vinod Aggarwal and Lisa Martin, both employed process-tracing to establish the possibility of a causal

since both Gary King and Sidney Verba are quantitatively oriented researchers. On the other hand, Robert Keohane's voluminous research is largely of a qualitative character and, surprisingly, none of his previous studies are cited in *Designing Social Inquiry* as examples of the methods advocated therein.[26]

In contrast, in the present volume we present numerous examples of qualitative research on important policy-relevant problems, including research we ourselves have done. We do so not to imply that our own or others' work is methodologically flawless or worthy of emulation in every respect, but because the hardest methodological choices arise in actual research. Illustrating how such choices are made is vitally important in teaching students how to proceed in their own work. In addition, understanding methodological choices often requires sophisticated familiarity with the theories and cases in question, which reinforces the usefulness of using one's own research for examples.

Certainly King, Keohane, and Verba deserve the fullest praise and appreciation for their effort to improve qualitative research. *DSI*, despite our many disagreements with it, remains a landmark contribution. It is not alone in viewing the goals, methods, and requirements of case studies partly from the viewpoint of statistical methods. We choose to critique *DSI* in such detail not because it is the starkest example of this phenomenon, but because its clarity, comprehensiveness, and familiarity to many scholars make it an excellent vehicle for presenting our contrasting view of the differences, similarities, and comparative advantages of case study and statistical methods. In the next sections we define case studies and outline their advantages, limitations, and trade-offs, distinguishing between criticisms that in our view misapply statistical concepts and critiques that have real merit regarding the limits of case studies.

---

chain linking independent and dependent variables. (Aggarwal's use of process-tracing is described in Chapter 9; Lisa Martin's in the Appendix, "Studies That Illustrate Research Design.") Keohane graciously added that he recognized the importance of process-tracing used for this purpose.

26. The impact *DSI* has had on qualitative research in the social sciences since its publication in 1994 has not, so far as we know, been systematically assessed. Certainly the book has been widely read and consulted. In response to a question concerning *DSI's* impact (letter to Alexander L. George, April 27, 2003), Robert Keohane notes that the book's advice about observable implications has caught on in much of the field. He cites a number of specific papers by Mark Pollock and Erica Gould who have cited *DSI's* emphasis on observable implications. Dan Nielson and Michael Tierney, "Delegation to International Organizations: Agency Theory and World Bank Environmental Reform," *International Organization*, Vol. 57, No. 2 (April 2003), pp. 241–276, does the same. The clearest published reference to *DSI* on this score appears in Lisa Martin's *Democratic Commitments* (Princeton, N.J.: Princeton University Press, 2000), p. 9.

A major new reassessment of *Designing Social Inquiry* has been provided by a team of specialists in a book edited by Henry Brady and David Collier,[27] in which the editors integrate their respective specializations in quantitative survey research and qualitative comparative studies. Their book provides a major scholarly statement on the relationship between quantitative and qualitative methods. While generous and specific in its praise for contributions made in *DSI*, Brady, Collier, and the contributors to their volume express major misgivings: First, *DSI*, "does not adequately address the basic weaknesses within the mainstream quantitative approach it advocates." Second, *DSI's* "treatment of concepts, operationalizations, and measurement" is regarded as "seriously incomplete." Third, Brady and Collier "disagree with *DSI's* claims that it provides a general framework for 'specific inference in qualitative research.'" They emphasize, as others have, *DSI's* "failure to recognize the distinctive strengths of qualitative methods," which leads its authors to "inappropriately view qualitative analysis almost exclusively through the optic of mainstream quantitative methods."

The present book has much in common with Brady and Collier's book. They emphasize, as we do, the need to "rethink the contributions" of quantitative and qualitative approaches and to indicate how scholars can most effectively draw on the respective strengths of each. Considerable attention is given to our emphasis on the importance of within-case analysis and process-tracing. Brady and Collier, and other distinguished scholars contributing to their book, share our criticism of *DSI's* almost exclusive focus on increasing the number of observations in order to increase "leverage." In their conclusion, Brady, Collier, and Jason Seawright develop a "multi-faceted approach to evaluating sources of leverage for addressing rival explanations."

Despite these important reservations and criticisms, Brady and Collier, as do we, regard *DSI* as a major contribution that has usefully stimulated important new work on the relation between quantitative and qualitative methods.

---

27. Henry E. Brady and David Collier, eds., *Rethinking Social Inquiry: Diverse Tools, Shared Standards* (Lanham, Md.: Rowman and Littlefield, 2004). The quotations that follow are from the uncorrected proof of the Preface, Chapter 1, and Chapter 13. Their book reprints important articles that have expressed criticism of *Designing Social Inquiry* by Larry Bartels, Ronald Rogowski, David Collier, James Mahoney, James Seawright; Gerardo Munck, Charles C. Ragin, Timothy J. McKeown, and Sidney Tarrow. It also reprints the reply made by Gary King, Robert O. Keohane, and Sidney Verba to comments on *Designing Social Inquiry* made in the symposium on their book in the *American Political Science Review*, Volume 89, Number 2 (June 1995), pp. 475–481.

Advantages and Limitations of Case Studies: Casting Off the Prism of Statistical Methods

In the 1960s and 1970s, definitions of case studies relied on distinctions between the study of a small versus a large number of instances of a phenomenon. Case studies were characterized as "small-n" studies, in contrast to "large-N" statistical studies. This distinction suggests that the difference in the number of cases studied is the most salient difference between statistical and case study methods; in our "bigger is better" culture, this language implies that large-N methods are always preferable when sufficient data is available for study, as Arend Lijphart implied in a 1971 article.[28] In fact, case studies and other methods each have particular advantages in answering certain kinds of questions.

One early definition, still widely used, states that a case is a "phenomenon for which we report and interpret only a single measure on any pertinent variable."[29] This definition, which case study researchers have increasingly rejected, has sometimes led scholars trained in statistical methods to misapply the "degrees of freedom problem" (which we discuss below) and to conclude that case studies provide no basis for evaluating competing explanations of a case.

We define a case as an instance of a class of events.[30] The term "class of events" refers here to a phenomenon of scientific interest, such as revolutions, types of governmental regimes, kinds of economic systems, or

---

28.   Arend Lijphart, "Comparative Politics and the Comparative Method," *American Political Science Review,* Vol. 65 (September 1971), pp. 682–693.

29.   Eckstein, "Case Studies and Theory in Political Science," p. 85. King, Keohane, and Verba reject the term "case" as subject to too many uses and substitute "observations" for "cases" (*Designing Social Inquiry,* p. 52), but this leads to ambiguity as well. See, for example, *DSI's* discussion of whether Eckstein viewed cases as having single or multiple observations, pp. 210–211. Our reading is that Eckstein envisioned multiple process-tracing observations in each case study despite his definition of a case as having one measure of the dependent variable. (In our view it is more precise to speak of one instance of the dependent variable, which may have several qualitative measures.) A full discussion of *DSI's* advice on how to generate additional observable implications of a theory is presented in Chapter 8.

30.   Alexander L. George, "Case Studies and Theory Development," paper presented at Carnegie-Mellon University, October 15–16, 1982, p. 45. For a similar definition by sociologists, see Charles Ragin's, "Introduction" in Charles Ragin and Howard Becker, eds., *What is a Case? Exploring the Foundations of Social Inquiry* (New York: Cambridge University Press, 1992), pp. 1–3. In the concluding chapter ("'Casing' and the Process of Social Inquiry"), Ragin emphasizes the importance for theory development of focusing research on specific subclasses of a phenomena, which he calls "casing" (pp. 217–226).

personality types that the investigator chooses to study with the aim of developing theory (or "generic knowledge") regarding the causes of similarities or differences among instances (cases) of that class of events. A case study is thus a well-defined aspect of a historical episode that the investigator selects for analysis, rather than a historical event itself. The Cuban Missile Crisis, for example, is a historical instance of many different classes of events: deterrence, coercive diplomacy, crisis management, and so on.[31] A researcher's decision about which class of events to study and which theories to use determines what data from the Cuban Missile Crisis are relevant to her or his case study of it.[32] Questions such as "what is this event a case of?" and "is this event a designated phenomenon?" are integral to selecting cases for study and designing and implementing research of these cases.[33]

There is potential for confusion among the terms "comparative methods," "case study methods," and "qualitative methods." In one view, the comparative method (the use of comparisons among a small number of cases) is distinct from the case study method, which in this view involves the internal examination of single cases. However, we define case study methods to include both within-case analysis of single cases and comparisons of a small number of cases, since there is a growing consensus that the strongest means of drawing inferences from case studies is the use of a combination of within-case analysis and cross-case comparisons within a single study or research program (although single-case studies can also play a role in theory development). The term "qualitative methods" is sometimes used to encompass both case studies carried out with a relatively positivist view of the philosophy of science and those implemented with a postmodern or interpretive view. We exclude postmodern narra-

---

31. The Cuban Missile Crisis is treated as a case of deterrence failure in Alexander L. George and Richard Smoke, *Deterrence in American Foreign Policy: Theory and Practice* (New York: Columbia University Press, 1974); as a case of coercive diplomacy in Alexander L. George, David K. Hall, and William E. Simons, *The Limits of Coercive Diplomacy* (Boston: Little, Brown, 1971); and as a case of crisis management in Ole R. Holsti, *Crisis, Escalation, War* (Montreal: McGill-Queen's University Press, 1972).

32. It is important to note that the definition of which independent variables are relevant to the class of events remains open to revision as the research proceeds. In conducting interviews, reading secondary accounts, or reviewing historical documents, the researcher may inductively discover independent variables that previous theories may have overlooked. This inductive side to identifying variables is open also to statistical researchers who are constructing their own data sets from primary and secondary sources, but it is closed to statistical studies that rely on existing data sets, as well as to the purely deductive development of formal models.

33. Ragin and Becker, eds., *What is a Case?*; and David Collier, "Translating Quantitative Methods for Qualitative Researchers: The Case of Selection Bias," *American Political Science Review*, Vol. 89, No. 2 (June 1995), pp. 461, 465.

tives from our view of case studies, though some of the more disciplined forms of discourse analysis approach our view of case studies. This book therefore hews to the traditional terminology in focusing on case studies as the subset of qualitative methods that aspires to cumulative and progressive generalizations about social life and seeks to develop and apply clear standards for judging whether some generalizations fit the social world better than others.

Strengths of Case Study Methods

Case studies are generally strong precisely where statistical methods and formal models are weak. We identify four strong advantages of case methods that make them valuable in testing hypotheses and particularly useful for theory development: their potential for achieving high conceptual validity; their strong procedures for fostering new hypotheses; their value as a useful means to closely examine the hypothesized role of causal mechanisms in the context of individual cases; and their capacity for addressing causal complexity.

CONCEPTUAL VALIDITY

Case studies allow a researcher to achieve high levels of conceptual validity, or to identify and measure the indicators that best represent the theoretical concepts the researcher intends to measure. Many of the variables that interest social scientists, such as democracy, power, political culture, state strength, and so on are notoriously difficult to measure. For example, a procedure that is "democratic" in one cultural context might be profoundly undemocratic in another. Thus, researchers must carry out "contextualized comparison," which "self-consciously seeks to address the issue of equivalence by searching for *analytically equivalent* phenomena—even if expressed in substantively different terms—across different contexts."[34] This requires a detailed consideration of contextual factors, which is extremely difficult to do in statistical studies but is common in case studies.

Whereas statistical studies run the risk of "conceptual stretching" by lumping together dissimilar cases to get a larger sample, case studies allow for conceptual refinements with a higher level of validity over a smaller number of cases. Research in comparative politics on democratic systems, for example, has proceeded in part through the conceptual development of "democracy with adjectives," where each adjective, such as

---

34.   Richard Locke and Kathleen Thelen, "Problems of Equivalence in Comparative Politics: Apples and Oranges, Again," *American Political Science Association: Comparative Politics Newsletter*, No. 8 (Winter 1998), p. 11.

a "federal," "parliamentary," "presidential," or "authoritarian" democracy, denotes a subtype or subclass with a smaller number of cases that are presumably more similar than those under the overall concept of "democracy."[35] A common path of theoretical development has been from broad generalizations, such as the "democratic peace" theory (which argues that democracies are less war-prone) into more contingent generalizations (such as the "interdemocratic peace" theory, which holds that democracies rarely fight other democracies; see Chapter 2). Often, when such phenomena are examined in more detail, they prove to exhibit "equifinality"; that is, they involve several explanatory paths, combinations, or sequences leading to the same outcome, and these paths may or may not have one or more variables in common.

Consequently, statistical research is frequently preceded by case study research to identify relevant variables and followed by case study work that focuses on deviant cases and further refines concepts.[36] For example, after a range of statistical studies suggested that democracies do not fight other democracies, case study researchers started to explore which aspects of democracy—democratic values, democratic institutions, the transparency of decision-making in democracies, and so on—might be responsible for this apparent "democratic peace." Should these case studies indicate, say, that transparency is an important causal factor whereas universal suffrage is not, then revised and new statistical tests are performed.

DERIVING NEW HYPOTHESES

Case studies have powerful advantages in the heuristic identification of new variables and hypotheses through the study of deviant or outlier cases and in the course of field work—such as archival research and interviews with participants, area experts, and historians. When a case study researcher asks a participant "were you thinking X when you did Y," and gets the answer, "No, I was thinking Z," then if the researcher had not thought of Z as a causally relevant variable, she may have a new variable demanding to be heard. The popular refrain that observations are

---

35. David Collier and Steven Levitsky, "Democracy with Adjectives: Conceptual Innovation in Comparative Research," *World Politics*, Vol. 49, No. 3 (April 1997), pp. 430–451. Collier and Levitsky also note the use of "diminished subtypes," or cases that lack a few attributes of the overall concept, such as "limited suffrage democracies" (pp. 437–442).

36. David Collier, "Comparative Historical Analysis: Where Do We Stand?" *American Political Science Association: Comparative Politics Newsletter*, No. 10 (Winter 1999), pp. 1–6.

theory-laden does not mean that they are theory-determined. If we ask one question of individuals or documents but get an entirely different answer, we may move to develop new theories that can be tested through previously unexamined evidence.

Statistical methods can identify deviant cases that may lead to new hypotheses, but in and of themselves these methods lack any clear means of actually identifying new hypotheses. This is true of all studies that use existing databases or that modify such databases only slightly or without recourse to primary sources. Unless statistical researchers do their own archival work, interviews, or face-to-face surveys with open-ended questions in order to measure the values of the variables in their model, they have no unproblematic inductive means of identifying left-out variables. Even statistical methods of "data mining" necessarily include only those variables that a researcher has already thought to code into a data base. Deductive theorizing can also identify new variables, but with the exception of purely deductive theories, inductive field research methods typically lie behind every newly identified variable.

EXPLORING CAUSAL MECHANISMS

Case studies examine the operation of causal mechanisms in individual cases in detail. Within a single case, we can look at a large number of intervening variables and inductively observe any unexpected aspects of the operation of a particular causal mechanism or help identify what conditions present in a case activate the causal mechanism. Our definition of causal mechanism (see Chapter 7) notes that such mechanisms operate only under certain conditions. Statistical studies, which omit all contextual factors except those codified in the variables selected for measurement or used for constituting a population of cases, necessarily leave out many contextual and intervening variables.

Researchers can also use theories on causal mechanisms to give historical explanations of cases. Historical explanation is quite different from the development and testing of variable-centered theories from the statistical study of a large number of cases. As statistical researchers frequently point out, correlation does not imply causation. If a prosecutor knows on the basis of criminological studies that 90 percent of acts of arson are perpetrated by the owner of the property that is burned down, this is not sufficient to convict a particular property owner of arson. The prosecutor needs to empirically establish that means, motive, and opportunity existed in this particular case. Ideally, the prosecutor will construct a complete and uninterrupted chain of evidence to establish how the specific crime may have been done by the particular individual accused, using forensic theories to bolster each point in the chain.

MODELING AND ASSESSING COMPLEX CAUSAL RELATIONS

A final advantage of case studies is their ability to accommodate complex causal relations such as equifinality, complex interactions effects, and path dependency.[37] This advantage is relative rather than absolute. Case studies can allow for equifinality, but to do so they produce generalizations that are narrower or more contingent. We find great value in such middle-range theories, but others may prefer theories that are more general even if this necessarily means they are more vague or more prone to counterexamples. Case studies also require substantial process-tracing evidence to document complex interactions. Analogously, statistical methods can model several kinds of interactions effects, but only at the cost of requiring a large sample size, and models of nonlinear interactions rapidly become complex and difficult to interpret. New statistical methods may be able to improve upon the statistical treatment of equifinality and interactions effects.[38]

Trade-offs, Limitations, and Potential Pitfalls of Case Studies

It is important to distinguish among the recurrent trade-offs, inherent limits, and examples of poor implementation of case study methods and not to misinterpret these aspects through the prism of statistical methods, as has been done in the past. Recurrent trade-offs include the problem of case selection; the trade-off between parsimony and richness; and the related tension between achieving high internal validity and good historical explanations of particular cases versus making generalizations that apply to broad populations. The inherent limitations include a relative inability to render judgments on the frequency or representativeness of particular cases and a weak capability for estimating the average "causal effect" of variables for a sample. Potential limitations can include indeterminacy and lack of independence of cases.

CASE SELECTION BIAS

One of the most common critiques of case study methods is that they are particularly prone to versions of "selection bias" that concern statistical researchers.[39] Selection biases are indeed a potentially severe problem in case study research, but not in the same ways as in statistical research.

---

37. Charles Ragin, *The Comparative Method: Moving Beyond Qualitative and Quantitative Strategies* (Berkeley: University of California Press, 1987).

38. Bear F. Braumoeller, "Causal Complexity and the Study of Politics," (unpublished manuscript, Harvard University, Cambridge, Mass., 2002).

39. Christopher H. Achen and Duncan Snidal, "Rational Deterrence Theory and Comparative Case Studies," *World Politics*, Vol. 41, No. 2 (January 1989), p. 160; and

Selection bias, in statistical terminology, "is commonly understood as occurring when some form of selection process in either the design of the study or the real-world phenomena under investigation results in inferences that suffer from systematic error."[40] Such biases can occur when cases or subjects are self-selected or when the researcher unwittingly selects cases that represent a truncated sample along the dependent variable of the relevant population of cases.[41] If for some reason a statistical researcher has unwittingly truncated the sample of cases to be studied to include only those whose dependent variable is above or below an extreme value, then an estimate of the regression slope for this truncated sample will be biased toward zero. In other words, in statistical studies selection bias always understates the strength of the relationship between the independent and dependent variables. This is why statistical researchers are admonished not to select cases on the dependent variable.[42]

In contrast, case study researchers sometimes deliberately choose cases that share a particular outcome. Practitioners and analysts of case study methods have argued that selection on the dependent variable should not be rejected out of hand. Selection of cases on the basis of the value of their dependent variables is appropriate for some purposes, but not for others. Cases selected on the dependent variable, including single-case studies, can help identify which variables are not necessary or sufficient conditions for the selected outcome.[43]

In addition, in the early stages of a research program, selection on the dependent variable can serve the heuristic purpose of identifying the potential causal paths and variables leading to the dependent variable of interest. Later, the resulting causal model can be tested against cases in which there is variation on the dependent variable.[44] Ideally, researchers

Barbara Geddes, "How the Cases You Choose Affect the Answers You Get: Selection Bias in Comparative Politics," *Political Analysis,* Vol. 2 (1990), pp. 131–150.

40.   David Collier and James Mahoney, "Insights and Pitfalls: Selection Bias in Qualitative Work," *World Politics,* Vol. 49, No. 1 (October 1996) p. 59.

41.   Ibid., p. 60; and King, Keohane, and Verba, *Designing Social Inquiry,* pp. 128–132.

42.   Collier and Mahoney, "Insights and Pitfalls," p. 60.

43.   Douglas Dion, "Evidence and Inference in the Comparative Case Study," in Gary Goertz and Harvey Starr, eds., *Necessary Conditions: Theory, Methodology, and Applications* (Lanham, Md.: Rowman and Littlefield, 2003), pp. 95–112; and Collier, "Translating Quantitative Methods for Qualitative Researchers," p. 464.

44.   Case study researchers in many instances should make comparisons between the subset of cases or types studied and the larger population, where there is more variance on the dependent variable (Collier and Mahoney, "Insights and Pitfalls," p. 63). Sometimes, such comparisons can be made to existing case studies in the literature, or the researcher might include "mini-case" studies, or less in-depth studies, of a wide number of cases in addition to full studies of the cases of greatest interest. To say

would like to have the functional equivalent of a controlled experiment, with controlled variation in independent variables and resulting variation in dependent variables, but the requisite cases for such research designs seldom exist.

A related issue is whether researchers' foreknowledge of the values of variables in cases—and perhaps their cognitive biases in favor of particular hypotheses—necessarily bias the selection of case studies.[45] Selection with some preliminary knowledge of cases, however, allows much stronger research designs; cases can be selected with a view toward whether they are most-likely, least-likely, or crucial for a theory, making the process-tracing test of a theory more severe. Also, within-case analysis often leads to the finding that the researcher's (or the literature's) preliminary knowledge of the values of the independent and dependent variables was incomplete or simply wrong, and case study researchers sometimes conclude that none of the proposed theories adequately explains a case. In addition, researchers selecting cases can benefit from knowledge of the findings of existing studies, and be guided by estimations of whether the theories of interest are strong and previously tested or new and relatively weak.[46] There are also methodological safeguards against investigator-induced bias in case studies, such as careful congruence testing and process-tracing.

Interestingly, statistical views of selection bias understate both the most severe and the most common kinds of selection biases in qualitative research. The most damaging consequences arise from selecting only cases whose independent *and* dependent variables vary as the favored hypothesis suggests, ignoring cases that appear to contradict the theory, and overgeneralizing from these cases to wider populations. This type of selection bias can occur even when there is variation in both independent and dependent variables and this variation covers the full range of values that these variables can assume.

Rather than *understating* the relationship between independent and dependent variables, as in the statistical view of selection bias, this selection bias can *understate or overstate* the relationship.[47] While this form of

---

that such comparisons are often useful for many research goals, however, is very different from arguing that they are always necessary for all research goals.

45. The standard protection against this bias in statistical studies is random selection, but as King, Keohane, and Verba note (*Designing Social Inquiry*, pp. 124–127), in studies of a small number of cases, random selection can be more likely to result in bias than intentional selection.

46. David Laitin, "Disciplining Political Science," *American Political Science Review*, Vol. 89, No. 2 (June 1995), p. 456.

47. Collier and Mahoney, "Insights and Pitfalls," pp. 71–72.

selection bias seems too obvious to require a warning to social scientists, case researchers may fail to realize that by implicitly or explicitly limiting their sample of cases (say, to history that is contemporary, Western, specific to one country, or easily researchable), they may bias their sample with regard to a wider set of cases about which they are trying to make inferences—unless they carefully define and limit the *scope* of their findings to a well-specified population that shares the same key characteristics as the cases studied.

This form of selection bias is far more common in political argumentation than in social science case studies. Several other case selection biases, however, are quite common in case study research and deserve increased attention. These include selection of cases based on their "intrinsic" historical importance or on the accessibility of evidence.

IDENTIFYING SCOPE CONDITIONS AND "NECESSITY"

A limitation of case studies is that they can make only tentative conclusions on *how much* gradations of a particular variable affect the outcome in a particular case or how much they generally contribute to the outcomes in a class or type of cases. Case studies are much stronger at identifying the scope conditions of theories and assessing arguments about causal necessity or sufficiency in particular cases than they are at estimating the generalized causal effects or causal weight of variables across a range of cases. More confident estimates of causal effects, the equivalent of beta coefficients in statistical studies, are possible in case studies only when there is a very well-controlled before-after case comparison in which only one independent variable changes, or more generally when extremely similar cases differ only in one independent variable. Otherwise, case studies remain much stronger at assessing *whether* and *how* a variable mattered to the outcome than at assessing *how much* it mattered.

Methodologists are working to reduce this limitation, however. Douglas Dion, for example, has focused on the role of case studies in testing theoretical claims that a variable is a necessary or sufficient condition for a certain outcome.[48] Dion convincingly argues that selection bias is not a problem in tests of necessity or sufficiency, that single counterexamples can falsify deterministic claims of necessity or sufficiency (if

---

48. The reader should note that any necessary condition can be inverted and stated as a sufficient condition, and vice versa. To say that "A is necessary for B" (for a specified population or set of scope conditions) is the same as saying "the absence of A is sufficient for the absence of B" (for the specified population or scope conditions). Thus from a methodological point of view any discussion of testing a necessary condition can be restated in terms of testing a sufficient condition, and vice versa.

measurement error can be ruled out), and that only small numbers of cases are required to test even probabilistic claims that a condition is almost always necessary or sufficient for an outcome.[49] These factors make case studies a powerful means of assessing claims of necessity or sufficiency.

It is important to distinguish carefully, however, among three kinds of claims of necessity or sufficiency. The most general claim would be that a single variable is necessary or sufficient for an outcome with respect to an entire population of cases. Unfortunately, few nontrivial single-variable relationships of necessity or sufficiency have been found to hold for large populations or wide-scope conditions in the social world. A second kind of claim is that a variable was either necessary or suffi-cient in a particular historical context or case for a specific historical outcome to have occurred. This kind of claim can only be tested counterfactually, and there is no infallible means of making such counterfactual tests.

The third and in our view most useful kind of assertion of necessity or sufficiency concerns the relationship of a variable to *conjunctions* of variables that are themselves necessary and/or sufficient for an outcome. Consider the following example. Let us assume that the variable A causes Y only in conjunction with B and C. Assume further that the conjunction ABC is sufficient for Y, and the conjunction BC cannot cause Y in the absence of A. In this instance, A is a necessary part of a conjunction that is sufficient for the outcome Y. Many different possible combinations of conjunctive necessity and sufficiency are possible. If equifinality is present, for example, the conjunction ABC itself may not be necessary for the outcome, which might arise through other causal paths that have little or nothing in common with ABC.[50]

Three caveats are in order regarding inferences of necessity or sufficiency. First, it is often not possible to resolve whether a causal condition identified as contributing to the explanation of a case is a *necessary*

---

49. See Dion, "Evidence and Inference," pp. 95–112.

50. One further variation on methods for assessing necessity and sufficiency is Charles Ragin's suggestion for using "fuzzy set" techniques to examine theories that make probabilistic assertions about conditions that are "almost always" or "usually" necessary or sufficient. Such relationships might be more commonly observed than deterministic relationships of necessity or sufficiency because measurement error, as well as the possibility of an irreducibly random element in human affairs, can never be conclusively eliminated. Charles Ragin, *Fuzzy-Set Social Science* (Chicago, Ill.: University of Chicago Press, 2000). We address Ragin's "fuzzy set methods" in Chapter 8 on comparative methods. We explore further in Chapter 11 some of the different types and implications of conjunctive conditions.

condition for that case, for the type of case that it represents, or for the outcome in general. It is often more appropriate to settle for a defensible claim that the presence of a variable "favors" an outcome, or is what historians often term a "contributing cause," which may or may not be a necessary condition. When a complex explanation identifies a number of contributing causes, it may be difficult, even with the help of counterfactual analysis, to offer a convincing argument that one condition or another was necessary to the outcome.

Second, whether a factor is necessary to an outcome in a case is a separate issue from *how much* it contributed to the magnitude of the outcome. One "last straw" may be necessary to break a camel's back, but it does not contribute as much to the outcome as the bales of straw that preceded it. As noted above, determining such relative causal weights for variables can be difficult to do with any precision in a single case or a small number of cases, but process-tracing evidence and congruence tests can provide useful evidence on this question.

Third, even when a plausible argument can be made that a factor is necessary to the outcome in a particular case, this does not automatically translate into a general claim for its causal role in other cases. If equifinality is present, the factor's necessity and causal weight may vary considerably across cases or types of cases.[51]

---

51.   A complex debate has emerged over whether, as Dion argues, claims of necessity should be tested only against cases that are positive on the outcome of interest, and claims of sufficiency should be tested only against cases that are positive on the independent variable of interest. Jason Seawright has used sophisticated Bayesian reasoning to argue, contra Dion, that studying diverse cases, in addition to looking for single cases that could disprove necessity or sufficiency, can yield stronger and more efficient tests of necessity and sufficiency; others dispute this. See Jason Seawright, "Testing for Necessary and/or Sufficient Causation: Which Cases Are Relevant?" *Political Analysis,* Vol. 10, No. 2 (Spring 2002), pp. 178–193; for the critiques of Seawright and his response see Kevin Clarke, "The Reverend and the Ravens," *Political Analysis,* Vol. 10, No. 2 (Spring 2002), pp. 194–197; Bear F. Braumoeller and Gary Goertz, "Watching Your Posterior: Sampling Assumptions, Falsification, and Necessary Conditions," pp. 198–203; and Seawright's rejoinder, "What Counts as Evidence? Prior Probabilities, Posterior Distributions, and Causal Inference," pp. 204–207. Without attempting to resolve this debate, we merely note that apart from Seawright's arguments, there may be reasons for selecting diverse cases to test theories, including those of necessity or sufficiency. Researchers are often testing not just one necessary condition hypothesis, for example, but also alternative hypotheses that may require different cases to test. Also, the causal mechanisms being tested may be different from the independent and dependent variables used to identify and select cases. We return to this question of case selection for testing claims of necessity and sufficiency in Chapter 2, which looks at the literature on whether it is a sufficient condition for peace between two countries if both of them are democratic.

THE 'DEGREES OF FREEDOM PROBLEM' AND CASE STUDIES:
MISAPPLICATION OF A STATISTICAL VERSION OF UNDERDETERMINATION

Analysts have occasionally criticized case studies for having a "degrees of freedom problem." This is the statistical term for the broader issue of underdetermination, or the potential inability to discriminate between competing explanations on the basis of the evidence. In our view, the statistical concept and nomenclature of "degrees of freedom" has often led to a misunderstanding of how the more generic problem of underdetermination can pose a challenge to case study methods.

In statistical methods—we focus for purposes of illustration on the example of multiple regression analysis—the term "degrees of freedom" refers to the number of observations minus the number of estimated parameters or characteristics of the population being studied (such as mean or variance). In a multiple regression analysis, the number of observations is taken as the number of cases (or the sample size) and the number of parameters is the number of independent variables and one additional parameter for the value of the intercept (the point at which the estimated regression line intercepts the axis on a graph). Thus, a study with 100 cases and 6 variables would have 100 - (6+1) or 93 degrees of freedom.

In a statistical study, degrees of freedom are crucial because they determine the power of a particular research design or the probability of detecting whether a specified level of explained variance is statistically significant at a specified significance level. In other words, as the sample size increases or the number of variables decreases—either of which would increase the degrees of freedom—lower and lower levels of explained variance are necessary to conclude with some confidence that the relationship being studied is unlikely to have been brought about by chance.

It is easy to see why this important consideration in the design of statistical research might seem directly applicable to case study research, which also uses the terms "case" and "variables." In a strictly literal sense, any study of a single case using one or more variables might seem to have zero or even negative degrees of freedom and be hopelessly indeterminate apart from simple tests of necessity or sufficiency. This is a fundamentally mistaken interpretation.

We have criticized above the definition of a case as a phenomenon in which we report only one measure on any pertinent variable. It is this definition that leads to the conclusion that case studies suffer from an inherent degrees of freedom problem. In fact, each qualitative variable has many different attributes that might be measured. Statistical researchers tend to aggregate variables together into single indices to get fewer independent variables and more degrees of freedom, but case study researchers do the reverse: they treat variables qualitatively, in many of their relevant dimensions. Statistical databases, for example, have created indices for "democracy," while qualitative researchers have been more active in measuring different attributes of or types of democracy, or what has been called "democracy with adjectives."[52]

In addition, within a single case there are many possible process-tracing observations along the hypothesized causal paths between independent and dependent variables. A causal path may include many necessary steps, and they may have to occur in a particular order (*other* causal paths, when equifinality is present, might involve different steps in a different order.) Some analysts emphasize that defining and observing the steps along the hypothesized causal path can lead to "a plethora of new observable implications for a theory" and circumvent the degrees of freedom problem.[53] Donald Campbell noted this in setting out to "correct some of my own prior excesses in describing the case study approach," arguing that:

I have overlooked a major source of discipline (i.e., degrees of freedom if I persist in using this statistical concept for the analogous problem in nonstatistical settings). In a case study done by an alert social scientist who has thorough local acquaintance, the theory he uses to explain the focal difference also generates predictions or expectations on dozens of other aspects of the culture, and he does not retain the theory unless most of these are also confirmed. In some sense, he has tested the theory with degrees of freedom coming from the multiple implications of any one theory.[54]

Thus, as long as competing theories make different predictions on the causal processes thought to have taken place in a case—and sufficient evidence is accessible for process-tracing and congruence testing—case study researchers may have the means to reject many of the possible alternative explanations of a case.[55]

We would go even further than Campbell on this issue. While Campbell states that "most" predictions or expectations a theory makes regarding a case must be confirmed in order for the theory to be retained, we would distinguish retaining a theory that has general utility in many cases from retaining a historical explanation of a particular case. A satisfactory historical explanation of a particular case needs to address and

---

52.   Collier and Levitsky, "Democracy with Adjectives," pp. 430–451.

53.   King, Keohane, and Verba, *Designing Social Inquiry*, p. 225.

54.   Donald Campbell, "Degrees of Freedom and the Case Study," *Comparative Political Studies*, Vol. 8, No. 8 (July 1975), pp. 179, 181–182.

55.   King, Keohane, and Verba, *Designing Social Inquiry*, pp. 119–120. King, Keohane, and Verba also acknowledge here that generating process-tracing observations can mitigate the problem of indeterminacy.

explain each of the significant steps in the sequence that led to the out-come of that case. If even one step in the hypothesized causal process in a particular case is not as predicted, then the historical explanation of the case needs to be modified, perhaps in a trivial way that is consistent with the original theory, or perhaps in a crucial way that calls into question the theory's general utility and its applicability to other cases. It is this insis-tence on providing a continuous and theoretically based historical expla-nation of a case, in which each significant step toward the outcome is ex-plained by reference to a theory, that makes process-tracing a powerful method of inference (a point that we take up in detail in Chapter 10).

The misguided focus on case studies' supposed "degrees of freedom problem" has diverted attention from a more fundamental problem of in-determinacy that affects all research methods, even experimental meth-ods. This is the problem that evidence, whether from a case or a database, can be equally consistent with a large or even infinite number of alterna-tive theories. The pragmatic (but necessarily incomplete) approach we and others suggest to this problem is that researchers limit themselves to testing alternative theories, which individuals have proposed, rather than worrying over the infinite number of potential theories that lack any pro-ponent. Even so, a particular database or case might not be able to dis-criminate between which of two or more competing explanations fits best. This is more a matter of how the evidence in a particular case matches up with competing hypotheses than a mechanical issue of the number of cases and the number of variables. This is why case study re-searchers seek crucial cases in order to be able to definitively test which of several theories fits best and, when such cases are not available, why they look for instances where a theory fails to fit a most-likely case or fits a least-likely one. When more than one competing explanation fits a case equally well, it may still be possible to narrow the number of plausible explanations, and it is also important to indicate as clearly as possible the extent to which the remaining hypotheses appear to be complementary, competing, or incommensurate in explaining the case.[56]

LACK OF REPRESENTATIVENESS

Case researchers do *not* aspire to select cases that are directly "representa-tive" of diverse populations and they usually do not and should not make claims that their findings are applicable to such populations except

---

56.   Olav Njølstad, "Learning From History? Case Studies and the Limits to The-ory-Building," in Olav Njølstad, ed., *Arms Races: Technological and Political Dynamics* (Newbury Park, Calif.: Sage Publications, 1990), pp. 220–246. See also our discussion of this problem in Chapter 2.

in contingent ways.[57] Statistical methods require a large sample of cases that is representative of and allows inferences about a larger population of cases from which the sample is drawn. Statistical researchers thus devote much effort to trying to make the sample as representative as possible. While useful and necessary in statistical studies, these practices are inappropriate and sometimes counterproductive when extended to case study methods or used to judge these methods, as some methodologists have urged.[58]

Case study methods involve a trade-off among the goals of attaining theoretical parsimony, establishing explanatory richness, and keeping the number the cases to be studied manageable. Parsimonious theories rarely offer rich explanations of particular cases, and such theories must be stated in highly general terms to be applicable across different types of cases.[59] Greater explanatory richness within a type of case usually leads to less explanatory power across other types of cases. In order to explain in rich detail different types of cases, it is usually necessary to give up theoretical parsimony and to study many cases. Case studies may uncover or refine a theory about a particular causal mechanism—such as collective action dynamics—that is applicable to vast populations of cases, but usually the effects of such mechanisms differ from one case or context to another.

In view of these trade-offs, case study researchers generally sacrifice the parsimony and broad applicability of their theories to develop cumulatively contingent generalizations that apply to well-defined types or subtypes of cases with a high degree of explanatory richness.[60] Case study researchers are more interested in finding the conditions under which specified outcomes occur, and the mechanisms through which they occur, rather than uncovering the frequency with which those conditions and their outcomes arise. Researchers often select cases with the

---

57.   Timothy McKeown, "Case Studies and the Statistical World View," *International Organization*, Vol. 53, No. 1 (Winter 1999), pp. 161–190.

58.   Stanley Lieberson, "Small N's and Big Conclusions," in Ragin and Becker, eds., *What is a Case? Exploring the Foundations of Social Inquiry*, pp. 108–109, 113, 116; Achen and Snidal, "Rational Deterrence Theory and Comparative Case Studies," pp. 160–161.

59.   Useful here is the reminder by King, Keohane, and Verba (*Designing Social Inquiry*, p. 20), that parsimony is not an unalloyed goal, and that "theory should be just as complicated as all our evidence suggests."

60.   Alexander L. George and Timothy McKeown, "Case Studies and Theories of Organizational Decision Making," in Robert Coulam and Richard Smith, eds., *Advances in Information Processing in Organizations*, Vol. 2 (Greenwich, Conn.: JAI Press, 1985), pp. 43–68; McKeown, "Case Studies and the Statistical World View."

goal of providing the strongest possible inferences on particular theories—most-likely or least-likely cases for a theory, or perhaps cases where the variables are at extreme values and the causal mechanisms are starkly evident. Researchers can also use deviant cases to help identify left-out variables.

In any of these research designs, the cases are necessarily unrepresentative of wider populations. Of course, in such research designs researchers must be careful to point out that they seek only contingent generalizations that apply to the subclass of cases that are similar to those under study, or that they seek to uncover causal mechanisms that may be in operation in a less extreme form in cases that have less extreme values on the pertinent variables. To the extent that there is a representativeness problem or a selection bias problem in a particular case study, it is often better described as the problem of "overgeneralizing" findings to types or subclasses of cases unlike those actually studied.[61]

SINGLE-CASE RESEARCH DESIGNS

Several of the above critiques of case study methods have converged into skepticism of the value of single-case studies. For example, *DSI* discourages research designs in which there is no variance on the dependent variable, and it also criticizes "single-observation" research designs.[62] As *DSI* argues, studies involving only a single observation are at great risk of indeterminacy in the face of more than one possible explanation, and they can lead to incorrect inferences if there is measurement error. This same text notes that a single case study can involve many observations, however, and in our view this greatly reduces these two problems.[63] Thus, in our view, several kinds of no-variance research designs can be quite useful in theory development and testing using multiple observa-

---

61. In some instances, critiques of particular case studies have overstated the problems of representativeness and selection bias by assuming that these studies have purported to offer generalizations that cover broad populations, whereas in fact these studies carefully circumscribed their claims to apply them only to cases similar to those studied. Collier and Mahoney ("Insights and Pitfalls," pp. 80–87) make this critique of Barbara Geddes's review of case studies and selection bias (Barbara Geddes, "How the Cases You Choose Affect the Answers You Get: Selection Bias in Comparative Politics," *Political Analysis*, Vol. 2 (1990), pp. 131–150).

62. King, Keohane, and Verba, *Designing Social Inquiry,* pp. 108, 208–211.

63. King, Keohane, and Verba, *Designing Social Inquiry,* pp. 208–211. A third potential problem *DSI* cites, the possibility of omitted variables or of some form of inherent probabilism, cannot be ruled out, regardless of methods, even when one has multiple observations.

DSI acknowledges that Harry Eckstein may also have intended for research designs of crucial, least-likely, and most-likely cases to use multiple observations from the same case to test alternative explanations (footnote, p. 210).

tions from a single case. These include the deviant, crucial, most-likely, and least-likely research designs, as well as single-case study tests of claims of necessity and sufficiency. Several influential works in comparative politics have used such single-case research designs to good effect.[64]

POTENTIAL LACK OF INDEPENDENCE OF CASES

One research design issue concerns whether cases are "independent" of one another. Here again, the statistical version of this problem does not apply to case studies, but a more fundamental concern does. In a statistical study, if a correlation is the result not of the hypotheses under consideration but of learning or diffusion from one case to the others, then the additional cases do not provide substantially new information and there are fewer degrees of freedom than the researcher thought (this is sometimes referred to as "Galton's Problem"). [65] In case studies, as in large-N research, there is a danger that the researcher will fail to identify a lack of independence between cases and will consequently reach false conclusions. This danger does not manifest itself as a "degrees of freedom" problem, however, and it is not necessarily amplified by the intentional selection of cases based on a preliminary knowledge of their variables (indeed, intentional selection can address the issue of the lack of independence of cases).

The question of whether the independence of cases is a relevant consideration depends on the research objectives of a particular study, what theory or hypothesis is being developed or tested, and how the comparison of cases is structured.[66] Process-tracing can inductively uncover linkages between cases and may thereby reduce the danger of any unanticipated lack of independence of cases. When learning or diffusion processes are anticipated or uncovered and taken into account, they need not undercut the value of studying partially dependent cases. Indeed, only perfectly dependent cases are capable of providing additional information.[67] Moreover, process-tracing can be particularly effective at examining the kinds of detailed sequences in learning and diffusion processes that can create relationships between cases, allowing researchers to gauge

---

64. Ronald Rogowski makes this point, citing works by Arend Lijphart, William Sheridan Allen, and Peter Alexis Gourevitch. (Ronald Rogowski, "The Role of Theory and Anomaly in Social-Scientific Inference," *American Political Science Review*, Vol. 89, No. 2 (June 1995), pp. 467–468.

65. George, "Case Studies and Theory Development," pp. 19–23; and King, Keohane, and Verba, *Designing Social Inquiry*, p. 222.

66. George, "Case Studies and Theory Development," p. 21.

67. King, Keohane, and Verba, *Designing Social Inquiry*, p. 222.

more accurately how much of the variance in outcomes is explained by learning or diffusion and how much is explained by other variables.[68]

A lack of independence of cases is useful in research that aims to test whether the lessons of an earlier case played a causal role in a later one. Hugh Heclo made use of this in studying the process of "political learning." Stephen Stedman's study of four sequential efforts at international mediation in Rhodesia's civil war also used the lack of case independence to identify possible learning from earlier cases. And, more generally, Jack Levy has suggested that intensive case studies that make use of process-tracing may be better suited than large-N quantitative studies for exploring the possibility of learning.[69]

Opportunities for Multi-Method Collaborative Research

The increasingly evident complementarity of case studies, statistical methods, and formal models is likely to lead toward more collaborative work by scholars using these various methods. The recent interest among rational choice theorists in using historical case studies to test their theories, for example, is an important step in this direction.[70] More generally, there are a variety of ways in which the three methods can be used together, either in a single study or sequentially.[71] Statistical analysis can help identify outliers or deviant cases, and case studies can then investigate why these cases are deviant, perhaps leading to the identification of omitted variables. Case studies can also explore the possible causal mechanisms behind the correlations or patterns observed in statistical studies, providing a check on whether correlations are spurious or potentially

---

68. George, "Case Studies and Theory Development," p. 21; see also commentaries on the studies by Hugh Heclo and Stephen Stedman in the Appendix, "Studies That Illustrate Research Design."

69. Hugh Heclo, *Modern Social Politics in Britain and Sweden* (New Haven, Conn.: Yale University Press, 1974); Stephen John Stedman, *Peacemaking in Civil War: International Mediation in Zimbabwe, 1974–1980* (Boulder, Colo.: Lynne Rienner, 1991); and Jack S. Levy, "Learning and Foreign Policy: Sweeping a Conceptual Minefield," *International Organization*, Vol. 48, No. 2 (Spring 1994), pp. 279–312. For a fuller discussion of the Heclo and Stedman studies, see the Appendix, "Studies That Illustrate Research Design." See also Jack Levy, "Explaining Events and Developing Theories: History, Political Science, and the Analysis of International Relations," in Colin Elman and Miriam Fendius Elman, eds., *Bridges and Boundaries: Historians, Political Scientists, and the Study of International Relations* (Cambridge, Mass.: MIT Press, 2001).

70. Bates et al., *Analytic Narratives*.

71. These techniques of multi-method research are discussed more fully in Andrew Bennett, "Where the Model Frequently Meets the Road: Combining Statistical, Formal, and Case Study Methods," presented at the American Political Science Association annual conference, Boston, Massachusetts, August 2002.

causal and adding details on how hypothesized causal mechanisms operate. Alternatively, when case studies lead to the specification of new variables or the refinement of concepts, statistical studies can explore whether these new variables and concepts are relevant to larger populations of cases. Formal models can be tested in case studies to see if their hypothesized causal mechanisms were in fact in operation, and the variables and concepts developed through case studies can be formalized in models.

Because case studies, statistical methods, and formal modeling are all increasingly sophisticated, however, it is becoming less likely that a single researcher can be adept at more than one set of methods while also attaining a cutting-edge theoretical and empirical knowledge of his field. Successful collaboration is therefore likely to take the form of several researchers working together using different methods, or of researchers more self-consciously building on the findings generated by scholars who have used different methods. In either form, effective collaboration requires that even as researchers become expert in one methodological approach, they must also become conversant with alternative approaches, aware of their strengths and limitations, and able to make informed reading of their substantive results. The next chapter shows how varied research methods have contributed to the progress of the democratic peace research program, from a broad hypothesis to a refined set of contingent generalizations.

Organization of the Book

This is a large book, and many readers may wish to focus on chapters that meet their current needs. Chapter 2 is about the research methods that political scientists have used to develop and study the democratic peace theory. It provides an extended illustration of what purposes are best served by different research methods; how knowledge accumulates within a research agenda; and how typological theories draw on the results of a large number of researchers. Chapter 2 reflects our strong belief that each research method is strong at answering particular kinds of questions, and that beyond the din of social scientists' sometimes heated disagreements, one can discern the cumulation of knowledge in the social sciences.

Part II is intended as a practical guide for graduate students. Chapter 3 introduces case study research design through a discussion of the method of structured, focused comparison. Chapter 4 covers the design of case studies; Chapter 5 discusses the work involved in actually carrying out the study; and Chapter 6 provides guidance for drawing implications for a theory from the findings of a case.

Part III addresses important methodological and epistemological issues of alternative case study methods and also discusses the use of typological theories. The section begins with Chapter 7, on the philosophical underpinnings of our methodological advice. Chapter 8, on comparative methods, focuses on the challenges of case methods that rely on the logic of controlled comparisons and highlights a need for methods that do not rely upon the covariance of variables. Chapter 9 discusses the congruence method, in which the researcher examines the correspondence between the values of the independent and dependent variables in a case. Chapter 10 discusses the method of process-tracing, and identifies its differences and similarities to historical explanation. Chapter 11, on the use of typological theories, provides guidance for the inductive and deductive construction of such theories, and the research designs supported by each. Chapter 12 offers additional advice on how to design research that will be relevant to policymakers; this chapter will also be useful to more senior academics who have not considered this issue.

We have also included an Appendix, "Studies that Illustrate Research Design," which briefly reviews the research designs of numerous books. This may be useful to graduate students who want to explore research designs in well-regarded studies; it may also be helpful to professors as they design classes in case study methods.

Chapter 2

Case Study Methods and Research on the Interdemocratic Peace

Political scientists have amassed growing evidence in the past three decades that democracies seldom if ever make war upon one another. This finding has sparked a rich literature on whether and how the international behavior of democracies is different from that of other kinds of regimes. Because the resulting "democratic peace" research program has developed so recently and rapidly, it has involved a broad range of sophisticated contemporary research methods and provides an excellent illustration of the methodological themes highlighted in Chapter 1.[1] Though disagreements among researchers over results and methods have often been sharp, it is clear that work on this subject by numerous scholars using several methods has achieved a progressively better understanding of when and how democracies use force, and the differences between their behavior and that of other types of regimes. Statistical methods, case studies, and formal models have all made important contributions to this cumulation of knowledge, and typological theories have been useful in synthesizing the literature on this topic, and in creating useful case study research designs.

This chapter analyzes the methodological lessons of the democratic peace research program, rather than directly engaging theoretical arguments about whether we should or should not expect democracies to be-

---

1. Of course, many different research programs in the social sciences illustrate the complementary nature of formal, statistical, and qualitative methods. For an analysis of how these methods have contributed to research in comparative politics, for example, see David Laitin, "Comparative Politics: The State of the Subdiscipline," in Ira Katznelson and Helen Milner, eds., *Political Science: State of the Discipline* (New York: Norton, 2002), pp. 630–659.

have differently from other kinds of regimes. One challenge in carrying out such an analysis is that the democratic peace research program has grown to encompass many different propositions. There is some evidence, for example, that democracies are more likely than other kinds of governments to ally with one another, trade with one another, form long-lasting intergovernmental organizations, accept mediation in disputes with one another, obey international law, avoid militarized disputes with one another short of war, and win the wars in which they choose to participate.[2] As the literature on these questions is vast and includes hypotheses with varying degrees of support, we focus on the hypothesis that democracies rarely if ever make war upon one another. We use the term "interdemocratic peace" to distinguish this hypothesis from the related argument, for which the evidence is more ambiguous, that democracies are generally less prone to war. The interdemocratic peace hypothesis is one of the earliest, most familiar, and best substantiated claims of the research program, and it has thus arguably generated the most methodologically diverse and sophisticated research.[3] This chapter assesses three methodological strands of the literature on this question that roughly succeeded one another.

The first generation of empirical research on the democratic peace, from the early 1960s through the late 1980s, for the most part utilized statistical methods to assess correlations between regime types and war. This research sought to establish whether democracies have been more peaceful generally or toward one another, and it attempted to determine whether correlations to this effect were spurious. The result was a fairly

---

2. For a listing of these and related hypotheses and the authors who introduced them, see James Lee Ray, "A Lakatosian View of the Democratic Piece Research Program," in Colin Elman and Miriam Fendius Elman, eds., *Progress in International Relations Theory: Appraising the Field* (Cambridge, Mass.: MIT Press, 2003), p. 221. As Ray points out, one of the most convincing arguments on behalf of the progressivity of the broader research program is that so many of the diverse auxiliary hypotheses that it has engendered have proven to have some merit.

3. Several of the auxiliary hypotheses have also involved sophisticated research using a variety of statistical, formal and case study methods. On the hypothesis that democracies tend to win the wars in which they participate, for example, see Dan Reiter and Alan Stam, *Democracies at War*, (Princeton, N.J.: Princeton University Press, 2002). This study uses both statistical and case study methods. See also David Lake, "Powerful Pacifists: Democratic States and War," *American Political Science Review*, Vol. 86, No. 1 (March 1992), pp. 24–37. For a critique of these works that turns on methodological issues, see Michael Desch, "Democracy and Victory: Why Régime Type Hardly Matters," *International Security*, Vol. 27, No. 2 (Fall 2002), pp. 5–47. For rejoinders, see David Lake, "Fair Fights? Evaluating Theories of Democracy and Victory"; Dan Reiter and Alan Stam, "Understanding Victory: Why Political Institutions Matter"; and Michael Desch, "Democracy and Victory: Fair Fights or Food Fights?" in *International Security*, Vol. 28, No. 1 (Summer 2003), pp. 154–194.

robust, but not unanimous consensus that democracies have rarely if ever fought wars against one another, but that they have engaged in war in general with about the same frequency as have other types of regime.

Yet adequate causal explanations must include two things: correlational or probabilistic statements associating purported causes with observed effects, *and* logically coherent and consistent assertions on the underlying causal mechanisms through which purported causes affect outcomes. As the focus of the research program began to shift from the "whether" to the "why" of the democratic peace, a second generation of research began to use case studies to test purported causal mechanisms more directly, develop more finely differentiated variables and typological theories, and identify new variables. This research was more cognizant of the possibility that the democratic peace might manifest the phenomenon of equifinality. In other words, as in the title of a book edited by Miriam Fendius Elman, there might be *Paths to Peace,* rather than one single path to peace among democracies.[4]

The third and most recent generation of literature on the interdemocratic peace has used formal models to refine theories on this phenomenon and has tested these revised theories with both statistical and case study research. Formal models have helped clarify the logic of how democratic institutions might both constrain democracies' foreign policy behaviors and inform other states of the credibility of commitments democratic leaders make regarding the possible use of force.

This chapter looks at these three generations of the literature on the interdemocratic peace. Yet this tripartite categorization of research on this topic should not be taken as suggesting that any one method has or will supplant others in the democratic peace research program or that the evolution of social science research programs generally proceeds from one method to another. Research using all three methods usually proceeds simultaneously and iteratively, as each method confronts new research tasks where another method is superior. Much useful work on the democratic peace remains to be done using all three approaches. As case studies and formal models refine the concepts and logic of democratic peace theories, statistical tests can fruitfully be redone using these new concepts and their associated measurements. Such tests will in turn help identify new sets of anomalous cases for further case studies, which can provide fertile ground for both inductive and formal refinements to extant theories, which will need to be tested by new statistical studies, and so on.

---

4. Miriam Fendius Elman, ed., *Paths to Peace: Is Democracy the Answer?* (Cambridge, Mass.: MIT Press, 1997).

The First Generation: Contributions of Statistical Methods

As James Lee Ray points out in his thorough review of the literature on the democratic peace, arguments for the existence of a democratic peace can be traced back to such liberal theorists as Immanuel Kant and Woodrow Wilson, and critiques of these arguments have an equally distinguished pedigree among realist thinkers like E. H. Carr and Hans Morgenthau and neorealists such as Kenneth Waltz.[5] Much of the contemporary research on this subject, however, can be traced back to a 1964 article by Dean Babst, a research scientist at the New York State Narcotic Addiction Control Commission.[6] In this four-page article, Babst concluded that "no wars have been fought between independent nations with elective governments between 1789 to 1941," and he calculated the difference between the proportions of democratic and mixed or nondemocratic dyads at war in World Wars I and II to be significant at the 1 percent level.[7] Yet Babst's article was theoretically underdeveloped, positing a monadic explanation (the purported reluctance of democratic publics to vote to take on the costs of war) for this dyadic result, and it did not control for important variables.

J. David Singer and Melvin Small rescued Babst's argument from obscurity among political scientists by critiquing it in a 1976 article that contended that the war involvement of democratic states between 1816 and 1965, in terms of duration and battle deaths, was not significantly different from that of other types of regimes. Singer and Small suggested that the absence of wars between democracies was due to the fact that democratic states rarely bordered upon one another, but they did not test this assertion.[8] In the late 1970s and 1980s, a rapidly expanding body of statistical research made three key contributions to the democratic peace research program. First, statistical studies refined the research question from whether democratic states were more peaceful in general to whether they were more peaceful only or primarily toward one another (the interdemocratic peace).[9] Some research continued on the monadic

---

5. James Lee Ray, *Democracies and International Conflict: An Evaluation of the Democratic Peace Process* (Columbia: University of South Carolina Press, 1995), pp. 1–9.

6. Ibid., p. 11.

7. Dean V. Babst, "Elective Governments: A Force for Peace," *Wisconsin Sociologist*, Vol. 3, No. 1 (1964), pp. 9–14.

8. Melvin Small and J. David Singer, "The War-Proneness of Democratic Regimes," *Jerusalem Journal of International Relations*, Vol. 1, No. 1 (1976), pp. 50–69.

9. Rudolph J. Rummel, *War, Power, Peace* (Beverly Hills, Calif.: Sage Publications, 1979); Steve Chan, "Mirror, Mirror, on the Wall . . . Are the Freer Countries More Pacific?" *Journal of Conflict Resolution*, Vol. 28, No. 4 (December 1984), pp. 617–648;

proposition that democracies might be more peaceful in general, but research increasingly focused on the stronger evidence for an inter-democratic peace.[10] Researchers also used statistical methods to test whether democracies have been less likely than other states to engage in conflicts short of war—both generally and vis-à-vis one another.[11] Some researchers also began to examine whether subtypes of states, such as states in transition to democracy, were more or less prone to war.[12] Second, many statistical studies tested for whether findings of an interdemocratic peace were spurious by controlling for the effects of numerous variables—including contiguity, wealth, alliance membership, relative military capabilities, rates of economic growth, and the presence of a hegemon.[13] Third, researchers using statistical methods theorized on and began to test the potential causal mechanisms behind an interdemocratic peace, often grouping them together under explanations relating to democratic norms or institutions or some interaction between the two.[14]

Erich Weede, "Democracy and War Involvement," *Journal of Conflict Resolution*, Vol. 28, No. 4 (December 1984), pp. 649–664; Michael Doyle, "Liberalism and World Politics," *American Political Science Review*, Vol. 80, No. 4 (December 1986), pp. 1151–1161; Nasrian Abdolali and Zeev Maoz, "Regime Types and International Conflict, 1817–1976," *Journal of Conflict Resolution*, Vol. 33, No. 1 (March 1989), pp. 3–35; and Zeev Maoz and Bruce Russett, "Normative and Structural Causes of Democratic Peace, 1946–1986," *American Political Science Review*, Vol. 87, No. 3 (September 1993), pp. 624–638.

10. David Rousseau et al., "Assessing the Dyadic Nature of the Democratic Peace," *American Political Science Review*, Vol. 90, No. 3 (September 1996), pp. 512–533.

11. T. Clifton Morgan and Valerie L. Schwebach, "Take Two Democracies and Call Me in the Morning: A Prescription for Peace?" *International Interactions*, Vol. 19, No. 4 (1992), p. 305; Bruce Bueno de Mesquita and David Lalman, *War and Reason* (New Haven, Conn.: Yale University Press, 1992); and William J. Dixon, "Democracy and the Peaceful Settlement of International Conflict," *American Political Science Review*, Vol. 88, No. 1 (March 1994), pp. 14–32.

12. Jack Snyder and Edward D. Mansfield make a monadic argument that states in transition to democracy are particularly prone to war. See Jack Snyder and Edward D. Mansfield, "Democratization and the Danger of War," *International Security*, Vol. 20, No. 1 (Summer 1995), pp. 5–38. In their subsequent book on this topic, these authors use both statistical tests and case studies to elaborate upon this argument. See Edward D. Mansfield and Jack Snyder, *Electing to Fight: Why Emerging Democracies Go to War* (Cambridge, Mass.: MIT Press, forthcoming).

13. Maoz and Russett, "Normative and Structural Causes of Democratic Peace"; and Stuart A. Bremer, "Democracy and Militarized Interstate Conflict, 1816–1965," *International Interactions*, Vol. 18, No. 3 (1993), pp. 231–249. For a more complete list of variables and studies, see Margaret Hermann and Charles Kegley, Jr., "Rethinking Democracy and International Peace: Perspectives From Political Psychology," *International Studies Quarterly*, Vol. 39, No. 4 (December 1995), pp. 511–533.

14. Maoz and Russett, "Normative and Structural Causes of Democratic Peace,"

On the first two tasks of refining the research question and testing for possible spuriousness, statistical methods greatly advanced the research program and achieved a growing consensus among researchers.[15] The conflict behavior of democracies and other regime types gained attention as a research program worthy of intensive study, even among skeptics of a democratic peace. Also, a consensus emerged that democracies are not markedly more peaceful in general, although some studies continue to challenge and qualify this conclusion.[16] The consensus view is also that democracies have fought wars substantially less frequently against one another than they have against other types of states, although opinions differ on the number and seriousness of exceptions to this generalization.[17] A weaker consensus emerged around the idea that democracies are less likely to engage in militarized disputes with one another short of war.[18]

Statistical methods proved less successful at explaining why an interdemocratic peace might exist. Researchers using statistical methods had theorized and rigorously defined several potential causal mechanisms that might explain the democratic peace, focusing on democratic institutions and democratic norms. However, the posited causal mechanisms were often contradictory, and no consensus existed on which of these variables caused an interdemocratic peace. Statistical methods proved inadequate to test these mechanisms for three reasons. First, they

---

pp. 624–638; and Dixon, "Democracy and the Peaceful Settlement of International Conflict."

15.   For similar assessments of where the consensus lies on these issues, see Ray, *Democracies and International Conflict;* Bear F. Braumoeller, "Causal Complexity and the Study of Politics," *Political Analysis,* Vol. 13, No. 3 (2003), pp. 209–233; Bueno de Mesquita and Lalman, *War and Reason;* and Elman, ed., *Paths to Peace.*

16.   Rousseau et al., "Assessing the Dyadic Nature of the Democratic Peace."

17.   For an account that uses statistical methods to question the existence of an interdemocratic peace, see David E. Spiro, "The Insignificance of the Liberal Peace," *International Security,* Vol. 19, No. 2 (Fall 1994), pp. 50–86. In subsequent published correspondence, Bruce Russett critiques Spiro's argument, particularly Spiro's assumption that dyadic data points lack independence and offers some of the most convincing statistical tests yet for the existence of an interdemocratic peace (Bruce Russett, "Correspondence: The Democratic Peace," *International Security,* Vol. 19, No. 4 (Spring 1995), pp. 164–184). For an additional account that finds Russett's statistical tests more convincing, see Braumoeller, "Causal Complexity and the Study of Politics." For an additional account that questions the statistical validity of the finding of an interdemocratic peace, see Henry Farber and Joanne Gowa, "Polities and Peace," *International Security,* Vol. 20, No. 2 (Fall 1995), pp. 123–146.

18.   Dixon, "Democracy and the Peaceful Settlement of International Conflict," pp. 14–32; Elman, ed., *Paths to Peace,* p. 48.

faced daunting measurement problems.[19] One of the most methodologically sophisticated efforts to test for the normative versus institutional causes of the democratic peace, by Bruce Russett and Zeev Maoz, illustrates these problems. Maoz and Russett use well-established and straightforward measures to control for wealth, economic growth, and contiguity. They also employ careful measures of more complex variables such as alliance membership and ratios of military capabilities. Their measurement of democratic institutions is more complex, though there is at least some consensus on this issue, as many quantitative studies have joined Maoz and Russett in relying on the "Polity II" data set, or modified versions of this data set.[20] The most difficult measurement problem, however, is that there is no easy way to quantify the slippery variable of "democratic norms" and no widely accepted database for this variable. Consequently, Maoz and Russett used the longevity of political regimes as a proxy for the prevalence of their norms, and they used the average number of recent deaths from domestic political violence or executions within a dyad as a measure of the "democraticness" of that dyad's norms.[21] Clearly, these proxy measures are problematic, as authoritarian and totalitarian states that persist for decades may minimize the use of domestic violence by monopolizing the instruments of force and creating powerful police and intelligence institutions that deter domestic violence and political opposition.

To some extent, even measurement problems on complex variables like democratic norms can be addressed, and statistical researchers have proven adept at devising creative ways of measuring complex variables. One study by Bear Braumoeller, for example, has developed a dedicated definition and data set for looking at democratic norms as they relate to the democratic peace. This study even measures the differences between the norms of elites and those of mass publics.[22] This is a very labor-

---

19.   On the difficulties of conceptualizing and measuring democracy, and on the strengths and weaknesses of various statistical databases in doing so, see Gerardo Munck and Jay Verkuilen, "Conceptualizing and Measuring Democracy: Evaluating Alternative Indices," *Comparative Political Studies*, Vol. 35, No. 1 (February 2002), pp. 5–34.

20.   Ted Gurr et al., "The Transformation of the Western State: The Growth of Democracy, Autocracy, and State Power Since 1800," *Studies in Comparative International Development*, Vol. 25, No. 1 (1990), pp. 73–108. The "Polity" data set, begun in the 1970s, has been updated several times, and the current "Polity IV" version is available at <http://weber.ucsd.edu/?kgledits/Polity.html>.

21.   Maoz and Russett, "Normative and Structural Causes of Democratic Peace," p. 630.

22.   Braumoeller, "Causal Complexity and the Study of Politics."

intensive task and it is all but impossible to implement for states for which extensive and dedicated polling data is not available. More generally, data sets that quantify or dichotomize variables can achieve reproducible results across many cases (external validity), but only at the cost of losing some of the ability to devise measures that faithfully represent the variables that they are designed to capture (internal validity).

A second problem is that statistical methods are not well suited to testing causal mechanisms in the context of particular cases. These methods are optimized for assessing correlations across cases or among data points within a case, rather than for testing whether every aspect of a case is consistent with a hypothesized causal process. In contrast to statistical methods, if process-tracing shows that a single step in a hypothesized causal chain in a case study is not as the theory predicts, then the variable in question cannot explain that case without modification, even if it does explain most or even all other cases. If, for example, we find a case in which a democratic public clamored for going to war, the hypothesized propensity of democratic citizens to avoid voting upon themselves the cost of war cannot explain this case, even if it might explain other cases. Conversely, if a complex hypothesis involved one hundred steps and ninety-nine of these were as predicted in a case, a statistical test would confirm the hypothesized process at a high level of significance, but a case study analysis would continue to probe the missing step.

Third, the relative infrequency of both wars and contiguous democracies presents a sharp methodological limitation for statistical research. Given the small number of potential wars between democracies, the existence of even a few wars between democracies or the omission of a single relevant variable could call into question the statistical support for an interdemocratic peace.[23] Because there are at least twenty hotly debated potential exceptions or near-exceptions to the assertion that democracies have never fought wars with one another, the results of statistical studies remain provisional despite the emerging consensus that an interdemocratic peace exists.[24] For case study researchers, this is an opportunity rather than a problem: it is easily possible for the field as a whole to intensively study every one of the possible exceptions to the democratic peace and to also include a number of comparative cases of mixed dyads and nondemocratic dyads.

---

23. Ray, *Democracies and International Conflict;* and Spiro, "The Insignificance of the Liberal Peace."

24. Ray, *Democracies and International Conflict*, pp. 86–87.

The Second Generation: Case Study Contributions

As one researcher argued in the 1990s, "generalizations about the democratic peace are fine—we have many of them—but now is the time to explore via comparative case studies the causal chains, if they exist."[25] The
limitations of statistical methods as applied to the democratic peace were
greatest precisely where case study methods had the most to contribute.[26]
Case studies on the democratic peace in the past decade illustrate the
comparative advantages of qualitative methods and offer commendable
examples of alternative research designs.

One of the main advantages of case studies is their ability to serve the
heuristic purpose of inductively identifying additional variables and generating hypotheses.[27] Statistical methods lack accepted procedures for inductively generating new hypotheses. Moreover, case studies can analyze
qualitatively complex events and take into account numerous variables
precisely because they do not require numerous cases or a restricted
number of variables. Case study researchers are also not limited to variables that are readily quantified or those for which well-defined data sets
already exist. Case studies on the democratic peace have thus identified
or tested several new variables, including issue-specific state structures,
specific norms on reciprocity and the use of deadly force, leaders' perceptions of the democraticness of other states, transparency, and the distinction between status quo and challenger states.[28]

Second, process-tracing can test individual cases regarding the claims
made about causal mechanisms that might account for a democratic
peace. Miriam Elman, for example, asserts that

---

25.   Correspondence of Kalevi Holsti, cited in Elman, ed., *Paths to Peace*, p. 44.

26.   Elman, ed., *Paths to Peace*, p. 43.

27.   Harry Eckstein, "Case Studies and Theory in Political Science," in Fred
Greenstein and Nelson Polsby, eds., *Handbook of Political Science*, Vol. 7 (Reading,
Mass.: Addison-Wesley, 1975), pp. 79–138; Alexander L. George, "Case Studies and
Theory Development," in Paul G. Lauren, ed., *Diplomacy: New Approaches in Theory,
History, and Policy* (New York: Free Press, 1979), pp. 43–68.

28.   See, respectively, Susan Peterson, "How Democracies Differ: Public Opinion,
State Structure, and the Lessons of the Fashoda Crisis," *Security Studies*, Vol. 5, No. 1
(Autumn 1995), pp. 3–37; William Hoeft, *Explaining Interdemocratic Peace: The Norm of
Cooperatively Biased Reciprocity* (Ph.D. dissertation, Georgetown University, 1993); John
M. Owen, "How Liberalism Produces Democratic Peace," *International Security*, Vol.
19, No. 2 (Fall 1994), pp. 87–125; Bernard Finel and Kristin Lord, "The Surprising Logic
of Transparency," *International Studies Quarterly*, Vol. 43, No. 2 (June 1999), pp. 315–339;
and Ray, *Democracies and International Conflict*, p. 196.

The quantitative empirical analyses that find that democracy is associated with peace are correlational studies, and provide no evidence that leaders actually consider the opponent's regime type in deciding between war and peace. These studies focus primarily on foreign policy outcomes and ignore the decision-making process. If we want to move beyond correlation to causation, we need to reveal the decision-making processes of aggressive and pacific states.[29]

Both proponents and critics of the existence of a democratic peace agree on the importance of process-tracing on causal mechanisms, and researchers who had once relied largely on statistical methods have turned to case study methods because of these methods' ability to test causal mechanisms.[30] Some have combined statistical and case study techniques.[31] Since the 1990s, scholars have used case study methods to test many of the hypothesized causal mechanisms and independent variables listed above, but there is not yet a consensus on which causal mechanisms might account for a democratic peace. However, case studies have been able to rule out the presence of some causal mechanisms in important cases. For example, the assertion that democratic mass publics oppose wars with other democracies does not hold for the Fashoda Crisis between Britain and France in 1898.[32]

Third, case studies can develop typological theories (theories on how different combinations of independent variables interact to produce different levels or types of dependent variables). Researchers have begun to identify the conditions under which specified types of democracies behave in various contexts to produce specific types of conflict behavior within democratic or mixed dyads.[33] The resulting theories usually focus on interactions among combinations of variables, rather than variables considered in isolation.

The development of typological theories thus involves differentiating configurations of independent and dependent variables into qualitatively different "types," such as types of war or types of democracy. The task of

---

29.   Elman, ed., *Paths to Peace*, p. 33.

30.   Owen, "How Liberalism Produces Democratic Peace," p. 91; Christopher Layne, "Kant or Cant: The Myth of Democratic Peace," *International Security*, Vol. 19, No. 2 (Fall 1994), pp. 12–13; and Ray, *Democracies and International Conflict*, pp. 151; 158–159.

31.   See Mansfield and Snyder, *Electing to Fight;* and Edgar Kiser, Kriss A. Drass, and William Brustein, "Ruler Autonomy and War in Early Modern Europe," *International Studies Quarterly*, Vol. 39, No. 1 (March 1995), pp. 109–138.

32.   Ray, *Democracies and International Conflict;* and Peterson, "How Democracies Differ."

33.   Elman, ed., *Paths to Peace*, pp. 40–41.

defining "war" and "democracy" is challenging for both statistical and case study researchers, and they respond to it differently. Statistical researchers attempt to develop rigorous but general definitions, with a few attributes that apply across a wide number of cases. Case study researchers usually include a larger number of attributes to develop more numerous types and subtypes, each of which may apply to a relatively small number of cases.[34] In the context of the democratic peace, for example, case study researchers have suggested differentiating between centralized and decentralized democracies, and among democracies where leaders and mass publics either share or have different norms regarding the use of force vis-à-vis other democracies.[35] It is also useful to distinguish among different kinds of peace. Alexander George has suggested, for example, that it is important to distinguish among three types of peace: "precarious peace," which is the temporary cessation of hostilities when one side remains dissatisfied with the status quo and continues to see force as a legitimate means of changing it; "conditional peace," such as the situation that existed during the Cold War, when the threat of mutual destruction by nuclear weapons helped deter war; and "stable peace," when two states no longer even consider or plan for the possibility of using force against one another.[36]

Two examples illustrate particularly well the kind of typological theories that case studies can develop to model complex interactions of variables. The first is Susan Peterson's model of how war was averted in the Fashoda Crisis in ways that are not entirely consistent with either liberal or realist views of the democratic peace. Peterson argues that systemic variables (such as military balance) interacted with state institutions and the preferences of leaders and public opinion in France and Britain to avert war. In Britain, she argues, the dovish Prime Minister Lord Robert Cecil (the Earl of Salisbury) was constrained by a strong and hawkish cabinet, parliament, and public, and was pushed into more confrontational policies than he would have liked. In France, the hawkish Foreign Minister Theophile Delcasse was constrained by a more dovish parliament and public, as well as by France's military inferiority, but not by his own cabinet. As a result, France pushed harder for concessions and Salisbury was more willing to make them than realists might expect, while

34. David Collier and Steven Levitsky, "Democracy with Adjectives: Conceptual Innovation in Comparative Research," World Politics, Vol. 49, No. 3 (April 1997), pp. 430–451; and Elman, ed., Paths to Peace, pp. 35–39.

35. Elman, ed., Paths to Peace, pp. 36–37; 41.

36. Alexander L. George, "Foreword" in Arie Kacowicz, ed., A Stable Peace Among Nations (Lanham, Md.: Roman and Littlefield, 2000), pp. xii–xiii.

traditional liberal theories on the democratic peace have difficulty explaining the British public's willingness to go to war against France.[37]

A second example is Randall Schweller's study of how democracies behave with regard to preventive war. Like Peterson, Schweller incorporates both systemic and domestic variables, looking at how domestic structures affect state decisions on preventive wars during ongoing power shifts. Schweller concludes that only nondemocratic states wage preventive wars against rising opponents, and that democracies seek accommodation with rising democracies and form counterbalancing alliances against rising nondemocratic challengers.[38]

Both these studies define useful subtypes of democracies, but not every subtype is useful or progressive. Researchers might allow their subjective biases to intrude, leading them to define away anomalies through the creation of subtypes. As Miriam Elman argues, for example, "defining democracy as a regime in an independent state that ensures full civil and economic liberties; voting rights for virtually all the adult population; and peaceful transfers of power between competing political groups makes it fairly easy to exclude numerous cases of warring democracies."[39] The creation of a new subtype is warranted if it helps explain not only the aspects of a case that led to the creation of this subtype, but also other unexplained dimensions of the case or of other cases. The assertion that "new" or "transitional" democracies are more war-prone and should be treated differently from other cases that might fit the democratic peace, for example, may warrant the creation of a new subtype. It posits testable correlations and causal mechanisms and suggests dynamics that should make states in transitions from as well as into democracy more war-prone.[40] More questionable is the exclusion from assertions on the "democratic peace" of civil wars, like the U.S. Civil War.[41] Also debatable is the exclusion from some data sets of conflicts that fall somewhat below the arbitrary figure of 1,000 battle deaths, such as the conflict between Finland and Britain during World War II.[42]

While case study methods are particularly amenable to creating subtypes and differentiating variables, they have no monopoly on such inno-

---

37.   Peterson, "How Democracies Differ."

38.   Randall L. Schweller, "Domestic Structure and Preventive War: Are Democracies More Pacific?" *World Politics*, Vol. 44, No. 2 (January 1992), pp. 235–269. The U.S. invasion of Iraq in 2003 may constitute an important exception to Schweller's argument.

39.   Elman, *Paths to Peace*, p. 21.

40.   Snyder and Mansfield, "Democratization and the Danger of War."

41.   Spiro, "The Insignificance of the Liberal Peace."

42.   Ibid. See also Elman, ed., *Paths to Peace*, pp. 22–23.

vations. Studies using statistical methods have addressed the behavior of "democratizing" states and have examined the behavior of states that have democratic institutions but not democratic norms.[43] Also, once case studies identify potentially useful subtypes, if a sufficient number of cases in the subtype exists statistical tests can assess whether these subtypes are indeed correlated with the specified outcome. In this way, case studies can often help develop sharper concepts, subtypes, or measurement procedures that can then be incorporated into statistical studies, though this can require considerable effort in recoding the cases in existing statistical datasets.

Examples of Case Study Research Design in the Interdemocratic Peace Literature

The democratic peace literature provides some of the best examples of how to implement case studies. These examples illustrate the important point that there is no single "case study research design." Rather, different case study research designs use varying combinations of within-case analysis, cross-case comparisons, induction, and deduction for different theory-building purposes.[44] An excellent example of a case study research design using both within-case analysis and cross-case comparisons is *Paths to Peace*, edited by Miriam Elman. Elman carefully defines the class of cases to be studied—international crises between democratic, mixed, and nondemocratic dyads—while acknowledging that this class of cases cannot adequately test the assertion that democracies frequently resolve their conflicts with one another without resorting to war.[45] The alternative of trying to select "non-crisis" as well as crisis cases is obviously problematic, and crisis cases have the advantage of posing tough tests for hypotheses supporting the democratic peace. Moreover, Elman selects cases that provide substantial variance on the independent and dependent variables, and in contrast to many studies, includes cases of both wars and successful crisis management from all three types of dyads: demo-

43. Snyder and Mansfield, · "Democratization and the Danger of War"; and Braumoeller, "Causal Complexity and the Study of Politics."

44. There are, unfortunately, no good examples of a "crucial" or critical case in the democratic peace literature. As Eckstein argues, history seldom provides clear examples of cases that satisfy the demanding criteria of a crucial case. The second best alternative, Eckstein argues, are "most- likely" cases that a theory fails or "least-likely" cases that a theory passes (Harry Eckstein, "Case Studies and Theory in Political Science," in Fred Greenstein and Nelson Polsby, eds., *Handbook of Political Science*, Vol. 7, pp. 79–138). These constitute "tough tests" for the theory, and Elman provides examples of such tough tests (*Paths to Peace*, p. 47).

45. Elman, ed., *Paths to Peace*, pp. 47–52.

cratic dyads, mixed dyads, and nondemocratic dyads.[46] Elman also evaluates alternative hypotheses via process-tracing and cross-case comparison tests.

The democratic peace literature has also produced commendable examples of research designs that incorporate "least similar" and "most similar" cases. In the most similar case design, the researcher attempts to select cases that are similar in all of their independent variables except one and differ in their dependent variable. James Lee Ray uses this design to compare the cases of the Fashoda Crisis and the Spanish-American War.[47] Ray carefully addresses each of the standard categories of confounding variables identified by Donald Campbell and Julian Stanley, including "regression" (selection of cases with extreme scores on the variables of interest) and other kinds of selection bias, as well as "mortality" (the differential loss of respondents from the study: in this instance, the possibility that states may become more authoritarian as they see a war coming).[48] Ray obviates other standard problems, such as the effects of history, maturation, and changes in instrumentation, by selecting cases from the same year. Ray also addresses six other variables that might account for the different outcomes of the two cases: proximity, power ratios, alliances, levels of economic development, militarization, and political stability. Ray's systematic attention to these aspects of cross-case comparison, as well as his use of process-tracing evidence, bolsters his conclusions that Spain's autocracy contributed to the Spanish-American War and that democracy in France and Britain helped peacefully resolve the Fashoda Crisis.[49]

As for the research design of least similar cases, Carol and Melvin Ember and Bruce Russett use the logic of this design, together with the instruments of statistical research, to test assertions about the democratic peace. In a least similar cases design, the researcher selects cases that are dissimilar in all but one independent variable, but that share the same dependent variable. This can provide evidence that the single common independent variable, in this instance the democratic decision-making processes, may account for the common dependent variable. In their study, Ember, Ember, and Russett test the findings of studies on the democratic

46.   Ibid., pp. 47–52.

47.   Ray, *Democracies and International Conflict*, pp. 159–200.

48.   *Donald Campbell and Julian Stanley, Experimental and Quasi-Experimental Design for Research* (Chicago: Rand McNally, 1963).

49.   Ray, *Democracies and International Conflict*, pp. 159–200; Carol Ember, Melvin Ember, and Bruce Russett, "Peace Between Participatory Polities: A Cross-Cultural Test of the 'Democracies Rarely Fight Each Other' Hypothesis," *World Politics*, Vol. 44, No.4 (July 1992), pp. 573–599.

peace among modern states and test them against pre-industrial societies; they find support for the proposition that participatory decision-making processes are conducive to peace in otherwise very different industrial and pre-industrial societies.

Both the most similar and least similar designs for case study comparisons, which rely on the logic of John Stuart Mill's "method of difference" and "method of agreement," respectively, are subject to methodological limitations that Mill and others have identified.[50] In particular, the omission of relevant variables can entirely invalidate the results of cross-case comparisons in either design. Yet there are safeguards against this, as exemplified by Ray's careful attention to a wide range of alternative hypotheses to ensure that no relevant variables are omitted from the comparison. In addition, process-tracing (undertaken by Ray, by Ember, and by Russett) provides an additional check on the results of cross-case comparisons.

Critiques and Challenges of Case Study Methods as Applied to the Democratic Peace

The case study literature on the democratic peace reveals two problems in case study methods: the problem of case selection and that of reconciling conflicting interpretations of the same cases. On the issue of case selection, there is always the danger that case study researchers' subjective biases and commitments to certain theoretical propositions will lead them to select cases that over-confirm their favorite hypotheses (a different and potentially more serious problem than that addressed in standard discussions of selection biases in statistical studies, which result in truncated samples and under-confirmation of hypotheses).[51] Biased case selection can also arise from the fact that evidence on certain cases is more readily accessible than that on others and from the tendency for historically important cases to be overrepresented relative to studies of obscure—but theoretically illuminating—events. Miriam Elman argues, for example, that democratic peace case studies overemphasize cases involving the United States and that they have focused excessively on the study of the Fashoda Crisis and the Spanish-American War compared to possible exceptions of the democratic peace. She also maintains that demo-

---

50. Alexander L. George and Timothy J. McKeown, "Case Studies and Theories of Organizational Decision Making," in Robert Coulam and Richard Smith, eds., *Advances in Information Processing in Organizations*, Vol. 2 (Greenwich, Conn.: JAI Press, 1985), pp. 43–68.

51. David Collier and James Mahoney, "Insights and Pitfalls: Selection Bias in Qualitative Research," *World Politics*, Vol. 49, No. 1 (October 1996), pp. 56–91.

cratic dyads have been over-studied relative to mixed and nondemocratic dyads.[52] On the other hand, for some theory-building purposes mixed dyads are less interesting, and existing studies of wars in mixed and nondemocratic dyads may help fill this gap. Studies that show that states have initiated wars despite inferior military capabilities, for example, call into question assertions that military imbalances alone help explain cases of successful crisis management by democracies. Still, Elman is justified in arguing that more dedicated case studies of mixed and even nondemocratic dyads are needed for comparative research designs like Ray's study of the Spanish-American War and the Fashoda Crisis.

Yet the substantial convergence among supporters and critics of the democratic peace on which cases deserve study demonstrates that case selection is not an arbitrary process. Several cases have been mentioned by numerous scholars as possible deviant cases, or exceptions to the democratic peace, including the War of 1812, the U.S. Civil War, conflicts between Ecuador and Peru, the Fashoda Crisis, the Spanish-American War, and Finland's conflict with Britain in World War II. Many of the fourteen other possible exceptions to the democratic peace listed by Ray have also been cited by more than one author or subjected to more than one case study.[53] The initial focus on "near wars" between democracies and "near democracies" that went to war was appropriate for the first wave of case studies of the interdemocratic peace, as it offered tough tests of such a theory. As researchers accumulate adequate studies of these cases, they can branch out into more comparisons to mixed and nondemocratic dyads, as Elman has begun to do.

As researchers conduct multiple studies of particular cases, how can they reconcile or judge conflicting interpretations of the same cases? Olav Njølstad emphasizes this problem in case study research, noting that differing interpretations may arise from several sources. First, competing explanations or interpretations could be equally consistent with the process-tracing evidence, making it hard to determine whether both are at play and the outcome is overdetermined, whether the variables in competing explanations have a cumulative effect, or whether one variable is causal and the other spurious. Second, competing explanations may address different aspects of a case, and they may not be commensurate. Third, studies may simply disagree on the "facts" of the case.

Njølstad offers several useful suggestions on these problems.[54] These suggestions include: identifying and addressing factual errors, disagree-

---

52.   Elman, ed., *Paths to Peace*, pp. 47–52.

53.   Ray, *Democracies and International Conflict*, pp. 86–87.

54.   Olav Njølstad, "Learning From History? Case Studies and the Limits to The-

ments, and misunderstandings; identifying all potentially relevant theoretical variables and hypotheses; comparing various case studies of the same events that employ different theoretical perspectives (analogous to paying careful attention to all the alternative hypotheses in a single case study); identifying additional testable and observable implications of competing interpretations of a single case; and identifying the scope conditions for explanations of a case or category of cases.

The democratic peace literature illustrates how these suggestions work in practice. There is some factual disagreement on whether both British and French public opinion was bellicose in the Fashoda Crisis or whether British public opinion was substantially more supportive of going to war, and some argue that foreign policymaking was so dominated by elites in both cases that public opinion made little difference.[55] Similarly, there is some disagreement on the nature and salience of public opinion in Spain at the time of the Spanish-American War.[56]

On the Fashoda Crisis, there is disagreement on whether democracy in both states and a wide power imbalance overdetermined the peaceful outcome, whether they had cumulative effects, or whether one factor was more causal and the other more spurious.[57] This may be resolvable through more systematic analysis of process-tracing data, or careful counterfactual analysis, but likely will not be entirely determined to the satisfaction of a scholarly consensus.[58] The same is true of discussions on whether a large power disparity and a (perceived) absence of democracy

---

ory-Building," in Olav Njølstad, ed., *Arms Races: Technological and Political Dynamics* (Newbury Park, Calif.: Sage Publications, 1990), pp. 240–244. We disagree with Njølstad's suggestion that these approaches are substantially different from the standard methodological advice offered by those who have outlined the method of structured, focused comparisons between cases. See George, "Case Studies and Theory Development," and George and McKeown, "Case Studies and Theories of Organizational Decision Making," pp. 21–58.

55.   See, respectively, Kevin Wang and James Lee Ray, "Beginners and Winners: The Fate of Initiators of Interstate Wars Involving Great Powers Since 1495," *International Studies Quarterly*, Vol. 38, No. 1 (March 1994), pp. 139–154; Robert Bates et al., *Analytic Narratives* (Princeton, N.J.: Princeton University Press, 1998); Peterson, "How Democracies Differ"; and Ray, *Democracies and International Conflict*.

56.   Owen, "How Liberalism Produces Democratic Peace," pp. 87–125; and José Varela Ortega, "Aftermath of Splendid Disaster: Spanish Politics Before and After the Spanish-American War of 1898," *Journal of Contemporary History*, Vol. 15, No. 2 (April 1980), pp. 317–344.

57.   Ray, *Democracies and International Conflict*; Peterson, "How Democracies Differ;" and Layne, "Kant or Cant."

58.   Philip Tetlock and Aaron Belkin, eds., *Counterfactual Thought Experiments: Logical, Methodological, and Psychological Perspectives* (Princeton, N.J.: Princeton, University Press, 1996).

in Spain were both necessary conditions for the Spanish-American War.[59] In case study methods, as in statistical methods, scholars may at times have to live with some degree of indeterminacy when competing variables push in the same direction.

One disagreement that has been narrowed by additional research concerns the question of how to interpret Finland's decision to side with Germany against several democracies in World War II. Democratic peace proponents note that Finland did not undertake any offensive operations against democratic states, and the only attack against Finland by a democracy consisted of a single day of British bombing.[60] Critics argue that the Finnish case should be considered an important exception to the democratic peace because Finland became a co-belligerent with Germany and several democracies declared war on Finland.[61] Miriam Elman's careful case study of the Finnish case suggests that more centralized or semi-presidential democracies like Finland are more likely than decentralized democracies to engage in war with other democracies. She indicates that the Finnish parliament resisted aligning with Germany, but was overruled by the Finnish president. Thus, while the case does not fit neorealist theories arguing that systemic pressures are paramount, neither does it strongly vindicate interdemocratic peace theories.[62]

The Third Generation: Formal Modeling Contributions

Researchers have more recently begun to use formal models to help unravel the causal mechanisms that might explain the correlational and case study findings on the interdemocratic peace. We concentrate here on Kenneth Schultz's work on this subject, which provides an excellent exemplar both of formal work, and of multi-method research that tests a formal model with statistical and case study evidence.[63] Schultz frames his

59.   Ray, *Democracies and International Conflict*.

60.   Russett, "Correspondence: The Democratic Peace."

61.   Spiro, "The Insignificance of the Liberal Peace."

62.   Elman, ed., *Paths to Peace*, pp. 192–197.

63.   Kenneth A. Schultz, *Democracy and Coercive Diplomacy* (Cambridge: Cambridge University Press, 2001). Additional formal modeling work relevant to the interdemocratic peace includes Bueno de Mesquita and Lalman, *War and Reason;* Bruce Bueno de Mesquita, James D. Morrow, Randolph M. Siverson, and Alastair Smith, "An Institutional Explanation of the Democratic Peace," *American Political Science Review,* Vol. 92, No. 3 (September 1998), pp. 623–638; and George W. Downs and David Rocke, "Conflict, Agency, and Gambling for Resurrection: The Principal-Agent Problem Goes to War," *American Journal of Political Science,* Vol. 38, No. 2 (May 1994), pp. 362–380. For a discussion of these works and other applications of formal models to security stud-

research around the question whether democratic institutions primarily constrain or inform decisions on the use of force. The constraint theory argues that democratic publics are reluctant to vote upon themselves the costs of war, and will vote against any democratic leaders who use force unsuccessfully or unjustifiably. An alternative theory, which Schultz favors, emphasizes that the transparency inherent in democracy makes it hard for democratic leaders to bluff; a threat to use force will lack credibility when a democratic leader's opposition party or the public does not wish to use force. At the same time, transparency makes a democratic leader's threat of force highly credible when the opposition party or the public support the use of force. In this view, democratic leaders are more selective than authoritarian leaders in their threats to use force, and when they do threaten to use force, these threats carry high credibility when the opposition party supports them and low credibility when the opposition party vocally objects to the threat of force.[64]

Schultz provides a tight logic for his theory by developing it through a formal model of crisis bargaining that incorporates democratic leaders' preferences, opposition leaders' preferences, the information leaders have, and the signals they send to and receive from domestic audiences and the opposing actor in a crisis. This model highlights the bargaining problem, or the challenge that actors in a crisis face when they attempt to negotiate a peaceful outcome without complete information. In this view, the use of force, costly to all parties, is always to some degree suboptimal, as the side that ultimately loses on the battlefield would almost always have been better off conceding on the dispute prior to the costly resort to force (though if the public strongly favors war or the leader wants to have an international reputation for being "tough," there may be incentives to fight losing battles). Even when a negotiated outcome would be preferable for both parties, however, they may resort to force because they are unable to accurately assess each other's intentions and capabilities. Actors in a crisis have private information about their willingness and ability to fight, and they have incentives to misrepresent this information by bluffing to achieve a favorable outcome at the bargaining table. This is where the transparency of democratic politics enters in, helping to resolve the bargaining problem by making it hard for leaders to bluff but easy to issue credible threats when they have the support of the opposition party.

---

ies, see Andrew Kydd, "The Art of Shaker Modeling: Game Theory and Security Studies," in Detlef F. Sprinz and Yael Wolinsky-Nahmias, eds., *Models, Numbers, and Cases: Methods for Studying International Relations* (Ann Arbor: University of Michigan Press, 2004), pp. 344–366.

64. Schultz, *Democracy and Coercive Diplomacy*, pp. 3–18.

Schultz tests the implications of his formal model through a statistical analysis of 1,785 cases of militarized interstate disputes. In this test, he finds strong evidence that democratic institutions decrease the probability of a crisis being initiated by a threat of force, decrease the likelihood of resistance to a threat if one is issued, and decrease the probability of war.[65] Schultz further tests his model against fifty-six cases in which states attempted to deter threats made against their allies, finding a tendency for democratic governments to be more successful in their deterrent threats when their opposition parties support them (though this finding falls short of standard levels of statistical significance).[66] Schultz then turns to case studies so that his analysis can provide "both a statistical correlation that is consistent with the argument . . . and historical evidence that the hypothesized causal mechanisms underlie this correlation."[67] Here, Schultz studies one case where the credibility of a democratic government's threat to use force is confirmed by the support of its opposition party (the British side of the Fashoda Crisis) and several cases where a democratic government decided against threatening force or issued a threat that was less credible because of objections from the opposition party (the French side of the Fashoda Crisis, the British threat and use of force in the 1899 Boer War, French and British behavior in the 1936 Rhineland Crisis, and British behavior in the 1956 Suez crisis and the 1965 Rhodesian crisis).

Schultz's work in each methodological approach is generally rigorous and well done. He devotes ample attention to alternative explanations, including explanations that emphasize democratic norms (nonviolence and respect for democratic regimes) and neorealist variables (particularly alliance portfolios), as well as the constraining and informing aspects of democratic institutions. Schultz is careful not to overstate his findings, and his case studies are convincing in showing that opposition parties played an important role in forestalling, bolstering, or undercutting democratic leaders' threats to use force. He is not as systematic in treating the outliers in his statistical and case study work, however. Out of the thirty-two cases of extended-immediate deterrence in which the defending state had a competitive political system, for example, ten had outcomes that do not fit Schultz's argument. Yet he only discusses one of these cases (the British-Greek crisis over Crete in 1897) for the purpose of arguing that it might deserve recoding in a way that would make it fit his thesis. Similarly, the cases chosen for individual study all fit the argu-

---

65. Ibid., p. 158.

66. Ibid., pp. 169–170.

67. Ibid., p. 163.

ment; this is defensible in the early stages of an innovative research program such as Schultz's where the goal is to illustrate as much as test the mechanisms that might explain a correlational finding, but even so he might have paid more attention to anomalous cases that might have helped to delimit the scope conditions of his theory. Schultz justifiably notes that the cases that do not fit his theory tend to be the more spectacular and memorable ones, resulting in wars rather than negotiated settlements. Yet after listing World War I, World War II, and the Vietnam War as "some of the most prominent international conflicts of the last century" and indicating that they do not fit his theory, he does not discuss how these anomalies might be explained or how they might limit his findings.[68] Despite this shortcoming, Schultz's successful effort to integrate different methods is one worthy of emulation, as it demonstrates that the value of carrying out statistical and case study tests of a formal model is worth the considerable difficulties involved in doing so.

One final example illustrates how the latest work on the interdemocratic peace has been able to build on prior statistical, case study, and formal research toward a more complete and integrated theory of the interdemocratic piece. Charles Lipson's *Reliable Partners* uses the insights developed in Schultz's work, as well as other findings from formal theories on bargaining, contracting, audience costs, self-binding, and transparency, to construct a model of the superior ability of democracies to create credible and enforceable commitments or contracts with one another that make it unnecessary to use costly military force to resolve disputes.[69] Lipson's model aspires to explain not only the interdemocratic peace, but many of the other findings that have emerged from the broader democratic peace research program. Lipson tests his model against numerous brief case studies and the results of existing statistical studies. His goal is largely to integrate existing studies rather than to carry out exhaustive and detailed primary research or develop and test a single statistical model. Because Lipson conscientiously considers alternative explanations throughout, and because he has so many excellent prior studies to draw upon, what emerges is the most convincing and complete treatment of the interdemocratic peace thus far.

---

68. Ibid., pp. 241–242. Schultz points out in a footnote, without elaboration, that his model predicts that such deterrence failures by united democracies should not happen, but that a different model he used in earlier work allows for the possibility of resistance against united democracies (note 1, p. 242); the referenced work is Kenneth A. Schultz, "Domestic Opposition and Signaling in International Crises," *American Political Science Review*, Vol. 92, No. 4 (December 1998), pp. 829–844.

69. Charles Lipson, *Reliable Partners: How Democracies Have Made a Separate Peace* (Princeton, N.J.: Princeton University Press, 2003).

Methodological Suggestions for Future Research on the Interdemocratic Peace

We end this chapter by offering several suggestions for future research on the interdemocratic peace that will further enrich the development of typological theory on this subject. First, researchers can intensify efforts, like that undertaken by Braumoeller, to study states that have democratic institutions but lack democratic norms, as well as those that have democratic norms but lack democratic institutions. Researchers can then compare such cases to those that have both or neither of these attributes of democracy as a test of institutional and normative causal mechanisms.

Second, researchers can follow up Peterson's research on the interaction between leaders and publics by examining how leaders have tried to reconcile their own preferences with public opinion.

Third, researchers can look for other testable process-tracing implications of democratic peace assertions. For example, if norms and institutions affect the international use of force, they should also affect the conditions under which domestic police forces are allowed to use deadly force. William Hoeft, for example, has argued that the domestic police forces of democratic states are more likely to be allowed to use deadly force only to prevent the use of such force against themselves or others, whereas nondemocratic states allow the use of deadly force and of state-sanctioned executions for property crimes.[70] Also, researchers can look at civil-military relationships in democracies and in other regime types and at variations in civil-military relations among democracies and within democracies over time.[71]

Fourth, researchers can look at the origins of democratic norms and institutions and assess whether differing origins lead to different foreign policy behaviors. For example, do the foreign policies of democracies established through domestic revolutions against monarchs (France) differ from those created through anti-colonial uprisings (the United States), or those established through defeat in war and occupation by other democracies (Germany and Japan)? Does one democracy treat another differently depending on the origins of their respective norms and institutions?

Fifth, researchers might move beyond statistical, case study, and formal research to use surveys and other techniques to study the democratic peace. In particular, researchers might undertake surveys of the attitudes that elites and mass publics in democracies hold toward the use of force vis-à-vis other democracies and other types of regimes. Although recent

---

70. William Hoeft, "Explaining Interdemocratic Peace."

71. Elman, *Paths to Peace,* pp. 38–39.

research like that by Schultz and Lipson has focused on institutional and informational dynamics, one possible data bias regarding cases prior to the 1940s is that no systematic survey data exists on public and elite opinion. Moreover, although standard surveys indicate that citizens of contemporary democracies generally feel more warmly toward other democracies than toward other kinds of states, little dedicated survey work has been done on attitudes toward the possible use of force in ongoing disputes between democracies. There is thus a danger that the role of democratic values in promoting peace among democracies has been understated in works that emphasize institutions and information, although surveys might also help validate the role of institutions and information as well.

Sixth, researchers can look more assiduously for closely matched pairs of democratic and mixed dyads that might be amenable to most similar research designs like Ray's study of the Spanish-American War and the Fashoda Crisis. One possibility here is to undertake longitudinal studies of particular dyads, as John Owen has done in the case of U.S.-British relations. This allows a before-after comparison of dyadic relations after domestic developments that make one partner in the dyad more democratic.[72] Statistical methods can also carry out or augment such longitudinal comparisons.

Seventh, researchers might focus on the cases that pose anomalies to Schultz's theory that democracies find it hard to make convincing bluffs but easy to issue credible threats. This can help set the theory's scope conditions and perhaps uncover additional causal mechanisms that explain Schultz's anomalies.

Finally, researchers should look for relationships between democracies that have varying levels of power imbalances. This can test whether democratic norms function to the point of altruism or whether democracies are willing to exploit materially weaker democracies through the use or threat of force short of war.

In sum, the interdemocratic peace literature amply demonstrates the complementary nature of alternative methods and the value of combining them or using them sequentially for the research tasks to which they are best suited. We turn now to a detailed examination of the methods that have allowed case study researchers to contribute to the cumulation of knowledge in this and many other research programs.

---

72. Owen, "How Liberalism Produces Democratic Peace," pp. 87–125.

A Pedagogical Note to Parts II and III

Readers of this book who are or will be teaching Ph.D.-level courses on qualitative methods may be interested in how the materials presented in Part II were developed. The origins of the method of structured, focused comparison were already described in some detail in the Preface. This note indicates, first, how the method was developed and tested in the Ph.D.-level research seminar Alex George taught over a period of years at Stanford. Then, a brief commentary is provided on Parts II and III, which follow, to indicate that they provide a manual for case study methods.

In the seminar, students first read the current description of the method. Then, each student selected a book of interest that consisted of a study of a single case or comparative cases. For this assignment each student employed the requirements of structured, focused comparison as a basis for critiquing the chosen book's methodology. Students prepared written evaluations of the relevance and utility of the structured, focused method's requirements for developing an incisive critique of their chosen book. Was the method useful for this purpose, and how might it be made more useful? After critiquing their chosen study in this way, students then consulted published reviews of that book to judge what their use of the structured, focused method had added. Generally, they found that use of structured, focused comparison added substantially to the published reviews. This assignment gave students useful hands-on experience with the method. It also contributed, together with classroom discussion, to the clarification and further development of the method.

For their second assignment, students prepared a research design on a problem they were considering as a possible topic for a Ph.D. dissertation. Students were asked to assess whether the five research design tasks (described below in Chapter 4) were helpful in preparing research designs for a possible dissertation, what problems they encountered, and what they had learned from the experience. Each student's research design paper was discussed in the class and the writer of the paper then produced an addendum to his or her paper indicating what had been learned as a result of the discussion.

The modus operandi of the research seminar has been described in this note in order to indicate that the chapters that follow in Part II and Part III are the result of sustained efforts over a period of years to develop and refine the method of structured, focused comparison and related material in Parts Two and Three. Many students who took the seminar later drew upon that experience in their Ph.D. dissertations. The seminar became a required course at Stanford for all Ph.D. students in comparative politics and was taken by most Ph.D. students in international relations.

We emphasize in this book the critical importance of *research designs*. After a brief discussion of the essential components of the structured, focused method in Chapter 3, we discuss in Chapter 4, "Phase One: Designing Case Study Research," five interrelated requirements for developing effective research design. This chapter should be used as a reference guide to be read not just once, but as often as necessary; first, in initial efforts to develop a research design and, then, as needed to redesign one's research strategy to better approximate the desiderata set forth in the chapter. Readers planning to undertake case study research would be well advised to use the criteria for research design identified in that chapter to see how well they enable one to critique and build on existing publications of interest to them. In teaching these research seminars, we found it a quite useful first step to have students familiarize themselves with the challenge of good research design by applying these criteria as guidelines for reviewing existing studies.

Research design is an integral part of the method of structured, focused comparison. Readers should keep in mind, as emphasized in Chapter 4, that the guidelines for research design are intimately interrelated and must be integrated to produce an appropriate set of general questions to ask of each case in order to obtain the data needed to meet the study's research objectives. "Appropriate" general questions are those highly likely to provide the data from the case studies that will be needed when one turns to drawing conclusions from the cases that contribute to meeting the research objectives of the study. The reader's attention is called also to the Appendix, which describes the variety, flexibility, and ingenuity of research designs in some thirty studies within the field of American politics, comparative politics, and international relations. Reading these accounts will be helpful in designing one's own study.

Chapter 5, "Phase Two: Carrying Out the Case Studies" provides guidance and cautions for doing case study analyses in ways likely to provide good data. And Chapter 6, "Phase Three: Drawing the Implications of Case Study Findings for Theory," discusses various methods for using case results to meet the research objectives of a study.

Part III closely examines additional research methods available to case researchers, and presents chapters on process-tracing and typological theory, which we see as two of a researcher's most important tools for empirically identifying causal mechanisms and for modeling phenomena that reflect complex causation. Graduate students may wish to consult these chapters as they select their methods, and then later as a check that they are using their chosen methods in a disciplined way.

Chapter 7 in Part III surveys recent developments in philosophy of science that are relevant for theory-oriented case study research. We call attention in particular to the emergence of the scientific realism school, which supports the emphasis we give to the role of causal mechanisms in explanation and to within-case analysis and process-tracing.

Chapter 8 provides a detailed discussion of the limitations of "controlled comparison," which is still the standard comparative method. This chapter also discusses various ways to cope with these limitations. We offer an alternative to controlled comparison, the within-case method, which makes use of process-tracing in analyzing individual cases. Chapter 9 calls attention to another within-case method, the congruence method, which does not make use of process-tracing. Illustrations of both types of within-case analysis are provided.

Chapter 10 provides a detailed discussion of process-tracing, its different types and uses. Accompanying it is a discussion of similarities and differences between theory-oriented process-tracing and historical explanation.

Chapter 11 presents one of the most important contributions of our book: a discussion of how to develop typological theories of problems characterized by equifinality and complex causation. "Equifinality," a term used in general systems theory, is referred to by some scholars as multiple causality. It identifies a pervasive characteristic of social phenomena, namely the fact that *different* causal processes can lead to *similar* outcomes of a given dependent variable. Equifinality complicates the task of theory development and testing and must be taken into account in the design and implementation of all research, not just case study investigation. We emphasize also that many real-world problems are characterized by considerable causal complexity, which also complicates the task of theory development. Both equifinality and causal complexity are discussed in detail at various points in the book. Both can be dealt with effectively in theory-oriented case study research that develops more limited conditional generalizations in lieu of broad-spanning universal or probabilistic generalizations.

Finally, we note in Chapter 12 the kind of theory for which case study research is particularly applicable. This is "middle-range" theory, to distinguish it from efforts to develop and apply broad-spanning paradigmatic theories such as realism, liberalism, and constructivism. In contrast, middle-range theory focuses on specific subtypes of a general phenomenon—for example, not all but each specific type of military intervention and not all but each type of effort to employ a particular variant of coercive diplomacy. This approach contributes greatly by filling in the theoretical vacuum left by these general paradigmatic models.

Middle-range theories carefully delimit the scope of their findings to each particular subclass of a general phenomenon. Individual middle-range theories of each specific subclass constitute building blocks for constructing broader but also internally differentiated theories of a general phenomenon. Middle-range theories, as noted in Chapter 12, are particularly relevant for the development of policy-relevant theoretical findings—or "generic knowledge," as they are sometimes called—of strategies and problems repeatedly encountered in different contexts in the conduct of foreign policy.

In sum, Parts II and III provide a manual for developing theory through a variety of case study methods. We have attempted to make this manual as "user-friendly" as possible. We hope that it provides an important, usable approach for efforts to raise the standards for case study research and to explicate the procedures for doing so, the two objectives for our study we have pursued for several decades.

Part II
How to Do Case Studies

Chapter 3

The Method of Structured, Focused Comparison

The method and logic of structured, focused comparison is simple and straightforward. The method is "structured" in that the researcher writes general questions that reflect the research objective and that these questions are asked of each case under study to guide and standardize data collection, thereby making systematic comparison and cumulation of the findings of the cases possible. The method is "focused" in that it deals only with certain aspects of the historical cases examined. The requirements for structure and focus apply equally to individual cases since they may later be joined by additional cases.

The method was devised to study historical experience in ways that would yield useful generic knowledge of important foreign policy problems. The particular challenge was to analyze phenomena such as deterrence in ways that would draw the explanations of each case of a particular phenomenon into a broader, more complex theory. The aim was to discourage decision-makers from relying on a single historical analogy in dealing with a new case.[1]

---

1. This discussion draws upon earlier publications: Alexander L. George, "Case Studies and Theory Development: The Method of Structured, Focused Comparison," in Paul Gordon Lauren, ed., *Diplomacy: New Approaches in History, Theory, and Policy* (New York: Free Press, 1979), pp. 43–68; Alexander L. George, "The Causal Nexus Between Cognitive Beliefs and Decision-Making Behavior," in Lawrence S. Falkowski, ed., *Psychological Models in International Politics* (Boulder, Colo.: Westview Press, 1979), pp. 95–124; and Alexander L. George and Timothy J. McKeown, "Case Studies and Theories of Organizational Decision Making," in Robert F. Coulam and Richard A. Smith, eds., *Advances in Information Processing in Organizations*, Vol. 2 (Greenwich, Conn.: JAI Press, 1985), pp. 21–58.

An extension of structured, focused comparison is proposed by Patrick J. Haney in

Before we discuss each of these two characteristics of structured, focused comparison, it will be instructive to show how they improve upon previous case study approaches. Following the end of World War II, many political scientists were quite favorably disposed toward or even enthusiastic about the prospect of undertaking individual case studies for the development of knowledge and theory. Many case studies were conducted, not only in the field of international relations but also in public administration, comparative politics, and American politics. Although individual case studies were often instructive, they did not lend themselves readily to strict comparison or to orderly cumulation. As a result, the initial enthusiasm for case studies gradually faded, and the case study as a strategy for theory development fell into disrepute.[2] In 1968 James Rosenau critiqued case studies of foreign policy and called attention to their nonscientific, noncumulative character. These studies of foreign policy by political scientists and historians, Rosenau observed, were not conducted in ways appropriate for scientific inquiry. In his view, most of them lacked "scientific consciousness" and did not accumulate. Individual studies may have made interesting contributions to knowledge, but a basis for systematic comparison was lacking.[3]

---

his *Organizing for Foreign Policy Crisis* (Ann Arbor, Mich.: University of Michigan Press, 1997). Haney develops ways of surveying cases that are capable of combining the advantages of structured, focused comparison with large-N analysis. He suggests that the findings of a number of studies that address the same problem can be combined and the results averaged—i.e., a form of what statisticians refer to as "meta-analysis." This particular case survey method was proposed earlier by Robert Yin and Karen A. Heald, "Using the Case Survey Method to Analyze Policy Studies," *Administrative Science Quarterly*, Vol. 20, No. 3 (September 1975), pp. 371–381. The rather obvious limitations of the case survey approach are noted by Yin and Heald.

A cogent statement of key research steps in small-n research is provided by Ronald Mitchell and Thomas Bernauer in "Empirical Research in International Environmental Policy: Designing Qualitative Case Studies," *Journal of Environment and Development*, Vol. 7, No. 1 (March 1998), pp. 4–31.

Dwaine Medford outlines a way of extending and generalizing structured, focused comparisons that focus on the actor's cognitive processes in Charles F. Hermann, Charles W. Kegley, Jr., and James N. Rosenau, eds., *New Directions in the Study of Foreign Policy* (Boston, Mass.: Allen & Unwin, 1987).

See also our commentary on the important work by Thomas Homer-Dixon in the Appendix, "Studies That Illustrate Research Design."

2.   Of course, as noted in Chapter 10, well-researched case studies that are largely descriptive and atheoretical are useful in providing a form of vicarious experience for students and others interested in a particular phenomenon, and sometimes they provide data that can be of some use in case studies devoted to theory development.

3.   James N. Rosenau, "Moral Fervor, Systematic Analysis, and Scientific Consciousness in Foreign Policy Research," in Austin Ranney, ed., *Political Science and Public Policy* (Chicago, Ill.: Markham, 1968), pp. 197–238.

Writers in other fields of political science offered similar critiques of extant case studies. In 1955, Roy Macridis and Bernard Brown criticized the old "comparative politics" for being, among other things, not genuinely comparative. These earlier studies consisted mainly of single case studies which were often essentially descriptive and monographic rather than theory-oriented. In the field of public administration, similar concerns were expressed, and, in the field of American politics, an important critique of the atheoretical case study was presented by Theodore Lowi.[4]

What, then, are some of the requirements that case study research must meet to overcome these difficulties?

First, the investigator should clearly identify the universe—that is, the "class" or "subclass" of events—of which a single case or a group of cases to be studied are instances. Thus, the cases in a given study must all be instances, for example, of only one phenomenon: either deterrence, coercive diplomacy, crisis management, alliance formation, war termination, the impact of domestic politics on policymaking, the importance of personality on decision-making, or whatever else the investigator wishes to study and theorize about. The identification of the class or subclass of events for any given study depends upon the problem chosen for study.

Second, a well-defined research objective and an appropriate research strategy to achieve that objective should guide the selection and analysis of a single case or several cases within the class or subclass of the phenomenon under investigation. Cases should not be chosen simply because they are "interesting" or because ample data exist for studying them.

Third, case studies should employ variables of theoretical interest for purposes of explanation. These should include variables that provide some leverage for policymakers to enable them to influence outcomes.

We turn now to a discussion of the two characteristics of the method of structured, focused comparison. From the statistical (and survey) research model, the method of structured, focused comparison borrows the device of asking a set of standardized, general questions of each case, even in single case studies. These questions must be carefully developed to reflect the research objective and theoretical focus of the inquiry. The use of a set of general questions is necessary to ensure the acquisition of comparable data in comparative studies. This procedure allows researchers to avoid the all too familiar and disappointing pitfall of traditional, in-

---

4. Roy C. Macridis and Bernard E. Brown, eds., *Comparative Politics: Notes and Readings* (Homewood, Ill.: Dorsey Press, 1955); Herbert Kaufmann, "The Next Step in Case Studies," *Public Administration Review*, Vol. 18 (Winter 1958), pp. 52–59; and Theodore J. Lowi, "American Business, Public Policy, Case-Studies and Political Theory," *World Politics*, Vol. 16, No. 1 (July 1964), pp. 671–715.

tensive single case studies. Even when such cases were instances of a class of events, they were not performed in a comparable manner and hence did not contribute to an orderly, cumulative development of knowledge and theory about the phenomenon in question. Instead, each case study tended to go its own way, reflecting the special interests of each investigator and often being unduly shaped by whatever historical data was readily available. As a result, idiosyncratic features of each case or the specific interests of each investigator tended to shape the research questions. Not surprisingly, single case studies—lacking "scientific consciousness"—did not accumulate.

The method also requires that the study of cases be "focused": that is, they should be undertaken with a specific research objective in mind and a theoretical focus appropriate for that objective. A single study cannot address all the interesting aspects of a historical event. It is important to recognize that a single event can be relevant for research on a variety of theoretical topics. For example, the Cuban Missile Crisis offers useful material for developing many different theories. This case may be (indeed, has been) regarded and used as an instance of deterrence, coercive diplomacy, crisis management, negotiation, domestic influence on foreign policy, personality involvement in decision-making, etc. Each of these diverse theoretical interests requires the researcher to adopt a different focus, to develop and use a different theoretical framework, and to identify a different set of data requirements. A researcher's treatment of a historical episode must be selectively focused in accordance with the type of theory that the investigator is attempting to develop.

One reason so many case studies of a particular phenomenon in the past did not contribute much to theory development is that they lacked a clearly defined and common focus. Different investigators engaged in research on a particular phenomenon tended to bring diverse theoretical (and nontheoretical) interests to bear on their case studies. Each case study tended to investigate somewhat different dependent and independent variables. Moreover, many case studies were not guided by a well-defined theoretical objective. Not surprisingly, later researchers who had a well-defined theoretical interest in the phenomenon often found that earlier studies were of little value for their purposes.

It is important for researchers to build self-consciously upon previous studies and variable definitions as much as possible—including studies using formal, statistical, and qualitative methods. "Situating" one's research in the context of the literature is key to identifying the contribution the new research makes. Of course, researchers will sometimes find it necessary to modify existing definitions of variables or add new ones, but they must be precise and clear in doing so and acknowledge that this reduces the comparability to or cumulativity with previous studies.

It should be noted that a merely formalistic adherence to the format of structured, focused comparison will not yield good results. The important device of formulating a set of standardized, general questions to ask of each case will be of value only if those questions are grounded in—and adequately reflect—the theoretical perspective and research objectives of the study. Similarly, a selective theoretical focus for the study will be inadequate by itself unless coupled with a relevant set of standardized general questions.

In comparative case studies, structure and focus are easier to achieve if a single investigator not only plans the study, but also conducts all of the case studies. Structured, focused comparison is more difficult to carry out in collaborative research when each case study is undertaken by a different scholar. Collaborative studies must be carefully planned to impress upon all participants the requirements of structure and focus. The chief investigator must monitor the conduct of case studies to ensure that the guidelines are observed by the case writers and to undertake corrective actions if necessary. Properly coordinating the work of case writers in a collaborative study can be a challenging task for the chief investigator, particularly when the contributors are well-established scholars with views of their own regarding the significance of the case they are preparing.

This can be seen in comparing two collaborative studies. One study of Western democratic political opposition brought together a distinguished group of scholars, each studying the democratic opposition in a Western democracy. The study was not tightly organized to meet the requirement of a structured comparison, so the organizer of the study was left with the difficult task of drawing together the disparate findings of the individual case studies for comparative analysis in the concluding chapter.[5] In contrast, Michael Krepon and Dan Caldwell developed a tight version of structured, focused comparison for their collaborative study of cases of U.S. Senate ratification of arms control treaties. They

---

5.   Robert A. Dahl, *Political Oppositions in Western Democracies* (New Haven, Conn.: Yale University Press, 1966). As Sidney Verba notes in his detailed commentary on this book, it "highlights a problem that arises in the multiauthored book. There are great advantages in having a large number of country specialists, but specialists are hard to discipline. In *Political Oppositions,* the major theoretical chapters that attempt to tie together the individual country chapters are found at the end of the book. . . . If we want to have as collaborators men of the stature of the authors of this book, we must let them go their own way." Sidney Verba, "Some Dilemmas in Comparative Research," *World Politics,* Vol. 20, No. 1 (October 1967), pp. 116–118.

closely monitored the individual authors' adherence to the guidelines and intervened as necessary to ensure that they adhered to the original or revised guidelines.[6]

The next chapter provides a more specific discussion of procedures for the design and implementation of case studies—either single case analyses or comparative investigations that are undertaken within the framework of the structured, focused method.

---

6. Michael Krepon and Dan Caldwell, eds., *The Politics of Arms Control Treaty Ratification* (New York: St. Martin's Press, 1991). We are indebted to Michael Krepon for providing us with a detailed account of how he and Caldwell accomplished this difficult task.

Chapter 4

Phase One: Designing Case Study Research

There are three phases in the design and implementation of theory-oriented case studies. In phase one, the objectives, design, and structure of the research are formulated. In phase two, each case study is carried out in accordance with the design. In phase three, the researcher draws upon the findings of the case studies and assesses their contribution to achieve the research objective of the study. These three phases are interdependent, and some iteration is often necessary to ensure that each phase is consistent and integrated with the other phases.[1] The first phase is discussed in this chapter, and phases two and three in the chapters that follow.

Phase one—the research design—consists of five tasks. These tasks are relevant not only for case study methodology but for all types of systematic, theory-oriented research. They must be adapted, of course, to different types of investigation and to whether theory testing or theory development is the focus of the study. The design phase of theory-oriented case study research is of critical importance. If a research design

---

1.   The procedure of organizing such studies on the basis of these three phases was introduced by Alexander L. George and Richard Smoke in their book *Deterrence in American Foreign Policy: Theory and Practice* (New York: Columbia University Press, 1974). It has proven to be a useful organizing device in subsequent studies and has also provided a framework for reviewing and evaluating existing studies. We are omitting here a fourth phase, presentation of the results of the study, that was mentioned in Alexander L. George and Timothy J. McKeown, "Case Studies and Theories of Organizational Decision Making," in Robert F. Coulam and Richard A. Smith, eds., *Advances in Information Processing in Organizations*, Vol. 2 (Greenwich, Conn.: JAI Press, 1985), pp. 21–58. Some of the observations therein are discussed in the treatment of Phase Two in the present study.

proves inadequate, it will be difficult to achieve the research objectives of the study. (Of course, the quality of the study depends also on how well phases two and three are conducted.)

Task One: Specification of the Problem and Research Objective

The formulation of the research objective is the most important decision in designing research. It constrains and guides decisions that will be made regarding the other four tasks.

The selection of one or more objectives for research is closely coupled with identification of an important research problem or "puzzle." A clear, well-reasoned statement of the research problem will generate and focus the investigation. A statement that merely asserts that "the problem is important" is inadequate. The problem should be embedded in a well-informed assessment that identifies gaps in the current state of knowledge, acknowledges contradictory theories, and notes inadequacies in the evidence for existing theories. In brief, the investigator needs to make the case that the proposed research will make a significant contribution to the field.

The research objective must be adapted to the needs of the research program at its current stage of development. Is there a need for testing a well-established theory or competing theories? Is it important to identify the limits of a theory's scope? Does the state of research on the phenomenon require incorporation of new variables, new subtypes, or work on different levels of analysis? Is it considered desirable at the present stage of theory development to move up or down the ladder of generality?[2] For example, as noted in Chapter 2, in the 1990s the democratic peace research program moved largely from the question of whether such a peace existed to that of identifying the basis on which democratic peace rests. It now needs to go further to explain how a particular peace between two democratic states developed over time. Similarly, in the 1960s deterrence theory needed to bring in additional variables to add to excessively parsimonious and abstract deductive models.

In general, there are six different kinds of theory-building research objectives. Arend Lijphart and Harry Eckstein identified five types. We outline these below and add a sixth type of our own:[3]

---

2.   Giovanni Sartori, "Concept Misformation in Comparative Politics," *American Political Science Review,* Vol. 64, No. 4 (December 1970), pp. 1033–1053.

3.   Arend Lijphart, "Comparative Politics and the Comparative Method," *American Political Science Review,* Vol. 65, No. 3 (September 1971), pp. 682–693; and Harry Eckstein, "Case Studies and Theory in Political Science," in Fred Greenstein and Nel-

- *Atheoretical/configurative idiographic* case studies provide good descriptions that might be used in subsequent studies for theory building, but by themselves, such cases do not cumulate or contribute directly to theory.
- *Disciplined configurative* case studies use established theories to explain a case. The emphasis may be on explaining a historically important case, or a study may use a case to exemplify a theory for pedagogical purposes. A disciplined configurative case can contribute to theory testing because it can "impugn established theories if the theories ought to fit it but do not," and it can serve heuristic purposes by highlighting the "need for new theory in neglected areas."[4] However, a number of important methodological questions arise in using disciplined configurative case studies and these are discussed in Chapter 9 on the congruence method.
- *Heuristic* case studies inductively identify new variables, hypotheses, causal mechanisms, and causal paths. "Deviant" or "outlier" cases may be particularly useful for heuristic purposes, as by definition their outcomes are not what traditional theories would anticipate. Also, cases where variables co-vary as expected but are at extremely high or low values may help uncover causal mechanisms.[5] Such cases may not allow inferences to wider populations if relationships are nonlinear or involve threshold effects, but limited inferences might be possible if causal mechanisms are identified (just as cancer researchers use high dosages of potential carcinogens to study their effects).
- *Theory testing* case studies assess the validity and scope conditions of single or competing theories. As discussed in Chapter 6, it is important in tests of theories to identify whether the test cases are most-likely, least-likely, or crucial for one or more theories. Testing may also be devised to identify the scope conditions of theories (the conditions under which they are most- and least-likely to apply).
- *Plausibility probes* are preliminary studies on relatively untested theories and hypotheses to determine whether more intensive and laborious testing is warranted. The term "plausibility probe" should not be used too loosely, as it is not intended to lower the standards of evidence and inference and allow for easy tests on most-likely cases.

---

son Polsby, eds., *Handbook of Political Science*, Vol. 7 (Reading, Mass.: Addison-Wesley, 1975), pp. 79–138.

4. Eckstein, "Case Studies and Theory," p. 99.

5. Stephen Van Evera, *Guide to Methods for Students of Political Science* (Ithaca, N.Y.: Cornell University Press, 1997).

- *"Building Block" studies of particular types or subtypes* of a phenomenon identify common patterns or serve a particular kind of heuristic purpose. These studies can be component parts of larger contingent generalizations and typological theories. Some methodologists have criticized single-case studies and studies of cases that do not vary in their dependent variable.[6] However, we argue that single-case studies and "no variance" studies of multiple cases can be useful if they pose "tough tests" for theories or identify alternative causal paths to similar outcomes when equifinality is present.[7] (See also the more detailed discussion of "building blocks" theory below.)

Researchers should clearly identify which of these six types of theory-building is being undertaken in a given study; readers should not be left to find an answer to this question on their own. The researcher may fail to make it clear, for example, whether the study is an effort at theory testing or merely a plausibility probe. Or the researcher may fail to indicate whether and what kind of "tough test" of the theory is supposedly being conducted.[8]

These six research objectives vary in their uses of induction and deduction. Also, a single research design may be able to accomplish more than one purpose—such as heuristic and theory testing goals—as long as it is careful in using evidence and making inferences in ways appropriate to each research objective. For example, while it is not legitimate to derive a theory from a set of data and then claim to test it on the same data, it is sometimes possible to test a theory on different data, or new or previously unobserved facts, from the same case.[9]

---

6. Gary King, Robert O. Keohane, and Sidney Verba, *Designing Social Inquiry: Scientific Inference in Qualitative Research* (Princeton, N.J.: Princeton University Press, 1994).

7. David Collier, "Translating Quantitative Methods for Qualitative Researchers: The Case of Selection Bias," *American Political Science Review,* Vol. 89, No. 2 (June 1995), pp. 461–466; and Ronald Rogowski, "The Role of Theory and Anomaly in Social-Science Inference," *American Political Science Review,* Vol. 89, No. 2 (June 1995), pp. 467–470. Theory development via building blocks is useful also in the absence of equifinality. Contingent generalizations are possible, and indeed easier to formulate, when equifinality is not present. For an example of this approach see George and Smoke, *Deterrence in American Foreign Policy.*

8. Joseph Grieco criticizes Robert O. Keohane's *After Hegemony: Cooperation and Discord in the World Political Economy* (Princeton, N.J.: Princeton University Press, 1984) on both counts in his detailed criticism of the research design in this important study, to which Keohane replies in David A. Baldwin, ed., *Neorealism and Neoliberalism: The Contemporary Debate* (New York: Columbia University Press, 1993).

9. Van Evera, *Guide to Methods.*

Specific questions that need to be addressed in designating the research objectives include:

- What is the phenomenon or type of behavior that is being singled out for examination; that is, what is the class or subclass of events of which the cases will be instances?
- Is the phenomenon to be explained thought to be an empirical universal (i.e., no variation in the dependent variable), so that the research problem is to account for the lack of variation in the outcomes of the cases? Or is the goal to explain an observable variation in the dependent variable?
- What theoretical framework will be employed? Is there an existing theory or rival candidate theories that bear on those aspects of the phenomenon or behavior that are to be explained? If not, what provisional theory or theories will the researcher formulate for the purpose of the study? If provisional theories are lacking, what theory-relevant variables will be considered?
- Which aspects of the existing theory or theories will be singled out for testing, refinement, or elaboration?
- If the research objective is to assess the causal effects or the predictions of a particular theory (or independent variable), is that theory sufficiently specified and operationalized to enable it to make specific predictions, or is it only capable of making probabilistic or indeterminate predictions? What other variables and/or conditions need to be taken into account in assessing its causal effects?

Researchers' initial efforts to formulate research objectives for a study often lack sufficient clarity or are too ambitious. Unless these defects are corrected, the study will lack a clear focus, and it will probably not be possible to design a study to achieve the objectives.

Better results are achieved if the "class" of the phenomenon to be investigated is not defined too broadly. Most successful studies, in fact, have worked with a well-defined, smaller-scope *subclass* of the general phenomenon.[10] Case study researchers often move down the "ladder of generality" to contingent generalizations and the identification of more circumscribed scope conditions of a theory, rather than up toward broader but less precise generalizations.[11]

---

10. For illustrative examples, see the Appendix, "Studies That Illustrate Research Design."

11. A similar point is made by Robert Keohane in his critique of structural realism. He notes that it is desirable to select a smaller subclass of a phenomenon in order "to achieve greater precision" of a theory. This entails "narrowing" the "domain of a the-

Working with a specified subclass of a general phenomenon is also an effective strategy for theory development. Instead of trying in one study to develop a general theory for an entire phenomenon (e.g., all "military interventions"), the investigator should think instead of formulating a typology of different kinds of interventions and proceed to choose one type or subclass of interventions for study, such as "protracted interventions." Or the study may focus on interventions by various policy instruments, interventions on behalf of different goals, or interventions in the context of different alliance structures or balances of power. The result of any single circumscribed study will be one part of an overall theory of intervention. Other studies, focusing on different types or subclasses of intervention, will be needed to contribute to the formulation of a general theory of interventions, if that is the broader, more ambitious research program. If the typology of interventions identifies six major kinds of intervention that are deemed to be of theoretical and practical interest, each subtype can be regarded as a candidate for separate study and each study will investigate instances of that subtype.

This approach to theory development is a "building block" procedure. Each block—a study of each subtype—fills a "space" in the overall theory or in a typological theory. In addition, the component provided by each building block is itself a contribution to theory; though its scope is limited, it addresses the important problem or puzzle associated with the type of intervention that led to the selection and formulation of the research objective. Its generalizations are more narrow and contingent than those of the general "covering laws" variety that some hold up as the ideal, but they are also more precise and may involve relations with higher probabilities.[12] In other words, the building block developed for a subtype is self sufficient; its validity and usefulness do not depend upon the existence of other studies of different subclasses of that general phenomenon.

If an investigator wishes to compare and contrast two or more different types of intervention, the study must be guided by clearly defined puzzles, questions, or problems that may be different from or similar to those of a study of a single subclass. For example, the objective may be to discover under what conditions (and through what paths) Outcome X occurs, and under what conditions (and through what paths) Outcome Y

---

ory." Robert O. Keohane, ed., *Neorealism and Its Critics* (New York: Columbia University Press, 1986), pp. 187–188.

12. For example, see the discussion in the Appendix of Ariel Levite, Bruce Jentleson, and Larry Berman, eds., *Foreign Military Intervention: The Dynamics of Protracted Conflict* (New York: Columbia University Press, 1992). See also the discussion of "middle-range" theory in Chapter 12.

occurs. Alternatively, the objective may be to examine under what conditions Policy A leads to Outcome Y and under what other conditions Policy A leads to Outcome X. Similarly, the focus may be on explaining the outcome of a case or a subclass or type of cases, or it may be on explaining the causal role of a particular independent variable across cases.

Task Two: Developing a Research Strategy: Specification of Variables

In the course of formulating a research objective for the study—which may change during the study—the investigator also develops a *research strategy* for achieving that objective. This requires early formulation of hypotheses and consideration of the elements (conditions, parameters, and variables) to be employed in the analysis of historical cases. Several basic decisions (also subject to change during the study) must be made concerning questions such as the following:

- What exactly and precisely is the dependent (or outcome) variable to be explained or predicted?
- What independent (and intervening) variables comprise the theoretical framework of the study?
- Which of these variables will be held constant (serve as parameters) and which will vary across cases included in the comparison?

The specification of the problem in Task One is closely related to the statement of what exactly the dependent variable will be. If a researcher defines the problem too broadly, he or she risks losing important differences among cases being compared. If a researcher defines the problem too narrowly, this may severely limit the scope and relevance of the study and the comparability of the case findings.[13] As will be noted, the definition of variance in the dependent variable is critical in research design.

In analyzing the phenomenon of "war termination," for instance, a researcher would specify numerous variables. The investigator would decide whether the dependent (outcome) variable to be explained (or predicted) was merely a cease-fire or a settlement of outstanding issues over which the war had been fought. Variables to be considered in explaining the success or failure of war termination might include the fighting capabilities and morale of the armed forces, the availability of

---

13. This research dilemma is discussed by Sidney Verba in his detailed commentary on Robert A. Dahl, ed., *Political Oppositions in Western Democracies* (New Haven, Conn.: Yale University Press, 1966), and in Sidney Verba, "Some Dilemmas in Comparative Research," *World Politics,* Vol. 20, No. 1 (October 1967), pp. 122–123.

economic resources for continuing the war, the type and magnitude of pressures from more powerful allies, policymakers' expectation that the original war aim was no longer attainable at all or only at excessive cost, the pressures of pro-war and anti-war opinion at home, and so on. The researcher might choose to focus on the outcome of the dependent variable (e.g., on cases in which efforts to achieve a cease-fire or settlement failed, but adding cases of successful cease-fires or settlements for contrast) to better identify the independent and intervening variables associated with such failures. Alternatively, one might vary the outcome, choosing cases of both successes and failures in order to identify the conditions and variables that seem to account for differences in outcomes.

Alternatively, the research objective may focus not on outcomes of the dependent variable, but on the importance of an independent variable—e.g., war weariness—in shaping outcomes in a number of cases.

We conclude this discussion of Task Two with a brief review of the strengths and weaknesses of the common types of case study research designs in relation to the kinds of research objectives noted above.

First, single case research designs can fall prey to selection bias or over-generalization of results, but all of the six theory-building purposes identified above have been served by studies of single well-selected cases that have avoided or minimized such pitfalls. Obviously, single-case studies rely almost exclusively on within-case methods, process-tracing, and congruence, but they may also make use of counterfactual analysis to posit a control case.[14]

For theory testing in single cases, it is imperative that the process-tracing procedure and congruence tests be applied to a wide range of alternative hypotheses that theorists and even participants in the events have proposed, not only to the main hypotheses of greatest interest to the researcher. Otherwise, *left-out variables* may threaten the validity of the research design. Single cases serve the purpose of theory testing particularly well if they are "most-likely," "least-likely," or "crucial" cases. Prominent case studies by Arend Lijphart, William Allen, and Peter Gourevitch, for example, have changed entire research programs by impugning theories that failed to explain their most-likely cases.[15]

---

14.   David Laitin, "Disciplining Political Science," *American Political Science Review*, Vol. 89, No. 2 (June 1995), pp. 454–456. We say "almost" since single case studies take place within the context of ongoing research programs, so that studies of single cases may draw comparisons to existing studies; thus, "the community of scientists," rather than the "individual researcher" is the relevant context in which to judge case selection.

15.   Rogowski, "The Role of Theory and Anomaly in Social-Scientific Inference"; Arend Lijphart, *The Politics of Accommodation: Pluralism and Democracy in the Netherlands* (Berkeley: University of California Press, 1968); William Sheridan Allen, *The Nazi*

Similarly, studies of single "deviant" cases and of single cases where a variable is at an extreme value can be very useful for heuristic purposes of identifying new theoretical variables or postulating new causal mechanisms. Single-case studies can also serve to reject variables as being necessary or sufficient conditions.[16]

Second, the research objective chosen in a study may require comparison of several cases. There are several comparative research designs. The best known is the method of "controlled comparison"—i.e., the comparison of "most similar" cases which, ideally, are cases that are comparable in all respects except for the independent variable, whose variance may account for the cases having different outcomes on the dependent variable. In other words, such cases occupy neighboring cells in a typology, but only if the typological space is laid out one change in the independent variable at a time. (See Chapter 11 on typological theories.)

As we discuss in Chapter 8 on the comparative method, controlled comparison can be achieved by dividing a single longitudinal case into two—the "before" case and an "after" case that follows a discontinuous change in an important variable. This may provide a control for many factors and is often the most readily available or strongest version of a most-similar case design. This design aims to isolate the difference in the observed outcomes as due to the influence of variance in the single independent variable. Such an inference is weak, however, if the posited causal mechanisms are probabilistic, if significant variables are left out of the comparison, or if other important variables change in value from the "before" to the "after" cases.

However, even when two cases or before-after cases are not perfectly matched, process-tracing can strengthen the comparison by helping to assess whether differences other than those in the main variable of interest might account for the differences in outcomes. Such process-tracing can focus on the standard list of potentially "confounding" variables identified by Donald Campbell and Julian Stanley, including the effects of history, maturation, testing, instrumentation, regression, selection, and mortality.[17] It can also address any idiosyncratic differences between the two

---

Seizure of Power: The Experience of a Single German Town, 1930–1935 (New York: Watts, 1965); and Peter Alexis Gourevitch, "The International System and Regime Formation: A Critical Review of Anderson and Wallerstein," *Comparative Politics*, Vol. 10, No. 3 (April 1978), pp. 419–438.

16. For an example, see Lijphart's study summarized in the Appendix, "Studies That Illustrate Research Design"; Douglas Dion, "Evidence and Inference in Comparative Case Study," *Comparative Politics*, Vol. 3, No. 2 (January 1998); and Collier, "Translating Quantitative Methods," p. 464.

17. Donald T. Campbell and Julian C. Stanley, *Experimental and Quasi-Experimental*

cases that scholars or participants have argued might account for their differences.

Another comparative design involves "least similar" cases and parallels John Stuart Mill's method of agreement.[18] Here, two cases are similar in outcome but differ in all but one independent variable, and the inference might be made that this variable contributes to the invariant outcome. For example, if teenagers are "difficult" in both postindustrial societies and tribal societies, we might infer that their developmental stage, and not their societies or their parents' child-rearing techniques, account for their difficult natures. Here again, left-out variables can weaken such an inference, as Mill recognized, but process-tracing provides an additional source of evidence for affirming or infirming such inferences.

Another type of comparative study may focus on cases in the same cell of a typology. If these have the same outcome, process-tracing may still reveal different causal paths to that outcome. Conversely, multiple studies of cases with the same level of a manipulable independent variable can establish under what conditions that level of the variable is associated with different outcomes. In either approach, if outcomes differ within the same type or cell, it is necessary to look for left-out variables and perhaps create a new subtype.

Often, it is useful for a community of researchers to study or try to identify cases in all quadrants of a typology. For example, Sherlock Holmes once inferred that a dog that did not bark must have known the person who entered the dog's house and committed a murder, an inference based on a comparison to dogs that do bark in such circumstances. To fully test such an assertion, we might also want to consider the behavior of non-barking non-dogs on the premises (was there a frightened cat?) and barking non-dogs (such as a parrot). The process of looking at all the types in a typology corresponds with notions of Boolean algebra and those of logical truth tables.[19] However, it is not necessary for each researcher to address all the cells in a typology, although it is often useful

---

Designs for Research (Chicago: Rand McNally College Publishing, 1963); for a good example, see James Lee Ray, *Democracies and International Conflict: An Evaluation of the Democratic Peace Proposition* (Columbia: University of South Carolina Press, 1995), pp. 158–200.

18.   For a detailed discussion of Mill's methods, see Chapter 8.

19.   Charles C. Ragin, *The Comparative Method* (Berkeley: University of California Press, 1987); Daniel Little, *Varieties of Social Explanation: An Introduction to the Philosophy of Science* (Boulder, Colo.: Westview Press, 1991); and Daniel Little, *Microfoundations, Method, and Causation: On the Philosophy of the Social Sciences* (New Brunswick, N.J.: Transaction Publishers, 1998).

for researchers to offer suggestions for future research on unexamined types or to make comparisons to previously examined types.

Finally, a study that includes many cases may allow for several different types of comparisons. One case may be most similar to another and both may be least similar to a third case. As noted below, case selection is an opportunistic as well as a structured process—researchers should look for whether the addition of one or a few cases to a study might provide useful comparisons or allow inferences on additional types of cases.

Task Three: Case Selection

Many students in the early stages of designing a study indicate that they find it difficult to decide which cases to select. This difficulty usually arises from a failure to specify a research objective that is clearly formulated and not overly ambitious. One should select cases not simply because they are interesting, important, or easily researched using readily available data. Rather, case selection should be an integral part of a good research strategy to achieve well-defined objectives of the study. Hence, the primary criterion for case selection should be relevance to the research objective of the study, whether it includes theory development, theory testing, or heuristic purposes.

Cases should also be selected to provide the kind of control and variation required by the research problem. This requires that the universe or subclass of events be clearly defined so that appropriate cases can be selected. In one type of comparative study, for example, all the cases must be instances of the same subclass. In another type of comparative study that has a different research objective, cases from different subclasses are needed.

Selection of a historical case or cases may be guided by a typology developed from the work in Tasks One and Two. Researchers can be somewhat opportunistic here—they may come across a pair of well-matched before-after cases or a pair of cases that closely fit "most similar" or "least similar" case research designs. They may also come upon cases that have many features of a most- or least-likely case, a crucial case, or a deviant case.

Often researchers begin their inquiry with a theory in search of a test case or a case in search of a theory for which it is a good test.[20] Either approach is viable, provided that care is taken to prevent case selection bias and, if necessary, to study several cases that pose appropriate tests for a

---

20. King, Keohane, and Verba, *Designing Social Inquiry,* pp. 17–18.

candidate theory once one is identified. Often, the researcher might start with a case that interests her, be drawn to a candidate theory, and then decide that she is more interested in the theory than in the case and conclude that the best way to study the theory is to select several cases that may not include the case with which the inquiry began. Some such iteration is usually necessary—history may not provide the ideal kind of cases to carry out the tests or heuristic studies that a research program most needs at its current stage of development.

Important criticisms have been made of potential flaws in case selection in studies with one or a few cases; such concerns are influenced by the rich experience of statistical methods for analyzing a large-N. David Collier and James Mahoney have taken issue with some widespread concerns about selection bias in small studies; we note four of their observations.[21] They question the assertion that selection bias in case studies is potentially an even greater problem than is often assumed (that it may not just understate relationships—the standard statistical problem—but may overstate them). They argue that case study designs with no variance in the dependent variable do not inherently represent a selection bias problem. They emphasize that case study researchers sometimes have good reasons to narrow the range of cases studied, particularly to capture heterogeneous causal relations, even if this increases the risk of selection bias. They point out (as have we) that case study researchers rarely "overgeneralize" from their cases; instead, they are frequently careful in providing circumscribed "contingent generalizations" that subsequent researchers should not mistakenly overgeneralize.

Task Four: Describing the Variance in Variables

The way in which variance is described is critical to the usefulness of case analyses in furthering the development of new theories or the assessment or refinement of existing theories. This point needs emphasis because it is often overlooked in designing studies—particularly statistical studies of a large-N. The researcher's decision about how to describe variance is important for achieving research objectives because the discovery of potential causal relationships may depend on how the variance in these variables is postulated. Basing this decision on *a priori* judgments may be risky and unproductive; the investigator is more likely to develop sensitive ways of describing variance in the variables after he or she has become familiar with how they vary in the historical cases examined. An it-

21.   David Collier and James Mahoney, "Insights and Pitfalls: Selection Bias in Qualitative Research," *World Politics*, Vol. 49, No. 1 (October 1996), pp. 56–91.

erative procedure for determining how best to describe variance is therefore recommended.[22]

The variance may in some instances be best described in terms of qualitative types of outcomes. In others, it may be best described in terms of quantitative measures. In either case, one important question is how many categories to establish for the variables. Fewer categories—such as dichotomous variables—are good for parsimony but may lack richness and nuance, while greater numbers of categories gain richness but sacrifice parsimony. The trade-off between parsimony and extreme richness should be determined by considering the purposes of each individual study.

In a study of deterrence, for example, Alexander George and Richard Smoke found it to be inadequate and unproductive to define deterrence outcomes simply as "successes" or "failures."[23] Instead, their explanations of individual cases of failure enabled them to identify different types of failures. This led to a typology of failures, with each type of failure having a different explanation. This typology allowed George and Smoke to see that deterrence failures exemplified the phenomenon of equifinality. The result was a more discriminating and policy-relevant explanatory theory for deterrence failures.[24]

The differentiation of types can apply to the characterization of independent as well as dependent variables. In attempting to identify conditions associated with the success or failure of efforts to employ a strategy of coercive diplomacy, one set of investigators identified important variants of that strategy.[25] In their study, coercive diplomacy was treated as an independent variable. From an analysis of different cases, four types of the coercive diplomacy strategy were identified: the explicit ultimatum, the tacit ultimatum, the "gradual turning of the screw," and the "try and see" variant. By differentiating the independent variable in this way, it was possible to develop a more discriminating analysis of the effectiveness of coercive diplomacy and to identify some of the factors that favored or handicapped the success of each variant. A very general or undifferentiated depiction of the independent variable would have

---

22. See also the discussion of this point in Chapter 9 on "The Congruence Method."

23. George and Smoke, *Deterrence in American Foreign Policy.*

24. See the Appendix, "Studies That Illustrate Research Design," for a fuller discussion of their study.

25. Alexander L. George, David K. Hall, and William E. Simons, *The Limits of Coercive Diplomacy* (Boston: Little, Brown, 1971); an extended second edition under the same title that examines additional cases was published in 1994, edited by Alexander L. George and William E. Simons (Boulder, Colo.: Westview Press).

"washed out" the fact that variants of coercive diplomacy may have different impacts on outcomes, or it might have resulted in ambiguous or invalid results. In addition, the identification of different variants of coercive diplomacy strategy has important implications for the selection of cases.

Task Five: Formulation of Data Requirements and General Questions

The case study method will be more effective if the research design includes a specification of the data to be obtained from the case or cases under study. Data requirements should be determined by the theoretical framework and the research strategy to be used for achieving the study's research objectives. The specification of data requirements should be integrated with the other four design tasks. Specification of data requirements structures the study. It is an essential component of the method of structured, focused comparison.

Whether a single-case study or a case comparison is undertaken, specification of the data requirements should take the form of general questions to be asked of each case. This is a way of standardizing data requirements so that comparable data will be obtained from each case and so that a single-case study can be compared later with others. Case study methodology is no different in this respect from large-N statistical studies and public opinion surveys. Unless one asks the same questions of each case, the results cannot be compared, cumulated, and systematically analyzed.

This is only to say—and to insist—that case researchers should follow a procedure of systematic data compilation. The questions asked of each case must be of a general nature; they should not be couched in overly specific terms that are relevant to only one case but should be applicable to all cases within the class or subclass of events with which the study is concerned. Asking the same questions of each case does *not* prevent the case writer from addressing more specific aspects of the case or bringing out idiosyncratic features of each case that may also be of interest for theory development or future research.

A problem sometimes encountered in case study research is that data requirements are missing altogether or inadequately formulated. The general questions must reflect the theoretical framework employed, the data that will be needed to satisfy the research objective of the study, and the kind of contribution to theory that the researcher intends to make. In other words, a mechanical use of the method of structured, focused comparison will not yield good results. The proper focusing and structuring of the comparison requires a fine-tuned set of general questions that are integrated with the four other elements of the research design. For example, in a comparative study of policymakers' approaches to strategy and tactics toward political opponents in the international arena, one might start by asking questions designed to illuminate the orientations of a leader toward the fundamental issues of history and politics that presumably influence his or her processing of information, policy preference, and final choice of action.[26] In this type of study, the investigator examines an appropriate body of material in order to infer the "answers" a political leader might have given to the following questions:

PHILOSOPHICAL QUESTIONS

- What is the essential nature of political life? Is the political universe essentially one of harmony or conflict? What is the fundamental character of one's political opponents?
- What are the prospects for eventual realization of one's fundamental political values and ideological goals? Can one be optimistic or pessimistic?
- In what sense and to what extent is the political future predictable?
- How much control or mastery can one have over historical developments? What is the political leader's (or elite's) role in moving and shaping history?
- What is the role of chance in human affairs and in historical development?

INSTRUMENTAL QUESTIONS

- What is the best approach for selecting goals or objectives for political action?
- How are the goals of action pursued most effectively?
- How are the risks of political action best calculated, controlled, and accepted?
- What is the best timing of action to advance one's interests?

---

26. See Alexander L. George, "The 'Operational Code': A Neglected Approach to the Study of Political Leaders and Decision-Making," *International Studies Quarterly*, Vol. 13, No. 2 (June 1969), pp. 190–222. The problem of judging the causal role of such beliefs in a policymaker's choice of action was discussed in Alexander L. George, "The Causal Nexus Between Cognitive Beliefs and Decision-Making Behavior: The 'Operational Code' Belief System," in Lawrence S. Falkowski, ed., *Psychological Models In International Relations* (Boulder, Colo.: Westview Press, 1979), pp. 95–124. Since then, numerous studies have been made of the "operational codes" of a variety of leaders using this standardized approach or a slight modification of it. This has facilitated comparison and cumulation of results. See, for example, the publications of Ole R. Holsti and Stephen G. Walker.

- What is the utility and role of different means for advancing one's interests?

Integration of the Five Design Tasks

The five design tasks should be viewed as constituting an integrated whole. The researcher should keep in mind that these tasks are interrelated and interdependent. For example, the way in which Task Two is performed should be consistent with the specification of Task One. Similarly, both the selection of cases in Task Three and the theoretical framework developed in Task Four must be appropriate and serviceable from the standpoint of the determinations made for Tasks One and Two. And finally, the identification of data requirements in Task Five must be guided by the decisions made for Tasks One, Two, and Three.

Yet a satisfactory integration of the five tasks usually cannot be accomplished on the first try. A good design does not come easily. Considerable iteration and respecification of the various tasks may be necessary before a satisfactory research design is achieved. The researcher may need to gain familiarity with the phenomenon in question by undertaking a preliminary examination of a variety of cases before finalizing aspects of the design.

Despite the researcher's best efforts, the formulation of the design is likely to remain imperfect—and this may not be apparent until the investigator is well into phase two or even phase three of the study. If these defects are sufficiently serious, the researcher should consider halting further work and redesigning the study, even if this means that some of the case studies will have to be redone. In drawing conclusions from the study, the researcher (or others who evaluate it) may be able to gain some useful lessons for a better design of a new study of the problem.[27]

---

27. For additional discussion of the critical importance of research design, see the "Pedagogical Note to Parts Two and Three."

Chapter 5

Phase Two: Carrying Out the Case Studies

The fifth task in a research design—the formulation of general questions to ask of each of the cases to be studied in phase two—allows the researcher to analyze each case in a way that will provide "answers" to the general questions.[1] These answers—the product of phase two—then constitute the data for the third phase of research, in which the investigator will use case findings to illuminate the research objectives of the study.

Usually one's first step in studying a case with which one is not already intimately familiar is to gather the most easily accessible academic literature and interview data on the case and its context. This preliminary step of immersing oneself in the case, known as "soaking and poking," often leads to the construction of a chronological narrative that helps both the researcher and subsequent readers understand the basic outlines of the case.[2]

---

1.   This chapter draws on earlier publications by Alexander L. George, "Case Studies and Theory Development: The Method of Structured, Focused Comparison," in Paul Gordon Lauren, ed., *Diplomacy: New Approaches in Theory, History, and Policy* (New York: Free Press, 1979), pp. 3–68; Alexander L. George, "The Causal Nexus Between Cognitive Beliefs and Decision-Making Behavior," in Lawrence S. Falkowski, ed., *Psychological Models in International Politics* (Boulder, Colo.: Westview Press, 1979), pp. 95–124; and Alexander L. George and Timothy J. McKeown, "Case Studies and Theories of Organizational Decision Making," in Robert F. Coulam and Richard A. Smith, eds., *Advances in Information Processing in Organizations*, Vol. 2 (Greenwich, Conn.: JAI Press, 1985), pp. 21–58.

2.   An interesting example of "soaking and poking" and a description of how it mixes inductive and deductive reasoning is found in Richard F. Fenno's *Homestyle* (Boston: Little, Brown, 1978). As noted in the review of his study in the Appendix, Fenno gives a detailed reconstruction of how his interview questions and research design evolved as he undertook subsequent interviews with members of Congress.

After a period of "soaking and poking," the researcher turns to the task of case study analysis, establishing the values of independent and dependent variables in a case through standard procedures of historical inquiry. (If appropriate, the researcher may be able to quantify and scale variables in some fashion.) The researcher should always articulate the criteria employed for "scoring" the variables so as to provide a basis for inter-coder reliability.

Next, the researcher develops explanations for the outcome of each case. This is a matter of detective work and historical analysis rather than a matter of applying an orthodox quasi-experimental design.[3] Social scientists performing case studies will need to familiarize themselves with the craft of the historian's trade—learning, for the context in which the case is embedded, the special difficulties presented by various kinds of evidence that may be available; using multiple weak inferences rather than single strong inferences to buttress conclusions; developing procedures for searching through large masses of data when the objectives of the search are not easily summarized by a few simple search rules.[4]

This chapter provides advice on these topics. The first three sections focus on the provisional nature of case explanations, and the challenges involved in weighing explanations offered by other researchers who have analyzed a given case, and the task of transforming a descriptive explanation for a case into an explanation that adequately reflects the researcher's theoretical framework. We then turn to issues that researchers encounter when working with a variety of primary and secondary materials. Notable issues with secondary sources include the biases of their authors, and a tendency to overestimate the rationality of the policy-making process while underestimating the complexity and the multitude of interests that may be at play. Scholars face numerous issues in assessing the evidentiary value of primary sources. Finally, we describe some of the tasks faced by those who critically read others' case studies, and urge that researchers make their methods as transparent as possible to the reader.

The Provisional Character of Case Explanations

Case explanations must always be considered to be of a provisional character. Therefore, the theoretical conclusions drawn from case study findings (in phase three) will also be provisional. The explanations pro-

---

3. For discussion of this point, see George and McKeown, "Case Studies and Theories of Organizational Decision Making," pp. 38–39.

4. The nature and requirements of historical explanations are discussed in Chapter 10.

vided by the case writer may be challenged by other scholars on one or another ground—for example, the original research may have overlooked relevant data or misunderstood its significance, failed to consider an important rival hypothesis, and so forth. If case explanations are later successfully challenged, the researcher will have to reassess the implications for any theory that has been developed or tested. Such a reassessment would also be necessary if new historical data bearing on the cases become available at a later date and lead to a successful challenge of earlier explanations.

In seeking to formulate an explanation for the outcome in each case, the investigator employs the historian's method of causal imputation, which differs from the mode of causal inference in statistical-correlational studies. These causal interpretations gain plausibility if they are consistent with the available data and if they can be supported by relevant generalizations for which a measure of validity can be claimed on the basis of existing studies. The plausibility of an explanation is enhanced to the extent that alternative explanations are considered and found to be less consistent with the data, or less supportable by available generalizations.

An investigator must demonstrate that he or she has seriously considered alternative explanations for the case outcome in order to avoid providing the basis for a suspicion, justified or not, that he or she has "imposed" a favored theory or hypothesis as the explanation. Such a challenge is likely if the reader believes that case selection was biased by the investigator's commitment to a particular theory or hypothesis.[5]

The Problem of Competing Explanations

A familiar challenge that case study methods encounter is to reconcile, if possible, conflicting interpretations of a case or to choose between them. This problem can arise when the investigator provides an explanation that differs from an earlier scholar's but does not adequately demonstrate the superiority of the new interpretation. As Olav Njølstad notes, competing explanations may arise from several sources.[6] There are different types of explanation stemming, for example, from historiographical is-

---

5. The need to avoid selecting cases that favor a particular theory and that constitute easy rather than tough tests of a theory was emphasized in Chapter 4.

6. This brief discussion draws from the fuller discussion of these problems in Chapter 2, "Case Study Methods and Research on the Interdemocratic Peace," which also provides illustrative materials. See also Olav Njølstad's chapter, "Learning from History? Case Studies and the Limits to Theory-Building," in Nils Petter Gleditsch and Olav Njølstad, eds., *Arms Races: Technological and Political Dynamics* (London: Sage Publications, 1990), pp. 220–245. Njølstad also offers several useful suggestions for dealing with these problems, which are summarized in Chapter 2.

sues such as the relative importance of ideology or historical context. Sometimes competing explanations can be equally consistent with the available historical evidence; this makes it difficult to decide which is the correct explanation or, alternatively, whether both interpretations may be part of the overall explanation—i.e., whether the outcome may be overdetermined. Another possibility is that each of the ostensibly competing explanations in fact addresses different parts of a complex longitudinal development. In such cases, the task of the investigator is to identify different turning points in the causal chain and to sort out which independent variables explain each step in the causal chain—for example, those explaining why a war occurred, those that explain the form of the attack, those that explain its timing, and so on. Still another possibility is that the key variable in one explanation is causal and the proposed causal variable in the other explanation is spurious.

The problem of apparently competing explanations may also arise when the rival interpretations address and attempt to explain different aspects of a case and therefore cannot be reconciled. When this happens, the investigator and readers of the case account should not regard the two interpretations as competing with each other. Another possibility is that the rival explanations emerge because the scholars advancing them have simply disagreed on the "facts" of the case.

In any case, if the data and generalizations available to the investigator do not permit him or her to choose from competing explanations, then both explanations for the case should be retained as equally plausible, and the implications of both for theory development should be considered in phase three of the study.

Transforming Descriptive Explanations Into Analytical Explanations

In addition to developing a specific explanation for each case, the researcher should consider transforming the specific explanation into the concepts and variables of the general theoretical framework specified in Task Two.[7] (In Harry Eckstein's terminology, such research is "disciplined-configurative" rather than "configurative-idiographic.") To transform specific explanations into general theoretical terms, the researcher's theoretical framework must be broad enough to capture the major elements of the historical context. That is, the set of independent and inter-

---

7. For an early discussion of the practice of transforming a historical explanation into an analytical one see Gabriel Almond et al., *Crisis, Choice, and Change: Historical Studies of Political Development* (Boston: Little, Brown, 1973). This study is among those summarized in the Appendix, "Studies That Illustrate Research Design."

vening variables must be adequate to capture and record the essentials of a causal account of the outcome in the case. The dividing line between what is essential and what is not is whether aspects of a causal process in a given case are expected or found to operate across the entire class of cases under consideration. For example, if some instance of organizational decision-making was decisively affected by the fact that one of the key participants in the decision process caught a cold and was unable to attend an important meeting, this would *not* constitute a basis for revising our theory of organizational decision-making to endogenize the susceptibility of actors to disease. It *would*, however, constitute a basis for a general argument about how outcomes are affected by the presence or absence of important potential participants.

Some historians will object to this procedure for transforming a rich and detailed historical explanation into a more abstract and selective one couched in theoretical concepts, arguing that unique qualities of the explanation inevitably will be lost in the process. This is undoubtedly true: some loss of information and some simplification is inherent in any effort at theory formulation or in theoretically formulated explanations. The critical question, however, is whether the loss of information and the simplification jeopardize the validity of the conclusions drawn from the cases for the theory and the utility of that theory. This question cannot be answered abstractly. The transition from a specific to a more general explanation may indeed lead a researcher to dismiss some of the causal processes at work in the case simply because they are not already captured by the general theory or because the researcher fails to recognize a variable's general significance. To say that avoiding these errors depends on the sensitivity and judgment of the researcher, while true, is not very helpful. One slightly more specific guideline is that researchers seem more susceptible to this error when trying to discern new causal patterns than when attempting to evaluate claims about some causal patterns already hypothesized to be operating in a particular case; and second, that the more fine-tuned and concrete the description of variance, the more readily the analysis will accommodate a more differentiated description of the causal processes at work.[8]

To the extent that the case study method has arisen from the practice of historians, it has tended to follow certain procedures that are not really appropriate for social scientists. One feature of most historians' work is a relative lack of concern with or discussion of methodological issues en-

---

8. See Chapter 4 for a discussion of Task Four and the critical importance of how variance in the variables is described, our caution against *a priori* decisions on such matters, and the desirability of making such determinations after preliminary analysis of the cases.

countered in the performance of research. We believe that case research-ers should explicitly discuss the major research dilemmas the case study researcher faced in the analysis of a case and the justifications for solving those dilemmas in a particular way. Therefore, we recommend that the investigator give some indication of how his or her initial expectations about behavior and initial data-collection rules were revised in the course of the study. This would permit readers to make a more informed analy-sis of the process by which a case and the conclusions based on the case were reached.

Most historians also rely heavily on chronological narrative as an or-ganizing device for presenting the case study materials. Preserving some elements of the chronology of the case may be indispensable for support-ing the theory-oriented analysis, and it may be highly desirable to do so in order to enable readers not already familiar with the history of the case to comprehend the analysis. Striking the right balance between a detailed historical description of the case and development of a theoretically-focused explanation of it is a familiar challenge. Analysts frequently feel it necessary to reduce the length of a case study to avoid overly long ac-counts that exceed the usual limits for journal articles or even books! The more cases, the more difficult this problem becomes.

There is no easy answer to this dilemma. Still, it has been dealt with in a reasonably effective way by a number of writers. A brief résumé of the case at the beginning of the analysis gives readers the essential facts about the development and outcome of the case. The ensuing write-up can blend additional historical detail with analysis.[9] Presentation of a case need not always include a highly detailed or exclusively chronologi-cal narrative. As a theory becomes better developed and as research fo-cuses on more tightly defined targets, there will be less need to present overly long narratives. Moreover, narrative accounts of a case can be sup-plemented by such devices as decision trees, sketches of the internal ana-lytical structure of the explanation, or even computer programs to dis-play the logic of the actors' decisions or the sequence of internal developments within the case.

Some Challenges in Attempting to Reconstruct Decisions

Scholars who attempt to reconstruct the policymaking process in order to explain important decisions face challenging problems. An important limitation of the analysis presented here is that it is drawn solely from the

9. See, for example, how this task was dealt with in studies such as Alexander L. George and Richard Smoke, *Deterrence in American Foreign Policy: Theory and Practice* (New York: Columbia University Press, 1974).

study of U.S. foreign policy.[10] We discuss first the task of acquiring reliable data on factors that entered into the policy process and evaluating their impact on the decision. Political scientists must often rely upon, or at least make use of, historians' research on the policy in question. Such historical studies can be extremely useful to political scientists, but several cautions should be observed in making use of these studies.

First, researchers should forgo the temptation to rely on a single, seemingly authoritative study of the case at hand by a historian. Such a shortcut overlooks the fact that competent historians who have studied that case often disagree on how best to explain it. As Ian Lustick has argued, "the work of historians is not . . . an unproblematic background narrative from which theoretically neutral data can be elicited for the framing of problems and the testing of theories."[11] Lustick approvingly notes Norman Cantor's argument that a historian's work represents "a picture of 'what happened' that is just as much a function of his or her personal commitments, the contemporary political issues with which s/he was engaged, and the methodological choices governing his or her work."[12] The danger here, Lustick argues, is that a researcher who draws upon too narrow a set of historical accounts that emphasizes the variables of interest may overstate the performance of favored hypotheses.

It is thus necessary to identify and summarize important debates among historians about competing explanations of a case, and wherever possible to indicate the possible political and historical biases of the contending authors. The researcher should translate these debates into the competing hypotheses and their variables as outlined in phase one. If there are important historical interpretations of the case that do not easily translate into the hypotheses already specified, the researcher should consider whether these interpretations should be cast as additional hypotheses and specified in terms of theoretical variables. The same procedures apply to the primary political debates among participants in the case and their critics. Even such overtly political debates may draw upon

---

10.   Similar problems arise in efforts by scholars to make use of archival materials and interviews from Soviet sources. See, for example, the correspondence between Mark Kramer, who expressed concern about the use of oral histories by Bruce J. Allyn, James G. Blight, and David A. Welch, and their responses in "Remembering the Cuban Missile Crisis: Should We Swallow Oral History?" *International Security*, Vol. 15, No. 1 (Summer 1990), pp. 212–218. See also "Commentaries on 'An Interview With Sergo Mikoyan'" by Raymond L. Garthoff, Barton J. Bernstein, Marc Trachtenberg, and Thomas G. Paterson in *Diplomatic History*, Vol. 14, No. 2 (Spring 1990), pp. 223–256.

11.   Ian S. Lustick, "History, Historiography, and Political Science," *American Political Science Review*, Vol. 90, No. 3 (September 1996), pp. 605–618.

12.   Ibid.

generalizable variables that historians and researchers may have overlooked.

One way to avoid the risk of relying on a single historical analysis would be to follow the practice of Richard Smoke, who at the outset of his research, asked several historians to help him identify the best available accounts of each of the cases he planned to study. Later, Smoke obtained reviews of the first drafts of his cases from eight historians and made appropriate changes.[13]

Second, social scientists making use of even the best available historical studies of a case should not assume that they will provide answers to the questions they are asking. As emphasized in Chapter 3 on "The Method of Structured, Focused Comparison," the political scientist's research objectives determine the general questions to be asked of each case. The historian's research objectives and the questions addressed in his or her study may not adequately reflect those of subsequent researchers.[14] We may recall that historians have often stated that if history is approached from a utilitarian perspective, then it has to be rewritten for each generation. History does not speak for itself to all successive generations. When new problems and interests are brought to a study of history by later generations, the meaning and significance of earlier historical events to the present may have to be studied anew and reevaluated. Hence, the study of relevant historical experience very much depends on the specific questions one asks of historical cases.

One of the key tasks during the "soaking and poking" process is to identify the gaps in existing historical accounts. These gaps may include archival or interview evidence that has not been examined or that had previously been unavailable. They may also include the measurement of variables the researcher identified in phase one that historians have not measured or have not measured as systematically as the explanatory goals of subsequent researchers require. It is also possible that researchers can make use of technologies, such as computer-assisted content analysis, that were not available to scholars writing earlier historical accounts.

Third, having identified possible gaps in existing accounts, the re-

---

13.   See the preface to Richard Smoke, *War: Controlling Escalation* (Cambridge, Mass.: Harvard University Press, 1977).

14.   The different ways historians and political scientists tend to define the task of explanation and the different questions they often ask of available data is discussed in helpful detail in Deborah Larson, "Sources and Methods in Cold War History: The Need for a Theory-Based Archival Approach," in Colin Elman and Miriam Fendius Elman, eds., *Bridges and Boundaries: Historians, Political Scientists, and the Study of International Relations* (Cambridge, Mass.: MIT Press, 2001), pp. 327–350. The dangers of using studies by historians that may reflect their selection bias are noted also by Lustick, "History, Historiography, and Political Science."

searcher must reckon with the possibility that good answers to his or her questions about each case can be obtained only by going to original sources—archival materials, memoirs, oral histories, newspapers, and new interviews. In fact, political scientists studying international politics are increasingly undertaking this task. In doing so, however, they face the challenging task of weighing the evidentiary value of such primary sources.

Fourth, the researcher should not assume that going to primary sources and declassified government documents alone will be sufficient to find the answers to his or her research questions. The task of assessing the significance and evidentiary worth of such sources often requires a careful examination of contemporary public sources, such as daily media accounts of the developments of a case unfolding over time. Contemporary public accounts are certainly not a substitute for analysis of archival sources, but they often are an important part of contextual developments to which policymakers are sensitive, to which they are responding, or which they are attempting to influence. Classified accounts of the process of policymaking cannot be properly evaluated by scholars unless the public context in which policymakers operate is taken into account.[15] We have at times found students who have become intimately familiar with hard-to-get primary source materials of a case but who have only a vague sense of the wider context because they have not taken the relatively easy (but often time-consuming) step of reading the newspapers or journals from the period.[16]

---

15. The importance of studying contemporary journalistic sources in order to understand part of the context in which policymakers were operating became a central methodological procedure in Deborah Larson's research. In conjunction with thorough research into archival sources, Larson spent a great deal of time going through contemporary journalists' accounts of developments, a procedure which helped her to appreciate the impact of events that came to the attention of policymakers on their perceptions and responses. Careful study of the public context of private deliberations was useful in evaluating the evidentiary significance of archival sources. See Deborah Welch Larson, *The Origins of Containment* (Princeton, N.J.: Princeton University Press, 1985). Larson amplifies and illustrates different ways in which contemporary newspaper accounts help the investigator to discern important elements of the context in which policymakers operate. See Larson, "Sources and Methods in Cold War History."

16. One example comes from the work of one of the present authors, Andrew Bennett. In an unpublished study of the 1929 stock market crash for the Federal Reserve Board, he found by reading the newspapers of the period that there are strong reasons to question the often-cited argument that the crash was caused by excessive speculation on margin credit rates "as low as 10 percent," or the supposedly common practice of buying stocks by putting up only 10 percent of their value as equity. In fact, while no systematic data exists for the margins typically set, most newspaper accounts suggest that margins of 40 to 50 percent or higher were the norm. Banks offered to lower margin rates to 10 percent as an extraordinary step to try halt the crash, based

Finally, research on recent and contemporary U.S. foreign policy must be sensitive to the likelihood that important data may not be available and cannot be easily retrieved for research purposes, e.g., important discussions among policymakers that take place over the telephone or within internal e-mail and fax facilities—the results of which are not easily acquired by researchers.

The Risk of Over-Intellectualizing the Policy Process

When academic scholars attempt to reconstruct how and why important decisions were made, they tend to assume an orderly and more rational policymaking process than is justified. For example, overly complex and precise formal models may posit decision-making heuristics that are "too clever by half," or that no individual would actually utilize. Also, scholars sometimes succumb to the common cognitive bias toward univariate explanations—explanations in which there appears to be a single clear and dominating reason for the decision in question. Instead, analysts should be sensitive to the possibility that several considerations motivated the decision.

In fact, presidents and top-level executives often seek multiple payoffs from any decision they take. Leaders known for their sophistication and skill, such as Lyndon B. Johnson, use this strategy to optimize political gains from a particular decision. Disagreements among scholars as to the particular reason for why a certain action was taken often fail to take this factor into account.

Several considerations can enter into a decision in other ways as well. Particularly in a pluralistic political system in which a number of actors participate in policymaking, agreement on what should be done can emerge for different reasons. It is sufficient that members of the policymaking group agree only on *what* to do without having to agree on *why* to do it. In some situations, in fact, there may be a tacit agreement among members of the group that not all those who support the decision have to share the same reason or a single reason for doing so. To obtain sufficient

---

on the assumption that the crash was caused by a liquidity crisis as plunging stock values led to margin calls on stocks and forced sales of those stocks. The fact that this measure failed to stem the crash, and that bond purchases were strong during the crash, suggest that perhaps the crash was caused not so much by loose margin credit as by the classic bursting of a speculative bubble, and a revaluation of the relative value of stocks versus bonds. This explanation is more in line with modern theories of stock market behavior. In any event, a simple reading of the newspapers reveals that explanations of the crash cannot unproblematically accept that margins were typically 10 percent.

consensus on a decision may be difficult for various reasons, and sufficient time and resources may not be available for achieving a completely shared judgment in support of the decision. In any action-oriented group, particularly one that operates under time pressure, it is often enough to agree on what needs to be done. It may not be feasible or wise to debate until everyone agrees not merely on what decision to take but also the precise reasons for doing so.

Assessing the Evidentiary Value of Archival Materials

Scholars doing historical case studies must find ways of assessing the evidentiary value of archival materials that were generated during the policymaking process under examination. Similarly, case analysts making use of historical studies produced by other scholars cannot automatically assume that these investigators properly weighed the evidentiary significance of documents and interviews.

Scholars are not immune from the general tendency to attach particular significance to an item that supports their pre-existing or favored interpretation and, conversely, to downplay the significance of an item that challenges it. As cognitive dissonance theory reminds us, most people operate with a double standard in weighing evidence. They more readily accept new information that is consistent with an existing mind-set and employ a much higher threshold for giving serious consideration to discrepant information that challenges existing policies or preferences.

All good historians, it has been said, are revisionist historians. That is, historians must be prepared to revise existing interpretations when new evidence and compelling new interpretations emerge. Even seemingly definitive explanations are subject to revision. But new information about a case must be properly evaluated, and this task is jeopardized when a scholar is overly impressed with and overinterprets the significance of a new item—e.g., a recently declassified document—that emerges on a controversial or highly politicized subject.

Analytical or political bias on the scholar's part can lead to distorted interpretation of archival materials. But questionable interpretations can also arise when the analyst fails to grasp the context of specific archival materials. The importance of context in making such interpretations deserves more detailed analysis than can be provided here, so a few observations will have to suffice.

It is useful to regard archival documents as a type of purposeful communication. A useful framework exists for assessing the meaning and evidentiary worth of *what* is communicated in a document, speech, or interview. In interpreting the meaning and significance of what is said, the analyst should consider *who* is speaking *to whom, for what purpose* and *under what circumstances.*[17] The evidentiary worth of what is contained in a document often cannot be reliably determined without addressing these questions. As this framework emphasizes, it is useful to ask what purpose(s) the document was designed to serve. How did it fit into the policymaking process? What was its relation to the stream of other communications and activities—past, present, and future?

It is also important to note the circumstances surrounding the document's release to the public, and to be sensitive to the possibility that documents will be selectively released to fit the political and personal goals of those officials who control their release. Much of the internal documentation on Soviet decision-making on the invasion and occupation of Afghanistan beginning in 1979, for example, was released by the government of Russian President Boris Yeltsin in the mid-1990s to embarrass the Soviet Communist Party, which was then on trial for its role in the 1991 Soviet coup attempt. Needless to say, the Yeltsin government did not release any comparable documents on its own ill-fated intervention in Chechnya in the mid-1990s.

In studying the outputs of a complex policymaking system, the investigator is well advised to work with a sophisticated model or set of assumptions regarding ways in which different policies are made in that system. For example, which actors and agencies are the most influential in a particular issue area? To whom does the leader turn for critical information and advice on a given type of policy problem? How do status differences and power variables affect the behavior of different advisers and participants in high-level policymaking?

Thus, it is advisable to observe a number of cautions in following the "paper trail" leading to a policy decision. Has a country's leader tipped his or her hand—at least in the judgment of participants in the pro-

---

17.   This framework was initially developed and employed in a study that examined methods for inferring the intentions, beliefs, and other characteristics of a political elite from its propaganda by means of qualitative content analysis. See Alexander L. George, *Propaganda Analysis: A Study of Inferences Made from Nazi Propaganda in World War II* (Evanston, Ill.: Row, Peterson, 1959; and Westport, Conn.: Greenwood Press, 1973), pp. 107–121.

In a personal communication (March 26, 2000), Jeremi Suri drew on his own research experience to emphasize the need to distinguish between various types of archival materials. Personal correspondence and diaries of historical actors can be very helpful in developing understanding of their general beliefs about political life, particularly since such materials are often not designed to persuade others; such sources can reflect the emotions experienced at different junctures. Also, the "incoming files" of various reading matter insofar as it can be established that it was read, may throw light on the actor's ideology or cultural beliefs and the role they may play in policymaking.

cess—regarding what he or she will eventually decide? What effect does such a perception—or misperception—have on the views expressed or written by advisers? Are some of the influential policymakers bargaining with each other behind the leader's back regarding what advice and options to recommend in the hope and expectation that they can resolve their differences and protect their own interests?[18] What role did policymakers play in writing their own public speeches and reports, and to what extent do specific rhetorical formulations represent these top officials' own words rather than those of speech writers and other advisers?

It is well known that those who produce classified policy papers and accounts of decisions often wish to leave behind a self-serving historical record. One scholar who recently spent a year stationed in an office dealing with national security affairs witnessed occasions on which the written, classified record of important decisions taken was deliberately distorted for this and other reasons.[19] Diplomatic historian Stephen Pelz reminds us that "many international leaders take pains to disguise their reasoning and purposes, and therefore much of the best work on such figures as Franklin D. Roosevelt consists of reconstructing their assumptions, goals, and images of the world from a variety of sources."[20]

In assessing the significance of "evidence" that a leader has engaged in "consultation" with advisers, one needs to keep in mind that he or she may do so for several different reasons.[21] We tend to assume that he or she consults in order to obtain information and advice before making a final decision—i.e., to satisfy his or her "cognitive needs." But he or she may consult for any one or several other reasons. The leader may want to obtain emotional support for a difficult, stressful decision; or the leader may wish to give important advisers the feeling they have had an opportunity to contribute to the decision-making process so that they will be more likely to support whatever decision the president makes—i.e., to build consensus; or the leader may need to satisfy the expectation (generated by the nature of the political system and its political culture and

---

18. Some of these possibilities are among the various "malfunctions" of the policymaking system discussed in Alexander L. George, *Presidential Decisionmaking and Foreign Policy: The Effective Use of Information and Advice* (Boulder, Colo.: Westview Press, 1980), chap. 6.

19. This observation was provided by a scholar who must remain anonymous.

20. Stephen Pelz, "Toward A New Diplomatic History: Two and a Half Cheers for International Relations Methods," in Elman and Elman, eds., *Bridges and Boundaries*, p. 100.

21. This paragraph and the next one draw on George, *Presidential Decisionmaking*, pp. 81ff.

norms) that important decisions will not be made without the participation of all key actors who have some relevant knowledge, expertise, or responsibility with regard to the matter being decided; that is, the president hopes to achieve "legitimacy" for a decision by giving evidence that assures Congress and the public that it was well-considered and properly made. (Of course, a leader's consultation in any particular instance may combine several of these purposes.)

This last purpose—consultation—is of particular interest in the United States. The public wants to be assured that an orderly, rational process was followed in making important decisions. Consider the development in recent decades of "instant histories" of many important decisions by leading journalists on the basis of their interviews with policymakers shortly after the event. Knowing that the interested public demands to know how an important decision was made, top-level policymakers are motivated to conduct the decision process in ways that will enable them to assure the public later that the decision was made after careful multisided deliberation. Information to this effect is given to journalists soon after the decision is made. Since "instant histories" may be slanted to portray a careful, multidimensioned process of policymaking, the case analyst must consider to what extent such an impression is justified and how it bears on the evidentiary worth of the information conveyed in the instant history and in subsequent "insider" accounts of how and why a particular decision was made.

To weigh archival type material effectively, scholars need to be aware of these complexities. An excellent example of a study that captures the dynamics of decision-making is Larry Berman's interpretation of President Johnson's decision in July 1965 to put large-scale ground combat troops into Vietnam. Some archival sources suggest that Johnson employed a careful, conscientious version of "multiple advocacy" in which he thoughtfully solicited all views. But according to Berman's analysis, Johnson had already decided what he had to do and went through the motions of consultation for purposes of consensus-building and legitimization of his decision.[22]

In another example, many scholars assumed that President Dwight D. Eisenhower's policymaking system was highly formalistic and bureaucratic, a perception shared by important congressional and other critics at the time. Working with this image of Eisenhower's decision-making style, scholars could easily misinterpret the significance of archival sources generated by the *formal* track of his policymaking. Easily

---

22. Larry Berman, *Planning a Tragedy: The Americanization of the War in Vietnam* (New York: Norton, 1982).

overlooked was the *informal* track, which preceded and accompanied the formal procedures, awareness of which led Fred Greenstein to write about the "hidden hand style" by which Eisenhower operated.[23] Now, a more sophisticated way of studying Eisenhower's policymaking has developed that pays attention to both the formal and informal policy tracks and to the interaction between them.

The relevance and usefulness of working with an analytical framework that considers both tracks is, of course, not confined to studying the Eisenhower presidency. The workings of the informal track are not likely to become the subject of a written archival document. It is important to use interviews, memoirs, the media, etc., to obtain this valuable material.

Another aspect of the importance of a contextual framework for assessing the evidentiary worth of archival sources has to do with the hierarchical nature of the policymaking system in most governments. We find useful the analogy of a pyramid of several layers. Each layer, beginning with the bottom one, sends communications upwards (as well as sideways), analyzing available data on a problem and offering interpretations of its significance for policy. As one moves up the pyramid, the number of actors and participants grows smaller but their importance (potential, if not actual) increases. As one reaches the layer next to the top—the top being the president—one encounters a handful of key officials and top advisers. At the same time, we find that researchers at times interview officials who are too high in the hierarchy to have had close involvement in or detailed recall of the events under study. Often, lower-level officials who worked on an issue every day have stronger recollections of how it was decided than the top officials who actually made the decision but who focused on the issues in question only intermittently. However, a researcher must take into account that even well-informed lower-level officials often do not have a complete or fully reliable picture of how and why a decision was made—i.e., the "Rashomon" problem, when different participants in the process have different views as to what took place.

This layered pyramid produces an enormous number of communications and documents that the scholar must assess. The possibility of erroneous interpretation of the significance of archival material is enormous. How do sophisticated historians and other scholars cope with this problem? What cautions are necessary when examining archival sources on top-level policymaking? How does a researcher deal with the fact that much of the material coming to the top-level group of policymakers from

---

23.   Fred I. Greenstein, *The Hidden-Hand Presidency: Eisenhower As Leader* (New York: Basic Books, 1982).

below is inconsequential? How does one decide which material coming from below to the top-level officials made a difference in the decision? How can one tell why he or she really decided as he or she did as against the justifications given for his or her decisions?

The analyst's search for documentary evidence on reasons behind top-level decisions can also run into the problem that the paper trail may end before final decisions are made. Among the reasons for the absence of reliable documentary sources on such decisions is the role that secrecy can play. Dean Rusk, Secretary of State during the Kennedy administration, later stated that secrecy "made it very difficult for many to reconstruct the Bay of Pigs operation, particularly its planning, because very little was put on paper. [Allen] Dulles, [Richard] Bissell, and others proposing the operation briefed us orally."[24]

No doubt there are important examples of scholarly disputes that illustrate these problems and indicate how individual analysts handled them. What general lessons can be drawn that would help train students and analysts? We have not yet found any book or major article that provides an adequate discussion of the problems of weighing the evidentiary worth of archival materials.[25] The most we can do, therefore, is to warn writers of historical case studies about some of these problems and to call attention to some of the methods historians and political scientists have employed in dealing with archival materials. Deborah Larson, for example, suggests that "to judge the influence of a memo written by a

---

24. As told to Richard Rusk in Daniel S. Papp, ed., *As I Saw It* (New York: Norton, 1990), cited by Richard Ned Lebow, "Social Science and History: Ranchers versus Farmers," in Elman and Elman, eds., *Bridges and Boundaries,* p. 132.

25. The most useful account we have found is the article by John D. Mulligan, "The Treatment of A Historical Source," *History and Theory,* Vol. 18, No. 2 (May 1979), pp. 177–196. Mulligan identifies various criteria historians employ for evaluating the authenticity, meaning, and significance of historical sources. He cites the observations on these issues made by a large number of distinguished historians and illustrates how each criterion applies to his own research, which focused on the importance of a correct evaluation of a primary source which sharply challenges accepted historical research on an aspect of the Civil War. This source was a personal letter, not a governmental document. Nonetheless, Mulligan's article illustrates the relevance of the framework we suggest, namely asking, "who says what to whom for what purpose in what circumstances?"

Also useful is the recent article by Cameron G. Thies, "A Pragmatic Guide to Qualitative Historical Analysis in the Study of International Relations," *International Studies Perspective,* Vol. 3, No. 4 (November 2002), pp. 351–372. This article includes a comprehensive list of sources that contributed to his essay. Readers may also want to consult the website "History Matters" <www.historymatters.gmu.edu.> which is designed for high school and college teachers of history. This website includes sections on "making sense of evidence" and "secrets of great history teachers."

lower-level official, one can look to see who initialed it. Of course, that a secretary of state initialed a memo does not prove that he read it, but it is a first step in analysis. Sometimes higher officials will make marginal comments—these can be quite important. Finally, paragraphs from memos written by lower officials sometimes appear in National Security Council policy memoranda."[26]

Problems in Evaluating Case Studies

Case writers should become familiar with the variety of critiques their work may face. The importance of understanding the history and context of a case makes the difficulties of critiquing qualitative research different from those of assessing quantitative work. Readers cannot easily judge the validity of the explanation of a case unless they possess a degree of independent knowledge of that case. This requires that reader-critics themselves possess some familiarity with the complexity of the case and the range of data available for studying it; knowledge of the existence of different interpretations offered by other scholars and of the status of the generalizations and theories employed by the case writer; and an ability to evaluate the case writer's use of counterfactual analysis or to provide plausible counterfactual analysis of their own. These are tough requirements for readers who must evaluate case studies, and simply to state these desiderata suffices to indicate that they are not easily met. Our own commentaries of case study research designs in the Appendix, "Studies That Illustrate Research Design," should be read with the caveat that we are not theoretical or historical experts on all the subjects of these studies. This is a problem also for those who review these books in academic journals.

Let us discuss some of the problems likely to be encountered by readers who attempt to evaluate case studies. Much of the preceding discussion is relevant to the task of evaluating case studies, and a few additional observations can be made.

The task of evaluating case studies differs depending on the research objective of the case. When the investigator's research objective is to explain a case outcome, the reader-critic must consider whether the case analyst has "imposed" a favored theory as the explanation. Have alternative theories that might provide an explanation been overlooked or inadequately considered? When the case writer pursues the different research objective of attempting to use case findings to "test" an existing

---

26.   Letter from Deborah Welch Larson to Alexander L. George, April 10, 1999.

theory, there are several questions the reader-critic has to consider in deciding whether such a claim is justified. Does the case (or cases) constitute an easy or tough test of the theory? Do case findings really support the theory in question? Do they perhaps also support other theories the investigator has overlooked or inadequately considered?

Reader-critics must consider the possibility that the case-writer has overlooked or unduly minimized potentially important causal variables, or has not considered the possibility or likelihood that the phenomenon is subject to multiple conjunctural causation or is affected by equifinality.

These and other problems in using case studies to develop or test theories are also discussed in Chapter 6. They are referred to here in order to emphasize that case writers should be familiar with the variety of criticisms that can be and often are made of their work.

In addition, we urge that case writers accept the obligation to assist readers in evaluating whether their case analyses have met relevant methodological standards. To meet this requirement, case writers should go as far as reasonably possible to make the analyses they offer transparent enough to enable readers to evaluate them. Transparency of case studies must be closely linked with standards for case studies. These standards include (but are not limited to) providing enough detail to satisfy as much as possible the criteria of replicability and of the validity and reliability of the way in which variables are scored. Certainly these standards are often difficult to meet in case study research, but case writers can often do more to at least approximate them. We strongly concur with the admonition of Gary King, Robert Keohane, and Sidney Verba that *"the most important rule for all data collection is to report how the data were created and how we came to possess them."*[27]

In sum, case analysts should strive to develop and make use of appropriate rules for qualitative analysis. As argued in earlier chapters, however, the development of such guidelines should not be regarded as a matter of simply extending to qualitative analysis all of the standard conventions for quantitative analysis. Some of these conventions apply also to qualitative analysis, but guidelines for case studies must take into account the special characteristics of qualitative methodology.[28]

---

27. Gary King, Robert O. Keohane, and Sidney Verba, *Designing Social Inquiry: Scientific Inference in Qualitative Research* (Princeton, N.J.: Princeton University Press, 1994), p. 51. Emphasis in original.

28. For a detailed analysis of this position, see Gerardo L. Munck, "Canons of Research Design in Qualitative Analysis," *Studies in Comparative International Development*, Vol. 33, No. 3 (Fall 1998). The author provides a systematic and balanced assess-

Conclusion

The present book was in process of publication when we became aware of a new guidebook on how to make use of primary historical sources. The author, Marc Trachtenberg, has produced a superb manuscript which is in draft form for the time being. Its title is *Historical Method in the Study of International Relations.*

Himself a leading diplomatic historian, Trachtenberg joined the political science department at UCLA several years ago. He has succeeded in bringing together historical and political science approaches to the study of international relations. This book will be an invaluable source for students and professors who want to integrate the perspectives of history and political science for insightful research on foreign policies.

We will not attempt to summarize the rich materials he presents. The titles of several chapters may be noted: Chapter 3, "The Critical Analysis of Historical Texts"; and Chapter 5, "Working with Documents." A chapter is also provided on "Diplomatic History and International Relations Theory"; another chapter provides a detailed analysis of America's road to war in 1941.

Trachtenberg's treatment of these issues is unusually user-friendly. It is written in an engaging style. It will become standard text for research on foreign policy. Trachtenberg provides many incisive examples to illustrate his points.

We may also recall the statement that Trachtenberg made some time ago: "The basic methodological advice one can give is quite simple: documents are not necessarily to be taken at face value, and one has to see things in context to understand what they mean. One has to get into the habit of asking why a particular document was written—that is, what purpose it was meant to serve."[29]

We have stressed in the preceding pages the necessity to regard archival sources as being instances of purposive communication. This advice is strongly reinforced by Deborah Larson on the basis of her experience in conducting in-depth research in archival sources in preparing her book *Origins of Containment.*[30] A recent article by Larson helps to fill the gap regarding the proper use of archival sources, at least for research on U.S.

---

ment of the canons for qualitative research imbedded in King, Keohane, and Verba, *Designing Social Inquiry.*

29.   In a letter to Alexander L. George (January 29, 1998), Marc Trachtenberg indicated that he is currently studying methods for assessing archival and other sources in research on international politics.

30.   Larson, *The Origins of Containment.*

foreign policy. In it she emphasizes that it is important to understand the purpose of a document and the events leading up to it in order to correctly interpret its meaning. . . . The author of a memorandum or speaker at a meeting may be trying to ingratiate himself with superiors, create a favorable impression of himself, put himself on the record in case of leaks, or persuade others to adopt his preferred policy. Whatever his goals, we cannot directly infer the communicator's state of mind from his arguments without considering his immediate aims.[31]

Larson also notes that study of contemporary accounts in leading newspapers sometimes can be essential for ascertaining the context of documents. "News accounts can help to establish the atmosphere of the times, the purpose of speeches or statements, or the public reaction to a statement. Newspapers help to show what information policymakers had and provide clues as to what events they regarded as important. . . . In this way, newspapers help us to recapture the perspective of officials at the time."[32]

---

31. Deborah Welch Larson, "Sources and Methods in Cold War History," pp. 327–350.

32. Ibid. See also the project "Oral History Roundtables: The National Security Project," established in 1998 by Ivo H. Daalder and I.M. Destler, sponsored by the Brookings Institution and the Center for International and Security Studies at the University of Maryland. This series of roundtables, published periodically, brings together former officials specializing in foreign and security affairs to discuss specific historical problems in which they were involved. Daalder and Destler plan a final summary report.

Chapter 6

Phase Three: Drawing the Implications of Case Findings for Theory

Case study findings can have implications both for theory development and theory testing. On the inductive side of theory development, plausibility probes and studies of deviant cases can uncover new or omitted variables, hypotheses, causal paths, causal mechanisms, types, or interactions effects. Theory testing aims to strengthen or reduce support for a theory, narrow or extend the scope conditions of a theory, or determine which of two or more theories best explains a case, type, or general phenomenon. While many works on research methods and the philosophy of science emphasize theory testing more than theory development, we see both enterprises as essential to constructing good theories.

Case study findings can have implications for theory development and testing on three levels. First, they may establish, strengthen, or weaken historical explanations of a case. This is where within-case methods like process-tracing come into play. If a theory posits particular causal mechanisms as an explanation of a particular case, but these prove to be demonstrably absent, then the theory is greatly weakened as an explanation for this case, though there is still the possibility of measurement error or omitted variables.

Yet a modified historical explanation of a case may not add to explanations of other cases that are dissimilar in some respects. Establishing the general applicability of a new or modified explanation of a case requires showing that it accurately explains other cases. Conversely, invalidating an existing theory as an explanation of one case does not necessarily imply that the theory poorly explains other, dissimilar cases; indeed, the existing theory may have earlier demonstrated a strong ability to explain cases.[1] Whereas some earlier approaches assumed or demanded that a new theory subsume or explain all of the phenomena explained by its predecessors, we do not require that this always be so. A new theory may be superior in explaining only some of the cases explained by its predecessor, or even only one case, while being inapplicable to others.

Second, and more generally, the finding that a theory does or does not explain a case may be generalized to the type or class of cases (e.g., deterrence) of which this case is a member. Here, the generalization depends on the precision and completeness with which the class of cases has been defined and the degree to which the case exemplifies the class. Generalization to cases not studied always entails some risk of mistaken inferences because they may differ from the case or cases studied in the values of potentially causal variables omitted from the theoretical framework.

Third and most broadly, case study findings may in some circumstances be generalized to neighboring cells in a typology, to the role of a particular variable in dissimilar cases, or even to all cases of a phenomenon. Here overgeneralization is a risk, since the analyst is generalizing cases that differ in the value of variables that have been already identified as causally related to the outcome. This is why case study researchers usually limit themselves to narrow and well-specified contingent generalizations about a type.[2] Still, some cases may constitute particularly strong tests of theories, allowing generalization beyond the particular cases studied.

This chapter looks at each of these kinds of generalization, first in theory development and then in theory testing. It concludes that improved historical explanations of individual cases are the foundation for drawing wider implications from case studies, as they are a necessary condition for any generalizations beyond the case. Contingent or typological generalizations are often the most useful kind of theoretical

---

1. The Bayesian approach to theory choice is one means of weighting the confidence we should place in an existing theory versus a new competing theory. Briefly, in the Bayesian approach, we increase our prior estimate of the likely truth of a theory when we encounter evidence that is likely only if the theory is true and unlikely if alternative explanations are true. This relies, however, on subjective prior probabilities that researchers assign to the truth of competing theories. The Bayesian defense of this practice is that as evidence accumulates, differences in the prior probabilities that different researchers assign to theories will "wash out" as new evidence forces researchers' confidence in theories to converge. For arguments on both sides of this issue, see John Earman, *Bayes or Bust? A Critical Examination of Bayesian Confirmation Theory* (Cambridge, Mass.: MIT Press, 1992).

2. David Collier and James Mahoney, "Insights and Pitfalls: Selection Bias in Qualitative Research," *World Politics*, Vol. 49, No. 1 (October 1996), pp. 59–91.

conclusions from case studies, as they build on and go beyond improved historical explanations but present limited risks of extending these conclusions to causally dissimilar cases. Findings that can be extended to different types of cases are less common, and often must be stated as only loose generalizations. However, they can be important turning points in research programs, drawing attention toward avenues for future research.

Theory Development

The development of theory via case studies should be distinguished from the deductive development of theory. Deductive methods can usefully develop entirely new theories or fill the gaps in existing theories; case studies can test deductive theories and suggest new variables that need to be incorporated. (The literature on deterrence, as noted below, provides an excellent example of this process.) But theory development via case studies is primarily an inductive process. This section highlights the usefulness of deviant cases for inductively identifying new variables or causal mechanisms. (Plausibility probes, which we do not discuss here, also focus directly on the goal of theory development, by aiming at clearer specification of a theory and its variables and by attempting to better identify which cases might prove most valuable for theory building.)

THEORY DEVELOPMENT AND HISTORICAL EXPLANATION OF SINGLE CASES
The outcome in a deviant case may prove to have been caused by variables that had been previously overlooked but whose effects are well known from other research. This leads to an improved historical explanation of the case, but not necessarily to any new generalizations from the case, unless the case is one in which the previously overlooked variables were not expected to have any effect.

An inductively derived explanation of a case can also involve more novel theories and variables. In this context, researchers are frequently advised not to develop a theory from evidence and then test it against the same evidence; facts cannot test or contradict a theory that is constructed around them. In addition, using the same evidence to create and test a theory also exacerbates risks of confirmation bias, a cognitive bias toward affirming one's own theories that has been well documented both in laboratory experiments and in the practices of social scientists.[3]

However, it is valid to develop a theory from a case and then test the

---

3. For a study that indicates that social scientists' explanations for the failures of their predictions appear to be biased in favor of their initial theories, see Philip Tetlock,

theory against additional evidence from the case that was not used to derive the theory. This makes the theory falsifiable as an explanation for the case, and can circumvent confirmation biases. Researchers, even when they are fairly expert on a case and its outcome (or the value of its dependent variable), are often ignorant of the detailed processes through which the outcome arose.[4] As a researcher begins to delve into primary sources, there are many opportunities to reformulate initial explanations of a case in ways that accommodate new evidence and also predict what the researchers should find in evidence they have not yet explored or had not even thought to look for. Researchers can also predict what evidence they should find in archives before these are made accessible or in interviews before they are carried out.[5] Indeed, in testing a historical explanation of a case, the most convincing procedure is often to develop an explanation from data in the case and then test it against other evidence in the case; otherwise, the only recourse is to test the explanation in other cases that differ in ways that may prevent generalization back to the original case.

THEORY DEVELOPMENT AND CONTINGENT GENERALIZATIONS

The study of a deviant case can lead a researcher to identify a new type of case. As we discuss in Chapter 11, this process can take place through a "building block" approach, with new case studies identifying subtypes or the causal processes that apply to a subtype of cases. Each case study thus contributes to the cumulative refinement of contingent generalizations on the conditions under which particular causal paths occur, and fills out the cells or types of a more comprehensive theory.

Historians often view efforts to generalize from historical case studies with suspicion. Yet one can generalize from unique cases by treating

---

"Theory-Driven Reasoning about Plausible Pasts and Probable Futures in World Politics: Are We Prisoners of Our Preconceptions?" *American Journal of Political Science,* Vol. 43, No. 2 (April 1999), pp. 348–349. Researchers should also be on guard against other cognitive biases, including the bias toward over-confidence in one's causal theories, a preference for uni-causal explanations, and a tendency toward assuming that causes resemble consequences in terms of scale, scope, or complexity.

4.   Researchers also often find that their preliminary knowledge of the values of the independent and dependent variables is mistaken, particularly if it is based on news accounts or secondary sources that do not use precise definitions. Thus even these variables can provide some use-novelty for researchers; however, as we note in our chapter on congruence testing, tests of the congruence of independent and dependent variables, even with the advantage of use-novelty, are challenging and often less conclusive than process-tracing tests.

5.   William Wohlforth suggests this practice in "Reality Check: Revising Theories of International Politics in Response to the End of the Cold War," *World Politics,* Vol. 50, No. 4 (July 1998), pp. 650–680.

them as members of a class or type of phenomenon; that is, as instances of alliance formation, deterrence, war initiation, negotiation, peace-keeping, war termination, revolution, and so on. This is often followed by distinguishing subclasses of each of the phenomena. Researchers can also develop "concatenated" theories by dividing a complex causal process into its specific component theories, or sequential stages, focusing on particular policy instruments or the views of designated actors. For example, Alexander George and Richard Smoke divided deterrence theory into a number of more specific theories which deterrence comprises: commitment theory, initiation theory, and response theory.[6] Similarly, Bruce Jentleson, Ariel Levite, and Larry Berman broke down protracted military interventions into sequential stages and the differing dynamics of getting in, staying in, and getting out.[7] Such designations help identify subtypes of undertakings and phenomena that occur repeatedly throughout history which can be grouped together and studied as a class or subclass of similar events. This can be done through statistical analysis when a sufficiently large number of cases of a particular phenomenon is available, or through qualitative analysis of a small number of instances.

Where should one draw the line in developing ever more finely grained types and subtypes? As Sidney Verba put it many years ago:

To be comparative, we are told, we must look for generalizations or covering laws that apply to all cases of a particular type. But where are the general laws? Generalizations fade when we look at particular cases. We add intervening variable after intervening variable. Since the cases are few in number, we end up with an explanation tailored to each case. The result begins to sound quite idiographic or configurative... In a sense we have come full circle. . . . As we bring more and more variables back into our analysis in order to arrive at any generalizations that hold up across a series of political systems, we bring back so much that we have a "unique" case in its configurative whole.[8]

Yet Verba did not conclude that the quest for theory and generalization is infeasible. Rather, the solution to this apparent impasse is to formulate the idiosyncratic aspects of the explanation for each case in terms

---

6.   Alexander L. George and Richard Smoke, *Deterrence in American Foreign Policy: Theory and Practice* (New York: Columbia University Press, 1974). See also the discussion of George and Smoke in the Appendix, "Studies That Illustrate Research Design."

7.   Bruce Jentleson, Ariel Levite, and Larry Berman, eds., *Foreign Military Intervention: The Dynamics of Protracted Conflict* (New York: Columbia University Press, 1992). This book is discussed in the Appendix, "Studies That Illustrate Research Design."

8.   Sidney Verba, "Some Dilemmas of Political Research," *World Politics*, Vol. 20, No. 1 (October 1967), pp. 113–114.

of general variables. "The 'unique historical event' cannot be ignored," Verba notes, "but it must be considered as one of a class of events even if it happened only once."[9]

One criterion that helps determine where to draw the line in the proliferation of subtypes is the notion of "leverage"—the desirability of having theories that explain as many dependent variables as possible with as few simple independent variables as possible. This is not the same as parsimony, or simplicity of theories. We agree with Verba and his co-authors Gary King and Robert Keohane that parsimony is "an assumption . . . about the nature of the world: it is assumed to be simple . . . but we believe [parsimony] is only occasionally appropriate . . . theory should be just as complicated as all our evidence suggest."[10]

The recognition that even unique cases can contribute to theory development strengthens the linkage between history and political science. Some of the particular qualities of each case are inevitably lost in the process of moving from a specific to a more general explanation. The critical question, however, is whether the loss of information and simplification jeopardizes the validity and utility of the theory. This question cannot be answered abstractly or *a priori*. Much depends upon the sensibility and judgment of the investigator in choosing and conceptualizing variables and also in deciding how best to describe the variance in each of the variables. The latter task in particular—the way in which variations for each variable are formulated—may be critical for capturing the essential features of "uniqueness." For this reason, investigators should develop the categories for describing the variance in each of their variables inductively, via detailed examination of how the value of a particular variable differs across many different cases.

THEORY DEVELOPMENT AND GENERALIZING ACROSS TYPES

The most general kind of finding from a deviant case is the specification of a new concept, variable, or theory regarding a causal mechanism that affects more than one type of case and possibly even all instances of a phenomenon. This specification of new concepts or variables, as Max Weber noted, is often one of the most important contributions of research.[11] Charles Darwin's theory of evolution, for example, was sparked by a small number of cases (particularly the small differences between

---

9. Ibid.

10. Gary King, Robert O. Keohane, and Sidney Verba, *Designing Social Inquiry: Scientific Inference in Qualitative Research* (Princeton, N.J.: Princeton University Press, 1994), pp. 29, 20.

11. Marianne Weber, *Max Weber: A Biography*, trans. Harry Zohn (New Brunswick,

finches on the South American mainland and those on the Galapagos Islands), but it posited new causal mechanisms of wide relevance to biological and even social systems.

When a deviant case leads to the specification of a new theory, the researcher may be able to generalize about how the newly identified mechanism may play out in different contexts, or he or she may only be able to suggest that it should be widely relevant. As an example of the former, Andrew Bennett, Joseph Lepgold, and Danny Unger undertook a study of burden sharing in the 1991 Gulf War partly because several countries' sizeable contributions to the Desert Storm coalition contradicted the collective action theories that then dominated the literature on alliances and would have predicted more free-riding. The authors found that pressure from the United States, the coalition leader, explained the large contributions by allies dependent on the United States for their security, most notably Germany and Japan. While pressure from a powerful state is not a novel hypothesis in explaining international behavior, the finding suggested that the collective action hypothesis was generally less determinative in alliance behavior than had been argued. While the temptation of free riding grows as one state becomes more powerful relative to others, so does the ability of the powerful state to coerce dependent allies as well. As these forces offset one another, other factors—domestic politics and institutions, the nature of the public good of alliance security, and so on—help tilt the balance toward or away from a contribution. In short, the authors developed fairly detailed contingent generalizations on how the understudied factor of alliance dependence would play out in different contexts.[12]

Theory Testing

When theories are fairly well developed, researchers can use case studies for theory testing. The goal here is rarely to refute a theory decisively, but rather to identify whether and how the scope conditions of competing theories should be expanded or narrowed. This is a challenging process: when a theory fails to fit the evidence in a case, it is not obvious whether the theory fails to explain the particular case, fails to explain a whole class of cases, or does not explain any cases at all. Should we blame a theory's

---

N.J.: Transaction Press, 1988), p. 278, cited in David Laitin, "Disciplining Political Science," *American Political Science Review*, Vol. 89, No. 2 (June 1995), p. 455.

12. See Chapter 11 for a more detailed discussion of this research as an example of typological theory. See also Andrew Bennett, Joseph Lepgold, and Danny Unger, "Burden-Sharing in the Persian Gulf War," *International Organization*, Vol. 48, No. 1 (Winter 1994), pp. 39–75.

failure on a flaw in the theory's internal logic or on contextual conditions that rendered the theory inapplicable (which would require only a narrowing of the theory's scope conditions to exclude the anomalous case), or on some combination of the two? We should not be too quick to reject general theories on the basis of one or a few anomalous cases, as these theories may still explain other cases very well. Conversely, there is a danger of too readily retaining a false theory by narrowing its scope conditions to exclude anomalous cases, or by adding additional variables to the theory to account for anomalies.

An additional difficulty in theory testing is that tests are partly dependent on the causal assumptions of theories themselves. For example, theories that posit simple causal relations, such as necessity, sufficiency, or linearity can be falsified by a single case (barring measurement error). Theories are harder to test if they posit more complex causal relations, such as equifinality and interactions effects. Still, such theories, which are often the kind that most interest case study researchers, may be subjected to strong tests if they assume high-probability (but not necessarily deterministic) relations between variables and posit a manageably small number of variables, interactions, and causal paths. Theories are hardest to subject to empirical tests if they involve the most complex types of causal relations, or what might be called "enigmatic" causality: complex interactions among numerous variables, low-probability relations between variables, and endogeneity problems or feedback effects. Such theories are difficult to test even with large numbers of cases to study. Although a single case can disprove a deterministic assertion, even many cases cannot *falsify* a probabilistic claim—it is only increasingly unlikely to be true if it fails to fit a growing number of cases.

While theories need to be developed into a testable form, a theory should not be forced into predictions beyond its scope; this leads to the creation of an easily discounted "straw man" version of the theory. A test could also be too tough if countervailing variables mask the causal effects of the variable under study.[13] Of course, researchers frequently disagree on whether a theory is being forced to "stick its neck out" sufficiently far, or whether it is being pushed into predictions beyond its rightful scope.[14] If an empirical test is beyond the domain of phenomena to which the the-

---

13.   See Stephen W. Van Evera, *Guide to Methods for Students of Political Science* (Ithaca, N.Y.: Cornell University Press, 1997), p. 34.

14.   See, for example, Colin Elman, "Horses for Courses: Why Not Neorealist Theories of Foreign Policy," *Security Studies,* Vol. 6, No. 1 (Autumn 1996), pp. 7–53. Elman critiques neorealist theories for claiming to eschew any testable predictions on individual states' foreign policies.

ory has been applied, then findings inconsistent with the theory limit its scope rather than falsify it.

How can a researcher avoid too readily rejecting or narrowing the scope conditions of a theory that is in fact accurate, or accepting or broadening the scope conditions of a theory that is in fact false or inapplicable? There are no infallible criteria for addressing all of the complications of generalizing the results of a case study's theory tests. A key consideration, however, is the issue of how tough an empirical test a case poses for a theory: How strongly do the variables predict the case's outcome, and how unique are the predictions the theory makes for the case?[15]

TESTING COMPETING EXPLANATIONS OF CASES

An explanation of a case is more convincing if it is more unique, or if the outcome it predicts "could not have been expected from the best rival theory available."[16] If a phenomenon has not previously received wide study, a theory can only make a rather weak claim to being the "best" explanation. For closely studied phenomena, however, the finding that a case fits only one explanatory theory is powerful evidence that the theory best explains the case. Of the five hypotheses considered in the study of burden-sharing in the 1991 Gulf War noted above (balance of threat, alliance dependence, collective action, domestic politics, and policymaking institutions) *only* the alliance dependence hypothesis fit the outcome and process of the German and Japanese contributions to the coalition. This highlighted the power of alliance dependence, since the variables identified by all the other hypotheses militated against this outcome.

---

15. In a similar formulation, Stephen Van Evera suggests that the probity of an empirical test depends on the certainty and uniqueness of the predictions a theory makes regarding the test. "Hoop tests" are those in which the predictions of a theory are certain but not unique. Failing such a test is damaging to a theory, but passing it is not definitive. "Smoking gun tests" are those in which a theory is unique but not certain. Passing such a test is strong corroboration, but failing it does not undermine a theory. "Doubly decisive" tests, when predictions are both unique and certain, are those in which either passage or failure is definitive. (Van Evera gives the example here of a bank camera, which can both convict those guilty of robbery and exculpate the innocent.) "Straw-in-the-wind" tests, with predictions of low certainty and uniqueness, are not definitive regardless of the outcome. See Van Evera, *Guide to Methods*, pp. 31–32.

16. Colin Elman and Miriam Fendius Elman, "How Not to be Lakatos Intolerant: Appraising Progress in IR Research," *International Studies Quarterly*, Vol. 46, No. 2 (June 2002), p. 240, citing M. Carrier, "On Novel Facts: A Discussion of Criteria for Non-Ad-Hocness in the Methodology of Scientific Research Programs," *Zeitschrift für allgemeine Wissenschaftstheorie*, Vol. 19, No. 2 (1988), pp. 205–231. In the philosophy of science, a theory that makes a unique prediction is said to have achieved "background theory novelty."

In testing competing historical explanations of a case, then, it is important to find instances where explanations make unique predictions about the process or outcome of the case. An excellent example of this is Scott Sagan's work on the safety of nuclear weapons from accidental or unauthorized use.[17] Sagan treats the safety of nuclear weapons as a subclass of the ability of complex organizations to manage hazardous technology. The latter problem has been addressed in two major theories: Charles Perrow's normal accidents theory, and the high reliability theory developed by a group of Berkeley scholars.[18] Neither of these two organizational theories had addressed the specific problem of nuclear weapons safety, but Sagan argues they each have implications for this issue.

Sagan notes that both theories often make ambiguous predictions.[19] Neither theory excludes the possibility of a serious accident, though the normal accident theory is more pessimistic. There is considerable overlap between the two in their predictions on the nuclear weapons cases of interest to Sagan, but he finds the theories to be at odds in several important respects. Sagan notes that "many of the specific conditions that the high reliability theorists argue will promote safety will actually reduce safety according to the normal accidents theorists." Conversely, he argues, the safety requirements posited by the high reliability school are impossible to implement in the view of normal accidents theorists.[20]

Sagan identifies historical situations, including several aspects of the Cuban Missile Crisis, in which the theories make different predictions about the level of safety achieved and the means through which it was attained.[21]

Sagan notes that his goal was to "deduce what each theory should predict about specific efforts to prevent the ultimate safety system failure—an accidental nuclear war—and then compare these predictions to the historical experiences of U.S. nuclear weapons command and control.

17.   Scott D. Sagan, *The Limits of Safety: Organizations, Accidents, and Nuclear Weapons* (Princeton N.J.: Princeton, University Press, 1993).

18.   Charles Perrow, *Normal Accidents: Living with High-Risk Technologies* (New York: Basic Books, 1984); and Todd LaPorte and Paula Consolini, "Working in Practice but Not in Theory: Theoretical Challenges of 'High Reliability Organizations,'" *Journal of Public Administration Research and Theory*, Vol. 1, No. 1 (January 1991), pp. 19–47.

19.   Sagan, *The Limits of Safety*, pp. 13, 49.

20.   Ibid., p. 45.

21.   Ibid., p. 51. A debate on Sagan's book was later published between Todd LaPorte, a leading adherent of the "high reliability" school and Charles Perrow, the founder of the "normal accidents" school. A comment on their exchange is provided by Scott Sagan in *Journal of Contingencies and Crisis Management*, Vol. 2, No. 4 (December 1994), pp. 205–240.

Which theory provides better predictions of what happened and more compelling explanations of why it happened? Which theory leads to the discovery of more novel facts and new insights? Which one is therefore a better guide to understanding?"[22] Sagan concludes that on the whole, the normal accidents school provides more accurate answers to these questions in the case of the Cuban Missile Crisis.

Sagan's reasoning is as follows: given that there have been no accidental nuclear wars, one can focus on the performance of the two theories in predicting and explaining the serious—though not catastrophic—failures in the safety of nuclear weapons that have occurred. An interesting feature is Sagan's effort to construct a tough test for the normal accidents theory in the impressive U.S. safety record with nuclear weapons, which appears to conform more closely to the optimistic predictions of high reliability theorists. That U.S. leaders attach high priority to avoiding accidental nuclear war, U.S. nuclear forces personnel are isolated from society and subject to strict military discipline, and the United States has adequate resources to spend on the safety of its nuclear weapons also favors the validity of the high reliability theory and poses a tough test for the normal accidents theory. Sagan nonetheless concludes on the basis of detailed process-tracing evidence that the lesser safety failures and near misses that did occur are comprehensible only in terms of the warnings of the normal accidents school. By arriving at this finding even in a very tough test, Sagan creates a convincing basis for generalizing beyond his cases to U.S. nuclear weapons safety as a whole.

TESTING CONTINGENT GENERALIZATIONS

To test contingent or typological generalizations, scholars must clearly specify the scope or domain of their generalizations. To what range of institutional settings, cultural contexts, time periods, geographic settings, and situational contexts do the findings apply? Here again, typological theorizing, as discussed in Chapter 11, provides a ready means for specifying the configurations of variables or the types to which generalizations apply. Tests of contingent generalizations can then consist of examining cases within the specified domain of the theory to see if their processes and outcomes are as the theory predicts. Conversely, researchers can test for cases beyond the specified scope conditions of the theory to determine if these scope conditions might be justifiably broadened.

The proper boundaries of contingent generalizations are a frequent subject of contention among theorists. An illuminating example concerns Theda Skocpol's study of social revolutions in France, Russia, and

China.[23] Barbara Geddes critiques Skocpol's analysis by arguing that in several Latin American countries, the causes of revolution that Skocpol identified were present, but no revolutions occurred, while in other countries in the region, revolutions took place even in the absence of the preconditions Skocpol noted.[24] Skocpol was careful to make her theory contingent, however, clearly indicating in her introduction and conclusion that her theory is not a general theory of revolutions, but a theory of revolutions in wealthy agrarian states that had not experienced colonial domination. Skocpol in fact explicitly states that her argument does not apply to three cases that Geddes raises (Mexico in 1910, Bolivia in 1952, and Cuba in 1959), so these cases do not contravene the scope conditions that Skocpol outlines.[25] A more appropriate critique of Skocpol would point out cases that fit within the domain Skocpol defined but that do not fit her theory, or criticize directly the way in which Skocpol defined the domain of her theory.[26]

GENERALIZING ACROSS TYPES: TOUGH TESTS AND MOST-LIKELY, LEAST-LIKELY, AND CRUCIAL CASES

It is difficult to judge the probative value of a particular test relative to the weight of prior evidence behind an existing theory. Harry Eckstein argues that "crucial cases" provide the most definitive type of evidence on a theory. He defines a crucial case as one "that *must closely fit* a theory if one is to have confidence in the theory's validity, or conversely, *must not fit* equally well with any rule contrary to that proposed." He adds that "in a crucial case it must be extremely difficult, or clearly petulant, to dismiss any finding contrary to the theory as simply 'deviant' (due to chance, or the operation of unconsidered factors)."[27]

---

23. Theda Skocpol, *States and Social Revolutions: A Comparative Analysis of France, Russia, and China* (Cambridge, U.K.: Cambridge University Press, 1979).

24. Barbara Geddes, "How the Cases You Choose Affect the Answers You Get: Selection Bias in Comparative Politics," in James A. Stimson, ed., *Political Analysis*, Vol. 2 (Ann Arbor: University of Michigan Press, 1990). This example of the Skocpol-Geddes debate is from Collier and Mahoney, "Insights and Pitfalls," pp. 80–82.

25. Collier and Mahoney, "Insights and Pitfalls," p. 81.

26. Along these lines, as Chapter 2 notes, there is a debate over whether new democracies should be excluded from tests of democratic peace theories. Some view the exclusion of new democracies from statistical tests of these theories as an arbitrary way to rescue the theories from anomalous findings. Others view the exclusion as legitimate, arguing that the causal mechanisms that create a democratic peace are only very weakly established in states in transition to democracy.

27. Harry Eckstein, "Case Studies in Political Science," in Fred Greenstein and Nelson Polsby, eds., *Handbook of Political Science*, Vol. 7 (Reading, Mass.: Addison-Wesley, 1975), p. 118. McKeown suggests that in this regard case study researchers use an in-

Eckstein notes the difficulties in identifying such crucial cases when theories and their predictive consequences are not precisely stated, but notes that the foremost problem is that truly crucial cases rarely occur in nature or the social world. Therefore, he suggests the alternative of tough tests which entail studying most-likely and least-likely cases. In a most-likely case, the independent variables posited by a theory are at values that strongly posit an outcome or posit an extreme outcome. In a least-likely case, the independent variables in a theory are at values that only weakly predict an outcome or predict a low-magnitude outcome. Most-likely cases, he notes, are tailored to cast strong doubt on theories if the theories do not fit, while least-likely cases can strengthen support for theories that fit even cases where they should be weak.

Many case study researchers have identified the cases they choose for study as most-likely or least-likely cases, but it is necessary to be explicit and systematic in determining this status. One must consider not only whether a case is most or least likely for a given theory, but whether it is also most or least likely for alternative theories. One useful means of doing so, as noted in Chapter 11 on typological theory, is to include a typological table that shows the values of variables in the case or cases studied for competing hypotheses. Such a table helps the researcher and reader identify which variables in a case may favor alternative theories, and helps the researcher to address systematically whether alternative theories make the same or different predictions on processes and outcomes in a given case.

In general, the strongest possible supporting evidence for a theory is a case that is least likely for that theory but most likely for all alternative theories, and one where the alternative theories collectively predict an outcome very different from that of the least-likely theory. If the least-likely theory turns out to be accurate, it deserves full credit for a prediction that cannot also be ascribed to other theories (though it could still be spurious and subject to an as-yet undiscovered theory). This might be called a toughest test case.[28] Theories that survive such a difficult test may prove to be generally applicable to many types of cases,

---

formal version of Bayesian logic. Timothy J. McKeown, "Case Studies and the Statistical World View," *International Organization*, Vol. 53, No. 1 (Winter 1999), pp. 161–190.

28. Similarly, Margaret Mooney Marini and Burton Singer define the "gross strength" of a causal inference on the role of a variable X as the overall evidence consistent with "X causes Y," and they define the "net strength" on X as the gross strength of X discounted by the gross strength of alternative variables and their underlying theories. Margaret Mooney Marini and Burton Singer, "Causality in the Social Sciences," in Clifford Clogg, ed., *Sociological Methodology*, Vol. 18 (1998), pp. 347–409. See also James Caporoso, "Research Design, Falsification, and the Qualitative-Quantitative Divide," *American Political Science Review*, Vol. 89, No. 2 (June 1995), p. 458.

as they have already proven their robustness in the presence of counter-vailing mechanisms.

The best possible evidence for weakening a theory is when a case is most likely for that theory and for alternative theories, and all these theories make the same prediction. If the prediction proves wrong, the failure of the theory cannot be attributed to the countervailing influence of variables from other theories (again, left-out variables can still weaken the strength of this inference). This might be called an easiest test case. If a theory and all the alternatives fail in such a case, it should be considered a deviant case and it might prove fruitful to look for an undiscovered causal path or variable. A theory's failure in an easiest test case calls into question its applicability to many types of cases.

One example of a theory that failed an easy test case comes from Arend Lijphart's study of the Netherlands, which cast doubt on David Truman's theory of "cross-cutting cleavages."[29] Truman had argued that mutually reinforcing social cleavages, such as coterminous class and religious cleavages, would lead to contentious politics, while cross-cutting cleavages would lead to cooperative social relations. In the Netherlands, however, Lijphart found a case with essentially no cross-cutting cleavages but a stable and cooperative democratic political culture. This cast doubt on Truman's theory not just for the Netherlands, but more generally.

Cases usually fall somewhere in between being most and least likely for particular theories, and so pose tests of an intermediate degree of difficulty. Short of finding toughest or easiest test cases, researchers should be careful to specify, for each alternative hypothesis, where the case at hand lies on the spectrum from most to least likely for that theory, and when the theory predicts outcomes that complement or contradict other theories' predictions.

For example, Graham Allison's study of the Cuban Missile Crisis, *Essence of Decision*, is in some respects a strong test case for the rational actor model, a moderate test of the organizational process model, and a strong test of the bureaucratic politics model.[30] However, it is not the strongest

29.   This example comes from Ronald Rogowski, "The Role of Theory and Anomaly in Social-Scientific Inference," *American Political Science Review*, Vol. 89, No. 2 (June 1995), pp. 467–468; the referenced works are Arend Lijphart, *The Politics of Accommodation: Pluralism and Democracy in the Netherlands* (Berkeley: University of California Press, 1975); and David Truman, *The Governmental Process: Political Interest and Public Opinion* (New York: Knopf, 1951).

30.   Graham Allison and Philip Zelikow, *Essence of Decision: Explaining the Cuban Missile Crisis,* 2nd ed. (Longman, N.Y.: Longman, 1999).

possible test of any model and just how strong it is depends on which of Allison's research questions is under consideration.

Let us consider the first two of Allison's three research questions as examples. On the question of "Why did the Soviet Union place missiles in Cuba?" rational actor considerations should have been strong given the clear strategic stakes. Organizational processes should not have been very strong because the Soviet Union was taking the initiative and had time to adapt its procedures. Bureaucratic politics should have been of moderate importance given the stakes involved for Soviet military budgets and missions. On the question of "Why did Kennedy react as he did?" rational actor considerations were constrained by the incomplete information and short time period, but strengthened by the president's direct involvement. On the other hand, the nature of the crisis favored U.S. decision-making that approximates the rational actor model. Organizational processes were a moderate constraint—the president's personal involvement could and did modify procedures, but the short time available limited possible adaptations. Bureaucratic politics should have been constrained by the president's role and the overriding importance of national concerns (rather than parochial institutional concerns). One could add details on what makes each question a most- or least- likely case for each of the models, but the general point is that many contextual factors must be taken into account and that they rarely all point in the same direction on the high likelihood of one theory and the low likelihood of others.

It is important to note that a case in which one variable is at an extreme value is not necessarily a definitive test. Rather, if the variables of competing explanations make the same prediction and are not at extreme values, this may represent an easy test that provides only weak evidence for the importance of the extreme variable. Such easy tests are not very probative, and if they are incorrectly used to infer strong support for a theory, they may constitute a problem of selection bias. Such a case may be more useful for the heuristic purpose of identifying the outsized causal mechanisms related to the extreme variable.

Conclusion

Generalizing the results of case studies is not a simple function of the number or diversity of cases studied. A researcher may study diverse cases that prove to have no common patterns, so that only unique historical explanations of each case are possible. Alternatively, a researcher may study a few cases or even one case and uncover a new causal mechanism that proves applicable to a wide range of cases. Single cases can also cast doubt on theories across a wide range of scope conditions, as Arend Lijphart's study of the Netherlands demonstrates. These extremes of a complete inability to generalize from a case and a warrant for broad generalizations from a single case are relatively infrequent. More common is the opportunity to use case study findings to incrementally refine middle-range contingent generalizations, either by broadening or narrowing their scope or introducing new types and subtypes through the inclusion of additional variables. Such refinements draw on both within-case analyses, which help test historical explanations of cases, and cross-case comparisons, which help identify the domains to which these explanations extend. This interplay among within-case analyses and comparative methods is the hallmark of typological theorizing, a subject to which we return in Chapter 11.

Part III
Alternative Methods and Select Issues

Chapter 7

Case Studies and the Philosophy of Science

Philosophical assumptions are unavoidable in everyday methodological choices at all phases of the design and execution of research. Although scholars can hold similar theoretical beliefs for very different epistemological reasons, once they begin to test, adapt, or change their beliefs, their differing philosophical assumptions often come to the fore. Thus, despite the complexity of the philosophy of science, we address in this chapter the philosophical underpinnings of case study methods.

Practicing social scientists need not continuously concern themselves with the intricacies of the latest "best practices" among philosophers of science—nor can the best practices be established with total confidence or beyond contention. Yet practicing social scientists can be too disengaged from developments in the philosophy of science. Many scholars in the field of international relations, for example, appear to have become too removed from these developments. This has resulted in a gap between our field's ontological assumptions, or its assumptions about the ultimately unobservable entities that generate the observable social world, and its epistemology, or its ideas about how to develop and model knowledge of how the world works.[1] Specifically, much of the discourse in the study of international relations is structured among "schools of thought"—neorealism, neoliberalism, and constructivism—that some scholars have consciously modeled after Thomas Kuhn's "paradigms" or

---

1.   Peter Hall, "Aligning Ontology and Methodology in Comparative Politics," in James Mahoney and Dietrich Reuschemeyer, eds., *Comparative Historical Analysis in the Social Sciences* (Cambridge: Cambridge University Press, 2003). Hall directs his argument toward the field of comparative politics, but it is also relevant to other fields in political science and to other social sciences.

Imre Lakatos' "research programs."[2] This parsing of our field into contending "isms" does not fit very well with the emphasis we and many other scholars have placed on causal explanation via causal mechanisms, which often cut across these schools of thought.[3] Nor does it address the importance of what Robert Merton termed "middle-range theory."[4] The focus on large schools of thought has usefully clarified our theories and allowed scholars to talk to (rather than past) one another, and it has simplified the task of teaching the field to our students. But to the extent that it has diverted attention from empirical puzzle-solving and problem-driven research, the field has suffered. Thus, introducing new ways of thinking about causal explanation can open up what has become a rather stylized debate among contending schools of thought and create space for research that is driven by local puzzles and recurrent policy-relevant problems as well as grand "isms."

In this chapter on the philosophy of science, the issues that we focus on bear directly on the pragmatic methodological choices facing social science researchers using qualitative methods. We first address the differences contemporary scholars have identified between the social and physical sciences. Next, we look at the problem of theoretical explanation and critique the "deductive-nomological" model of explanation, which involves explanation via reference to law-like statements of regularity. We outline as an alternative the use of theories about causal mechanisms to explain cases, and we address several challenges in defining causal mechanisms and distinguishing their epistemology from that of using

---

2. Thomas Kuhn, *The Structure of Scientific Revolutions* (Chicago: University of Chicago Press, 1962); Imre Lakatos, "Falsification and the Methodology of Scientific Research Programmes," in Imre Lakatos and Alan Musgrave, eds., *Criticism and the Growth of Knowledge* (New York: Cambridge University Press, 1970), pp. 91–196. The term "constructivism" and the group of scholars and ideas to which it applies remains more amorphous than the terms neoliberalism and neorealism (though these too are subject to debate), and some interpretations of constructivism are consistent with our own view of causal explanation and our emphasis on causal mechanisms. See, for example, Jeffrey Checkel, "The Constructivist Turn in International Relations Theory," *World Politics*, Vol. 50, No. 2 (January 1998), pp. 324–348.

3. For discussion of these schools of thought in a Lakatosian framework, see Colin Elman and Miriam Fendius Elman, "How Not to be Lakatos Intolerant: Appraising Progress in IR Research," *International Studies Quarterly*, Vol. 46, No. 2 (June 2002), pp. 231–262, and these authors' edited volume, *Progress in International Relations Theory: Appraising the Field* (Cambridge, Mass.: MIT Press, 2003). As the Elmans note, a key problem for efforts to render schools of thought as Lakatosian research programs is that Lakatos and his successors have not devised any defensible distinction between the untestable "hard core" assumptions of a research program and its testable "outer belt" theories.

4. Robert Merton, *Social Theory and Social Structure*, rev. ed. (New York: Free Press, 1957), pp. 36, 41, 45–46, 51–53, 68–69.

laws to explain cases. Finally, we discuss the close connection between the epistemology of causal mechanisms and the methodology of process-tracing, which allows close inspection of the observable implications of theorized causal mechanisms in the context of individual cases. We conclude that both process-tracing and typological theorizing are powerful methods for testing theories about causal mechanisms in individual cases and developing contingent generalizations about the conditions under which these mechanisms, and conjunctions of different mechanisms, operate in particular ways in specified contexts.

How Does the Philosophy of the Social Sciences Differ From That of the Physical Sciences?

A key difference between the physical sciences, which have shaped much of the philosophy of science, and the social sciences is that human agents are *reflective*—that is, they contemplate, anticipate, and can work to change their social and material environments and they have long-term intentions as well as immediate desires or wants. These observations have led to what has been termed the constructivist approach to international relations.[5] This approach, in part a reaction to the structuralist modern variants of *realpolitik* theories of international relations, emphasizes that structures are social as well as material, and that agents and structures are mutually constitutive. In other words, social and material environments both socialize and constrain individuals and enable them to take actions intelligible to others, including actions that intentionally change social norms and material circumstances. As David Dessler has persuasively argued, this constructivist ontology entirely encompasses structuralist ontologies because it takes into account social and material structures as well as the intended and unintended consequences of social interaction.[6] Agent-centered change is not unique to human agents—living beings from microbes to mammals can affect their environments—but intentional change is unique to human agents or nearly so.

The reflexivity of human agents suggests that the postmodern and hermeneutic critiques of the successors of the positivist tradition in the philosophy of science are more relevant in the social than in the physical sciences. Postmodernists emphasize that language—a key medium of hu-

---

5.　For an overview of constructivism and variants within it, see John Gerard Ruggie, "What Makes the World Hang Together? Neo-Utilitarianism and the Social Constructivist Challenge," *International Organization*, Vol. 52, No. 4 (Autumn 1998), pp. 855–886.

6.　David Dessler, "What's at Stake in the Agent-Structure Debate?" *International Organization*, Vol. 43, No. 3 (Summer 1989), pp. 441–474.

man interaction—is open to multiple interpretations, thus hampering any aspiration toward definitive explanatory theories. Hermeneuticists argue that the study of social phenomena cannot be independent of these phenomena because researchers are socialized into certain conceptions of science and society. Moreover, the results of research can change the behavior being studied; a new theory of the relationship between inflation and unemployment, for example, might lead investors and employers to change their behavior in ways that make the theory less valid. More generally, the very nature of the objects under study can change, as in the emergence of capitalism or state sovereignty. In short, there are no immutable foundational truths in social life.

Thus, most social generalizations are necessarily contingent and time-bound, or conditioned by ideas and institutions that hold only for finite periods; yet we need not concede fully to the postmodernist or hermeneutic critiques of social theorizing. Observation is theory-laden, but it is not theory-determined. Evidence can surprise us and force us to revise our theories and explanations. Language is subject to multiple interpretations, but not infinite ones, and sometimes it is fairly unambiguous. Moreover, important social structures like sovereignty or capitalism clearly are sufficiently recursive and long-lived that recognizable behavioral patterns can usefully be theorized upon for meaningful periods of time. Many postmodernists critique the ability of powerful actors to reproduce the social institutions that are the source of their power, but it is inconsistent to argue that relations of social power exist and persist and also to maintain that it is not useful to theorize about these relations or the continuity of language and meaning that they embody.[7]

Still, the reflexivity of social subjects does constrain social science theorizing in a variety of ways. Strategic interaction, self-fulfilling and self-denying prophecies, moral hazard, selection effects, and a range of other phenomena make the development of predictive theories far more difficult in the social sciences than in the physical sciences.[8] To cope with these difficulties, social scientists should distinguish here between theories that can explain and predict both processes and outcomes, which are common in the physical sciences, and those that can explain processes and outcomes but not predict them. The second kinds of theories, common in the social sciences, are also found in the physical sciences. Theories of evolutionary biology, for example, explain processes and *post*

---

7.   We set aside here the debate over the ways in which social power can be oppressive and those in which it serves useful purposes such as overcoming collective action problems.

8.   Robert Jervis, *System Effects: Complexity in Political and Social Life* (Princeton, N.J.: Princeton University Press, 1997).

facto outcomes, but they do not predict outcomes. While social scientists should aspire toward predictive theories—our own approach to the development of typological theories is meant to foster contingent generalizations with predictive (or at least diagnostic) power—they should also recognize the value of good historical explanations of cases as well as that of law-like generalizations.[9] The two are linked, in that historical explanations use theoretical generalizations to argue why in a particular context certain outcomes were to be expected, and good historical explanations (especially of cases with surprising outcomes) can lead to the development of better theories.[10] But the logic of historical explanation does differ from that of nomological generalization, as we note in Chapter 10.

These factors give theories in the social sciences a different "life-cycle" from those in the physical sciences. In the social sciences, much cumulation takes the form of increasingly narrow and more contingent (but also more valid) generalizations.[11] At the same time, fundamental changes in research programs are more frequent in the social sciences than in the physical sciences not just because of the "faddishness" or "subjectivity" of the social sciences, but because the objects of study change in reflexive ways.

In sum, while the reflexivity of human agents means that the philosophies of the social and physical sciences differ in important ways, we argue that progressive theorizing over long periods of time is possible in the social sciences. We also urge more explicit differentiation of various types of theory. We concur, moreover, with the scientific realist view that social facts exist independently of the observer and can be the subject of defensible causal inferences.

Theoretical Explanation: From the Deductive-Nomological Model to Causal Mechanisms

The traditional positivist model of explanation associated with Karl Popper, Karl Hempel, and Ernest Nagel posits that a "law or event is ex-

---

9. David Dessler, "Dimensions of Progress in Empirical Social Science: Toward a Post-Lakatosian Account of Scientific Development," in Elman and Elman, eds., *Progress in International Relations Theory,* pp. 381–404.

10. Clayton Roberts, *The Logic of Historical Explanation* (University Park: Pennsylvania State University Press, 1996).

11. Dessler, "Dimensions of Progress," pp. 381–404. On the other hand, the effort to build theories on the basis of individual-level causal mechanisms, whether these mechanisms are rational choice, cognitive, or socio-biological, does attempt to move toward more universal generalizations.

plained when it is shown to be something that is or was to be expected in the circumstances where it is found."[12] In this view, laws, or covering laws, are statements of regularity in the form of "if A, then B," and explanation consists of combining a law with initial conditions A to show that B was to be expected. While this model of explanation, developed by Hempel and Paul Oppenheim and later labeled as the "deductive nomological" or "D-N" model, remains intuitively appealing and widely used, it suffers from several serious shortcomings. First, it does not distinguish between causal and spurious regularities. Second, it does not indicate whether the outcome B was to be expected with 100 percent certainty or something less than certainty.[13] In this section, we elaborate briefly upon each of these challenges and indicate how they have driven philosophical debate toward the scientific realist notion of explanation via reference to *causal mechanisms.* We then define such mechanisms and indicate how case study methods provide a basis for inferences regarding causal mechanisms, and we identify some of the remaining challenges that beset mechanism-based explanations: the challenges of distinguishing mechanisms from laws or theories, delineating the relationship between observables and unobservables in the process of explanation, and making sense of probabilistic mechanisms.

The first flaw of the D-N model is that it does not distinguish between regularities that might be considered causal and those that clearly are not. The D-N model equates explanation with prediction, but some observations may be predictive without being causal or explanatory. For example, a sharp drop in a barometer's reading of air pressure may indicate that a storm is coming, but we would not argue that the barometric reading causes or explains the storm. Both the drop in barometric readings and the storm are caused by atmospheric conditions that work through mechanisms involving air pressure (as well as factors such as temperature and topography). Yet the D-N model allows the change in

---

12.   Dessler, "Dimensions of Progress," p. 386. This section draws heavily on Dessler and on Wesley Salmon, *Four Decades of Scientific Explanation* (Minneapolis: University of Minnesota Press, 1990). See also Wesley C. Salmon, "Scientific Explanation: Causation and Unification," in Wesley C. Salmon, *Causality and Explanation* (New York: Oxford University Press, 1998), pp. 68–78.

13.   A third problem with the D-N model is that it does not offer an explanation of laws themselves, as Hempel and Oppenheim acknowledged in an infamous footnote (note 33); Salmon makes this point in his "Scientific Explanation" (p. 69) and notes that Hempel and Oppenheim never resolved this issue and that Hempel even argued later that causality does not play a crucial role in scientific explanation, a stance that Salmon and others found unsatisfactory. We do not offer an explanation of laws themselves but rather, like Salmon, note that they invoke causal mechanisms that are ultimately unobservable.

barometric readings to count as an "explanation" of the storm, and cannot distinguish between the explanation via barometric readings and that via air pressure and other mechanisms.[14] In some instances, a good predictive capability may suffice to guide decisions or policy choices, and in the colloquial sense we may use the term "cause" for such phenomena. For many years, for example, smoking was considered on the basis of statistical evidence to be a "cause" of cancer, and the evidence was sufficiently strong to dissuade many people from smoking. Only recently have the intervening mechanisms through which smoking causes cancer become better understood, bringing us closer to a causal explanation in the scientific sense. A better understanding of the mechanisms through which smoking contributes to cancer can lead to better predictions on which individuals are more likely to develop cancer from smoking and better means of prevention and intervention to reduce the risk of cancer.

A second problem with the D-N model is that its predictions must be rendered with perfect certainty. If laws are to predict outcomes with absolute certainty, then the model founders in the physical sciences on the problem of quantum mechanics, which render quantum phenomena inherently probabilistic. In the social sciences, few nontrivial covering law type regularities hold with certainty across a wide variety of contexts.

For these reasons, philosophers and statisticians have labored mightily to construct a modification of the D-N model that would allow explanation to proceed in probabilistic terms rather than through exceptionless regularities. The "inductive statistical" (I-S) model, for example, argued for using high likelihood as the standard for explanation, but did not specify how likely an outcome must be to be considered law-like. Must a phenomenon be 99 percent likely, or only 51 percent likely? What about phenomena that are rare but occur with statistical regularity under specified circumstances? The problem, as the philosopher of science Wesley Salmon argues, is that the D-N model's two components –regularity and expectability—can conflict with one another. Salmon notes that "a particular event, such as a spontaneous radioactive decay, may be rather improbable, yet we know the ineluctably statistical laws that govern its occurrence. The nomic [regularity] side [of the D-N model] is fulfilled, but the expectability side is not."[15]

The failure of the I-S model prompted other attempts at probabilistic explanation. One of these is the "statistical relevance" or S-R model,

---

14.   On this and other counterexamples to the D-N model, see Salmon, *Four Decades,* pp. 46–47.

15.   Salmon, *Four Decades,* p. 120. Salmon develops this argument from the work of Peter Railton, "Explaining Explanation: A Realist Account of Scientific Explanation and Understanding" (Ph.D. dissertation, Princeton University, Princeton, N.J., 1980).

which suggests that factors are causal if they raise the probability with which an outcome is to be expected, whether or not the resulting probability was high or low. The S-R model and other probabilistic approaches to explanation remain unsatisfactory, however.[16] Salmon, a pioneer of the S-R approach, recounts his own intellectual evolution on this subject:

When I was busily expounding the statistical-relevance model . . . I was aware that explanation involves causality, but I hoped that the required causal relations could be fully explicated by means of . . . statistical concepts. A decade later, I was quite thoroughly convinced that this hope could not be fulfilled. Along with this realization came the recognition that statistical relevance relations, in and of themselves, have no explanatory force. They have significance for scientific explanation only insofar as they provide evidence for causal relations . . . causal explanation, I argued, must appeal to such mechanisms as causal propagation and causal interactions, which are not explicated in statistical terms. [17]

In Salmon's view, this failure to rescue the D-N model by rendering it in statistical or probabilistic terms led to the emergence of an alternative approach to scientific explanation. Whereas the D-N model explained events through general laws of nature, the alternative approach to explanation "made a strong identification between causality and explanation. Roughly and briefly, to explain an event is to identify its cause. The examples that furnish the strongest intuitive basis for this conception are cases of explanations of particular occurrences—for instance, the sinking of the *Titanic*."[18]

Salmon adds that the mechanism-based approach that he came to favor "makes explanatory knowledge into knowledge of the hidden mechanisms by which nature works. It goes beyond phenomenal descriptive knowledge into knowledge of things that are not open to immediate inspection. Explanatory knowledge opens up the black boxes of nature to

---

16. On the technical problems attending attempts at probabilistic explanation, see Salmon, *Four Decades*, pp. 61–89.

17. Salmon, *Four Decades*, p. 166; our emphasis. Salmon adds that he found "severe difficulties" with probabilistic accounts of causality, reinforcing his view that "causal concepts cannot be fully explicated in terms of statistical relationships; in addition, I concluded, we need to appeal to causal processes and causal interactions" (p. 168).

18. Salmon, "Scientific Explanation," p. 69. Salmon attributes the emergence of this approach to explanation to the works of Michael Scriven, citing, among other works, Scriven's "Explanations, Predictions, and Laws," in Herbert Feigl and Grover Maxwell, eds., *Scientific Explanation, Space, and Time*, Vol. 3, Minnesota Studies in the Philosophy of Science (Minneapolis: University of Minnesota Press, 1962), pp. 170–230.

reveal their inner workings. It exhibits the ways in which the things we want to explain come about."[19]

DEFINING CAUSAL MECHANISMS

The approach of explaining phenomena via causal mechanisms has gained a wide following among social scientists and philosophers of science.[20] The growing interest in causal mechanisms is of particular significance because it is shared by scholars who disagree on other important questions regarding theory and methodology. Yet there is no agreement on an exact definition of "causal mechanism." Some have defined causal mechanisms as being essentially indistinguishable from theories; Peter Hedstrom and Richard Swedburg, for example, define causal mechanisms as "analytical constructs that provide hypothetical links between observable events."[21] We prefer a scientific realist definition that places causal mechanisms on the ontological

19.   Salmon, *Four Decades*, pp. 182–183. Salmon contrasts this with the "unification approach" to explanation, which "holds that scientific understanding increases as we decrease the number of independent assumptions that are required to explain what goes on in the world. It seeks laws and principles of the utmost generality and depth." Salmon, *Four Decades*, p. 182. See also Salmon, "Scientific Explanation," pp. 68–78. Salmon suggests that the two conceptions of explanation are not incompatible, and he gives examples of phenomena that can be explained through either approach. We focus here on mechanism-based explanations without ruling out that some mechanisms may be of such a general character that they can provide unification-type explanations of diverse phenomena.

20.   See David Dessler, "Beyond Correlations: Toward a Causal Theory of War," *International Studies Quarterly*, Vol. 35, No. 3 (September 1991), pp. 337–355; Jon Elster, *Explaining Technical Change: A Case Study in the Philosophy of Science* (Cambridge: Cambridge University Press, 1983); Jon Elster, *Nuts and Bolts for the Social Sciences* (London: Cambridge University Press, 1989); Jon Elster, *Political Psychology* (London: Cambridge University Press, 1993); Daniel Little, *Varieties of Social Explanation: An Introduction to the Philosophy of Social Science* (Boulder, Colo.: Westview Press, 1991); Margaret Mooney Marini and Burton Singer, "Causality in the Social Sciences," in Clifford Clogg, ed., *Sociological Methodology*, Vol. 18 (1988), pp. 347–409; Richard W. Miller, *Fact and Method: Explanation, Confirmation and Reality in the Natural and Social Sciences* (Princeton, N.J.: Princeton University Press, 1987); Salmon, *Four Decades*; Andrew Sayer, *Method in the Social Sciences: A Realist Approach*, 2nd ed. (London: Routledge, 1992); Charles Tilly, "Means and Ends of Comparison in Macrosociology," *Comparative Social Research*, Vol. 16 (1997), pp. 43–53; Arthur Stinchcombe, "The Conditions of Fruitfulness of Theorizing About Mechanisms in Social Science," in Aage B. Sorensen and Seymour Spilerman, eds., *Social Theory and Social Policy: Essays in Honor of James S. Coleman* (Westport, Conn.: Praeger, 1993), pp. 23–41; and Peter Hedstrom and Richard Swedborg, "Social Mechanisms," *Acta Sociologica*, Vol. 39, No. 3 (1996), pp. 255–342.

21.   Peter Hedstrom and Richard Swedburg, *Social Mechanisms: An Analytical Approach to Social Theory* (Cambridge: Cambridge University Press, 1998), p. 13.

level.[22] In this view, theories and explanations are hypothesized models of how underlying mechanisms work. Roy Bhaskar, for example, states that "the construction of an explanation for . . . some identified phenomenon will involve the building of a model . . . which *if* it were to exist and act in the postulated way would account for the phenomenon in question."[23] Similarly, James Mahoney has defined a causal mechanism as "an unobservable entity that—when activated—generates an outcome of interest."[24] This introduces the notion that causal mechanisms are sufficient, in specific contexts, to bring about outcomes. Wesley Salmon also puts causal mechanisms on the ontological level, stating that "an intersection of two processes is a *causal interaction* if both processes are modified in the intersection in ways that persist beyond the point of intersection . . . causal processes are capable of transmitting energy, information, and causal influence from one part of spacetime to another."[25]

---

22.   Our above discussion of causal mechanisms resonates with the scientific realist school of thought in the philosophy of science. We are wary of using the term "scientific realism" too readily because there are almost as many versions of scientific realism as there are philosophers calling themselves realists. Fred Chernoff, for example, identifies six different versions of scientific realism; "Scientific Realism as a Meta-Theory of International Politics," *International Studies Quarterly*, Vol. 46, No. 2 (June 2002), p. 191. For our purposes, we do not need to analyze the many variants of scientific realism; we merely note for interested readers the connection between some of our arguments and a few of the propositions common among scientific realists.

One of the most widely used definitions of scientific realism, for example, is Richard Boyd's view that the terms of science refer to ontological entities that exist independently of the observer and that the laws or theories in mature sciences are approximately true. Richard Boyd, "Realism, Underdetermination and a Causal Theory of Evidence," *Nous*, Vol. 7 (1973), pp. 1–12. With regard to the social world, the argument that "social facts" or entities exist independently of the observer, while not universally accepted, is one that we endorse as a working proposition. The assertion that theories in some sciences are approximately true is more widely contested, and we see no need to take either side of this proposition for qualitative research to be fruitful. Our views have less in common with Boyd's version of scientific realism than with what Daniel Little has proposed as a "doctrine of causal realism for the social sciences." Little argues that causal explanation should be the goal of social science, and that causal mechanisms play a key role in causal explanation. See Daniel Little, *Microfoundations, Methods, and Causation: On the Philosophy of the Social Sciences* (New Brunswick, N.J.: Transaction Publishers, 1998), pp. 197–198.

23.   Roy Bhaskar, *The Possibility of Naturalism: A Philosophical Critique of the Contemporary Human Sciences* (Atlantic Highlands, N.J.: Humanities Press, 1979), p. 15.

24.   James Mahoney, "Beyond Correlational Analysis: Recent Innovations in Theory and Method," *Sociological Forum*, Vol. 16, No. 3 (2001), pp. 575–593. For similar views, see George Steinmetz, "Critical Realism and Historical Sociology," *Comparative Studies in Society and History*, Vol. 40, No. 1 (January 1998), pp. 177–178. For other scientific realist views on causal mechanisms, see Bhaskar, *The Possibility of Naturalism;* and Rom Harre, *The Principles of Scientific Thinking* (Chicago: University of Chicago Press, 1970).

25.   Salmon, "Scientific Explanation," p. 71. Salmon adds that "I have argued that

Building on these definitions, we define causal mechanisms as ultimately unobservable physical, social, or psychological processes through which agents with causal capacities operate, but only in specific contexts or conditions, to transfer energy, information, or matter to other entities. In so doing, the causal agent changes the affected entity's characteristics, capacities, or propensities in ways that persist until subsequent causal mechanisms act upon it. If we are able to measure changes in the entity being acted upon after the intervention of the causal mechanism and in temporal or spatial isolation from other mechanisms, then the causal mechanism may be said to have generated the observed change in this entity.[26] The inferential challenge, of course, is to isolate one causal mechanism from another, and more generally, to identify the conditions under which a particular mechanism becomes activated.

CAUSAL MECHANISMS AND THE COMMITMENT TO MICROFOUNDATIONS
Our definition of causal mechanisms raises the question of whether explanation via causal mechanisms, even if these are defined on the ontological rather than the theoretical level, is different from explanation via the D-N model, in which an outcome is explained if it is shown that it should have been expected under the circumstances. How is it different to say that outcomes were generated than to say that they were to be expected? The essential difference between the D-N model and explanation via causal mechanisms is that the D-N model invokes only one aspect of causality, the outcomes or effects of putatively causal processes. The D-N model also relies only upon two of the many sources of inference that David Hume identified: constant conjunction (or a positive correlation between the appearance of the hypothesized cause and the observed effect); and congruity of magnitude between purported causes and observed effects (a positive correlation between the magnitude of the hypothesized cause and that of the designated effect).

Gary King, Robert Keohane, and Sidney Verba pose a view of explanation in *Designing Social Inquiry (DSI)* that differs from our own in a subtle but important way by emphasizing the importance of causal effects—or the changes in outcome variables brought about by changes in

---

causal processes are precisely the kinds of causal connections that Hume sought but was unable to find" (p. 71).

26. Of course, the ability to isolate a causal mechanism from the operation of all other mechanisms, which would be the equivalent of a perfect experiment or a testable counterfactual proposition, is not attainable in practice. Experimental methods attempt to approximate such a perfect experiment, while observational methods, including most statistical as well as qualitative work in the social sciences, try to control for or rule out the effects of mechanisms other than the mechanisms being investigated.

the value of an independent variable—over that of causal mechanisms. These authors argue that the definition of causal effect is:

Logically prior to the identification of causal mechanisms. . . . We can define a causal effect without understanding all of the causal mechanisms involved, but we cannot identify causal mechanisms without defining the concept of causal effect. . . . We should not confuse a definition of causality with the nondefinitional, albeit often useful, operational procedure [process-tracing] of identifying causal mechanisms.[27]

This view risks conflating the definition of "causality" with that of "causal effect." The definition of causal effect is an ontological one that invokes an unobservable counter-factual outcome: the causal effect is the expected value of the change in outcome if we could run a perfect experiment in which only one independent variable changes. Statistical tests and controlled case study comparisons are operational procedures for estimating causal effects across cases. Usually, in the social sciences, these procedures are employed in nonexperimental settings that can only approximate the logic of experiments. Similarly, a "causal mechanism" invokes an ontological causal process, and process-tracing is an operational procedure for attempting to identify and verify the observable within-case implications of causal mechanisms. Consequently, this passage of *DSI* compares apples and oranges in juxtaposing an ontological notion (causal effects) and an operational procedure (process-tracing) rather than comparing ontology to ontology or procedure to procedure.

Albert Yee has made an opposite and equally fruitless assertion that causal mechanisms are "ontologically prior" to causal effects because one cannot have a causal effect without an underlying causal mechanism.[28] Such arguments are true but trivial, as they divert attention from the key point that causal effects and causal mechanisms are equally important components of explanatory causal theories. The more productive ques-

---

27. Gary King, Robert O. Keohane, and Sidney Verba, *Designing Social Inquiry: Scientific Inference in Qualitative Research* (Princeton, N.J.: Princeton, University Press, 1994), p. 86. This volume does give one example—drawn from research on whether a mass extinction of dinosaurs was caused by a large meteor hitting the earth (pp. 11–12)—that fits our approach of using process-tracing to construct historical explanations that provide evidence on theories. All the other examples in the book, however, focus on cross-case inferences on causal effects. Elsewhere, Robert Keohane has discussed causal explanation in ways that are quite similar to our own emphasis on causal mechanisms. See his "International Relations: Old and New," in Robert Goodin and Hans-Dieter Klingemann, eds., *Handbook of Political Science* (Oxford: Oxford University Press, 1996), pp. 463–465.

28. Albert S. Yee, "The Causal Effect of Ideas on Policies," *International Organization*, Vol. 50, No. 1 (Winter 1996), p. 84.

tion is whether case studies have comparative advantages in assessing causal mechanisms within the context of individual cases, while statistical methods have comparative advantages in estimating the causal effects of variables across samples of cases.

A more radical critique of the explanatory role of causal mechanisms is Milton Friedman's argument that all theories simplify reality by making *as if* assumptions. Friedman argues that successful explanatory theories are those that accurately predict outcomes based on assumptions that the entities under study behave *as if* the theory were true, even if the theory is not literally true as stated. He asserts that:

Truly important and significant hypotheses will be found to have "assumptions" that are wildly inaccurate representations of reality . . . the relevant question to ask about the "assumptions" of a theory is not whether they are descriptively "realistic," for they never are, but whether they are sufficiently good approximations for the purpose in hand. And this question can be answered only by seeing whether the theory works, which means whether it yields sufficiently accurate predictions.[29]

Firms operating in a market, for example, behave *as if* they know the underlying cost and demand functions posited by economic theory, even though they do not go through the actual complex mathematical calculations posited by economic theory.[30]

Friedman is right in the sense that all theories are simplifications of reality. His argument is also consistent with the D-N model, in that D-N explanations are satisfied by statements of regularity that invoke *as if* assumptions regardless of whether the posited causal mechanisms are in fact operative. But for this reason, Friedman's analysis confronts the same "barometer problem" that afflicts the D-N model: he cannot distinguish a good predictive relationship from a good causal explanation. In contrast, researchers seeking to explain phenomena via causal mechanisms must

29. Milton Friedman, "The Methodology of Positive Economics," in Daniel Hausman, ed., *The Philosophy of Economics* (Cambridge: Cambridge University Press, 1984), p. 218.

30. "As if" assumptions of the type Friedman deploys have been common among rational choice theorists, but notably, rational choice theorists have increasingly eschewed blanket "as if" assumptions and argued that their theories and the causal mechanism they posit should be evident in the decision-making processes and behavior of individuals. Prominent rational choice theorists Robert H. Bates, Barry R. Weingast, Avner Greif, Margaret Levi, and Jean-Laurent Rosenthal, for example, present an approach to combining and integrating rational choice theories with case narratives that to some degree examines the ways in which decisions were actually made. See these authors' book, *Analytic Narratives* (Princeton, N.J.: Princeton University Press, 1998).

acknowledge that their theories are in trouble if the mechanisms their theories posit are not consistent with the observed processes at a more detailed or micro level of analysis. For example, economists modify their theories when individuals act out of altruism or other social motives that deviate from the assumptions of rational choice theory. Notably, the 2002 Nobel Prize in economics was awarded to Daniel Kahneman for working toward more accurate microlevel mechanisms that identify common cognitive biases that depart from the assumptions of rational decision-making.

In contrast to approaches that emphasize causal effects or predictive capacity, which draw on regularity of association and congruity of magnitude as sources of causal inference, explanation via causal mechanisms also draws on spatial contiguity and temporal succession, two additional sources of causal inference discussed by Hume. In particular, explanation via causal mechanisms involves a commitment in principle to making our explanations and models consistent with the most continuous spatial-temporal sequences we can describe at the finest level of detail that we can observe. For example, the barometer cannot be characterized as having "explained" the weather, since we know from our observations at levels of greater detail that processes involving air pressure, temperature, and so on continually interact, accounting for both the barometer readings and the weather.

More generally, in this view an adequate explanation requires also the specification of hypotheses about a causal process that brought about the observed correlation.[31] Thus, while covering law explanations of the D-N type bear a superficial resemblance to mechanism-based explanations (in that a covering law explanation can simply be restated in more detailed and contingent terms to mimic a mechanism-based explanation), the two forms are profoundly different. Mechanism-based explanations are committed to realism and to continuousness and contiguity in causal processes.[32] While we can posit macrolevel social mechanisms and test

---

31. John Goldthorpe similarly argues that the idea of causation advanced by statisticians assumes that a statistical association "is created by some 'mechanism' opening 'at a more microscopic level' than at which the association is established." John H. Goldthorpe, "Causation, Statistics, and Sociology," *European Sociological Review*, Vol. 17, No. 1 (2001), pp. 1–20, cited in Henry Brady and David Collier, *Rethinking Social Inquiry: Diverse Tools, Shared Standards* (Lanham, Md.: Rowman and Littlefield, 2004), pp. 263–264.

32. As Martin Hollis notes, Friedman's version of the "as if" assumption "lets positive science dabble in unobservables, provided they are not thought more than useful fictions . . . I call this dabbling because there is no concession to the idea of unobservables existing in nature, as opposed to the model." Martin Hollis, *The Philoso-*

them against macrolevel phenomena, macrolevel theories must be consistent with what we know about individual-level behavior. In principle, a mechanism-based approach to explanation even requires that social theories be consistent with what we know about the chemical, electrical, and biological interactions within individuals' brains and bodies that generate their behavior. D-N explanations, in contrast, admit "as if" assumptions at high levels of generality, even if they are demonstrably untrue at lower levels of analysis.

Thus, causal mechanisms provide more detailed and in a sense more fundamental explanations than general laws do. The difference between a law and a mechanism is that between a static correlation ("if X, then Y") and a "process" ("X leads to Y through steps A, B, C"). As Jon Elster notes:

The scientific practice is to seek explanation at a lower level than the explanandum. If we want to understand the pathology of the liver, we look to cellular biology for explanation. . . . To explain is to provide a causal mechanism, to open up the black box and show the nuts and bolts. . . . The role of mechanisms is two-fold. First, they enable us to go from the larger to the smaller: from molecules to atoms, from societies to individuals. Secondly, and more fundamentally, they reduce the time lag between the explanans and explanandum. A mechanism provides a continuous and contiguous chain of causal or intentional links; a black box is a gap in the chain. . . . The success of the reduction is constrained by the extent to which macro-variables are simultaneously replaced by micro-variables. . . . The search for micro-foundations . . . is in reality a pervasive and omnipresent feature of science. . . . [33]

In our view, this commitment in principle to consistency between a theory and what is known at the lowest observable level of space and time does *not* rule out positing and testing theories on the macrolevel. The commitment to consistency with the microlevel also does not mean that the explanatory weight or meaningful variation behind any particular phenomenon occurs at this level. If all individuals behave the same in the same social structure, then the interesting causal and explanatory ac-

---

phy of Social Science: An Introduction (Cambridge: Cambridge University Press, 1994), p. 56.

33. Elster, *Explaining Technical Change,* pp. 23–24. In a more recent publication, Elster advances what he regards as "a somewhat more precise definition of the notion of a mechanism" than in his 1983 book. He does so, apparently, in order to move away from the position in his earlier book in which he regarded "the search for mechanisms as more or less synonymous with the reductionist strategy in science." Jon Elster, *Alchemies of the Mind: Rationality and the Emotions* (Cambridge: Cambridge University Press, 1999), pp. 3–5.

tion is at the level of the social structure, even if it must operate through the perceptions and calculations of individuals.

The acceptable level of generality of causal mechanisms will vary depending on the particular research question and research objectives under investigation.[34] As we note in Chapter 10 on process-tracing, social science research never delves into the finest level of detail observable. Macrosocial mechanisms can be posited and tested at the macrolevel, as is common in the field of economics, and this is often the most cost-effective way to test such mechanisms. All that the commitment to microlevel consistency entails is that individuals must have been capable of behaving, and motivated to behave as the macrolevel theory states, and that they did in fact behave the way they did because of the explicit or implicit microlevel assumptions embedded in the macrolevel theory.

Some simplification of the microfoundations of macrotheories is tolerable for the purposes of parsimony or pedagogy. At the frontiers of research, however, social scientists need to discard stylized simplifying assumptions and build upon the most accurate microlevel mechanisms that can be discerned. David Dessler gives a good example of this process from physics:

In the ideal gas model, the gas is said to behave *as if* the molecules occupy no volume and have no interactions. These are idealizations. They are useful because they lay bare the essential workings of a gas . . . the idealizations also restrict the model's range of applicability . . . the theory's explanatory power increases as its false assumptions are "relaxed"—that is, as the assumptions distorting, idealizing, or simplifying effects are removed. At each step in the process, *it is the assumptions that are true that carry the explanatory burden.* To the extent the theory remains false, its range and power are restricted.[35]

Thus, while our theories rely on simplifying assumptions, advancing beyond the boundaries of our knowledge requires that we make our assumptions as accurate as possible.

The commitment to consistency with the microfoundational level raises another question: must a causal mechanism involve the irreducibly smallest link between one entity and another, and at what point does in-

34. Daniel Little, for example, is among those who argue that all macro-social causal mechanisms must operate through the micro-social level of individual behavior. Little, *Microfoundations, Methods, and Causation,* p. 198.

35. Dessler, "Dimensions of Progress," p. 399. Dessler ties this discussion to Friedman's essay "Methodology of Positive Economics," 1953, stating in a footnote that "if predictive capacity is all that matters, the truth or falsity of a theory's assumptions are irrelevant. But if we are interested in *explanation* as well as prediction, the truth of theories becomes an issue" (p. 399, n. 34).

quiry into causal mechanisms stop? On this question it is useful to think of the frontiers of research as a potentially movable border between the observable world and the unobservable ontological level where causal mechanisms reside. This is most evident in the physical sciences. At one point in history, there were no microscopes to allow scientists to examine molecules or their observable implications, so it would not have been unreasonable to question the existence of "molecules." Once new instruments allowed scientists to observe molecules and their implications, it became unreasonable to disbelieve the broad outlines of the molecule model, and debates (and instruments of observation) moved on to examine the nature of atoms and then subatomic particles. Theoretical arguments in physics now focus on whether it is reasonable to believe in the esoteric mathematics of string theory, which posits the existence of additional dimensions for which there are as yet no readily observable implications, or whether inquiry can or must end with the seemingly impenetrable observational barrier that surrounds the odd implications of quantum effects.[36]

No matter how far down we push the border between the observable and the unobservable, some irreducibly unobservable aspect of causal mechanisms remains. At the frontier of our knowledge at any given time, our theoretical commitment to molecules, atoms, quantum mechanics, or string theory resembles an "as if" assumption about the underlying mechanism at the next level down. In this sense, the causal mechanism view, like the D-N model, ultimately does not offer an explanation of laws themselves at the frontiers of our knowledge. Unlike the D-N model, however, the causal mechanism model, at every point up to the potentially movable border of the unobservable, explains hypotheses or laws with reference to observable implications on underlying processes at a lower level of analysis.

Thus, the commitment to explanation via mechanisms differs from more general "as if" assumptions in that it pushes inquiry to the outer boundaries of what is observable and urges us to expand those boundaries rather than stop with demonstrably false "as if " assumptions at higher levels of analysis.[37] This process is less obvious in the social sci-

---

36.   John Gribbin notes an "ongoing debate about whether there could be an underlying layer of reality beneath quantum mechanics that operates in a much more common-sense way but produces the weird quantum effects that are visible to our experiments . . . such an underlying clockwork reality is indeed allowed by the theory and experiments, provided that you have the instantaneous communication between entangled entities." *Washington Post*, December 15, 2002, book review of Amir Aczel, *Entanglement: The Greatest Mystery in Physics* (New York: Four Walls Eight Windows, 2002).

37.   Similarly, Elster suggests that the distinction between laws and mechanisms "is

ences, but even here new instruments of observation and measurement at the macrolevel (public opinion polls, measures of GNP, and so on) and the microlevel (evidence on cognitive processes within the brain) are expanding the boundaries of what we can observe.[38]

The formulation of hypotheses about a particular causal mechanism, and the decision on whether to model these hypotheses at the micro- or macrolevel, is a theory-building choice of the investigator. At the microlevel, this choice is influenced by the state of knowledge about the causal process that is operating and the limits to observation posed by extant instruments for data collection. The formulation of a given hypothesis is provisional, being reformulated if we acquire additional information about the causal process at a lower microlevel or new tools that provide finer-grained observations. As in the example above of our changing understanding of how smoking causes cancer, "explanations" that are satisfactory at one point will later come to be considered insufficiently precise as new evidence becomes available at lower levels of analysis.

New insights about underlying mechanisms ideally take the form of simple and widely generalizable models, as is sometimes true in the physical sciences. In the social sciences, however, models built on detailed observations often take the form of complex and contingent generalizations (or middle-range theories) that describe a smaller subset of a phenomenon with a higher degree of precision or probability. Rational choice theorists, among others, emphasize the need for microlevel mechanisms at the level of individuals, but often argue that rational choice mechanisms operate almost universally in social life. We believe that the generality of causal mechanisms, including rational choice mechanisms, will vary, depending largely on the particular research question and the research objective under investigation.

The best examples of theories about social causal mechanisms at the

---

not a deep philosophical disagreement. A causal mechanism has a finite number of links. Each link will have to be described by a general law, and in that sense by a 'black box' about whose internal gears and wheels we remain ignorant. Yet for practical purposes—the purposes of the working social scientist—the place of emphasis is important. By concentrating on mechanisms, one captures the dynamic aspect of scientific explanation: the urge to produce explanations of ever finer grain." Elster, *Alchemies of the Mind*, p. 4. See also Little, *Microfoundations*, pp. 210–211.

38.   Similarly, Arthur Stinchcombe discusses causal mechanisms in a manner that evokes the movable border between mechanisms and theories, and indicates why some are tempted to define mechanisms as theoretical rather than ontological entities: "A mechanism becomes a theory when we can specify in a general way when the conditions for a theory for lower-level units of analysis hold so that the aggregate results of the operation of that mechanism hold at the higher level." Stinchcombe, "The Conditions of Fruitfulness of Theorizing About Mechanisms in Social Science," p. 31.

frontiers of the observable world are theories on cognitive mechanisms based on experiments on individual decision-making. These include prospect theory, schema theory, and other cognitive theories, as well as rational choice theory. More generally, theories about social mechanisms can be classified as positing agent-to-agent mechanisms (such as theories of persuasive communication, emulation, strategic interaction, collective action, or principle-agent relations) or structure-to-agent theories (evolutionary selection, socialization, and so on). Structural theories must ultimately work through or be consistent with the actions of individuals, but they can be modeled and tested at the macrolevel.[39] Often, as we note in Chapter 11, it is useful to develop models that incorporate both agent-centered and structure-centered mechanisms, so that theories can address how certain kinds of agents (personality types, for example) operate in certain kinds of social structures.

Causal Mechanisms, Contexts, and Complexity

Our definition of causal mechanisms states that these mechanisms operate only under certain conditions and that their effects depend on interactions with the other mechanisms that make up these contexts. In other words, a causal mechanism may be necessary, but not sufficient, in an explanation.[40]

In this regard, causal mechanisms are consonant with what Paul Humphreys has termed his "aleatory theory" of explanation. In this view, effects are brought about by bundles or configurations of mechanisms, some of which contribute to the effect and some of which may operate to counteract the effect or reduce its magnitude. Aleatory explanations take the form of "Y occurred because of A, despite B," where A is a set of contributing causes and B is a potentially empty set of counteracting causes. (The set A cannot be empty or we would not have an explanation for the occurrence of Y.) Salmon gives an example, modified from Humphreys, in which a car went off a road at a curve because of excessive speed and the presence of sand on the road and despite clear visibility and an alert driver. He notes that the addition of another mechanism or contextual

---

39. Similarly, Sidney Tarrow classifies social mechanisms into the categories of cognitive, rational, and environmental mechanisms. Sidney Tarrow, "Expanding Paired Comparison: A Modest Proposal," *APSA—Comparative Politics Section Newsletter*, Vol. 10, No. 2 (Summer 1999), pp. 9–12.

40. Andrew Sayer, *Method in Social Science*, pp. 107, 111, 121. Sayer emphasizes, as we do, that "the operation of the same mechanism can produce quite different results and, alternatively, different mechanisms may produce the same empirical results." Thus, Sayer takes into account the phenomena of equifinality and multifinality.

factor can change a contributing cause to a counteracting one, or vice versa: sand decreases traction on a dry road, but increases traction when there is ice on a road.[41] Here again, typological theorizing allows for this kind of interaction, as it can incorporate causal mechanisms that offset one another in some contexts and complement one another in others.

Similarly, Jon Elster discusses a number of psychological theories which posit mechanisms that are in tension with one another, such as the "sour grapes syndrome" in which one's desires are adjusted in accordance with the means of achieving them, and "the opposite mechanism," when one wants what one cannot have, precisely because one cannot have it.[42] Elster recognizes the challenge presented by such contradictory mechanisms and suggests the need to for identify the different conditions under which each applies: "Moving from a plurality of mechanisms to a unified theory would mean that we should be able to identify in advance the conditions in which one or the other mechanism would be triggered. . . . My own view is that the social sciences are currently unable to identify such conditions and are likely to remain so forever."[43]

This statement underscores that many scholars equate the context-dependence of causal mechanisms with complexity in social relations. Indeed, Elster's pessimism about the ability to identify the conditions under which mechanisms are triggered is similar to his skepticism on the usefulness of general theories in the social sciences. He argues that "the aim of such theories—to establish general and invariable propositions—is and will always remain an illusory dream. Despite a widespread belief to the contrary, the alternative to nomological thinking is not a mere description or narrative ideographic method. Between the two extremes there is a place and need for the study of mechanisms."[44]

We agree with Elster on the usefulness of thinking in terms of causal mechanisms, but in our view his conclusion on the impossibility of modeling the conditions under which they operate is too pessimistic. As we

---

41.   Salmon, *Four Decades*, pp. 166–167, citing Paul Humphreys, "Aleatory Theory of Explanation," *Synthese*, Vol. 48 (1981), pp. 225–232; and Paul Humphreys, "Aleatory Explanation Expanded," in Peter Asquith and Thomas Nickles, eds., *PSA 1982*, Vol. 2 (Lansing, Mich.: Philosophy of Science Association, 1983), pp. 208–223.

42.   Elster, *Political Psychology*, p. 2.

43.   Elster, *Political Psychology*, p. 5. Elster also notes that while his examples of mechanisms are essentially psychological, the construction of sociological causal mechanisms is also possible (pp. 6–7).

44.   Elster, *Political Psychology*, p. 2. Similarly, Charles Tilly notes that "big case comparisons are properly disappearing" and adds that "social scientists should shift to the search for general causal mechanisms in multiple, never repeated, structures and processes." Tilly, "Means and Ends of Comparison," p. 43.

argue in Chapter 11, typological theories provide a way to model complex interactions or causal mechanisms by including recurrent combinations of hypothesized mechanisms as distinct types or configurations.[45] In this regard, typological theories resemble the middle-range theories that Robert Merton advocated, situated as they are between the microlevel of individual causal mechanisms and the highly abstract level of general theories. Moreover, while complexity is in our view common in social phenomena, and many scholars are interested in causal mechanisms as vehicles of explanation because they can accommodate complexity, some causal mechanisms may be rather simple and general in character. Thus, complexity is not intrinsic to the definition of causal mechanisms, even though mechanisms operate in historical contexts that are often complex and mechanism-oriented theories can accommodate contingency or complexity.

Causal Mechanisms, Process-Tracing, and Historical Explanation

Several scholars interested in explanation via causal mechanisms have noted the relationship between such explanations and the methodology of process-tracing.[46] We elaborate on this relationship in Chapter 10. Briefly, process-tracing is one means of attempting to get closer to the mechanisms or microfoundations behind observed phenomena.[47] Process-tracing attempts to empirically establish the posited intervening variables and implications that should be true in a case if a particular explanation of that case is true. Theories or models of causal mechanisms must undergird each step of a hypothesized causal process for that process to constitute a historical explanation of the case.

As David Dessler has argued, there are two approaches to the explanation of events: a generalizing strategy (to show the event as an instance of a certain *type* of event) and particularization (detailing the sequence of happenings leading up to an event, without necessarily placing it in a larger class). The historical explanation relies on laws to explain each step toward a historical outcome, but the laws are used in piecemeal fashion

---

45. This is similar to the notion of theories as "repertoires of causal mechanisms." R.W. Miller, *Fact and Method*, p. 139. See also Dessler, "Beyond Correlations," p. 343.

46. Dessler, "Beyond Correlations;" Yee, "Causal Effects of Ideas;" and Little, *Microfoundations*.

47. Little, *Microfoundations*, pp. 211–213. Little adds the caveat that in order to distinguish causal from accidental accounts, process-tracing should be combined with comparative or statistical study of multiple cases. This is consistent with our own emphasis on combining within-case and comparative analysis and on multi-method research more generally.

at each step of the path leading to the outcome. Dessler notes that much explanatory progress in the social sciences, and also in physical and medical sciences, consists of improving historical as well as theoretical explanations. Progress in historical explanation consists of "*using* existing theories and laws and acquiring a more precise characterization of the initial conditions and the event itself."[48]

At the same time, improved historical explanations help to improve theories. As we discuss in Chapter 6, we may change our theories or limit their scope if, for example, we find that they do not explain a most-likely case that they should easily be able to explain. The inductive side of process-tracing can also contribute to the development of general theories on the mechanisms underlying the processes observed in a case.[49] Additionally, our approach of combining typological theorizing with process-tracing is an attempt to make use of both generalizing and particularizing explanations, placing cases as instances of a class of events while also giving detailed historical explanations of each case. Case study researchers often ask the two basic questions Dessler identifies: "What is this a case of?" and "From what historical pathway did this event emerge?"

Conclusion

The philosophical issues raised in this chapter have important and direct implications for the practice of the qualitative research methods detailed in subsequent chapters, particularly case comparisons and process-tracing. We conclude, therefore, by emphasizing three practical implications for qualitative methods. First, regarding the goals of social science research, we do not need to view ourselves as the poor relatives of the physical sciences or eschew attempts at causal and potentially even predictive theories. The changing and reflective nature of social subjects makes social science theories more provisional and time-bound than those in the physical sciences, but does not prevent cumulative and progressive theorizing over long periods of time in the form of middle-range theories. Theoretical progress in the social sciences can consist of advances in puzzle-driven research programs, increasingly complete and convincing historical explanations, and theories that are stronger at ex-

---

48.   Dessler, "Dimensions of Progress," p. 395.

49.   This proposition is rejected by some rational choice theorists. Edgar Kiser and Michael Hechter argue that causal mechanisms cannot be derived inductively, but only from general theories. Edgar Kiser and Michael Hechter, "The Role of General Theory in Comparative Historical Sociology," *American Journal of Sociology*, Vol. 97, No. 1 (July 1991), pp. 4, 6, 23, 24.

plaining social behavior than at predicting it. Progress is not limited to the development of general theories or schools of thought with greater validity, scope, or predictive capability—as desirable as these kinds of progress may be.

Second, an attempt to explain by reference to causal mechanisms, which in principle requires consistency with the finest level of detail observable, provides a powerful source of causal inference when carried out through the method of process-tracing, which examines processes within single cases in considerable detail. In practice, process-tracing need not always go down to the finest level of detail observable, but by avoiding *as if* assumptions at high levels of analysis and insisting on explanations that are consistent with the finest level of detail observable, process-tracing can eliminate some alternative explanations for a case and increase our confidence in others.

Finally, typological theorizing, which combines methods of both cross-case comparison and process-tracing, is a powerful way to create middle-range theories that are consistent with both the historical explanations of individual cases and the general theoretical patterns evident across cases. Such theorizing makes very limited assumptions about whether a causal mechanism operates in similar ways across different contexts. At the same time, typological theorizing attempts to outline the conditions under which a particular causal mechanism has a defined effect, and the differing effects it has in different contexts, by modeling recurrent combinations and interactions of mechanisms. In short, typological theorizing offers the promise of cumulation without losing sensitivity to context.

Chapter 8

Comparative Methods: Controlled Comparison and Within-Case Analysis

In this chapter we discuss comparative methods—the case study methods that attempt to approximate the conditions of scientific experiments. Comparative methods involve the nonstatistical comparative analysis of a small number of cases. Perhaps the best known and still dominant variant of comparative methods is controlled comparison, the study of two or more instances of a well-specified phenomenon that resemble each other in every respect but one.[1] When two such cases can be found, controlled comparison provides the functional equivalent of an experiment that enables the investigator to make use of experimental logic to draw causal inferences. This possibility gives controlled comparison considerable appeal.

Yet such control is very difficult to achieve.[2] Researchers urgently

---

1. Arend Lijphart uses the term "comparable cases" for what we call "controlled comparison," a term we prefer because of the explicit reference to the requirement that comparison be controlled. Lijphart reserves the term "comparative method" for the comparable cases strategy. See Lijphart, "The Comparable-Cases Strategy in Comparative Research," *Comparative Political Studies*, Vol. 8, No. 2 (July 1975), pp. 158–177. The term "controlled comparison" appears to have been originated by Fred Eggan, "Social Anthropology and the Method of Controlled Comparison," *American Anthropologist*, new series, Vol. 56, No. 1, Part 1 (October 1954), pp. 743–763.

2. The following discussion draws upon and elaborates materials presented earlier in Alexander L. George, "Case Studies and Theory Development," paper presented to the Second Annual Symposium on Information Processing in Organizations, Carnegie Mellon University, October 15–16, 1982, and Alexander L. George and Timothy J. McKeown, "Case Studies and Theories of Organizational Decision Making," in Robert F. Coulam and Richard A. Smith, eds., *Advances in Information Processing in Organizations*, Vol. 2 (Greenwich, Conn.: JAI Press, 1985), pp. 21–58. For an excellent review of developments in comparative methods, see David Collier, "The Comparative Method:

need an alternative to the experimental paradigm for several reasons. It is generally extremely difficult to find two cases that resemble each other in every respect but one, as controlled comparison requires. The familiar alternative of using statistical analysis to achieve the functional equivalent of an experiment often runs into the problem that there is an insufficient number of cases for many phenomena of interest.[3] Even in the relatively few cases in which genuine experimentation is possible, it is often ethically problematic and sometimes forbidden.

Many writers have noted that the impossibility of applying experimental methods or making perfectly controlled comparisons bedevils rigorous application of the comparative method and have discussed several ways to minimize the difficulties.[4] In this chapter, we survey some of the most important alternatives to controlled comparison methodologists have proposed. We start by discussing John Stuart Mill's methods, the foundational work on comparative methods. We then discuss equifinality—the fact that different causal explanations often exist for similar outcomes—and the difficult challenges it poses to comparative methods. Next we discuss a number of alternatives to Mill's methods, including Qualitative Comparative Analysis (QCA), before-after case study designs, counterfactual analysis, and others. Unfortunately, practically all efforts to make use of the controlled comparison method fail to achieve its strict requirements. This limitation is often recognized by investigators employing the method, but they proceed nonetheless to do the best they

Two Decades of Change," in Dankwart A. Rustow and Kenneth Paul Erickson, eds., *Comparative Political Dynamics: Global Research Perspectives* (New York: Harper Collins, 1991), pp. 8–11. A revised version of Collier's article was published in Ada Finifter, ed., *Political Science: The State of the Discipline II* (Washington, D.C.: American Political Science Association, 1993).

3.   The editors of an important assessment of the possible utility of counterfactual analysis note that experimental and statistical methods cannot play an important role in the study of international relations: "There appear to be large classes of questions in the study of global conflict and cooperation for which experimental control is out of the question and statistical control is of limited usefulness." Philip E. Tetlock and Aaron Belkin, eds., *Counterfactual Thought Experiments in World Politics* (Princeton, N.J.: Princeton University Press, 1996), p. 38.

4.   Gary King, Robert O. Keohane, and Sidney Verba term this problem "the fundamental problem of causal inference." See Gary King, Robert O. Keohane, and Sidney Verba, *Designing Social Inquiry: Scientific Inference in Qualitative Research* (Princeton, N.J.: Princeton, University Press, 1994) pp. 79–80; 208–210. Charles Ragin and Jeremy Hein emphasize that "most applications of comparative methodology resort to truncated, rhetorical comparison that gives the appearance but have little of the substance of a natural experiment . . . [the] two-case comparison is limited in its ability to test theories regarding causal regularities." Charles C. Ragin and Jeremy Hein, "The Comparative Study of Ethnicity," in John H. Stanfield III and Rutledge M. Dennis, eds., *Race and Ethnicity in Research Methods* (Newbury Park, Calif.: Sage, 1993), p. 255.

can with an admittedly imperfect controlled comparison. They do so because they believe that there is no acceptable alternative and no way of compensating for the limitations of controlled comparison.[5]

One alternative, proposed by Gary King, Robert Keohane, and Sidney Verba, focuses on the observable implications of a theory for independent and dependent variables, and not for intervening variables. In effect, it puts any processes that occur between independent and dependent variables in a "black box." We discuss this alternative—and our substantial reservations about it—in this chapter.

We end by briefly discussing how the within-case methods of congruence and process-tracing can serve as an alternative and supplement to comparative methods. These tools do not seek to replicate the logic of scientific experimentation. Instead, they seek to increase our confidence in a theory: the congruence method seeks to show that a theory is congruent (or not congruent) with the outcome in a case. Process-tracing seeks to uncover a causal chain coupling independent variables with dependent variables and evidence of the causal mechanisms posited by a theory. These methods are discussed in detail in Chapters 9 and 10.

Mill's Methods: Their Uses and Limitations

As numerous writers have noted, the essential logic of the comparative method is derived from John Stuart Mill's *A System of Logic* (1843).[6] In this work, Mill discussed the "method of agreement" and the "method of difference," which are sometimes referred to as the "positive" and "negative" comparative methods.[7] The (positive) method of agreement attempts to identify a similarity in the independent variable associated with a common outcome in two or more cases. The (negative) method of difference attempts to identify independent variables associated with different outcomes. A third method identified by Mill was the method of concomitant variations, a more sophisticated version of the method of difference. Instead of observing merely the presence or absence of key variables, concomitant variation measures the quantitative variations of

---

5.   See, for example, Arend Lijphart, "The Comparable-Cases Strategy in Comparative Research," and his earlier "Comparative Politics and the Comparative Method," *American Political Science Review*, Vol. 65, No. 3 (September 1971), pp. 682–693.

6.   See, for example, Arend Lijphart, "Comparative Politics and the Comparative Method," p. 688. For additional discussion of Mill's methods, see Chapter 11.

7.   Neil J. Smelser, "The Methodology of Comparative Analysis," in Donald P. Warwick and Samuel Osherson, eds., *Comparative Research Methods* (Englewood Cliffs, N.J.: Prentice Hall, 1973), p. 52.

the variables and relates them to each other, a method that is in some sense a precursor to statistical methods.

Mill himself emphasized the serious obstacles to making effective use of these methods in social science inquiry. He noted that the multiplicity and complexity of causes of social phenomena make it difficult to apply the logic of elimination relied upon by the methods of agreement and difference, thereby making it difficult to isolate the possible cause of a phenomenon. Mill judged the method of difference to be somewhat stronger than the method of agreement, and he also proposed the method of concomitant variation to deal with some of the limitations of the other two methods.

Mill, then, was pessimistic regarding the possibility of satisfactory empirical applications of these logics in social science inquiry. Other logicians and methodologists have subsequently expressed strong reservations.[8]

Since the logics associated with Mill's methods are integral to the strategy of controlled comparison, one must scrutinize studies that employ this strategy. One must judge how well the investigator has managed to achieve "control" among the cases, whether the logic of these methods has been correctly employed in making causal inferences, and whether the theoretical conclusions drawn from a study have been weakened by an inability to identify or control all of the operative variables that may have influenced the outcomes of the cases.

---

8. See, for example, Morris R. Cohen and Ernest Nagel, *An Introduction to Logic and Scientific Method* (New York: Harcourt, Brace, 1934). Detailed explications and critical examinations of Mill's methods are provided by a number of writers. In an early essay, "Intelligent Comparisons," in Ivan Vallier, ed., *Comparative Methods in Sociology* (Berkeley: University of California Press, 1971), Morris Zelditch provided a constructive, balanced discussion of the possibility of using Mill's methods as providing "rules" for the design of comparative research. He concluded that such "rules" had limitations and were not sufficient to be used as "mechanical procedures." Among more recent, detailed critiques of Mill's methods, see, for example, Brian Barry, "Methodology Versus Ideology: The 'Economic' Approach Revisited," in Elinor Ostrom, ed., *Strategies of Political Inquiry* (Beverly Hills, Calif.: Sage Publications, 1982), pp. 123–147; Stanley Lieberson, "Small N's and Big Conclusions: An Examination of the Reasoning in Comparative Study Based on a Small Number of Cases," *Social Forces*, Vol. 70, No. 2 (December 1991), pp. 307–320; and Lieberson, "More on the Uneasy Case for Using Mill-Type Methods in Small-N Comparative Studies," *Social Forces*, Vol. 72, No. 4 (June 1994), pp. 1225–1237; Irving M. Copi and Carl Cohen, *Introduction to Logic*, 9th ed. (New York: Macmillan, 1994), chap. 12, "Causal Connections: Mill's Methods of Experimental Inquiry," pp. 479–525; Daniel Little, "Evidence and Objectivity in the Social Sciences," *Social Research*, Vol. 60, No. 2 (Summer 1993), pp. 363–396; Daniel Little, *Varieties of Social Explanation: An Introduction to the Philosophy of Social Science* (Boulder, Colo.: Westview Press, 1991), pp. 35–37; and Charles Tilly, "Means and Ends of Comparative Macrosociology," in Lars Mjoset et al., eds., *Methodological Issues in Comparative Social Science* (Greenwich, Conn.: JAI Press, 1997), pp. 43–53.

Mill's methods can work well in identifying underlying causal relations only under three demanding assumptions. First, the causal relation being investigated must be a deterministic regularity involving only one condition that is either necessary or sufficient for a specified outcome. Second, *all* causally relevant variables must be identified prior to the analysis (whereas Mill's methods are applicable only for explaining single-cause hypotheses). Third, cases that represent the full range of all logically and socially possible causal paths must be available for study.

These well-known requirements strongly constrain and limit the usefulness of Mill's methods. The methods of agreement and difference both utilize the logic of what Mill called the "method of elimination." Mill explained that his use of the logic of elimination was analogous to its use in the theory of equations "to denote the process by which one or another of the elements of the question is excluded, and the solution is made to depend on the relation between the remaining elements only."[9]

In the method of agreement, the investigator employs the logic of elimination to exclude as a candidate cause (independent variable) for the common outcome (dependent variable) in two or more cases those conditions that are not present in both cases. A cause or condition that survives this method of elimination can be regarded as *possibly* associated ("connected," in Mill's terminology) with the case outcome. An inherent weakness of this method of causal inference is that another case may be discovered later in which the same outcome is not associated with the variable that survived the elimination procedure in the comparison of the two earlier cases. Thus, that variable cannot be regarded as either a necessary or sufficient condition for that type of outcome.[10] Thus, the possibil-

---

9. John Stuart Mill, as quoted in Amitai Etzioni and Frederick I. Dubow, eds., *Comparative Perspectives: Theories and Methods* (Boston: Little, Brown, 1970), pp. 207–208.

10. Douglas Dion, "Evidence and Inference in Comparative Case Study," *Comparative Politics*, Vol. 30, No. 2 (January 1998), pp. 127–145; Gary Goertz and Harvey Starr, eds., *Necessary Conditions: Theory, Methodology, and Applications* (Lanham, Md.: Rowman and Littlefield, 2003). Of course, it remains true that a given condition may be necessary or sufficient in one case but not others. We must distinguish here among claims that a variable is necessary or sufficient in a case, in a recurrent conjunction, or in all cases. A claim that a variable is necessary or sufficient to an outcome in a case asserts that the variable was necessary or sufficient in the causal context or background of all the other variables extant in the case. Ultimately, any such claim is untestable, as we cannot re-run the same history while changing only one variable. A claim that a variable X is part of a conjunction, say, XYZ that is necessary or sufficient to outcome Q can be disproved. An instance of Q in which XYZ was lacking can disprove a claim of necessity for XYZ, while the absence of Q in the presence of XYZ would disprove a claim that XYZ was sufficient. Note, however, that cases in which X was present without Y or Z and cases in which Y and Z were present but X was absent cannot disprove claims that X is part of a necessary or sufficient conjunction XYZ. A claim that X is nec-

ity remains that the common condition identified for the similar outcome in two cases may turn out to be a "false positive."

In the method of difference—in which two cases having different outcomes are compared—the investigator employs the logic of elimination to exclude as a candidate cause (independent variable) for the variance in the outcome (dependent variable) any condition that is present in both cases. On the face of it, the logic is quite simple: a condition present in both cases cannot account for the difference in case outcomes. However, conditions that were not present in both cases can only be regarded as *possibly* causally associated with the variance in case outcomes, for these conditions may not be present in other cases with the same outcome. In that event, the attribution of causal significance to the conditions that seemed to be associated with the variance in outcome in the first two cases would constitute a "false positive."

In sum, in exercises that use the method of agreement and difference, the investigator cannot be sure that all of the possibly relevant independent variables have been identified or that the study has included a sufficient variety of cases of the phenomenon. Hence, inferences in both methods of agreement and difference may be spurious and invalid. On the other hand, if a much larger number of independent variables are included, we may well encounter the problem of underdetermination (also known as "too many variables, too few cases"). This dilemma cannot easily or adequately be resolved so long as the investigator relies solely on the logic of elimination and does not find sufficiently comparable cases that provide the functional equivalent of experimental control. However, as we shall note later, Mill's methods may still be of some use if combined with process-tracing.

This logic of causal inference for small-n comparisons is highly problematic if the phenomenon being investigated has complex, multiple determinants rather than—as in the simple examples of Mill's methods discussed above—a single independent variable of presumed causal significance. Thus, in the example of the method of agreement cited above, the investigator might eventually discover that a condition that was "eliminated" as being neither necessary nor sufficient was in fact associated with the outcome *when and only when an additional condition, one not included in the initial study, was also present.* Meanwhile, failure to discover this additional condition might lead the investigator to prematurely discard the first condition's significance on the ground that it was not always associated with the type of outcome in question. This highlights the possibility of "false negatives" when applying the logic of elim-

---

essary for all cases of Q is easily disproved by a case of Q lacking X, and a claim that X is sufficient for all Q is disproved by a case with X lacking Q.

ination that goes along with the other possibility, already alluded to, of false positives.[11]

It has been argued that, nonetheless, Mill's methods are useful tools for eliminating causes that are *neither* necessary *nor* sufficient conditions. Scholars do seem to use Mill's methods for this purpose. However, it is not always clear whether they recognize that the variables excluded as neither necessary nor sufficient may still have considerable causal significance when combined with other variables. This is a matter of considerable importance since we believe that there are few nontrivial theories in the social sphere strong enough to support general claims of necessity or sufficiency for single variables, and that indeed the causation of many phenomena of interest to social science researchers is complex and lacks nontrivial necessary or sufficient conditions.

Another major difficulty in employing the logic of elimination occurs when different instances of the phenomenon under investigation have *alternative determinants*—what Mill referred to as the problem of "plurality of causes." This condition is termed "equifinality" in general systems theory and is also sometimes called "multiple causality." Equifinality is present in many social phenomena. For such phenomena, the *same* type of outcome can emerge in different cases via a *different* set of independent variables. With the method of agreement we cannot be certain that the outcome is associated *only* with a given independent variable. If that phenomenon is subject to plurality of causes, we may sooner or later encounter one or more additional cases in which the outcome occurs in the absence of the conditions with which it was earlier associated.[12]

---

11.   Insofar as we can tell from reading Mill's disquisition, he barely touches upon this obstacle. The possibility of "false negatives" from applying the logic of elimination is missed entirely in Cohen and Nagel's otherwise robust critique of the methods of agreement and difference. On the other hand, the possibility of false negatives and false positives was clearly recognized by Zelditch, "Intelligent Comparisons," pp. 299, 300, 306; and more recently by Ragin who uses different terms, "illusory commonalities" and "illusory differences." See Charles C. Ragin, *The Comparative Method: Moving Beyond Qualitative and Quantitative Strategies* (Berkeley: University of California Press, 1987), pp. 43, 47, 48.

12.   The problems for the comparative method created by a "plurality of causes" (which he refers to as multiple causation) plays a prominent role in Ragin's discussion. See, for example, Ragin, *The Comparative Method*, pp. x, xii, 15, 20, 25, 37, 39, 43, 46, 47. Ragin does not use the term "equifinality." The phenomenon of equifinality is noted also in Ragin's book, *Fuzzy-Set Social Science* (Chicago: University of Chicago Press, 2000). It was briefly noted earlier by Zelditch, "Intelligent Compromises," p. 296. Equifinality is also noted and emphasized as an important constraint on developing viable general laws by Benjamin A. Most and Harvey Starr, *Inquiry, Logic, and International Politics* (Columbia: University of South Carolina Press, 1989), chap. 5. Most and Starr use the phrase "domain specific laws" to characterize the phenomenon of equifinality. They use the term "substitutability" to characterize the opposite of

Some specialists on comparative method have proposed another variant of Mill's methods, which they call the "indirect method of difference." Charles Ragin describes this variant as involving "a double application of the method of agreement." First, the investigator identifies instances of a similar outcome of a phenomenon to see if they display a similar independent variable. If they do, then cases in which that outcome is absent are examined to see if they lacked the independent variable associated with the outcome. Ragin discusses the uses and limitations of this indirect method, noting that it "suffers some of the same liabilities as the method of agreement in situations of multiple causation" as well as with phenomena that are affected by "conjunctural causation."[13] More generally, Ragin issues a useful warning against "mechanical" application of Mill's methods.

Some research designs use both the methods of agreement and difference, such as *States and Social Revolutions* by Theda Skocpol, and *Shaping the Political Arena* by Ruth Berins Collier and David Collier. The Colliers describe the methodology of their important study as having two components: they combine Mill's methods of agreement and difference with process-tracing over time within each country to further probe explanations.[14]

There has been considerable controversy in recent years among specialists in comparative politics regarding the utility of Mill's methods for research in their field. A proponent is Theda Skocpol, who strongly asserted their value for comparative historical analysis and stated that was the approach taken in her book *States and Social Revolutions*. There is no reference in her book to Mill's own sober cautions regarding the difficulty of applying these methods in research on most social phenomena. However, Skocpol did make passing reference to the "inevitable difficulties in applying the method according to its given logic" since "often it is impos-

---

equifinality (what is termed "multifinality" in general systems theory), namely the fact that similar independent variables can trigger different outcomes. Most and Starr discuss at some length the difficulties equifinality and multifinality create for efforts to develop unconditional generalizations or "laws" in much research on international relations. Most and Starr also emphasize the importance of what we refer to as process-tracing and middle-range theories of limited scope for subclasses of a phenomenon.

13. Ragin, *The Comparative Method*, pp. 39–44, 46. In his more recent book, Ragin again cautions against being overly impressed with "the relatively simple and straightforward research design" of the method of difference. Ragin, *Fuzzy-Set Social Science*, p. 9.

14. Ruth Berins Collier and David Collier, *Shaping the Political Arena* (Princeton, N.J.: Princeton University Press, 1991), p. 5.

sible to find exactly the historical cases that one needs for the logic of a certain comparison." Recognizing this and other difficulties, she concluded: "Still, comparative historical analysis does provide a valuable check, or anchor, for theoretical speculation." And, continuing, she came close to recognizing that she had supplemented use of Mill's methods with what we call process-tracing, which is employed in within-case analysis. As Skocpol noted, comparative historical analysis making use of Mill's methods "encourages one to spell out the actual causal arguments suggested by grand theoretical perspectives." In the book itself, however, and in a subsequent essay on comparative methodology, she did not regard historical case analysis as making up for the limitations of Mill's methods.[15] In an essay with Margaret Somers, Skocpol recognized that Mill himself "despaired of the possibility of effectively applying the analytic methods he discussed to socio-historical phenomena," but she wrote that "complete retreat in the face of difficulties is surely unnecessary."[16]

Skocpol's understanding and use of Mill's methods was sharply challenged by a number of other scholars, including Elizabeth Nichols. Nichols, however, did not call attention to the importance of process-tracing as a method of compensating for the limitations of Mill's methods or recognize the ancillary role it played in Skocpol's study. This was left to Jack Goldstone, who explicitly notes the importance of process-tracing in Skocpol's study and, more generally, in comparative history, writing that "History in this sense is the heart of comparative case-study methods. . . . The key to comparative case-studies in macro sociology is *this unraveling of historical narratives.*" He called the procedure "process-tracing." In his commentary on Skocpol's study, William Sewell observed that she relied more on process-tracing than on quasicontrolled comparison. Similarly, Charles Tilly has bluntly stated that John Stuart Mill's own warnings rule out the application of his experimental methods to social processes and has called for more emphasis on the role of causal mechanisms in causal analysis.[17] Stephen Van Evera, however, frequently refers to the

15. Theda Skocpol, *States and Social Revolutions* (Cambridge: Cambridge University Press, 1979), pp. 37–40; and Theda Skocpol and Margaret Somers, "The Uses of Comparative History in Macrosocial Inquiry," *Comparative Studies in Society and History,* Vol. 22, No. 2 (April 1980), pp. 174–197.

16. Skocpol and Somers, "The Uses of Comparative History in Macrosocial Inquiry," p. 194.

17. Elizabeth Nichols, "Skocpol on Revolutions: Comparative Analysis vs. Historical Conjuncture," *Comparative Social Research,* Vol. 9 (1986), pp. 163–186; and Skocpol's rejoinder, "Analyzing Causal Configuration in History: A Rejoinder to Nichols," *Com-*

usefulness of Mill's methods, usually adding that they can be adapted for various purposes. It is not entirely clear, however, what this entails.[18]

The controversy over the utility of Mill's methods is part of a much broader debate among specialists in comparative politics over approaches to theory and methodology. Adherents of rational choice theory, cultural analysis, and structural approaches have also participated in this debate. We will not summarize the voluminous literature this debate has engendered here, but merely reemphasize our contention that process-tracing is an essential supplement to all forms of case comparisons to reduce the dangers of false positives and false negatives.[19]

---

parative Social Research, Vol. 9 (1986), pp. 187–194. In her response to Nichols, Skocpol clearly recognizes that she relied on the equivalent of process-tracing as a check on her methods of comparison (p. 189). See also Jack Goldstone, "Methodological Issues in Comparative Macrosociology" (forthcoming), and his "Revolution, War, and Security" (manuscript 1995). In his major work, *Revolution and Rebellion in the Early Modern World* (Berkeley: University of California Press, 1991), Goldstone provides a detailed discussion of the importance of case studies and process-tracing for explaining macro-political phenomena. See also William H. Sewell, Jr., "Three Temporalities: Toward An Eventful Sociology," in Terrence J. MacDonald, ed., *The Historic Turn in the Human Sciences* (Ann Arbor: University of Michigan Press, 1966); and Tilly, "Means and Ends of Comparative Macrosociology," pp. 43–53. David Waldner notes that Mill's methods can be combined with process-tracing and adds that causal mechanisms are needed for purposes of explanation. David Waldner, *State Building and Late Development* (Ithaca, N.Y.: Cornell University Press, 1999), pp. 230–235. A detailed commentary on Theda Skocpol's *States and Social Revolutions* is presented in James Mahoney, "Nominal, Ordinal, and Narrative Appraisal in Macro-Causal Analysis," *American Journal of Sociology*, Vol. 104, No. 4 (January 1999), pp. 1154–1196.

18.   Stephen Van Evera, *Guide to Methods for Students of Political Science* (Cambridge, Mass.: Defense and Arms Control Studies Program, MIT Press, 1996). Van Evera believes that Mill's methods are an aid to inductive theory making (p. 10), that the method of difference can be used in controlled comparisons to infer the operation of the antecedent conditions that must be present for theory to apply (p. 37). However, he also observes that "the method of difference is a fairly weak instrument for theory testing" and that the method of agreement is even weaker, but he does not elaborate (p. 47). And, in an interesting reference to one of his own studies some years ago, Van Evera indicates that only after its publication did he realize that he had employed process-tracing and that it had contributed to his theory testing (p. 11, footnote 24). The usefulness of the method of difference, despite its limitations, is defended also by John S. Odell, "Case Study Methods in International Political Economy," *International Studies Perspectives*, Vol. 2, No. 2 (May 2001), pp. 161–176.

19.   Of particular interest is a special issue of *Comparative Social Research* (Vol. 16, 1997) devoted to methodological issues. Wide-ranging and valuable discussion of theoretical and methodological issues can be found in the publications of the comparative politics section of the American Political Science Association. Similar issues are intensively discussed in sociology as well. In addition to important publications by Charles Ragin, these developments in the social sciences as a whole are discussed in MacDonald, ed., *The Historic Turn in the Human Sciences*.

The Implications of Equifinality for Theory Building

We are particularly concerned about the inability of Mill's methods to accommodate equifinality. The fact that *different* causal patterns can lead to *similar* outcomes has profound implications for efforts to develop empirical theory (or general laws). Robert Jervis states that equifinality offers "a real problem" for political scientists because "it constitutes a menace to one of [their] prime methodologies."[20]

Equifinality challenges and undermines the common assumption that similar outcomes in several cases must have a common cause that remains to be discovered. This assumption misdirects the attention of the investigator by leading him or her to believe that the task of empirical inquiry is to discover a single causal pattern for cases that have similar values on the dependent variable. Instead, a major redefinition of the task of developing theory is required when a phenomenon is governed by equifinality. The task becomes that of discovering *different* causal patterns that lead to similar outcomes. When a phenomenon is governed by equifinality, the investigator's task is to produce a *differentiated* empirically based theory that identifies different causal patterns that produce similar outcomes. If this research task is taken seriously, investigators cannot content themselves with a claim that they have at least discovered a common causal factor for all or many cases that have similar outcomes on the dependent variable. Such an explanation is incomplete, and even if justified, it leaves unanswered the question of the causal weight of the common factor in the total explanation.

Some investigators may attempt to deal with the challenge posed by equifinality by claiming only than that the relationship embodied in the single causal proposition is probabilistic. However, a quantitative description of that probability is usually left unspecified, since it would require considerable additional empirical research either on the total universe of relevant cases or a sample.

The phenomenon of equifinality also complicates efforts to assess a deductive theory's ability to make successful predictions. Sensitivity to the possibility that the phenomenon in question is subject to equifinality requires the investigator to consider the likelihood that some undetermined number of outcomes that the deductive theory predicts or fails to predict can be predicted by another deductive theory. In addition, equifinality also calls attention to the possibility that successful predic-

---

20. Robert Jervis, "International History and International Politics: Why Are They Studied Differently?" in Colin Elman and Miriam Fendius Elman, eds., *Bridges and Boundaries: Historians, Political Scientists, and the Study of International Relations* (Cambridge, Mass.: MIT Press, 2001), p. 392.

tions may not be necessarily valid explanations, since another theory may be able to claim to explain as well as to predict those outcomes.

Gary King, Robert Keohane, and Sidney Verba do not consider the implications of equifinality for research design and theory building in *Designing Social Inquiry*. In their sparse discussion of equifinality, they seem concerned primarily to claim that equifinality is not inconsistent with their definition of causal inference and their prescriptions on how to achieve such inferences.[21] In contrast, we give considerable emphasis to the widespread prevalence of equifinality and to several ways of taking it into account in the design and interpretation of research—for example, by developing typological theories. Charles Ragin also provides a detailed discussion of equifinality and its implications for research and theory in *Fuzzy-Set Social Science*.[22]

Similarly, there is little attention in *Designing Social Inquiry* (*DSI*) to comparative politics and to ways of doing good comparative work.[23] Not surprisingly, specialists in comparative politics have expressed important reservations about this book—for example, in the June 1995 issue of the *American Political Science Review*. King, Keohane, and Verba display little interest in important developments and controversies in the comparative politics field in the past two decades, summarized so well by David Collier in his article "The Comparative Method: Two Decades of Change."[24]

Extensions and Adaptations to Mill's Methods

QUALITATIVE COMPARATIVE ANALYSIS

The method of Qualitative Comparative Analysis (QCA) is a sophisticated extension of Mill's methods developed by Charles Ragin that relies on Boolean algebra and relaxes some of the assumptions necessary for the direct use of Mill's methods. QCA still requires rather restrictive conditions to arrive at valid causal inferences. Consequently, Ragin faces the same problem that Mill confronted: the challenge of reconciling his nondeterministic view of causality with the determinism necessary to make QCA effective.[25]

QCA allows for the possibility of equifinality. It can also use interval data by adding nominal categories to represent interval values (though this adds to the complexity of the analysis and represents a loss of infor-

21.   King, Keohane, and Verba, *Designing Social Inquiry*, pp. 87–89.

22.   Ragin, *Fuzzy-Set Social Science*, pp. 102 ff.

23.   King, Keohane, and Verba, *Designing Social Inquiry*, pp. 44–45; 212–213.

24.   David Collier, "The Comparative Method: Two Decades of Change,"

25.   Ragin, *The Comparative Method*, pp. 98, 113.

mation from truly continuous variables). These are key advances over Mill's methods, but QCA still requires sufficiency at the level of conjunctions of variables to reach definitive results. Also, QCA requires the inclusion of all causally relevant variables to prevent spurious inferences. In addition, the results of QCA are unstable, in that adding a single new case or changing the coding of one variable can radically change the results of the analysis.[26] Moreover, because QCA assumes that various conjunctions of variables may be sufficient to an outcome, then the presence of two such conjunctions does not make the outcome any more likely or certain than one alone. In other words, in terms of the Boolean algebra upon which QCA is based, "1+1=1," where the first two numerals are each a sufficient conjunction and the third is a positive outcome. Yet if the conjunctions in question are not fully sufficient, regardless of the values of omitted variables, a combination of two nearly sufficient conjunctions would usually be more likely to produce an outcome than either conjunction alone, barring an offsetting interaction between the conjunctions.

For these reasons, Ragin warns against the "mechanical" use of QCA for causal inference.[27] He also notes that cases with the same values on independent variables may exhibit different values on dependent variables, which should spur the researcher to examine these cases more closely to determine if there are important omitted variables on which the cases differ.[28] For example, in one of the most interesting and ambitious applications of QCA, Timothy Wickham-Crowley coded twenty cases of actual and potential peasant support for guerrilla movements in Latin America, but did not focus on several cases with similar independent variables but different outcomes. Closer examination of these cases might have identified omitted variables and strengthened the conclusions of Wickham-Crowley's QCA analysis.[29]

In short, with QCA, as with Mill's methods, it is necessary to supplement case comparisons with process-tracing of cases in order to relax the restrictive and unrealistic assumptions necessary for definitive results from comparisons alone.[30] It may often be preferable to use the less restrictive assumptions of typological theory as a guide to the selection of

26. John Goldthorpe, "Current Issues in Comparative Macrosociology," in Lars Mjoset et al., eds., *Comparative Social Research*, Vol. 16, p. 20, n. 8, 9.

27. Ragin, *The Comparative Method*, p. 98.

28. Ibid., p. 113.

29. Timothy P. Wickham-Crowley, "A Qualitative Comparative Approach to Latin American Revolutions," in Charles C. Ragin, ed., *Issues and Alternatives in Comparative Social Research* (Leiden, N.Y.: E.J. Brill, 1991), pp. 82–109.

30. Dietrich Rueschemeyer and John Stephens, "Comparative Approach to Latin American Revolutions," in Ragin, ed., *Issues and Alternatives*, pp. 82–109.

cases for study and to draw contingent generalizations from these cases in ways that are less restrictive than the method of QCA.

ATTEMPTS TO ACHIEVE CONTROLLED COMPARISON THROUGH STATISTICAL ANALYSIS AND SOME ALTERNATIVES

Since perfectly comparable cases for comparative analysis seldom exist, some analysts have sought to enlarge the number of cases under study so that statistical techniques can be used. The use of statistical techniques is widely accepted in experimental settings and in social settings where the assumption of unit homogeneity is unproblematic (in other terms, when large numbers of like cases are available). However, the use of statistical techniques on small numbers of cases is more limited and involves sharp trade-offs. To "increase the number of cases" so that statistical techniques are possible, researchers must often change the definitions of variables and the research question and must make assumptions of unit homogeneity or similarity of cases that may not be justified.

A remedy often proposed is simply to redefine and broaden the research problem to make it possible to identify a large enough number of cases to permit statistical analysis. For example, Neil Smelser has suggested that the investigator may resort to the "replication of the suspected association at a different analytical level" to multiply the number of observations at another level of analysis.[31] As an illustration of this practice, Smelser cited Emile Durkheim's study of suicide in the military. Another often-proposed remedy is to reduce the number of variables to be considered to those few regarded as of particular importance.

Various suggestions have been made for finding some way to deal with imperfect controlled comparison or to accept that it is inevitable. Smelser, for example, calls attention to "the method of heuristic assumption." This is a "crude but widely employed method of transforming potentially operative/independent variables into parameters," a method that has on occasion proven helpful in a variety of investigations.[32] Arend Lijphart, while acknowledging that it is difficult to find cases that are comparable enough and that one seldom can find cases similar in every respect but one, believes that "these objections are founded on a too exacting scientific standard" and that useful research can be accomplished by studies that approximate the standard as closely as possible.[33]

---

31. Neil J. Smelser, "The Methodology of Comparative Analysis," in Warwick and Osherson, *Comparative Research Methods,* pp. 77–78. Smelser integrated much, but not everything of relevance to the present chapter, in a later book, *Comparative Methods in the Social Sciences* (Englewood Cliffs, N.J.: Prentice Hall, 1976).

32. Smelser, "The Methodology of Comparative Analysis," p. 55.

33. Lijphart, "Comparative Politics and the Comparative Method," p. 688.

Other writers believe that the quest for controlled comparison should be abandoned in favor of a quite different approach. Adam Przeworski and Henry Teune distinguish between a "most similar" design (the closely matched case of controlled comparison) and a "most different" research design. The former, they argue, runs into serious difficulties by failing to eliminate rival explanations. A most different design, in contrast, deliberately seeks cases of a particular phenomenon that differ as much as possible, since the research objective is to find similar processes or outcomes in diverse cases. For example, if teenagers are rebellious in both modern Western societies and tribal societies, then it may be their developmental stage, and not their societies or their parents' child-rearing techniques, accounts for their rebelliousness.

One source of semantic confusion here is that the most similar design parallels the logic of Mill's method of difference, while the most different design corresponds with Mill's method of agreement. (Mill's terms come from a comparison of the dependent variables, while Przeworski and Teune focus on comparison of the independent variables.) Here again, as Mill recognized, left-out variables can weaken such an inference; however, process-tracing provides an additional source of evidence for affirming or discrediting such inferences. Przeworski has suggested that the utility of the "most different" design approach has contributed to the considerable success of some of the literature on democratization, such as the works of Guillermo O'Donnell, Philippe Schmitter, and Laurence Whitehead. These analysts, Przeworski maintains, were forced to distill from highly diverse cases the set of common factors that possessed the greatest explanatory power.[34]

We have discussed in some detail the difficulty of implementing the solution offered by Lijphart and other scholars to the problem of "too many variables, too few cases"—namely, to find comparable cases so closely matched that they provide the functional equivalent of an experiment. However, while it is generally recognized that history seldom provides the investigator with cases that achieve the necessary "control," there are rare exceptions.[35] More frequently available are the aforemen-

---

34. Adam Przeworski expressed these views in a personal communication to David Collier, as noted in Collier, "The Comparative Method: Two Decades of Change." Arend Lijphart believes that the "most different systems" design does not fit the definition of the comparative method and "should be assigned to the category of statistical analysis." See "The Comparable-Cases Strategy in Comparative Research," pp. 164–165.

35. One such case occurred during the Berlin Crisis of 1961. Two groups of presidential advisers to John F. Kennedy comparable in all respects except one—their image of the Soviets—came up with different assessments of the threat implicit in Khrushchev's ultimatum and, consistent with that, made different policy recommendations. See

tioned "most similar" and "least similar" methods and several others to which we now turn.

Instead of trying to find two different cases that are comparable in all ways but one, the investigator may be able to achieve "control" by dividing a single longitudinal case into two sub-cases.[36] In this connection, David Collier calls attention to the classic study by Donald Campbell and Julian Stanley in which they noted that the logic of experimental design can be approximated in "quasi-experiments."[37] They had reference to observational studies of a phenomenon occurring in a natural setting in which an event or a choice occurs at some point in time, creating the approximation of an experimental intervention. This permits the investigator to identify a "before-after" configuration within the sequential development of a longitudinal case. They also warned of the pitfalls of too simple an application of this approach.

One of the difficult requirements of a before-after research design is that only one variable can change at the moment that divides the longitudinal case neatly in two. Campbell and Stanley emphasize that the values of the observed variables should not be examined only immediately before and after the event, but also well before and well after it. As David Collier writes: "Causal inferences about the impact of discrete events can be risky if one does not have an extended series of observations."[38] Campbell and Stanley suggested, and subsequent research has demonstrated, that when this type of quasi-experimental research design is imaginatively and carefully employed, it can be extremely useful in policy evaluation research.

The most common challenge for the before-after design is that for most phenomena of interest, more than one variable changes at a time. It is therefore important to do process-tracing not just on the main variables

Alexander L. George, "The Causal Nexus Between Cognitive Beliefs and Decision-Making Behavior," in Lawrence S. Falkowski, ed., *Psychological Models in International Politics* (Boulder, Colo.: Westview Press, 1979), pp. 116–119.

36.   This possibility was recognized by Lijphart. He called attention to "maximizing comparability" by analyzing a single country diachronically, a procedure which "generally offers a better solution to the control problem than comparison of two or more [cases]." See "Comparative Politics and the Comparative Method," p. 689.

37.   Collier, "The Comparative Method," p. 19. The reference is to the book by Donald T. Campbell and Julian C. Stanley, *Experimental and Quasi-Experimental Designs for Research* (Chicago: Rand McNally, 1963).

38.   Ibid., pp. 20–21. Collier, too, provides a useful discussion of some of the difficulties encountered in attempts to employ quasi-experimental research designs.

of interest that changed at a particular time, but also on the other potential causal variables that changed at the same time. This can help establish whether the variables of interest were causal and whether the other variables that changed in the same period were not, or at least that they do not account for all of the change in the outcome. Such process-tracing can focus on the standard list of potentially "confounding" variables identified by Campbell and Stanley, including the effects of history, maturation, testing, instrumentation, regression, selection, and mortality.[39] It can also address whatever other idiosyncratic differences between the two cases might account for their differences.

Interesting examples of the before-after research design include Robert Putnam's *Making Democracy Work*. Putnam argues that the Italian government's reform of 1970 established regional governments for the first time in Italy, providing a type of natural experiment. Other socioeconomic and cultural variables could be held constant for the most part while the structure of political institutions was abruptly altered by the reform. This historical development gave Putnam an opportunity to evaluate the impact of this structural reform on the identities, power, and strategies of political actors.[40]

A more complex form of the before-after design or pathway analysis is employed by the Colliers in *Shaping the Political Arena*. They develop "critical junctures," defined as periods of significant change, to serve as a common framework that is hypothesized as producing distinct regimes.

THE USE OF A COUNTERFACTUAL CASE OR MENTAL EXPERIMENT

Another way of attempting to achieve controlled comparison when two historical cases closely resembling each other cannot be located is to match the given case with an invented one that does.[41] The case is, of

---

39. Campbell and Stanley, *Experimental and Quasi-Experimental Design for Research.* For a good example, see James Lee Ray, *Democracies and International Conflict: An Evaluation of the Democratic Peace Proposition* (Columbia: University of South Carolina Press, 1995), pp. 158–200.

40. For a more detailed summary of Robert Putnam, *Making Democracy Work: Civic Traditions in Modern Italy* (Princeton, N.J.: Princeton University Press, 1993), see the Appendix, "Studies That Illustrate Research Design."

41. An important contribution to explicating standards for counterfactual analysis is Tetlock and Belkin, eds., *Counterfactual Thought Experiments in World Politics.* These authors and most of the contributors to their volume take a sober view regarding the feasibility of plausible counterfactuals. At one point the editors state that "we seem to be stuck with quite literally a third-rate method" (p. 37). They highlight difficult-to-meet criteria for valid counterfactuals and urge analysts to be clearer and stricter in efforts to employ counterfactuals. See also Alexander L. George and Jane E. Holl, *The Warning-Response Problem and Missed Opportunities in Preventive Diplomacy* (New York: Car-

course, a hypothetical one derived through counterfactual analysis of the existing case or, as it is sometimes referred to, the "mental experiment." As James Fearon, Philip Tetlock, Aaron Belkin, and others have noted, resort to counterfactual analysis, either explicitly or implicitly, is a common practice in many types of research. Fearon asserts that "the common condition of too many variables and too few cases makes counterfactual thought experiments a necessary means for strong justification of causal claims."[42] The use of mental experiments in the service of theory development has a long and distinguished history, including Albert Einstein's development of relativity theory.

However, counterfactual analysis, though frequently employed, has lacked strong criteria and standards for distinguishing good practice from the highly speculative and less disciplined uses of the method. Additional discussion of standards for counterfactual analysis appears in Chapter 10, but several criteria can be stated here. First, since a counterfactual case necessarily builds upon an existing case, it will be difficult to invent an acceptable one *unless* the investigator has already constructed a plausible explanation for the existing case based on a well-validated and explicit theory. This step is important, obviously, because the counterfactual varies what are thought to be the critical variables that presumably accounted for the historical outcome. If the investigator has an erroneous or questionable explanation for the historical case, then the counterfactual analysis is likely to be flawed.[43] Similarly, if the generalization underlying the historical explanation is a probabilistic one, certain factors varied in the counterfactual exercise may have made the event less probable, but it might have occurred anyway in the absence of those factors.

Second, the relationship among variables hypothesized by the invented case must also be supported by a well-validated theory, as in the

---

negie Corporation of New York, 1997); Deborah Welch Larson's study of missed opportunities during the U.S.-Soviet Cold War, *Anatomy of Distrust: U.S.-Soviet Relations During the Cold War* (Ithaca, N.Y.: Cornell University Press, 1997); and Bruce Jentleson, ed., *Opportunities Missed, Opportunities Seized: Preventive Diplomacy in the Post–Cold War World* (Lanham, Md.: Rowman and Littlefield, 1999). We have benefited from discussions about counterfactuals with Aaron Belkin and Deborah Larson.

42.   James D. Fearon, "Counterfactuals and Hypothesis Testing in Political Science," *World Politics*, Vol. 43, No. 2 (January 1991), pp. 169–195. Cited material is from p. 194. In a subsequent essay, Fearon takes a very sober view regarding the feasibility of developing acceptable counterfactual analysis for most social science cases. James D. Fearon, "Causes and Counterfactuals in Social Science," in Tetlock and Belkin, eds., *Counterfactual Thought Experiments in World Politics*, pp. 65–67.

43.   Tetlock and Belkin, eds., *Counterfactual Thought Experiments in World Politics*, does not appear to give sufficient emphasis to this requirement.

historical case. In other words, the explanation for the counterfactual case must be plausible.

Third, when many variables are part of a historical explanation (as is often the case), it is difficult to formulate a counterfactual that includes variation of all the causal variables.

Fourth, a historical explanation does not necessarily imply a counterfactual argument that the event would not have happened if the causal variable had been different. There could be causal substitution—i.e., some other set of causes might have substituted for the variable in question and caused the same outcome.

Fifth, the independent variable in the existing case that is varied in order to produce an invented one must be autonomous; that is, it must be separable from other independent variables that have operated to produce the outcome in the first case. When several independent variables are interconnected so that conjunctural causation exists, as is often the case for problems that engage the interest of social scientists, it becomes difficult to invent a usable new case via counterfactual analysis by altering only one variable, and the complexity of the interconnected variables may be difficult to identify with any reliability.

Sixth, if the explanation for the historical case consists of a series of events in sequence over time—i.e., chains of causation involving path dependency—rather than a single, simple circumscribed event, then constructing an acceptable counterfactual becomes much more difficult. For this would require either a complex counterfactual that involves a long chain of causation involving many variables and conditions, or a more limited counterfactual that focuses on a change in only one of the many events in the chain of causation. Conversely, a counterfactual case is easier to construct if one or only a few decisive points in the historical case determined the outcome. Short-term causation is generally easier to address with a counterfactual than causation that involves a longer-term process.

Summarizing the preceding discussion of the special difficulties encountered with the controlled comparison method, it is not surprising that investigators should differ in their judgment of its utility for theory development. Not all investigators believe that the problems are so intractable as to warrant abandoning controlled comparison studies altogether. Nonetheless, practically all efforts to make use of the controlled comparison method fail to achieve its strict requirements. This limitation is often recognized by investigators employing the method, but they proceed nonetheless to do the best they can with an admittedly imperfect controlled comparison. They do so because they believe that there is no acceptable alternative and no way of compensating for the limitations of controlled comparison.

We conclude, however, that it is desirable to develop alternatives to controlled comparison. The major alternative we propose is "within-case" causal analysis to be discussed briefly in this chapter and more fully in Chapter 10.

An Alternative Proposed by King, Keohane, and Verba

In *Designing Social Inquiry (DSI)*, Gary King, Robert Keohane, and Sidney Verba express grave reservations, as we do, regarding the feasibility of meeting the strict requirements of controlled comparison (though they acknowledge its utility if carefully matched cases provide adequate control).[44] Yet they do not raise in any detail the other ways of meeting the requirements of controlled comparison that are discussed earlier in this chapter. Instead, they propose a different method for assessing theories, one that focuses almost exclusively on the observable implications of a theory for independent and dependent variables, but with little attention to intervening variables or within-case means of assessing them (with one exception—a discussion of research on the extinction of dinosaurs). *DSI* expresses a strong preference for this alternative, which forms the centerpiece of the book.

The method of testing theory by its observable implications for independent and dependent variables is indeed an alternative, a familiar one in discussions of methodology. Since the authors claim that this method fills a major gap in qualitative methodology, it deserves to be taken seriously and to be subjected to questioning, which follows below. Critical reviews of *Designing Social Inquiry* focus mainly on other issues, and we will not summarize all the questions these reviews have raised.[45]

Although *DSI* does not refer to the problem of "too many variables, too few cases" in so many words, it recognizes the importance of the problem, calling it "the Fundamental Problem of Inference." This problem exists because "we cannot rerun history at the same time and the same place with different values of our explanatory variable each time—as a true solution to the fundamental problem of causal inference would require."[46] This statement conveys a recognition of the great difficulty of employing the experimental method for analyzing historical

---

44. King, Keohane, Verba, *Designing Social Inquiry*, pp. 199–207.

45. Most of these critical reviews and additional commentary are republished in Henry Brady and David Collier, eds., *Rethinking Social Inquiry: Diverse Tools, Shared Standards* (Lanham, Md.: Rowman and Littlefield, 2004). Charles Ragin states that Part One, "Diversity-Oriented Research," of his book, *Fuzzy-Set Social Science,* is a rebuttal of *Designing Social Inquiry.*

46. King, Keohane, and Verba, *Designing Social Inquiry*, p. 91.

cases. It also is the foundation for their quite measured view of the feasibility of controlled comparison.

DSI discusses "two possible assumptions that [in principle] enable us to get around the fundamental problem." They emphasize that these assumptions, "like any other attempt to circumvent the Fundamental Problem of Causal Inference, always involve some untestable assumptions."[47] One of these assumptions is that of "unit homogeneity—the assumption that *"two units* [cases] *are homogenous when the expected values of the dependent variables from each unit are the same when our explanatory variable takes on a particular value."*[48] At the same time, however, *DSI* recognizes that such an assumption is often unjustified; two cases "might differ in some unknown way that would bias our causal inference."[49] To this qualification we add that the assumption of unit homogeneity is not justified when the phenomenon in question is affected by equifinality—i.e., when similar outcomes on the dependent variable have different causes.

DSI maintains that the concept of unit homogeneity (or a somewhat less demanding assumption of "constant causal effects") "lies at the base of all scientific research."[50] However, this assertion is not squared with the prevalence of equifinality. In stating that this assumption underlies "the method of comparative case studies," *DSI* overlooks the fact that the comparative method, combined with process-tracing, can be and has been employed to analyze and account for *differences* between cases—that is, cases that do *not* exemplify unit homogeneity.

In fact, in the end *DSI* does not place much confidence in the validity and usefulness of the unit homogeneity assumption; the authors say that obtaining it "is often impossible" and it is important for researchers to understand the "degree of heterogeneity" in units examined and estimate as best they can "the degree of uncertainty—or likely biases" that must be attributed to any inference drawn from the comparison.[51] Such a statement overlooks once again that when equifinality is present, a different procedure is necessary instead of an effort to assess the degree of uncertainty involved in comparing the cases.

It is clear, however, that *DSI* shares our belief that the requirements for strict, controlled comparison are difficult to meet and, therefore, serious questions arise concerning the utility of this method. *DSI* returns to this problem in a detailed discussion of the severe difficulty of establish-

---

47. Ibid.

48. Ibid.; emphasis in original.

49. Ibid., pp. 91–92.

50. Ibid., p. 93.

51. Ibid., pp. 93–94.

ing adequate controls in research and emphasizes the care that must be taken in employing research designs for comparative research that attempt to find matching cases: "matching is one of the most valuable small n strategies. . . . [But we] need to be aware that matching is, like all small n studies, subject to dangers that randomization and a large n would have eliminated."[52] Nonetheless, they maintain, "one very productive strategy is to choose case studies via matching but [make] observations within cases according to other criteria."[53]

In terms of the discussion in the comparative politics literature about whether researchers should select cases that are as similar as possible or as different as possible, the authors of *DSI* "recommend a different approach," namely one that foregoes or minimizes reliance on the comparative method and focuses instead on identifying the potential observations in a single case "that maximizes leverage over the causal hypothesis."[54]

At the same time, *DSI* concedes that comparative small-n studies that use careful matching techniques can produce useful results, even though matching can never be complete or reliable. They mention three studies that they regard as having been reasonably successful in matching cases.[55] *DSI* concludes with a somewhat more receptive view of small-n studies that achieve adequate, if not perfect, controls than in their earlier comments: "With appropriate controls—in which the control variables are held constant, perhaps by matching—we may need to estimate the causal effect of only a single explanatory variable, hence increasing the leverage we have on a problem."[56]

Let us examine more closely *DSI*'s preferred method of assessing theories via their observable implications. The method they espouse is well known, but it is spelled out in great detail and considerably extended in *Designing Social Inquiry*. The familiar concern with "too many variables, too few cases" takes the form of concern with "too few observations." One merit of their discussion is its emphasis on the possibility of attributing a large number of observations to a theory even when working with a single instance or a small number of cases. In the final chapter of the book, "Increasing the Number of Observations," two strategies for doing

52.   Ibid., pp. 199–206.

53.   Ibid., p. 204.

54.   Ibid., p. 205.

55.   These are Seymour Martin Lipset, *The First New Nation: The United States in Comparative and Historical Perspective* (New York: Basic Books, 1963); David Laitin, *Hegemony and Culture: Politics and Religious Change Among the Yoruba* (Chicago: University of Chicago Press, 1986); and Atul Kohli, *The State and Poverty in India: The Politics of Reform* (New York: Cambridge University Press, 1987).

56.   King, Keohane, and Verba, *Designing Social Inquiry*, p. 206.

so are presented.[57] First, the reader is presented with a "very simple formal model." The simplification of the model includes use of a linear regression assumption and a focus "on the causal effect of one variable"; all other variables "are controlled" in the model "in order to avoid omitted variable bias or other problems."

However, discussion of this model in *DSI* and the example chosen address not a single case or small-n research, but a large-N type of study. This would seem an inappropriate example for addressing the problem in qualitative research. The possibility of multicollinearity is recognized, but finessed by suggesting it could be dealt with by more observations; besides, assurance is given that "it is often possible to select observations so as to keep the correlation between the causal variable and the control variable low."[58] Later, the assumption of linearity is addressed and nonlinearity is briefly discussed. In the end, the authors of *DSI* acknowledge that they cannot provide a precise answer to the question of how many observations will be enough, which will always apply, and that "most qualitative research situations will not exactly fit the formal model," although its "basic intuitions do apply much more generally."[59]

The authors then turn to the second strategy for increasing the number of observations by "making many observations from few." This is accomplished by "reconceptualizing" a qualitative research design "to extract many more observations from it."[60] Since *DSI* rests much of its argument on this strategy, we need to examine it closely. The book suggests three ways for avoiding the possibility of an insufficient number of observations in any particular study. "We can observe more units, make new and different measures of the same units, or do both—observe more units while using new measures."[61]

The first of these suggestions is similar to that advanced by Arend Lijphart for increasing the numbers of cases, as *DSI* acknowledges.[62] The second method "involves a *partial* replication of the theory or hypothesis that uses a *new dependent variable* but keeps the same explanatory variables" (emphasis added). The problem here is that changing the dependent variable alters the research objective of the study—and, indeed, the

---

57.   Ibid., pp. 213–217.

58.   Ibid., p. 215.

59.   Ibid., p. 216.

60.   Ibid., p. 217.

61.   Ibid., p. 218. *Designing Social Inquiry* also notes (pp. 219–220) that an alternative to doing so is to work with subunits of the phenomenon in question.

62.   Ibid., p. 217.

theory itself—since the choice of a new dependent variable changes the nature of the phenomenon that is to be explained or predicted.

This criticism applies with even greater force to *DSI*'s third proposal: for "a new (or greatly revised) hypothesis implied by our original theory that uses a new dependent variable and applies the hypothesis to new instances."[63] *DSI* explicitly acknowledges that this suggestion involves "new variables and new units. The measures used to test what are essentially new hypotheses that are derived from the original ones may be quite different from those used thus far."[64] They acknowledge that this "may involve the introduction of explanatory variables not applicable to the original unit."[65]

The second and third ways of increasing the number of observations put the technical requirements of their method ahead of the objective of testing the *initial* theory. They endorse changing the starting theory when necessary to obtain a large number of observable implications of some other, perhaps related, theory. A similar critical observation is made by Charles Ragin in commenting on *DSI*'s effort to gain analytic leverage through empirical disaggregation. Most such attempts "undermine the question that inspired the investigation in the first place."[66]

We should make clear that the reservations expressed here do not question the *general* desirability of attempting to identify observable implications *of a given theory*, both within and among cases, in order to facilitate the task of assessing *it*. Our disagreement with *DSI* is that we believe the search for observable implications should be confined to those clearly relevant to the original theory. *DSI* anticipates this criticism by saying that the changes in an original theory suggested by their second and third ways of increasing observations should be consistent with the original theory. This is a basic prerequisite of their approach which rests on the questionable assumption that the different observations are not independent of each other and are not independent of the original outcome variable of the starting theory.

In our view, switching the effort to assess a given theory by altering it raises serious questions. First, how can one decide whether one has correctly assigned observable implications to a theory? This is the question of the validity of the imputed observations. Second, are all of the observations imputed to a theory equally important for assessing that theory? *DSI* makes only passing reference to both of these questions in its re-

63. Ibid., p. 218.

64. Ibid., p. 224.

65. Ibid., p. 225.

66. Ragin, *Fuzzy-Set Social Science*, p. 206.

peated emphasis on increasing the number of observations. For example: "Maximizing leverage is so important and so general that we strongly recommend that researchers routinely list *all possible* observable implications."[67] Similarly, readers are enjoined to "collect data on as many of its [the theory's] observable implications as possible."[68]

Following such advice may lead to indiscriminate listing of all questionable implications of a theory. Little guidance is given for distinguishing between genuine, questionable, and highly speculative implications of a theory, as a more Bayesian approach to theory testing would require. The emphasis on all *observable* implications, moreover, fails to indicate the importance of identifying strong, valid implications of a theory even if they are not readily observable at present. *DSI*'s method also fails to emphasize the importance of focusing on the particular implications that would provide a tough test of the theory.[69] The consequences of stretching to get all possible observable implications are not trivial. Implications of a questionable character can weaken the claim that the theory in question received a valid test and that it really increases "leverage."

In sum, *DSI*'s proposal for achieving scientific inference in qualitative research fails to address squarely the need to ensure that observations imputed to a theory achieve *quality, validity,* and *relevance.* In a brief discussion of a hypothetical example it is stated that observations "should be used even if they are not the implications of greatest interest."[70] On the other hand, the authors of *DSI* do make passing reference to the need for

---

67. King, Keohane, and Verba, *Designing Social Inquiry,* p. 30; emphasis added.

68. Ibid., p. 24. In his comment on King, Keohane, and Verba, *Designing Social Inquiry,* James Caporoso is critical of *Designing Social Inquiry*'s emphasis on obtaining as many observable implications as possible. He urges a more refined perspective, one that would engage in tough tests of a theory. James Caporoso, "Research Design, Falsification, and the Qualitative-Quantitative Divide," *American Political Science Review,* Vol. 89, No. 2 (June 1995), p. 458. And Ronald Rogowski expresses "fear that devout attention" to *Designing Social Inquiry*'s insistence on many observable implications "may paralyze rather than stimulate, scientific inquiry in comparative politics." Ronald Rogowski, "The Role of Theory and Anomaly in Social-Scientific Inference," *American Political Science Review,* Vol. 89, No. 2 (June 1995), pp. 457–459; 456, 470.

69. This criticism was made also by James Caporoso in the *American Political Science Review* symposium. He is critical of *Designing Social Inquiry*'s tendency "to see falsification in terms of deriving many implications of a theory. . . we should consider which of our theories' implications are least likely to be compatible with a particular outcome. Outcomes are overdetermined. . . . Instead of finding data that corresponds to theory, why not first ask which of the outcomes implied by the theory are least likely to be true if the theory is not true?" Caporoso, "Research Design, Falsification, and the Qualitative-Quantitative Divide," p. 458. For a detailed statement of our views regarding ways of testing theories, see Chapters 6 and 11.

70. King, Keohane, and Verba, *Designing Social Inquiry,* p. 31.

valid observations: "there are situations where a single case study (as always containing many observations) is better than a study based on more observations, *each one of which is not as detailed or certain.*"[71] More generally, a serious tension exists between *DSI*'s emphasis on the desirability of increasing "leverage"—i.e., explaining as much as possible with as little as possible—which encourages listing all possible observations, and the importance of ensuring that the observations imputed to a theory achieve the quality, validity, and relevance needed to assess the theory.[72]

DSI also misunderstands process-tracing, which it incorrectly represents as simply another way to obtain more observable implications of a theory. *DSI*'s major interest in briefly discussing process-tracing toward the end of the book is to label it as consistent with the authors' own approach. "From our perspective," they state, "process-tracing and other approaches to elaborations of causal mechanisms increase the number of theoretically relevant observations."[73] This overlooks the fact that within-case observations and methods for analyzing them in their particular historical context are different from cross-case comparisons and methods, which necessarily simplify or omit the contexts of the cases studies. In this context *DSI* refers briefly to the "within-case" approach of Alexander George and Timothy McKeown. However, it is mislabeled as "within-observation explanation" and asserts that it should be regarded as nothing more than "a strategy of redefining the unit of analysis in order to increase the number of observations."[74]

Working with this mischaracterization of process-tracing, *DSI* then concedes that it and related efforts to get at "psychological underpinnings of a hypothesis developed for units at a higher level of aggregation are very valuable approaches." This is coupled with an insistence that process-tracing and related approaches should be regarded as "extensions of the more fundamental logic of analysis we have been using, not ways of by-passing it."[75]

We instead characterize process-tracing as a procedure for identifying steps in a causal process leading to the outcome of a given dependent variable of a particular case in a particular historical context. As Sidney Tarrow pointed out in his commentary on *DSI*, noting that although it refers to process-tracing favorably, it errs in assimilating it "to their favorite goal of increasing the number of theoretically relevant observations."

---

71.   Ibid., p. 67.

72.   Ibid., pp. 29–31; 123.

73.   Ibid., p. 228.

74.   Ibid., pp. 226–227.

75.   Ibid., p. 228.

That is, *DSI* errs in regarding each step in a causal process as nothing more than an observable implication that can be attributed to a theory. In process-tracing, as Tarrow correctly notes, the goal is not, as *DSI* would have it, to aggregate the individual steps in a causal chain "into a larger number of data points but to *connect* the phases of the policy process and enable the investigator to identify the reasons for the emergence of a particular decision through the dynamic of events." As Tarrow writes, "process-tracing is different *in kind* from observation accumulation and is best employed in conjunction with it"—as was indeed the case, for example, in the study by Lisa Martin (1992) that *DSI* cites so favorably.[76]

To be sure, the components of process-tracing in single case studies can be used as *DSI* indicates. But to do so ignores the quite *different* use of process-tracing we propose for identifying an intervening causal process between independent variables and outcomes on the dependent variable. Process-tracing is a *different* method for testing theory than *DSI*'s method. This *distinction between two different methods* for testing theories (*DSI*'s and ours) is missing in *Designing Social Inquiry*.

DSI's misunderstanding of process-tracing leads to a failure to recognize that it can often provide an alternative method for testing theories. Thus, by utilizing process-tracing, a theory can be assessed by identifying a causal chain that plausibly links the independent variable of a theory with its dependent variable. Process-tracing does *not* regard each component of the intervening space between independent and dependent variables as simply an "observable implication" but rather as a step in a causal chain. Such a causal chain, if there is sufficient data for identifying it, can—and should—be supported by appropriate causal mechanisms.

There is another important issue that *DSI* deals with in an idiosyncratic way. The authors make no reference to assessing the predictive or explanatory power of a theory, a subject much emphasized by other writers. Instead, *DSI* focuses solely on assessing the validity of a theory via its observable implications; this is not equated to or related to a given theory's predictive or explanatory power. Perhaps this question is ignored because *DSI* favors assessing a theory's validity and usefulness not by its ability to explain or predict variance on a given dependent variable, but by the considerable number and variety of observable implications it can

---

76.   Sidney Tarrow, "Bridging the Quantitative-Qualitative Divide in Political Science," *American Political Science Review,* Vol. 89, No. 2 (June 1995), p. 472; emphasis in original. It may be noted, however, that *Designing Social Inquiry*'s reference to Lisa Martin, *Coercive Cooperation: Explaining Multilateral Economic Sanctions* (Princeton, N.J.: Princeton University Press, 1992) does not mention that she recognized the importance of process-tracing and its contribution to her study. *Designing Social Inquiry*, p. 5. For a discussion of Martin's study, see the Appendix, "Studies That Illustrate Research Design."

generate which they believe increases a theory's "leverage"—i.e., its ability to explain more with less.[77]

Why do *DSI*'s authors not assert that the observable implications of a theory, once established, constitute its predictive capacity? The answer would seem to be that the subjects of observable implications as construed by *DSI* can vary so widely and, as already noted, that the initial theory itself changes during the process of searching for observable implications. Accordingly, it would make little sense to regard the totality of the various observed implications as reflecting the theory's ability to predict or explain a given dependent variable. A large number of observable implications does not give assurance that the *revised* theory is capable of predicting variation in the values of the dependent variable that was postulated in the *initial* theory. If one wants to focus on the task of establishing the predictive and explanatory power of a *given* theory, then the congruence method discussed in Chapter 9 should be of interest.

In any case, as this chapter has noted, a variety of procedures, including that proposed in *Designing Social Inquiry*, for dealing with the "too many variables, too few cases" problem are available from which researchers can choose.

In *DSI* the phenomenon of equifinality—i.e., when the same type of outcome in different cases may have quite different causes—is recognized in the discussion of research on revolutions.[78] The authors later provide a more detailed discussion of "multiple causality" (a phrase sometimes used by social scientists as a synonym for equifinality). However, the discussion (especially in its hypothetical research examples) confuses equifinality with something quite different—namely the fact that explanations of complex phenomena encompass a number of independent variables.[79]

Within-Case Methods of Causal Inference: The Congruence and Process-Tracing Approaches

There is an alternative that compensates for the limits of both statistical and comparative case analyses: within-case analysis.[80] The methods we

---

77. On the meaning and importance attributed to a theory's "leverage," see King, Keohane, and Verba, *Designing Social Inquiry*, pp. 29–31.

78. Ibid., p. 31.

79. The confusion is illustrated by the following statement: "The fact that some dependent variables, and perhaps all interesting social science-dependent variables, *are influenced by many causal factors* does not make our definition of causality problematic." Ibid., p. 89; emphasis supplied.

80. The following discussion draws upon material presented in several previous pa-

have discussed in this chapter are all what Charles Ragin has termed "variable-oriented" approaches; they attempt to establish the causal powers of a particular variable by comparing how it performs in different cases. In contrast, we stress within-case analysis. David Collier has emphasized that "within-case comparisons are critical to the viability of small-n analysis."[81]

This alternative approach focuses not on the analysis of variables across cases, but on the causal path in a single case. Within-case analysis may be used also in conjunction with studies making cross-case comparisons or for the development of typological theories. Indeed, our position is that within-case analysis is essential to such studies and can significantly ameliorate the limitations of Mill's methods.

Chapter 9 considers the congruence procedure, which can be employed either in a single case study or for each case in a comparative study. Unlike the greater flexibility of the controlled comparison method, it requires a theory that predicts outcomes on the basis of specific initial conditions. Depending on how developed a theory is, its predictions may be abundant and precise, or scarce and highly general. Working with the preexisting theory, the researcher establishes the value of independent and dependent variables in the case at hand, and then compares the observed value of the dependent variable with that predicted by the theory, given the observed independent variables. If the outcome of the dependent variable is consistent with the theory's prediction, then the *possibility* of a causal relationship is strengthened.

The congruence and process-tracing methods for making causal inferences provide alternatives to controlled comparison, and therefore constitute the basis for a different type of comparative method. The results of individual case studies, each of which employs within-case analysis, can be compared by drawing them together within a common theoretical framework without having to find two or more cases that are similar in every respect but one. The process-tracing method is discussed in detail in Chapter 10.

pers and publications; also Ragin, *The Comparative Method*; George, "Case Studies and Theory Development"; George and McKeown, "Case Studies and Theories of Organizational Decision Making"; and George, "The Causal Nexus," pp. 116–119.

81. Collier, "The Comparative Method" p. 17.

Chapter 9

The Congruence Method

The congruence method occupies a special place in our conception of how a single case or a small number of cases can be used for theory development. As we noted in Chapter 8, the method of controlled comparison requires the investigator to find two cases similar in every respect but one. Since this requirement is difficult to meet, an alternative approach is often needed—one that does not attempt, as a controlled comparison does, to achieve the functional equivalent of an experiment. The alternative we propose is the within-case method of causal interpretation, which may include congruence, process-tracing, or both, and which does not operate according to the structure or causal logic of experiments. This chapter discusses the congruence method, and we turn to process-tracing in Chapter 10.

The essential characteristic of the congruence method is that the investigator begins with a theory and then attempts to assess its ability to explain or predict the outcome in a particular case. The theory posits a relation between variance in the independent variable and variance in the dependent variable; it can be deductive or take the form of an empirical generalization. The analyst first ascertains the value of the independent variable in the case at hand and then asks what prediction or expectation about the outcome of the dependent variable should follow from the theory. If the outcome of the case is consistent with the theory's prediction, the analyst can entertain the possibility that a causal relationship may exist. Of course, the finding of mere consistency between a theory's predictions and case outcomes may not be significant, and in this chapter we discuss several questions that can guide researchers as they assess the significance of preliminary findings.[1]

The congruence method has several attractive features. The investigator does not have to trace the causal process that leads from the independent variable to the case outcome; so the method does not require a great deal of data about the case being studied. Because the congruence method does not use process-tracing, it does not require a search for data that might establish a causal process from independent to dependent variables. (However, process-tracing can be combined with the congruence method to assess whether the congruence between independent and dependent variables is causal or spurious and also to enrich theories that only posit a relationship between independent and dependent variables and have nothing to say about the intervening variables and causal process that connect them.)

The congruence method offers considerable flexibility and adaptability. It can contribute to theory development in several ways; it can be employed in a disciplined-configurative type of case study, a plausibility probe, or in a crucial case (or tough test) of an existing theory.[2] The theory employed in the congruence method may be well-established and highly regarded, or it may be formulated or postulated by the investigator for the first time on the basis of a hunch that it may turn out to be important.

Often, however, available theories lack clarity and internal consistency so that they cannot make specific predictions and thus cannot be tested in any rigorous way. Nonetheless, investigators often succumb to the temptation to attribute predictive or explanatory power to such theories, leading to spurious or inconclusive tests of loosely formulated theories. The priority is not to test such theories, but to refine them if possible so that they can be tested. The congruence method may contribute to such refinement and development. An investigator may be able to clarify and refine a theory through its use in case studies, making it more nearly testable. As noted in Chapter 4, an investigator must establish the level of concreteness and differentiation with which variance in the dependent variable will be measured. How well this task is performed may well determine whether one can find congruence between the independent variable in the theory and outcomes on the dependent variable. This point is demonstrated later in this chapter.

A final attractive feature of the congruence method is that it can be

1.   Gary King, Robert O. Keohane, and Sidney Verba, *Designing Social Inquiry: Scientific Inference in Qualitative Research* (Princeton, N.J.: Princeton University Press, 1994).

2.   We use Harry Eckstein's categorization of ways in which a case study can contribute—in all stages, as he said—to theory development and testing.

used either as a within-case method or, when coupled with a counter-factual case, as a form of controlled comparison. The latter possibility is discussed later in this chapter.[3]

An important general standard for congruence tests is "congruity": similarities in the relative strength and duration of hypothesized causes and observed effects.[4] This does not mean that causes must resemble their effects or be on the same scale, and researchers must avoid the common bias toward assuming this should be the case. For example, there is a temptation to assume that large or dramatic effects must have large and dramatic causes, but this is not necessarily true. Researchers must take into account theoretical reasons why the effects of hypothesized causes might be amplified, diminished, delayed, or sped up (through expectations effects). Once this has been done, it is possible to address the question of whether the independent and dependent variables are congruent; that is, whether they vary in the expected directions, to the expected magnitude, along the expected dimensions, or whether there is still unexplained variance in one or more dimensions of the dependent variable.

Although consistency between a theory's predictions and case outcomes is often taken as providing support for a causal interpretation (and, for that matter, for assessing deductive theories generally), researchers must guard against unjustified, questionable imputation of a causal relationship on the basis of mere consistency, just as safeguards have been developed in statistical analysis to deal with the possibility of spurious correlation.

There are several ways in which this problem can be addressed. The investigator can employ process-tracing to attempt to identify a causal path (the causal chain) that depicts how the independent variable leads to the outcome of the dependent variable. (We note the close connection between process-tracing and causal mechanisms in Chapter 7.)

The usefulness of combining the congruence method with process-tracing was demonstrated in the innovative study by Yuen Foong Khong, *Analogies at War*. Earlier examples of the use of process-tracing in case studies to elaborate (or assess) the causal standing of an explanation first derived by applying a deductive theory include the studies by Vinod

---

3.   Stephen Van Evera suggests several other elaborations of the congruence method and discusses its usefulness for testing theory, creating theory, and inferring the antecedent conditions of a theory. We find it difficult to assess the utility of the two variants of the congruence approach he identifies and must await more research efforts to employ them. Stephen Van Evera, *Guide to Methods for Students of Political Science* (Ithaca, N.Y.: Cornell University Press, 1997), pp. 58–63, 69–70, 72–74.

4.   Margaret Mooney Marini and Burton Singer, "Causality in the Social Sciences," in Clifford Clogg, ed., *Sociological Methodology*, Vol. 18 (1988), pp. 347–409.

Aggarwal in *Liberal Protectionism,* and by David Yoffie in *Power and Protectionism: Strategies of the Newly Industrializing Countries.*[5] (The studies by Khong and Aggarwal are discussed later in this chapter.)

Another way in which the investigator can attempt to deal with the limitations of the congruence method is to provide a plausible or convincing argument that the deductive theory or empirical generalization being employed is powerful and well validated, that it fits the case at hand extremely well, and that it is not rivaled by competing theories or at least is better than conceivable alternative theories. By invoking the superior standing of the theory employed or by resorting to process-tracing, the investigator may be satisfied that the within-case approach suffices and need not be buttressed by across-case comparisons.

When an investigator lacks confidence in the results of the congruence method employed in the within-case mode, he or she may supplement it by making use of counterfactual analysis. That is, the investigator invents a new case that is presumably similar to the original case in every respect but one (keeping in mind the limitations of counterfactuals discussed in Chapter 8).

The next section discusses the concepts of spuriousness, causal priority, and causal depth, three possible relationships between independent and dependent variables that researchers should consider as they assess preliminary findings that the outcome in a case is congruent with a theory. The two sections that follow provide more specific advice on how researchers can assess whether a finding is spurious and whether the independent variable is a necessary condition for the outcome of the dependent variable. We then discuss how the congruence method can be used to assess the causal role of beliefs in decision-making, highlighting the difficulty of ascertaining how decision-makers come to their decisions and noting how several scholars have coped with this challenge. Finally,

---

5.   Yuen Foong Khong, *Analogies at War: Korea, Munich, Dien Bien Phu and the Vietnam Decisions of 1965* (Princeton, N.J.: Princeton University Press, 1992); Vinod Aggarwal, *Liberal Protectionism* (Berkeley, Calif.: University of California Press, 1985); and David Yoffie, *Power and Protectionism: Strategies of the Newly Industrializing Countries* (New York: Columbia University Press, 1983). We may recall also Bruce Russett's discussion many years ago of the utility of case studies for assessing the causal status of statistical correlations. Russett recommended that for this purpose investigators make greater use of an iterative research strategy, one that alternates statistical-correlational studies of large numbers of cases with intensive single case analysis. Bruce Russett, "International Behavior Research: Case Studies and Cumulation," in Michael Haas and Henry S. Kariel, eds., *Approaches to the Study of Political Science* (Scranton, Penn.: Chandler Publishing Co., 1970), pp. 425–443. The strategy of combining large-N statistical study with a few intensive case studies was followed by Russett's student, Paul Huth, in *Extended Deterrence and the Prevention of War* (New Haven, Conn.: Yale University Press, 1988).

we consider how the congruence method can be used to add to studies of deductive theories that put a "black box" around decision-making and strategic interaction, emphasizing the usefulness of process-tracing as a way to strengthen results by identifying a causal process that could lead from the independent to the dependent variable.

Spuriousness, Causal Priority, and Causal Depth

To assess the possible causal significance of congruity in a case, the researcher should ask two questions inspired by the logic of experiment. First, is the consistency spurious or of possible causal significance? Second, is the independent variable a necessary condition for the outcome of the dependent variable, and how much explanatory or predictive power does it have? The latter question is important, since a condition may be necessary but still contribute little to the explanation or prediction of the outcome in question.

Except for tests of deterministic theories stated in terms of necessity and sufficiency, a single congruence test is not strong enough to provide confirmation or falsification of theories.[6] More than one theory may be equally congruent with the outcome, or the outcome may be caused by other factors not identified by any of the theories considered. Researchers must be sensitive to the issues of spuriousness, causal priority, and causal depth in judging the strength of inferences made on the basis of congruence tests. A few comments on each of these three issues are needed. *Spuriousness* occurs when the observed congruence of the cause C and effect E is artificial because both C and E are caused by some third factor Z (whether or not Z has been identified in a competing theory):

Alternatively, the putative cause C lacks *causal priority* if C is necessary for E, but C is itself only an intervening variable wholly or largely caused by a necessary prior variable Z. In this instance, both Z and C are necessary for E, but C has no independent explanatory value:

$$Z \dashrightarrow C \dashrightarrow E$$

A third possibility is that C can be defined as lacking *causal depth* if a third variable Z would have brought about E even in the absence of C. In this instance, it does not matter whether or not Z is related to C. In other

6. Daniel Little, "Causal Explanation in the Social Sciences," *The Southern Journal of Philosophy*, Vol. 34 Supplement (1995), pp. 31–56.

words, Z has greater causal depth because it appears to be necessary and sufficient for E, and Z may act through C or through some other variable X. In contrast to the example of causal priority, C is not in this instance a necessary condition for E.[7]

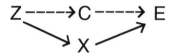

Thus, the appearance of congruence, especially when only one or primarily one theory is considered, cannot support an inference of causality, nor does the lack of congruence deny a possible causal role. Moreover, even if a congruence test suggests that a variable played a causal role in a given case, this does not mean that this theory proposes causal factors that are necessary, sufficient, or causal in any sense in other cases where contextual and conjunctive variables are different.

These problems of spuriousness, causal priority, and causal depth underscore that congruence tests by themselves may be inconclusive when several competing theories are involved. In such circumstances, for causal relations short of necessity or sufficiency, congruence tests are very difficult unless all the effects of the theories in question have been established with precision and confidence through previous testing. The problem is that alternative theories may focus on the same independent variables but point to different causal mechanisms that relate these variables to the observed outcome. The theories compete in logic, but may or may not make different predictions on the outcome. Theories may also be complementary, addressing different variables without contradicting one another logically. Such complementary theories may either reinforce or counteract one another's predicted effects.

A real-world example, drawn from Andrew Bennett's research on the rise and fall of Soviet military interventionism in the Third World in the 1970s and 1980s, illustrates these issues. The "Reagan Doctrine" and "Soviet economic stringency" explanations for Soviet retrenchment in the 1980s are complementary, and they both pointed toward an increased likelihood of Soviet retrenchment. Retrenchment occurred, but the congruence method alone cannot tell us if both explanations were important factors, if only one was primarily responsible for the outcome, or if neither was causal and the result was driven by other variables.[8]

7.   Richard Miller, *Fact and Method* (Princeton, N.J.: Princeton University Press, 1987); and David Dessler, "The Architecture of Causal Analysis," unpublished manuscript, 1992.

8.   Andrew Bennett, *Condemned to Repetition? The Rise, Fall, and Reprise of Soviet-Russian Military Interventionism, 1973–1996* (Cambridge, Mass.: MIT Press, 1999).

Now consider the problem of competing explanations. A competitor to the Reagan Doctrine theory is the "hard-line reactive theory," which holds that the Reagan Doctrine aid, rather than speeding up Soviet retrenchment, galvanized a hard-line coalition in the Soviet Union and delayed the retrenchment in Soviet foreign policy.[9] These competing views on the effects of the Reagan Doctrine complement the economic stringency view and are consistent with the outcome of retrenchment. The difference is that the Reagan Doctrine theory suggests that U.S. aid to Afghan rebels, in addition to Soviet economic constraints, led to the Soviet withdrawal from Afghanistan; the hard-line theory could suggest that Soviet economic constraints, despite the delays and hedging caused by the hard-line coalition, caused the Soviet withdrawal. These competing versions can be tested for congruence with the timing, nature, and completeness of the Soviet withdrawal.

This example also illustrates why it is important not to summarily dismiss explanations that seem inconsistent with the outcome. In this case, trends in Soviet forces for power projection appeared to be inconsistent with the Soviet retrenchment, as these forces actually grew through much of the 1980s. However, the strengthening of these forces might help explain why Soviet retrenchment did not take place sooner or more precipitously.

Bennett's research on Soviet interventionism also employed an additional kind of congruence test. The research objective was to test a relatively new theory, learning theory, as an explanation for patterns of Soviet military intervention. This required first establishing whether there was any unexplained variance after accounting for the combined effects of more established theories. Bennett thus canvassed these theories and assessed their individual and collective congruence with both the rise and fall of Soviet interventionism. Bennett concluded that these theories collectively provided a more complete explanation of the rise of Soviet interventionism in the 1970s than of its fall in the 1980s (which is consistent with the fact that many analysts in the late 1970s expected such interventionism to continue to increase). This test suggested that it was not possible to reject out of hand that a learning explanation might account for some of the variance in Soviet policies.

Multivariate congruence testing can be complex, but it is also a familiar form of historical analyses and arguments. One historian may argue that the structure of the international system and the bipolar distribution of power between the United States and the Soviet Union made the Cold War inevitable. Another may argue that the Cold War arose from not just

---

9. Diego Cordovez and Selig Harrison, *Out of Afghanistan: The Inside Story of the Soviet Withdrawal* (Oxford: Oxford University Press, 1995), pp. 245–246.

the distribution of power, but also from the specific domestic political dynamics in the United States and Soviet Union and despite the lack of any immediate danger of a military invasion by one superpower against the other. A third might argue that this balance of contributing and counteracting forces underdetermines the emergence of the Cold War unless one takes Stalin's personality into account.

Two injunctions can help clarify such debates. First, it is important to consider a wide range of potentially causal factors, to specify the predicted contributing and counteracting effects of each, and to identify where underlying causal arguments are complementary and competing. Second, it is useful to guard against the bias of what has been termed "explanatory overdetermination."[10] When called upon to predict events, theorists and experts often give underdetermined accounts, yet when these same observers are asked to explain past events, their accounts make these events seem overdetermined. For example, almost no scholars predicted the collapse of the Soviet Union and the end of the Cold War, but afterwards many scholars pointed to numerous, seemingly overdetermining "causes" of these outcomes. Careful use of congruence testing, and inclusion of all the candidate theories, might instead lead to the conclusion that these outcomes were underdetermined, or at least that their timing and particular course could have been quite different if a few variables had been changed.

We now discuss how researchers can assess their preliminary findings of congruity.

How Plausible is the Claim of Congruity?

The possibility that consistency between the values of the independent and dependent variable in a given case is not spurious—and possibly causal—gains a measure of support if the relationship can be supported by a general law or statistical generalization. For example, a causal inference drawn from the observed consistency between an independent cognitive variable(s) such as the actor's *belief* and some aspect of that individual's *behavior* can be supported by psychological theories of cognitive balance that call attention to the fact that individuals generally (at least under certain conditions) strive to achieve consistency between their beliefs and their actions. This, of course, is a very general theory. If more specific generalizations or theories could be adduced, the imputation of a causal relation would be strengthened. Typically, the stronger and more

---

10. Jack Snyder, "Richness, Rigor, and Relevance in the Study of Soviet Foreign Policy,"

precise the version of a more general theory, the more confidence we ought to attach to claims that consistency is not spurious.[11]

Is the Independent Variable a Necessary Condition for the Outcome of the Dependent Variable?

If the consistency identified appears to be causal and not spurious, the investigator may attempt to assess whether the independent variable is a necessary condition for the outcome in question. This question, of course, may be difficult to resolve. Efforts to do so will require the investigator to move beyond within-case analysis. Ideally, one would try to find other cases in which the same type of outcome occurred in the absence of that independent variable. If such a case(s) were discovered, then the independent variable could not be regarded as a necessary condition.[12]

When one or more comparable cases are not available, then the investigator can resort to analytical imagination to think of hypothetical cases that might help to judge whether the same type of outcome might occur in the absence of that independent variable. In other words, the investigator resorts to counterfactual analysis and mental experiments in an effort to create a controlled comparison.[13] Disciplined use of analytical imagination will at least provide a safeguard against the temptation to move too quickly and confidently from the earlier judgment that consistency was not spurious to the further inference that the independent variable is a necessary condition for the occurrence of that type of outcome.[14] If the grounds for regarding the independent variable as a necessary condition are shaky or dubious, as is often likely to be the case, then it is advisable

---

11.   Justification for this view may be found in Bayesian decision theory. For a discussion, see Alexander L. George and Timothy J. McKeown, "Case Studies and Theories of Organizational Decision Making," in Robert F. Coulam and Richard A. Smith, eds., *Advances in Information Processing in Organizations,* Vol. 2 (Greenwich, Conn.: JAI Press, 1985), pp. 31–32.

12.   Similarly, if the investigator wishes to assess whether the condition in question qualifies as a "sufficient" one for the occurrence of the type of outcome in question, it would be necessary to look for other cases in which that condition was always coupled with that type of outcome. A single case in which it was not, of course, would negate its status as a sufficient condition. In any event, failure to negate the condition as being either a necessary or sufficient condition would remain a provisional finding subject to rejection if negative cases were encountered in the future.

13.   The requirements for disciplined, effective use of counterfactual analysis are discussed in Chapters 8 and 10.

14.   Of course, even if a plausible claim can be advanced that the independent variable is probably or possibly a necessary condition for the occurrence of a given type of outcome, it is not thereby also a sufficient condition for that outcome.

to claim no more than that the type of independent variable in question appears to favor—make more likely—the occurrence of a certain type of outcome. In other words, the independent variable is a contributing cause, though neither necessary nor sufficient.

Analysts should also address the question, "Is the independent variable that is causally related to this particular outcome of the case also consistent with *other* possible outcomes?" In the analysis of a single case, history provides only one outcome of the dependent variable. Accordingly, it is easy to overlook the possibility that other outcomes, had they occurred, might *also* have been consistent with the value of that independent variable. Once again, if the investigator cannot locate cases in which the independent variable with the same value was accompanied by diverse outcomes, he or she can resort to disciplined imagination to assess this possibility. To do so, the investigator should immerse himself or herself in the rich details of the historical case being examined; this may enable him or her to envisage with greater confidence that the outcome might well have gone in different directions even with the independent variable held constant, had variation occurred in other operative independent variables. If there is reason to believe this might have been so, the investigator must assign weaker general predictive and explanatory power to the independent variable in question. It should be noted that broadening the assessment of the causal status of the independent variable (or theory) in question requires that the investigator take into account that other independent variables in the case may have played a role in producing that outcome.

Still another question can be asked: "Is it possible to conceive of any outcomes of the historical case that would *not* have been consistent with the independent variable?" Investigators should attempt to identify outcomes that would be inconsistent with the independent variable and associated conditions because this highlights the need to construct falsifiable theories. By immersing oneself in the historical case, the investigator might envisage a number of other possible outcomes interestingly different from the historical outcome that would also have been consistent with the implications of the independent variable. If so, then the independent variable (of the deductive or empirical theory in question) may be part of the explanation, but its ability to discriminate among alternative outcomes and its predictive power are much weakened.[15] On the

---

15. Deductive theories are more useful if they are capable of making specific predictions of discrete outcomes rather than highly generalized predictions that can be equally met by a number of quite different outcomes. Structural-realist theory, for example, suffers from this limitation. Not only is it capable of making only probabilistic predictions (that, in addition, are not quantified), even its correct predictions are often

other hand, if the investigator cannot envisage other outcomes that could also plausibly occur in the case in question, then there would be reason to attribute stronger predictive power to the independent variable or theory of which it is a part.

Similarly, if all or many of the conceivable outcomes would be consistent with the theory, then its explanatory power may be limited or negligible. Conversely, if other outcomes might have occurred that were not consistent with the theory, then the investigator has additional presumptive evidence of the explanatory power of the theory at least for the actual or the other conceivable outcomes identified.

A hypothetical example will illustrate and clarify how questions of this kind, which attempt to replicate the logic of controlled experiment, can contribute to making more refined and more valid causal interpretations in single-case analysis.

In our hypothetical example, the first actor takes an action (independent variable XX) that appears to have a particular impact on the second actor's behavior (outcome A). The investigator finds that independent variable XX (but not YY or ZZ) is consistent with outcome A. The investigator now asks whether XX can explain and predict *only* outcome A. Or would outcomes B, C, and D—outcomes that did not occur in this case—also have been consistent with XX? If so, while XX may be part of the explanation, its explanatory (and predictive) power is diminished since other explanatory variables are needed to round out the explanation of why the second actor's response was A (and not B, C, or D). These interpretations of the explanatory power of XX are summarized in Figure 9.1.

A more refined analysis is possible. Suppose that although outcome A differs in interesting respects from outcomes B, C, and D, all four outcomes share a certain characteristic—for example, that all are conciliatory responses by the second actor to the first actor's action (though the precise nature of the conciliatory response varies). Suppose further that out-

---

of a very general character. For example, although it is true that during World War II structural realist theory would have successfully predicted conflict developing between the United States and the Soviet Union after their cooperation in defeating Nazi Germany, the theory could not predict whether postwar U.S.-Soviet conflict would result in a spheres-of-influence agreement, a withdrawal of the United States from Europe in favor of a hemispheric "Fortress America" security policy, a relatively benign collaborative-competitive relationship, a cold war, or World War III. These are highly different outcomes of a very consequential nature. Other variables, not encompassed by structural-realist theory, would have to be considered to try to predict or explain which of these outcomes would occur. We are not criticizing the structural-realist theory for being unable to do more than it was able to do. Structural-realist theory is not designed to make highly specific predictions.

Figure 9.1. Possible Outcomes of an Independent Variable.

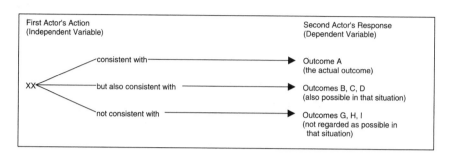

comes G, H, and I are all hard, refractory responses to the first actor's behavior. If so, then XX acquires added explanatory and predictive power
of a quite useful kind, for it discriminates between conciliatory and refractory responses (though not by itself between variants of a conciliatory
response).[16]

From this hypothetical example we turn to a more general discussion
of using the congruence mode to assess the causal role of an actor's beliefs in his or her decision-making.

Use of the Congruence Method to Assess the Causal Role of Beliefs in Decision-Making

Specialists who focus on decision-making approaches in the study of foreign policy have long emphasized the importance of cognitive variables.[17] Attention has centered on how decision-makers' general beliefs

---

16.   This illustrates the observation made in Chapter 4 that a causal relationship may
be sensitive to the level of concreteness or abstraction with which the investigator
defines the value and variance of the dependent variable. To extend our hypothetical
example further, let us assume that the action XX taken by the first actor is coupled
with his displaying a particular image of the opponent that views the second actor as a
limited adversary who is interested in moderating conflict and in striving for accom-
modations. In certain types of situations, this will encourage the second actor to
choose a conciliatory response of some kind. What type of conciliatory response he
chooses will be influenced by other beliefs that further refine his general propensity
for making a conciliatory response. For example, the second actor's belief regarding
the utility and role of different means for advancing one's interest may come into play,
influencing him to prefer option *A* rather than option *B*, *C*, or *D*. In other words, a
combination of several beliefs may further narrow his choice propensities. (Other combinations, of course, are also possible.)

17.   This brief discussion draws on the fuller discussion in Alexander L. George,
"The Causal Nexus Between Cognitive Beliefs and Decision-Making Behavior: The
'Operational Code' Belief System," in Lawrence S. Falkowski, ed., *Psychological Models
in International Politics* (Boulder, Colo.: Westview Press, 1979).

about international politics can affect their choices of policy. However, important methodological issues arise in attempting to assess the role that such beliefs play in two different phases of the process of decision-making: the processing of information and analysis that *precedes* the decision taken, and the *actual choice of policy*. The foregoing discussion of the congruence method is relevant for addressing these issues.

General support for the assumption that a policymaker's beliefs about international politics influence his or her decisions is provided by cognitive consistency theory. But an individual's beliefs and behavior are not always consistent with one another for various reasons. While a decision-maker's beliefs play an important role in information processing that precedes actual choice of action, variables other than these beliefs affect the choices made. For example, the policymaker's decisions will likely be influenced by the need to obtain sufficient support for whatever policy he or she decides upon, by the need for compromise, by domestic or international constraints on the leader's freedom of action, etc. These factors may run in a direction that significantly modifies or is contrary to his or her preferred option.

It is more useful, therefore, to regard an individual's general beliefs as introducing two types of *propensities*, not determinants, into his or her decision-making: diagnostic propensities, which extend or restrict the scope and direction of information processing and shape the decision-maker's diagnosis of a situation; and choice propensities, which lead him or her to favor certain types of action alternatives over others (but which may give way or be altered in response to decisional pressures).

Thus, psychological consistency theory cannot by itself provide robust support to conclusions from congruence method studies of the role of beliefs in decision-making. Causal interpretations in such studies must be disciplined by the methodological questions noted above.

STEPHEN WALKER'S STUDY OF HENRY KISSINGER
Confidence that consistency between an individual's beliefs and actions is of causal significance is enhanced if it is encountered repeatedly in a sequence of decisions taken by an actor over a period of time. This observation played an important role in Stephen Walker's pioneering study of the role of Henry Kissinger's beliefs in his negotiations with North Vietnamese leaders.[18] In this study, Walker developed highly systematic and

---

18. Stephen G. Walker, "The Interface between Beliefs and Behavior: Henry Kissinger's Operational Code and the Vietnam War," *Journal of Conflict Resolution,* Vol. 21, No. 1 (March 1977), pp. 129–168. More recently, Walker has written a much expanded version of this article in which he undertakes a two-sided analysis of the interaction between the United States and Vietnam whereas his earlier study looked only at

explicit methods for employing the congruence procedure. He also addressed the important question of whether Kissinger's actions were better explained by situational or role variables than by his beliefs. Walker advanced a plausible argument that Kissinger's operative beliefs were idiosyncratic in important respects and not easily accounted for by situational or role variables. That is, the set of Kissinger's beliefs and his policy actions consistent with those beliefs probably would not have been displayed by anyone else in his position. Walker noted that the Nixon administration's policy on Vietnam was controversial and that there were policy preferences that competed with Kissinger's. Moreover, the position of national security adviser that Kissinger occupied at that time was not precisely defined. This permitted the incumbent considerable latitude. For these and other reasons, Walker concluded, Kissinger's role in the prolonged bargaining process with North Vietnamese leaders exemplifies both "action indispensability" and "actor indispensability" as defined by Fred Greenstein.[19]

KHONG'S STUDY OF HISTORICAL ANALOGIES

The causal role of beliefs in decision-making was the subject of an exemplary study by Yuen Foong Khong.[20] Khong decided to focus not on operational code beliefs, as Stephen Walker had, but rather on the role historical analogies play in policymaking. Khong confronts the nettlesome problem of how the analyst can decide whether historical analogies are used by policymakers merely to *justify* decisions they take or whether analogies actually have a causal impact on the information processing that precedes decisions and the choice of a policy option. Drawing on Alexander George's "Causal Nexus" paper, Khong assesses the role of several historical analogies held by top-level U.S. policymakers at critical junctures of the Vietnam crisis: the February 1965 decision to initiate slow-squeeze graduated air attacks on North Vietnam and the July 1965 decision to expand substantially the deployment of U.S. combat forces.

In analyzing these two decisions, Khong examines three historical analogies of previous crises that U.S. policymakers were familiar with: Munich, the Korean War, and Dien Bien Phu. He finds evidence in historical materials and from interviews that each of these analogies was present in the minds of U.S. policymakers in 1965. However, by means of an

the effect of Kissinger's beliefs on U.S. policy. Stephen G. Walker, "The Management and Resolution of Conflict in a `Single' Case," in Zeev Maoz et al., eds., *Multiple Paths to Knowledge* (forthcoming).

19.   Fred I. Greenstein, *Personality and Politics* (Chicago: Markham, 1969).

20.   Yuen Foong Khong, *Analogies at War*.

ingenious and complex research strategy that uses both the congruence method and process-tracing, Khong concludes that the Korean analogy played the most influential role in U.S. decisions to use slowly graduated air attacks and then to put in large-scale ground forces.

Only a brief account of the essence of his rich analysis can be presented here. First, Khong built on the distinction mentioned above between diagnostic propensities and choice propensities that are implicit in the beliefs held by policymakers by distinguishing six different but closely related diagnostic tasks. (Although he labels all six tasks as "diagnostic," they do include choice propensities; in effect, he collapses the distinction between diagnostic and choice propensities.) Khong emphasizes that historical analogies are often used by policymakers to perform diagnostic tasks.

His six diagnostic tasks are: a definition of the new situation, facilitated by comparing it with a past one; a judgment of what is at stake; an implicit prescription as to how the new situation should be dealt with— i.e., the "solution" to the problem or type of policy response needed; an assessment of the moral acceptability of the implied prescription; an assessment of the likelihood of its success; and an estimate or warning of the dangers and risks of the implicit policy should it be adopted.

Khong labels this set of diagnostic tasks the Analogical Explanation (AE) Framework. He converts these six diagnostic tasks into a set of general standardized questions to be asked of each of the historical analogies; these are a central feature of his research design.[21] The answers to these questions satisfy the data requirements for comparing the role the analogies played in information processing. The study, therefore, constitutes an explicit example of the method of structured, focused comparison: it is only by asking the same general questions of each case that systematic comparison becomes possible.

Khong establishes the implications that each of the three historical analogies had for these diagnostic tasks via process-tracing by making a careful analysis of the available historical record and through interviews with U.S. policymakers. He then employs the congruence method to assess the implications of each analogy's answer to the six diagnostic tasks for the various policy options that were being considered at the time.

The question for Khong, then, was which of the various policy options under consideration were consistent with the diagnostic implications of the analogy and which were not. Khong employs a version of the congruence method discussed earlier in this chapter for each of the his-

---

21. Ibid., p. 62.

Figure 9.2. The Lessons of Korea and the Option Chosen.

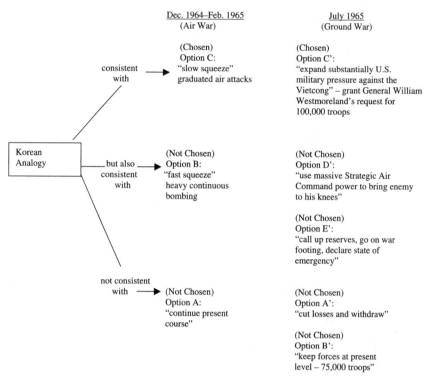

Dec. 1964–Feb. 1965
(Air War)

July 1965
(Ground War)

(Chosen)
Option C:
"slow squeeze"
graduated air attacks

(Chosen)
Option C':
"expand substantially U.S.
military pressure against the
Vietcong" – grant General William
Westmoreland's request for
100,000 troops

consistent
with

Korean
Analogy

but also
consistent
with

(Not Chosen)
Option B:
"fast squeeze"
heavy continuous
bombing

(Not Chosen)
Option D':
"use massive Strategic Air
Command power to bring enemy
to his knees"

(Not Chosen)
Option E':
"call up reserves, go on war
footing, declare state of
emergency"

not consistent
with

(Not Chosen)
Option A:
"continue present
course"

(Not Chosen)
Option A':
"cut losses and withdraw"

(Not Chosen)
Option B':
"keep forces at present
level – 75,000 troops"

AE Framework:
1. Definition of situation: Aggression
2. Stakes: Vital
3. Implicit prescription: Intervene
4. Morally acceptable to intervene: Yes
5. Likelihood of success: Good
6. Dangers: Chinese intervention

torical analogies. We reproduce in Figure 9.2 his analysis for the Korean analogy.[22]

Having established the answers to the diagnostic tasks each analogy suggested, Khong then looks for congruity between an analogy's diagnosis and the policy options that were under consideration by policymakers. According to Khong's analysis, the Korean analogy's answers to the six diagnostic tasks were highly consistent with the policy decision actually taken from December 1964 to February 1965 period to employ a "slow squeeze" version of graduated air attacks. But it was also consistent with a policy option calling for heavy, continuous bombing that was not taken. This left unanswered for the moment why the "slow squeeze"

---

22. Ibid., p. 139.

version of air attacks was chosen. A further challenge for analysis was raised by Khong's finding that the Munich analogy had identical implications for these two policy options. Similar results emerged when the congruence method was used to compare the implications of the Korean and Munich analogies for the various policy options under consideration in July 1965.

Thus, as Khong notes, both historical analogies supported the case for either of the two options. But Khong argues persuasively that the Korean analogy was more influential in the two decisions of February and July. He arrives at this conclusion by attributing decisive importance to the different answers the two analogies provided for the sixth diagnostic task. The Korean analogy carried a strong fear that resort to the stronger of the two options in both February and 1965 would trigger Chinese intervention in the Korean War. This particular vision of the Korean War was deeply etched in the historical memory of U.S. policymakers in 1965. Khong cites ample evidence from archival and interviews in support of this observation.

In contrast, the Munich analogy did not warn of the dangers of making a hard response to aggressions by the Japanese and Germans in the 1930s. Although the Munich analogy could account, as did the Korean analogy, for the rejection of the nonintervention options in 1965, it was unable to suggest why, among the intervention options, the least hard one was selected.[23]

In this excellent study, Khong has shown how an imaginative, disciplined research design that combines congruence and process-tracing methods can be used to confront the extremely complicated, difficult task of distinguishing between a justificatory role and an information processing function of historical analogies in foreign policy decision-making. His study is the most rigorous and disciplined treatment we know of for dealing with the theoretical and methodological issues associated with determining whether historical analogies are being used by policymakers solely to justify their decisions or whether the analogies play a genuine causal role in the information processing that leads to the decisions taken. Khong states his conclusions with appropriate cautions, noting a number of limitations and questions that remain, but he has raised the discussion of this difficult problem to a new level of analytical sophistication.[24]

---

23. Ibid., p. 190.

24. In otherwise highly favorable reviews of Khong's book, Deborah Larson and Jack Levy both suggest that a broader research design that considered additional explanatory variables would have been useful. Larson notes that Khong's analysis of U.S. decisions in the Vietnam War lacks "explanatory breadth." That is, "focusing solely on the admittedly important decisions of February and July 1965 overlooks . . .

RITTBERGER'S STUDY OF GERMANY'S POST-UNIFICATION FOREIGN POLICY

A study organized by Volker Rittberger also employed both the congruence method and process-tracing, this time to assess competing theories for predicting German foreign policy after the unification of the two Germanies.[25] The bulk of literature on this question predicted that post-unification German foreign policy would be dominated by the question of whether its improved power position should lead to a significant change in its foreign policy. The research question posed in Rittberger's study was whether there would be continuity or significant change in post-unification foreign policy. Three theories were formulated and submitted to a carefully constructed empirical test: neorealism (and a modified version of it that introduced variation in security pressures); utilitarian liberalism; and constructivism (which holds that state actors follow a logic of appropriateness whose behavior is shaped by international and societal norms).

---

international and domestic conditions." Continuing, she notes, "American involvement in Vietnam was determined by many causal factors, including the bipolar distribution of power, concern for the credibility of extended deterrence, memories of the anti-Communist hysteria that followed the loss of China, and belief in the domino theory." Deborah Welch Larson, *American Political Science Review*, Vol. 87, No. 3 (September 1993), pp. 812–813. We note that Khong would most likely agree with Larson's point, but observe that his study did not embrace the broader objective of explaining "American involvement in Vietnam." Levy's incisive explication and commentary on Khong's study is also coupled with a suggestion of a broader research design. See Jack S. Levy, "Learning from Experience in U.S. and Soviet Foreign Policy," in Manus I. Midlarsky, John A. Vasquez, and Paul V. Gladkov, eds., *From Rivalry to Cooperation: Russian and American Perspectives on the Post–Cold War Era* (New York: Harper Collins, 1994), pp. 56–86.

One may note also that Khong's use of psychological theories is limited to certain cognitive theories. He does not attempt to connect his analysis to the phenomenon of "decisional stress" often experienced by decision-makers when they must make important, highly consequential decisions under the three well-known cognitive limits on rationality: inadequate information, inadequate knowledge for evaluating likely outcomes of different options, and lack of a single utility function that encompasses the several values at stake. Resort to historical analogies is one way of coping with decisional stress. In his next to last chapter, Khong explains his failure to address this question by noting that psychological theories have focused mainly on cognitive, not emotional factors. Also, Khong does not clarify how his analogical explanation framework relates to conventional cost-benefit analysis. Finally, it would be perhaps difficult for readers to understand the case Khong makes (pp. 10–11, 48–50) that Vietnam decision-making qualifies as a "most likely" case for testing hypotheses that historical analogies are used by policymakers for justification and advocacy, and as a "least likely" case for hypotheses which hold that analogies actually influence decisions taken.

25. Volker Rittberger, ed., *German Foreign Policy Since Unification: Theories and Case Studies* (Manchester: Manchester University Press, 2001). See particularly pp. 1–7, 299–321.

To conduct an empirical test of these three theories, the authors selected four issue areas that provide a representative cross-section of German foreign policy and that include both issues of "high politics" and
"low politics." These are German security policy within NATO; German
constitutional policy vis-à-vis the European Union; German foreign trade
policy within the European Union and the General Agreement on Tariffs
and Trade (GATT); and German human rights policy within the United
Nations. The research design included a before-after component that enabled the authors to evaluate the extent to which post-unification Germany changed its foreign policy behavior. Three independent variables
were included in the research design: power position, domestic interests,
and social norms. The methodology of structured, focused comparison
was employed in a series of case studies, each consisting of one or more
observations of *post*-unification policy on a particular issue and one or
more observations of *pre*-unification foreign policy on the same issue.

The congruence procedure was the centerpiece of the research design. The degree of consistency between a theory's predictions and the
observed values of the dependent variable was regarded as the most important indication of its explanatory power. This test was employed in a
differentiated manner that took into account tough tests and easy ones,
dealt with instances in which several theories made correct predictions,
and evaluated evidence based on additional observable implications a
theory was able to make. These additional observable implications were
studied via process-tracing, except for the implications of neorealism,
which does not lend itself to the process-tracing procedure.

Post-unification German foreign policy was found to display a mix-
ture of continuity and change. The evaluation of each theory called attention to its successful and unsuccessful predictions. The study found that
the eight cases examined strongly disconfirmed neorealism. The modified variant of neorealism did better. Social norms associated with
constructivist theory turned out to yield the best explanation of post-
unification German foreign policy, capturing both cases of continuity and
change as well as hard and easy tests. Liberalism's explanatory power
seemed to depend on the policy network structure that dominated in a
particular issue.[26]

Use of the Congruence Method in Studies of Deductive Theories that "Black Box" Decision-Making and Strategic Interaction

The congruence method can be useful also in the studies that work with
deductive theories that "black box" decision-making or strategic interac-

---

26. Ibid.

tion. Such studies employ a deductive theory to make predictions of outcomes in a single case or in a number of cases too few to permit statistical analysis. The research objective is often to test the performance of the deductive theory in question or to identify and bound its scope. If its performance proves to be inadequate—i.e., a number of incorrect predictions occur that can not be attributed to measurement errors—then one must ask whether the internal structure or contents of the theory are flawed and in need of reformulation. If so, the congruence method may be used to develop and refine the provisional theory.

These uses of the congruence method have been applied in international relations studies that work with structural-realist, rational choice, or game theories, all of which involve black box decision-making and strategic interaction, and also in studies that directly examine internal decision-making processes and the dynamics of strategic interaction. Use of the congruence method (though it is not known by this name) also is employed in small-n case studies that focus on theories of macro-political processes.

What is involved in using the congruence method in research projects which, as an initial simplification, black box or set aside internal processes of decision-making or strategic interaction? The first step is to formulate a version of the general deductive theory being employed—whether it be structural realism, rational choice, or game theory—that addresses more specifically the phenomenon being studied. This first step can be noted in studies such as those by Barry Posen, Vinod Aggarwal, David Yoffie, and Bruce Bueno de Mesquita.[27]

A second step is to identify historical cases whose outcomes will enable the investigator to apply the congruence method to test, assess, or refine the theory's predictive and explanatory power. Selection of cases is a critical decision in research design and it is discussed in detail in Chapter 4. Suffice it to note here that the investigator must avoid "selection bias" and be clear about whether a representative sample of the universe of cases of the phenomenon is necessary to satisfy the research objective and to reach an acceptable statement of the nature and scope of the findings. It is a common misunderstanding to assume or to insist that all small-n studies must somehow satisfy the requirement of a representative sample, and that the findings of a small-n study must be capable

---

27.   Barry R. Posen, *The Sources of Military Doctrine: France, Britain, and Germany Between the World Wars* (Ithaca, N.Y.: Cornell University Press, 1984); Aggarwal, *Liberal Protectionism;* Yoffie, *Power and Protectionism;* and Bruce Bueno de Mesquita, *The War Trap* (New Haven, Conn.: Yale University Press, 1981).

of projecting a valid probability distribution of outcomes for the entire universe.[28]

A third step is to match the predictions and expectations of the theory with the outcomes of the cases to see if they are consistent. If consistency is noted, then the investigator should address the several questions that were discussed earlier in this chapter regarding the causal significance that can be properly inferred from congruence. Outcomes not consistent with the predictions and expectations of the theory should receive special attention. How can one account for these discrepant cases? How can the possibility of measurement error be correctly assessed, and how can that be distinguished from the possibility that the internal composition and logic of the deductive theory are faulty?

A fourth step is possible and we strongly recommend that it be undertaken. Process-tracing of the case should be employed for several purposes: to help assess whether the consistency noted is spurious or causal; to identify any possible intervening causal process that connects the deductive theory with the case outcomes; and to provide an explanation for deviant cases that the theory failed to predict correctly. Process-tracing was used for these purposes by Aggarwal, Yoffie, and Posen, but not by Bueno de Mesquita.

AGGARWAL'S STUDY OF TRADE REGIMES

Aggarwal's study was one of a number of studies in political economy undertaken by Ph.D. students at Stanford under the direction of Robert Keohane (with Alexander George serving as a second reader). The starting point for all these studies was the assumption that the best way to study problems of trade relations between the United States and its weaker trading partners (and also to study the development and possible transformation of international trade regimes) was to adapt structural realist theory for the specific issue-area and actors involved. (This assumption was substantially modified as students encountered the problem of developing causal inferences and explanations for outcomes of trading episodes.) The initial research design focused on the relative power advantage the United States possessed which, according to structural realist theory, should lead to outcomes favorable to the United States. When such favorable outcomes in trading episodes occurred, it might be assumed that realist theory provided an adequate explanation and could have predicted these outcomes.

However, Aggarwal realized that mere congruence of outcomes with

---

28.   This misconception is addressed in more detail in Chapter 1, "Case Studies and Theory Development."

the general predictions and expectations of structural-realist theory did not necessarily provide a reliable explanation—that it was not an adequate test of the theory. Hence, Aggarwal engaged in process-tracing of each trading episode to ascertain whether he could identify a causal process that supported the role attributed to the structural variable. He felt it necessary to proceed in this fashion since it was not possible to undertake a large-N statistical study for this purpose. In addition, to understand and explain a number of those deviant cases in which the outcomes were *not* as favorable to the United States as its relative power advantage would have predicted, Aggarwal undertook a detailed analysis of the dynamics of the trading interaction and engaged in process-tracing to identify how the actors' decision-making and their strategic interaction in bargaining with each other might have led to an outcome not predicted by the theory.

Hence, Aggarwal was not satisfied to settle for the familiar fall-back position that structural realism is a probabilistic theory that does not claim to predict all cases successfully. Instead, Aggarwal attempted to explain discrepant cases and, if possible, to enrich and differentiate the theory. He referred to these cases as anomalies and argued that in the absence of a large number of cases to permit statistical analysis, "a second approach, known as 'process-tracing,' is an effective and potentially superior substitute. In process-tracing, the decision-making procedure in a negotiation is systematically analyzed with an eye to identifying the degree to which participants appear to respond to international systemic or other constraints."[29]

As the third and fourth steps emphasize, one should not be satisfied merely with a finding of consistency. Since the data required for adequate process-tracing are often not available, the checks regarding the causal significance of consistency noted earlier should be undertaken.

Congruence and Structural-Realist Theory

Studies that use structural-realist theory to predict outcomes are in special need of supplementary process-tracing or other checks. Kenneth Waltz's structural-realist theory is not a fully developed deductive theory; it can make only very general probabilistic predictions, since it does not quantify its probabilistic claims. Strictly speaking, a finding that the outcomes of cases are consistent with probabilistic predictions is not an adequate basis for assuming a causal relationship exists *unless* other explanations for the outcomes are considered and eliminated. And even

---

29. Aggarwal, *Liberal Protectionism*, p. 16.

when support for some kind of causal relationship can be mustered, one must still establish whether the independent variable is either a necessary or sufficient condition for the outcome in question, and how much it contributes to a full explanation of the outcome.

In other words, partial, incomplete deductive theories based on structural realism often lack "operationalization"—i.e., the fine-tuning and specification of the theory that permits case-specific rather than general probabilistic prediction of outcomes for each of the cases examined. The only fully operationalized variant of a structural realist theory of which we are aware is that developed by Bruce Bueno de Mesquita in *The War Trap*.

In striking contrast to *The War Trap* is the case that Christopher Achen and Duncan Snidal offered for rational deterrence theory. They made no effort to formulate the level of specification and refinement of the theory needed to make concrete predictions; therefore, the theory they provided was a quite primitive and nonfalsifiable deductive theory. That is, any outcome—whether deterrence succeeded or failed in particular cases —would be "explainable" by the vague rational deterrence theory they espoused. Even more disconcerting in the argument these authors made on behalf of the superiority of a rational deterrence theory was their failure to address the requirements of a full-fledged, operationalized deductive theory.[30]

Even when operationalized, deductive theories may fail to identify or provide a satisfactory account of the causal mechanism that links the theory to the outcomes in question. Proponents of deductive theories based on rational choice or game theory might say that a causal mechanism is implicit in the internal logic of such deductive theories and needs no further explication or demonstration if the theory generates successful predictions. Yet some proponents of rational choice theory have recently emphasized the need to couple and integrate the rational choice framework with detailed case studies that make use of process-tracing in order to establish intervening causal processes.[31]

---

30. Christopher H. Achen and Duncan Snidal, "Rational Deterrence Theory and Comparative Case Studies," *World Politics,* Vol. 41, No. 2 (January 1989), pp. 143–169. Critical observations of their article made here draw on Alexander L. George and Richard Smoke in their rebuttal of the Achen-Snidal article and were reinforced by George Downs in his characterization of their article as a "weak" version of deterrence theory and emphasizing the requirements for developing a "strong" version. The three articles by Achen and Snidal, George and Smoke, and Downs appear in *World Politics,* Vol. 41, No. 2 (January 1989).

31. Robert Bates et al., *Analytic Narratives* (Princeton, N.J.: Princeton University Press, 1998).

We stated earlier that the congruence method applies not only to theories that focus on the causal role of beliefs in decision-making but, as has now been discussed, also to deductive theories associated with the structural realist theory of international relations and more generally to rational choice and game theories.

Chapter 10

Process-Tracing and Historical Explanation

In the last few decades process-tracing has achieved increasing recognition and widespread use by political scientists and political sociologists. David Collier observes that "refinements in methods of small-n analysis have substantially broadened the range of techniques available to comparative researchers." He emphasizes, as we do, that "within-case comparisons are critical to the viability of small-n analysis" and have contributed to the move "to historicize the social sciences."[1] Similarly, Charles Tilly emphasized the importance of what we call process-tracing in urging that theoretical propositions should be based not on "large-N statistical analysis" but on "relevant, verifiable causal stories resting in differing chains of cause-effect relations whose efficacy can be demonstrated independently of those stories."[2]

David Laitin emphasizes the importance of theoretically oriented narratives and process-tracing which, he states, have made a "fundamental contribution . . . in finding regularities through juxtaposition of historical cases. . . . If statistical work addresses questions of propensities, narratives address the questions of process."[3] Jack Goldstone urges that

1. David Collier, "The Comparative Method: Two Decades of Change," in Ada Finifter, ed., *Political Science: The State of the Discipline* (Washington, D.C.: American Political Science Association, 1993), pp. 8–11; 110–112.

2. Charles Tilly, "Means and Ends of Comparison in Macrosociology," *Comparative Social Research*, Vol. 16 (1997), pp. 43–53. The quotation is from p. 48.

3. David D. Laitin, "Comparative Politics: The State of the Subdiscipline," paper presented at the Annual Meeting of the American Political Science Association in Washington, D.C., September 2000, which appears in Helen V. Milner and Ira Katznelson, eds., *Political Science: The State of the Discipline* (New York: Norton, 2002). Quoted material is from pp. 2–5.

process-tracing be emphasized in efforts to explain macrohistorical phenomena: "To identify the process, one must perform the difficult cognitive feat of figuring out *which* aspects of the initial conditions observed, in
conjunction with *which simple principles* of the many that may be at work,
would have *combined* to generate the observed sequence of events."[4]

Another leading contributor to comparative politics, Peter Hall, also
stresses the importance of "theory-oriented process-tracing." Hall observes that "we might usefully turn to the techniques that George (1979)
initially termed 'process-tracing' [which] points us in the right methodological direction." He concludes, "In short, process-tracing is a methodology well-suited to testing theories in a world marked by multiple interaction effects, where it is difficult to explain outcomes in terms of two or
three independent variables—precisely the world that more and more social scientists believe we confront."[5]

Process-tracing finds a place also in the constructivist approach. Alexander Wendt recognizes that the core of descriptions of causal mechanisms is "process-tracing, which in social science ultimately requires case
studies and historical scholarship."[6]

This chapter considerably develops our analyses of process-tracing,
dating back to 1979. The process-tracing method attempts to identify the
intervening causal process—the causal chain and causal mechanism—between an independent variable (or variables) and the outcome of the dependent variable. Suppose that a colleague shows you fifty numbered
dominoes standing upright in a straight line with their dots facing the
same way on the table in a room, but puts a blind in front of the dominoes so that only number one and number fifty are visible. She then
sends you out of the room and when she calls you back in you observe
that domino number one and domino number fifty are now lying flat
with their tops pointing in the same direction; that is, they co-vary. Does
this mean that either domino caused the other to fall? Not necessarily.
Your colleague could have pushed over only dominoes number one and
fifty, or bumped the table in a way that only these two dominoes fell, or

---

4. Jack Goldstone, *Revolution and Rebellion in the Early Modern World* (Berkeley: University of California Press, 1991), pp. 50–62. Emphasis is in the original.

5. Peter A. Hall, "Aligning Ontology and Methodology in Comparative Politics,"
paper presented at the Annual Meeting of the American Political Science Association
in Washington, D.C., September 2000, pp. 14, 18.

6. Alexander Wendt, *Social Theory of International Politics* (Cambridge: Cambridge
University Press, 1999), pp. 80–85, 90, 152–156, 370–373. An endorsement of process-tracing appears also in John Ruggie's discussion of the concept of "narrative explanatory protocol," "What Makes the World Hang Together?" *International Organization*, Vol. 52, No. 4 (Autumn 1998), pp. 855–885.

that all the dominoes fell at once. You must remove the blind and look at the intervening dominoes, which give evidence on potential processes. Are they, too, lying flat? Do their positions suggest they fell in sequence rather than being bumped or shaken? Did any reliable observers hear the sound of dominoes slapping one another in sequence? From the positions of all the dominoes, can we eliminate rival causal mechanisms, such as earthquakes, wind, or human intervention? Do the positions of the fallen dominoes indicate whether the direction of the sequence was from number one to number fifty or the reverse?

These are the kinds of questions researchers ask as they use process-tracing to investigate social phenomena. Tracing the processes that may have led to an outcome helps narrow the list of potential causes. Yet even with close observation, it may be difficult to eliminate all potential rival explanations but one, especially when human agents are involved—for they may be doing their best to conceal causal processes. But process-tracing forces the investigator to take equifinality into account, that is, to consider the alternative paths through which the outcome could have occurred, and it offers the possibility of mapping out one or more potential causal paths that are consistent with the outcome and the process-tracing evidence in a single case. With more cases, the investigator can begin to chart the repertoire of causal paths that lead to a given outcome and the conditions under which they occur—that is, to develop a typological theory.

Process-tracing is an indispensable tool for theory testing and theory development not only because it generates numerous observations within a case, but because these observations must be linked in particular ways to constitute an explanation of the case. It is the very lack of independence among these observations that makes them a powerful tool for inference. The fact that the intervening variables, if truly part of a causal process, should be connected in particular ways is what allows process-tracing to reduce the problem of indeterminacy (the problem often misidentified in case studies as the degrees of freedom problem).

Process-tracing is fundamentally different from methods based on covariance or comparisons across cases. In using theories to develop explanations of cases through process-tracing, *all* the intervening steps in a case must be as predicted by a hypothesis (as emphasized later in this chapter), or else that hypothesis must be amended—perhaps trivially or perhaps fundamentally—to explain the case. It is not sufficient that a hypothesis be consistent with a statistically significant number of intervening steps.

Process-tracing complements other research methods. While process-tracing can contribute to theory development and theory testing in ways that statistical analysis cannot (or can only with great difficulty), the two methods are *not* competitive. The two methods provide different and complementary bases for causal inference, and we need to develop ways to employ both in well-designed research programs on important, complex problems.[7]

Nor is process-tracing incompatible with rational choice approaches. Process-tracing is a research *method*; rational choice models are *theories*. Many proponents of the rational choice approach agree that its efficacy must be judged in part by empirical testing of decision-making processes; process-tracing provides the opportunity to do so. In fact, scholars are using process-tracing within a general rational choice framework to construct detailed historical case studies (or analytic narratives).[8] Elements of a rational choice approach have been used, together with other theories, in developing rounded, more comprehensive explanations of complex events.[9] Similarly, case study methods can be used to test and refine theoretical insights built from deductive frameworks developed in game theory.[10]

However, even when rational choice theory or other formal models predict outcomes with a fairly high degree of accuracy, they do not constitute acceptable causal explanations unless they demonstrate (to the extent the evidence allows) that their posited or implied causal mechanisms were in fact operative in the predicted cases. Adequate causal explanations require empirically substantiated assertions about both the causal effects of independent variables and causal mechanisms or the observed processes that lead to outcomes.

Since process-tracing shares some of the basic features of historical explanation, we discuss the logic of historical explanation and indicate its similarities and differences with various types and uses of process-tracing.[11] Process-tracing takes several different forms, not all of which

---

7. Chapter 2 illustrates the use of both methods in one research program.

8. Robert Bates et al., *Analytic Narratives* (Princeton, N.J.: Princeton University Press, 1998).

9. See, for example, Jack S. Levy, "The Role of Crisis Management in the Outbreak of World War I," in Alexander L. George, ed., *Avoiding War: Problems of Crisis Management* (Boulder, Colo.: Westview Press, 1991), pp. 62–102; and Brent Sterling, "Policy Choice During Limited War" (Ph.D. dissertation, Georgetown University, Washington D.C., 1998).

10. Steven Weber's book, summarized in the Appendix, "Studies That Illustrate Research Design," illustrates how this can be done. See also Glenn Snyder and Paul Diesing, *Conflict Among Nations* (Princeton, N.J.: Princeton University Press, 1977).

11. For a detailed, rounded discussion of the similarities and differences between historical explanation and uses of history by political scientists to develop and test generalizations of theoretical interest, see "Symposium: History and Theory," *International Security*, Vol. 22, No. 1 (Summer 1997), pp. 5–85.

are seen in historical studies; and process-tracing also has quite a few uses, several of which are not usually encountered in historical studies. These differences stem from process-tracing's emphasis on theory development and theory testing.

Process-tracing can sometimes be used for theory testing and is frequently valuable in theory development. Many theories available thus far on problems of interest in international relations, comparative politics, and U.S. politics are probabilistic statements that do not specify the causal process that leads from the independent variables associated with the theory to variance in the outcomes.[12] Such theories cannot generate predictions or hypotheses about what should be observed regarding this process.[13] For example, the first generation of studies on the democratic peace thesis were correlational studies that seem to indicate that democratic states do not fight each other or seldom do so. While a number of ideas were put forward as possible explanations for this phenomenon, they were not well enough specified to permit use of detailed process-tracing of individual cases to assess whether there is evidence of the causal process implied by these hypotheses.[14]

When case studies employing process-tracing cannot *test* theories that are underspecified, they can play an important role in *development* of theories.[15] Case studies can do so for the democratic peace theory, for example, by identifying one or more causal processes that explain how the fact that two states are both democratic enables them to avoid war-threatening disputes or to resolve disputes without engaging in war or threats of it.

The first part of this chapter briefly discusses several kinds of process-tracing and several kinds of causal processes. Various techniques of process-tracing can be employed for different purposes in different phases and approaches to theory development and testing. The second part of the chapter discusses a variety of uses of process-tracing, emphasizing its use in theory building and development. We also indicate how

---

12.   Theories can be tested in two different ways: by assessing the ability of a theory to predict outcomes, and by assessing the ability of a theory to predict the intervening causal process that leads to outcomes (which we discuss in the present chapter).

13.   Over the years, Jack Levy has published a number of articles that emphasize the failure of much early quantitative research on international relations to provide theoretical specification of possible intervening causal processes in correlational findings.

14.   For a review of this literature, see Miriam Fendius Elman, ed., *Paths to Peace: Is Democracy the Answer?* (Cambridge, Mass.: MIT Press, 1997).

15.   An example of research that makes this kind of contribution is Alexander George and Richard Smoke, *Deterrence in American Foreign Policy*, which is summarized in the Appendix, "Studies That Illustrate Research Design."

process-tracing can be an effective tool for testing theories that are well enough specified to make predictions about processes and causal mechanisms.[16] The chapter concludes by considering the similarities and differences between process-tracing and historical explanation.

Varieties of Process-Tracing

DETAILED NARRATIVE

The simplest variety of process-tracing takes the form of a detailed narrative or story presented in the form of a chronicle that purports to throw light on how an event came about. Such a narrative is highly specific and makes no explicit use of theory or theory-related variables. It may be supportable to some extent by explanatory hypotheses, but these remain tacit. Historical chronicles are a familiar example of what is at best an implicit, atheoretical type of process-tracing.[17]

It should be noted, however, that narrative accounts are not without value. Such atheoretical narratives may be necessary or useful steps toward the development of more theoretically oriented types of process-tracing. A well-constructed detailed narrative may suggest enough about the *possible* causal processes in a case so that a researcher can determine what type of process-tracing would be relevant for a more theoretically oriented explanation.

Some philosophers of history who have tried to clarify the "logic" of historical explanation reject the view that historical explanation requires no more than a description of a sequence of events. They maintain that each step or link in a causal process should be supported by an appropriate law—i.e., a statement of regularity (posited as either universalistic or probabilistic). At the same time, they acknowledge that such "laws" in microcausal explanations are usually so numerous and so platitudinous that historians do not bother to list them in the interest of maintaining the flow of the narrative, unless the explanation offered is controversial.[18]

---

16. This chapter cites a number of studies that have employed process-tracing; some thirty such examples are briefly summarized in the Appendix, "Studies That Illustrate Research Design."

17. Harry Eckstein labels this type of study as "configurative-ideographic"; Arend Lijphart refers to it as an "atheoretical case study." Harry Eckstein, "Case Study and Theory in Political Science," in Fred I. Greenstein and Nelson W. Polsby, eds., *Handbook of Political Science*, Vol. 7 (Reading, Mass.: Addison-Wesley Press, 1973), pp. 79–138; and Arend Lijphart, "Comparative Politics and the Comparative Method," *American Political Science Review*, Vol. 65, No. 3 (September 1971), pp. 682–693.

18. See Clayton Roberts, *The Logic of Historical Explanation* (University Park: Pennsylvania State University Press, 1996). See the discussion of historical explanation below.

USE OF HYPOTHESES AND GENERALIZATIONS

In a more analytical form of process-tracing, at least parts of the narrative are accompanied with explicit causal hypotheses highly specific to the case without, however, employing theoretical variables for this purpose or attempting to extrapolate the case's explanation into a generalization.

A still stronger form of explanation employs some generalizations—laws either of a deterministic or probabilistic character—in support of the explanation for the outcome; or it suggests that the specific historical explanation falls under a generalization or exemplifies a general pattern.

ANALYTIC EXPLANATION

A substantially different variety of process-tracing converts a historical narrative into an *analytical* causal explanation couched in explicit theoretical forms. The extent to which a historical narrative is transformed into a theoretical explanation can vary. The explanation may be deliberately selective, focusing on what are thought to be particularly important parts of an adequate or parsimonious explanation; or the partial character of the explanation may reflect the investigator's inability to specify or theoretically ground all steps in a hypothesized process, or to find data to document every step.

MORE GENERAL EXPLANATION

In another variety of process-tracing, the investigator constructs a general explanation rather than a detailed tracing of a causal process. The investigator may do this either because the data or theory and laws necessary for a detailed explanation are lacking or because an explanation couched at a higher level of generality and abstraction is preferred for the research objective. A decision to do so is consistent with the familiar practice in political science research of moving up the ladder of abstraction.[19] Such process-tracing does *not* require a minute, detailed tracing of a causal sequence. One may opt for a higher level of generality of explanations in within-case analysis, just as researchers using statistical methods often create larger cells either to obtain categories of broader theoretical significance or to obtain enough cases (in a smaller number of larger cells) to permit statistical analysis.

Process-tracing can be applied also to the explanation of macro-phenomena, as it often is in economics, as well as to microprocesses. The

---

19. Giovanni Sartori, "Concept Misformation in Comparative Politics," *American Political Science Review,* Vol. 64, No. 4 (December 1970), pp. 853–864; and David Collier and Steven Levitsky, "Democracy With Adjectives: Concept Innovation in Comparative Research," *World Politics,* Vol. 49, No. 3 (April 1997), pp. 430–451.

method of process-tracing does not necessarily focus on the individual decision-making level of analysis.

Forms of Causal Processes

The process-tracing technique must be adapted to the nature of the causal process thought to characterize the phenomenon being investigated. Several different types of causal processes can be distinguished.[20] The simplest form is linear causality, a straightforward, direct chain of events that characterizes simple phenomena. However, many or most phenomena of interest in international relations and comparative politics are characterized by more complex causality, for which the assumption of linearity is misplaced.

In a more complex form of causality the outcome flows from the *convergence* of several conditions, independent variables, or causal chains. An example of this type of complex explanation occurs in Theda Skocpol's study of revolutions referred to in Chapter 8.

A still more complex form involves *interacting* causal variables that are not independent of each other. Case study methods provide opportunities for inductively identifying complex interaction effects. In addition, typological theories (discussed in Chapter 11) can capture and represent interaction effects particularly well. Statistical methods can also capture interaction effects, but they are usually limited to interactions that reflect simple and well-known mathematical forms.

Another type of causal process to which the technique of process-tracing can be applied occurs in cases that consist of a sequence of events, some of which foreclose certain paths in the development and steer the outcome in other directions. Such processes are *path-dependent*. A different kind of within-case analysis and process-tracing is needed for dealing with phenomena of this kind. The investigator must recognize the possibility of path dependency in order to construct a valid explanation. Path dependency can be dealt with in several ways, for example by identifying key decision points or branching points in a longitudinal case (as in Jack Levy's study of developments during the six-week crisis that led to World War I and in Brent Sterling's study of policy choices during limited wars).[21] However, the investigator must avoid assuming that certain outcomes were necessarily excluded once and for all by the resolu-

---

20.   For a similar discussion of different types of causal relations, see Robert Jervis, *System Effects: Complexity in Political and Social Life* (Princeton, N.J.: Princeton University Press, 1997), pp. 34–60.

21.   Levy ("The Role of Crisis Management in the Outbreak of World War I") and Sterling ("Policy Choice During Limited War") articles.

tion of an earlier branching point. One or another final outcome may have become only less likely at that stage, but the way in which subsequent branching points were resolved may have increased its probability.

Such considerations are particularly relevant when the branching points are decisions taken by policymakers. A decision taken at one point that reduces the likelihood of achieving a desired policy goal may be recouped by changes in the situation that give policymakers a second chance to accomplish a desired goal or to avoid a poor outcome. In brief, path dependency at early points in the development of a longitudinal case should not be assumed to determine the outcome. Process-tracing can assess to what extent and how possible outcomes of a case were restricted by the choices made at decision points along the way. Assessments of this kind may be facilitated by counterfactual analysis.

Perhaps enough has been said to emphasize and illustrate that there are a number of distinctively different types of process-tracing just as there are different types of causal processes. *The challenge in using process-tracing is to choose a variant of it that fits the nature of the causal process embedded in the phenomenon being investigated.*

Uses of Process-Tracing

Case studies are useful, as Harry Eckstein and Arend Lijphart noted many years ago, at all stages in the formation, development, and testing of theories.[22] Moreover, deductive theories (including rational choice theories) and empirical theories derived inductively can be employed using one or another type of process-tracing. Those who cite Achen and Snidal's critique of existing case studies of deterrence often overlook the

---

22.   Both Eckstein and Lijphart offer typologies of case studies; their terminology differs but the types they identify are similar with two exceptions. Lijphart does not designate a category for Eckstein's "plausibility probe," and he adds the quite important "deviant case" for which Eckstein does not make explicit provision. The similarities and differences between their listings of types of cases are as follows:

Lijphart	*Eckstein*
"atheoretical case study" <————————————————>	"configurative-ideographic"
"interpretative case study" <———————————————>	"disciplined-configurative"
"hypothesis-generating case study" <—————————>	"heuristic"
(?) <———————————————————————————————————————>	"plausibility probe"
"theory-confirming case study" <————|	
	|————>	"crucial case" and "tough tests"
"theory-infirming case study" <————|	
"deviant case study" <—————————————————————>	(?)

authors' emphasis on the critical importance of case studies for theory development and testing:

> Although many of our comments have criticized how case studies are used in practice, we emphatically believe they are essential to the development and testing of social science theory. . . . In international relations, only case studies provide the intensive empirical analysis that can find previously unnoticed causal factors and historical patterns. . . . The [case study] analyst is able to identify plausible causal variables, a task essential to theory construction and testing. . . . Indeed, analytic theory cannot do without case studies. Because they are simultaneously sensitive to data and theory, case studies are more useful for these purposes than any other methodological tool.[23]

The study of macro- as well as microlevel phenomena benefits from uses of process-tracing. The utility of process-tracing is not restricted to the study of the intentional behavior of actors and organizations; it is also applicable, as in Theda Skocpol's study of *States and Revolution*, to investigations of any hypothesized causal process. An interest in studying process is to be seen also in the use of simulations, as in the recent work of Bruce Bueno de Mesquita and Frans Stokman.[24] And, as is increasingly clear, process-tracing is particularly important for generating and assessing evidence on causal mechanisms.[25]

More generally, process-tracing offers an alternative way for making causal inferences when it is not possible to do so through the method of controlled comparison. In fact, process-tracing can serve to make up for the limitations of a particular controlled comparison. When it is not possible to find cases similar in every respect but one—the basic requirement of controlled comparisons—one or more of the *several* independent variables identified may have causal impact. Process-tracing can help to assess whether each of the potential causal variables in the imperfectly matched cases can, or cannot, be ruled out as having causal significance. If all but one of the independent variables that differ between the two

---

23. Christopher H. Achen and Duncan Snidal, "Rational Deterrence Theory and Comparative Case Studies," *World Politics*, Vol. 41, No. 2 (January 1989), pp. 167–168.

24. Bruce Bueno de Mesquita and Frans N. Stokman, eds., *European Community Decision Making: Models, Applications, and Comparisons* (New Haven, Conn.: Yale University Press, 1994).

25. Scientific realists who have emphasized that explanation requires not merely correlational data, but also knowledge of intervening causal mechanisms, have not yet had much to say on methods for generating such knowledge. The method of process-tracing is relevant for generating and analyzing data on the causal mechanisms, or processes, events, actions, expectations, and other intervening variables, that link putative causes to observed effects.

cases can be ruled out via a process-tracing procedure that finds no evidence that they were operating in the two cases, a stronger (though still not definitive) basis exists for attributing causal significance to the remaining variable. The case for it is strengthened, of course, if process-tracing uncovers evidence of the role of that variable in the process leading to the outcome.[26]

In the same way, process-tracing can ameliorate the limitations of John Stuart Mill's methods of agreement and difference. For example, process-tracing offers a way of assessing *hypotheses* regarding causal relations suggested by preliminary use of Mill's methods, as in Theda Skocpol's study.[27] More generally, process-tracing can identify single *or different* paths to an outcome, point out variables that were otherwise left out in the initial comparison of cases, check for spuriousness, and permit causal inference on the basis of a few cases or even a single case. These potential contributions of process-tracing make case studies worthwhile even when sufficient cases exist for use of statistical methods.

Process-tracing may be a unique tool for discovering whether the phenomenon being investigated is characterized by equifinality (or "multiple convergence" as it is referred to by some scholars). Process-tracing offers the possibility of identifying different causal paths that lead to a similar outcome in different cases. These cases, in turn, can serve as building blocks for empirical, inductive construction of a typological theory.[28] Process-tracing encourages the investigator to be sensitive to the possibility of equifinality. Case studies employing process-tracing are particularly useful as a supplement in large-N statistical analyses, which are likely to overlook the possibility of equifinality and settle for a statement of a probabilistic finding regarding only one causal path at work.

Process-tracing is particularly useful for obtaining an explanation for deviant cases, those that have outcomes not predicted or explained adequately by existing theories. Deviant cases are frequently encountered in large-N studies and usually noted as such without an effort to explain why they are deviant. Process-tracing of deviant cases offers an opportunity to differentiate and enrich the general theory. Witness, for example, the exemplary study of the International Typographical Union (I.T.U.) by

---

26. See James Lee Ray, *Democracies and International Conflict: An Evaluation of the Democratic Peace Proposition* (Columbia: University of South Carolina Press, 1995), pp. 158–200.

27. For discussion, see Chapter 8.

28. For a detailed discussion of equifinality and typological theory, see Chapters 8 and 11.

Seymour Martin Lipset, Martin Trow, and James S. Coleman. They noted that the record of the I.T.U. contradicted the "iron law of oligarchy" advanced by Robert Michels in his classic study, *Political Parties*, which argued that inherent in any large-scale social organization were motivations and means that led leaders of its bureaucratic structure to place protection and exercise of their position ahead of commitment to democratic internal procedures. Contradicting the generalization, the I.T.U. governed itself through an elaborate and largely effective democratic system. The I.T.U., as Lipset describes it in a subsequent "biography" of their study, was an example of what he later learned that Paul Lazarsfeld called a deviant case. The authors' study of the I.T.U. investigated whether there were new or specific factors present in this deviant case that explained its departure from the iron law of oligarchy. A historical-structural study of the I.T.U. employing survey research data and making some use of process-tracing uncovered causal mechanisms and social and psychological processes that provided an explanation for the special deviant character of the union.[29]

The identification and analysis of deviant cases and of cases characterized by equifinality are useful for developing *contingent generalizations* that identify the conditions under which alternative outcomes occur. The importance of developing conditional generalizations of limited scope, a form of middle-range theory, is emphasized at various points in the present study.[30]

In developing a theory about a particular phenomenon such as deterrence via analytic induction, as in the Alexander George and Richard Smoke study (summarized in the Appendix, "Studies That Illustrate Research Design"), process-tracing provided an explanation for each of the small number of cases examined. At the outset, each case was regarded as a possible deviant case. When explanations for the outcome of individual cases vary, the results can be cumulated and contribute to the development of a rich, differentiated theory about that phenomenon.

---

29. Seymour M. Lipset, Martin Trow, and James S. Coleman, *Union Democracy* (Glencoe, Ill.: Free Press, 1956). Lipset later provided a remarkably interesting account of the origins and development of the study in "The Biography of a Research Project: Union Democracy," in Philip E. Hammond, ed., *Sociologists at Work*, (New York: Doubleday Anchor Books, 1967), pp. 111–139.

Another example of deviant case analysis is illustrated in Lijphart's *Politics of Accommodation*, summarized in the Appendix. Stephen Van Evera emphasizes the importance of studying deviant cases, which he refers to as "outlier" cases, for theory development. See Stephen Van Evera, *Guide to Methods for Students of Political Science* (Ithaca, N.Y.: Cornell University Press, 1997), pp. 22–23, 69.

30. See, for example, Chapter 12.

Assessing Predictions

If a theory is sufficiently developed that it generates or implies predictions about causal processes that lead to outcomes, then process-tracing can assess the predictions of the theory. In this use, process-tracing evidence tests whether the observed processes among variables in a case match those predicted or implied by the theory. To be sure, as noted earlier in this chapter, many available theories have not been developed to the point that they are capable of making predictions about causal processes. Under these circumstances, process-tracing of cases relevant to the theory can identify causal processes not yet identified by the theory. In this way, process-tracing contributes not to the *testing* of the theory, but to its further *development*.

Assessing Alternative Hypothesized Processes

We note in particular that process-tracing needs to consider the possibility of alternative processes that lead to the outcome in question. It is important to examine the process-tracing evidence not only on the hypothesis of interest, but on alternative hypotheses that other scholars, policy experts, and historians have proposed. Too often, researchers focus great attention on the process-tracing evidence on the hypothesis that interests them most, while giving the process-tracing evidence that bears on alternative explanations little attention or using it only to explain variance that is not adequately explained by the hypothesis of interest. This can create a strong confirmation bias, and it can overstate the causal weight that should be accorded to the hypothesis of interest.

Lawrence Mohr has given a useful account of the need to avoid confirmation bias, following Michael Scriven's *modus operandi* method and his metaphor of a detective:

... when X causes Y it may operate so as to leave a "signature," or traces of itself that are diagnostic. In other words, one can tell when it was X that caused Y because certain other things that happened and are observed unequivocally point to X. At the same time, one knows the signature of other possible causes of Y and one may observe that those traces did *not* occur. By using this technique, one can make a strong inference that X either did or did not cause Y in a certain case. For the present purpose, moreover, one notes in passing the affinity of this approach for the study of a single case. The kind of example of the *modus operandi* approach that is frequently given reminds one of the work of a detective or a diagnostician.[31]

---

31.   Lawrence B. Mohr, "The Reliability of the Case Study as a Source of Informa-

Yet as Mohr himself points out, the theory in question may not leave an observable signature. It is also possible that the predictions about causal process attributed to, or claimed by, the theory may be questionable or ambiguous. Moreover, proving the negative and demonstrating that a particular process did not occur can be notoriously difficult. Both detectives and researchers face these difficulties. But the main difficulty may be that the theory is not sufficiently specified to allow one to identify confidently a causal process it predicts or is capable of predicting.

As Mohr's detective metaphor suggests, when well-specified theories are available, process testing can proceed forward, from potential causes to effects; backward, from effects to their possible causes; or both. The use of process-tracing to verify the predictions of a theory should also ordinarily involve attempts to test and eliminate alternative causal processes (derived from other theories) that might lead to the same outcome. For example, the detective usually pursues several suspects and clues, constructing possible chronologies and causal paths backward from the crime scene and forward from the last known whereabouts of the suspects. With theories, as with suspects, the evidence might not be sufficient to eliminate all but one. In addition, alternative theories and the causal processes they specify may be complementary rather than mutually exclusive. Since more than one theory may be consistent with the process-tracing evidence, several may have contributed to the observed effect or even overdetermined it.

On the other hand, when theories make genuinely competing process predictions, the process-tracing evidence may be incomplete in ways that do not permit firm conclusions on which theory fits better. The detective's colleague, the district attorney, would remind us that a potential causal path cannot explain a case if it does not establish an uninterrupted causal path from the alleged cause to the observed outcome. The inaccessibility of evidence at one point in this path does not disprove the cause, but does make it harder to eliminate competing theories beyond a reasonable doubt.

ASSESSING THE CAUSAL POWER OF AN INDEPENDENT VARIABLE

Most case studies are outcome-oriented; they focus on explaining variance in the dependent variable. But when researchers or policymakers

tion," in Robert F. Coulam and Richard A. Smith, eds., *Advances in Information Processing in Organizations*, Vol. 2 (Greenwich, Conn.: JAI Press Inc., 1985), pp. 65–97. The quote is from pp. 82–83. Mohr cites Michael Scriven, "Maximizing the Power of Causal Investigations: The Modus Operandi Method," in Gene V. Glass, ed., *Evaluation Studies Review Annual*, Vol. 1 (Beverly Hills, Calif.: Sage, 1976), pp. 101–118.

wish to assess the causal power of a particular factor—such as an independent variable that policymakers can manipulate—they have an interest in exploring the contingent conditions under which similarity or variance in the independent variable leads to different outcomes.[32] Research on the strategy of coercive diplomacy, for example, treats it as an independent variable and develops a typology of such strategies to investigate variations in outcome of these strategies.

We differ with many methodologists in that we argue that a theory can be derived or modified based on the evidence within a case, and still be tested against *new facts* or *new evidence* within the same case, as well as against other cases. Detectives do this all the time—clues lead them to develop a new theory about a case, which leads them to expect some evidence that in the absence of the new theory would have been wildly unexpected, and the corroboration of this evidence is seen as strong confirmation of the theory.

This process relies on Bayesian logic—the more unique and unexpected the new evidence, the greater its corroborative power. For example, in *The Limits of Safety*, Scott Sagan made process-tracing predictions on particular kinds of evidence regarding nuclear accidents that would be true if his theory were true, but that would have been highly unlikely if the alternative explanations were true.[33] Another example comes from research on schizophrenia. When researchers looking at brain chemistry proposed a chemical mechanism that might help explain schizophrenia, they unexpectedly found that this same chemical mechanism was involved in the brain's reaction to the inhalation of cigarette smoke. The proposed mechanism thus appeared to explain the long-known but unexplained fact that some schizophrenics tend to be chain-smokers. In other words, schizophrenics may have unconsciously been using chain-smoking to ameliorate the brain chemistry abnormalities that caused their schizophrenia. As the researchers were not looking for or expecting an explanation of schizophrenic's chain-smoking, this finding is a heuristically independent confirmation. Although the study involved many schizophrenics, the logic of this kind of confirmation does not derive

---

32. Here, we can use process-tracing inductively. It may even be possible to study all known cases in which a variable assumed a certain value, if the number of such cases is manageably small. If the number of cases is large, then the researcher may choose to narrow the context to cases in a particular country or time period, or he may choose cases in ways that achieve a specified range of values or variables that interact with the manipulable variable of interest.

33. Scott D. Sagan, *The Limits of Safety: Organization, Accidents, and Nuclear Weapons* (Princeton, N.J.: Princeton University Press, 1993).

from sample size and it applies in single cases of the kind that historians often investigate.[34]

VALIDITY OF CONCLUSIONS BASED ON SINGLE CASE STUDIES

Some political scientists argue that causal explanation *requires* case comparisons and that single-case studies have limited uses in theory building. James Lee Ray, for example, has argued that causal linkages cannot be identified within the context of one case.[35] Similarly, the authors of *Designing Social Inquiry* (*DSI*) argue that the single observation is not a useful technique for testing hypotheses or theories unless it can be compared to other observations by other researchers. They add that single cases cannot exclude alternative theories, and that their findings are limited by the possibility of measurement error, probabilistic causal mechanisms, and omitted variables.[36]

Indeed, the conclusions of single case studies are much stronger if they can be compared to other studies, but we suspect that most historians would join us in arguing that the limitations attributed to single case studies are not categorical. As *DSI* acknowledges, its view of the limits of single case studies is based in part on its definition of a case having only one observation on the dependent variable, and it notes that "since one case may actually contain many potential observations, pessimism is actually unjustified." Thus, while process-tracing may not be able to exclude all but one of the alternative theories in a single case, if some competing theories make similar process-tracing predictions, many single case studies can exclude at least some explanations. Process-tracing in single cases, for example, has the capacity for disproving claims that a single variable is necessary or sufficient for an outcome. Process-tracing in a single case can even exclude all explanations but one, if that explanation makes a process-tracing prediction that all other theories predict would be unlikely or even impossible.

As for measurement error, case study research is less prone to some kinds of measurement error because it can intensively assess a few variables along several qualitative dimensions, rather than having to quantify variables across many cases. Similarly, probabilistic causal mechanisms and the potential for omitted variables pose difficult challenges and limits to all research methods, but they do not necessarily invalidate

---

34.   Denise Grady, "Brain-Tied Gene Defect May Explain Why Schizophrenics Hear Voices," *New York Times*, January 21, 1997, p. C–3.

35.   Ray, *Democracy and International Conflict*, p. 132.

36.   Gary King, Robert O. Keohane, and Sidney Verba, *Designing Social Inquiry: Scientific Inference in Qualitative Research* (Princeton, N.J.: Princeton University Press, 1994), pp. 208, 210–211.

the use of single case studies. The inductive side of process-tracing may identify potential omitted variables through the intensive study of a few cases, and single case studies have changed entire research programs when they have impugned theories that failed to explain their most-likely cases.[37]

In before-after research designs, discussed in Chapter 8, the investigator can use process-tracing to focus on whether the variable of interest was causally linked to any change in outcome and to assess whether other independent variables that change over time might have been causal. In Donald Campbell's and Julian Stanley's terms, the potential confounding variables of greatest interest in a before-after design are maturation effects (the effects of a unit maturing from one developmental stage to another) and the effects of history (exogenous changes over time).[38] For example, in Andrew Bennett's comparison of the Soviet decision to intervene in Afghanistan in 1979 to the Soviet withdrawal from that country in 1989, he needed to look at several variables that had changed in the intervening decade. In particular, it was essential to use process-tracing to assess the respective roles of changes in Soviet leaders' views on the use of force, changes in the Soviet government (such as Mikhail Gorbachev's political reforms), and changes in Soviet interactions with other actors (such as the emergence of a U.S. policy of providing aid to the Afghan rebels). Process-tracing evidence in this study indicated that U.S. aid to Afghan rebels likely delayed a Soviet withdrawal, but made a more complete withdrawal more likely. Soviet democratization had little effect because it largely took place after 1989, and changes in Soviet ideas fit both the specifics and timing of the Soviet withdrawal and associated Soviet policies.[39]

We have emphasized the use of process-tracing to develop and refine many theories that are not yet capable of generating testable predictions about causal processes and outcomes. Such a procedure need not degenerate into an atheoretical and idiosyncratic enterprise. When a researcher uncovers a potential causal path for which there is no pre-existing theory, there are several possible approaches for converting this atheoretical finding into an analytical result couched in terms of theoretical variables. For example, deductive logic or study of other cases may suggest a gen-

37.   This point is emphasized by Ronald Rogowski, "The Role of Theory and Anomaly in Social Scientific Inference," *American Political Science Review,* Vol. 89, No. 2 (June 1995), p. 467.

38.   See Donald T. Campbell and Julian C. Stanley, *Experimental and Quasi-Experimental Designs for Research* (Chicago: Rand McNally College Publishing, 1973).

39.   Andrew Bennett, *Condemned to Repetition? The Rise, Fall, and Reprise of Soviet-Russian Military Intervention, 1973–1996* (Cambridge, Mass.: MIT Press, 1999).

eralizable theory that includes the novel causal path. If so, it may be possible to specify and operationalize that new theory and assess it by means of a plausibility probe involving other cases. Or the novel causal path may be identified as an exemplar of an existing theory that the investigator had overlooked or had thought to be irrelevant. The newly identified causal process may then contribute to the evaluation of the existing theory. Finally, it is possible that the novel causal path may have to remain ungeneralizable and unconnected to a useful theory for the time being.

The Limits of Process-Tracing

There are two key constraints on process-tracing. Process-tracing provides a strong basis for causal inference only if it can establish an uninterrupted causal path linking the putative causes to the observed effects, at the appropriate level(s) of analysis as specified by the theory being tested. Evidence that a single necessary intervening variable along this path was contrary to expectations strongly impugns any hypothesis whose causal effects rely on that causal path alone. The inferential and explanatory value of a causal path is weakened, though not negated, if the evidence on whether a certain step in the putative causal path conformed to expectations is simply unobtainable. Also, theories frequently do not make specific predictions on all of the steps in a causal process, particularly for complex phenomena. When data is unavailable or theories are indeterminate, process-tracing can reach only provisional conclusions.

Another potential problem for process-tracing is that there may be more than one hypothesized causal mechanism consistent with any given set of process-tracing evidence. The researcher then faces the difficult challenge of assessing whether alternative explanations are complementary in the case, or whether one is causal and the other spurious. Even if it is not possible to exclude all but one explanation for a case, it may be possible to exclude at least some explanations and thereby to draw inferences that are useful for theory-building or policymaking.

Olav Njølstad has emphasized this problem in case study research, noting that differing interpretations may arise for several reasons. First, competing explanations or interpretations could be equally consistent with the available process-tracing evidence, making it hard to determine whether both are at play and the outcome is overdetermined, whether the variables in competing explanations have a cumulative effect, or whether one variable is causal and the other spurious. Second, competing explanations may address different aspects of a case, and they may not be commensurate. Third, studies may be competing and commensurate, and they may simply disagree on the facts of the case.

Njølstad offers several useful suggestions on these problems, although we disagree with his suggestion that these are substantially different from the standard methodological advice offered in discussion in Chapter 3. These suggestions include: identifying and addressing factual errors, disagreements, and misunderstandings; identifying all potentially relevant theoretical variables and hypotheses; comparing various case studies of the same events that employ different theoretical perspectives (analogous to careful attention to all the alternative hypotheses in a single case study); identifying additional testable and observable implications of competing interpretations of a single case; and identifying the scope conditions for explanations of a case or category of cases.[40]

Summary on Process-Tracing

Process-tracing provides a common middle ground for historians interested in historical explanation and political scientists and other social scientists who are sensitive to the complexities of historical events but are more interested in theorizing about categories of cases as well as explaining individual cases. We do not regard process-tracing as a panacea for theory testing or theory development. It can require enormous amounts of information, and it is weakened when data is not accessible on key steps in a hypothesized process. In a particular case, limited data or underspecified theories (or both) may make it impossible to eliminate plausible alternative processes that fit the available evidence equally well. Both false positives, or processes that appear to fit the evidence even though they are not causal in the case at hand, and false negatives, processes that are causal but do not appear to be so, are still possible through measurement error or under-specified or misspecified theories.

Process-tracing has many advantages for theory development and theory testing, however, some of them unique. It is a useful method for generating and analyzing data on causal mechanisms. It can check for spuriousness and permit causal inference on the basis of a few cases or even a single case. It can greatly reduce the risks of the many potential inferential errors that could arise from the isolated use of Mill's methods of comparison, congruence testing, or other methods that rely on studying covariation. It can point out variables that were otherwise left out in the initial model or comparison of cases, and it can lead inductively to the explanation of deviant cases and the subsequent derivation of new hypotheses.

Process-tracing is particularly useful at addressing the problem of

---

40. Olav Njølstad, "Learning from History? Case Studies and the Limits to Theory-Building," in Nils Petter Gleditsch and Olav Njølstad, eds., *Arms Races: Technologies and Political Dynamics* (Newbury Park, Calif.: Sage, 1989), pp. 240–244.

equifinality by documenting alternative causal paths to the same outcomes and alternative outcomes for the same causal factor. In this way, it can contribute directly to the development of differentiated typological theories. Finally and most generally, process-tracing is the only observational means of moving beyond covariation alone as a source of causal inference. Whether it is pursued through case studies, correlations, experiments, or quasi-experiments, it is an invaluable method that should be included in every researcher's repertoire. It can contribute in ways that statistical methods can do only with great difficulty, and it is often worthwhile even when sufficient cases exist for the concurrent use of statistical methods. The power of process-tracing for both theory testing and heuristic development of new hypotheses accounts in part for the recent "historical turn" in the social sciences and the renewed interest in path-dependent historical processes.

However, we do not regard the within-case methods such as process-tracing as competitive with case comparisons or statistical analysis; rather, both within-case and cross-case analyses are important for advancing theory testing and theory development. The two methods provide different and complementary bases for causal inference. Case studies are superior at process-tracing, which relates to the causal mechanism component of causal explanation. Statistical studies are better at measuring the observed probability distribution relating measures of an independent variable to measures of outcomes across a large number of cases, which relates to the component of causal explanation defined as causal effects.[41] More attention needs to be given to developing ways in which researchers working with each method can complement one another in well-designed research programs, because it is seldom possible for a single researcher to apply both methods with a high level of proficiency. We turn now to a discussion of the logic of historical explanation.

Process-Tracing and Historical Explanation: Similarities and Differences

The question is sometimes asked whether process-tracing is similar to historical explanation and whether process-tracing is anything more than "good historical explanation." It is not unreasonable to respond to such

---

41. For a formal definition of causal effects, see Keohane, King, and Verba, *Designing Social Inquiry*, pp. 76–82. For an illustration of how case studies and statistical studies contribute complementary kinds of knowledge to a research program, see Chapters 1 and 2 and Andrew Bennett and Alexander L. George, "An Alliance of Statistical and Case Study Methods: Research on the Interdemocratic Peace," *Newsletter of the APSA Organized Section in Comparative Politics*, Vol. 9, No. 1 (Winter 1998), pp. 6–9.

an observation by asking what is a good historical explanation! We indicated earlier in this chapter how a process-tracing explanation differs from a historical narrative, and emphasized the desirability for certain research purposes of converting a purely historical account that implies or asserts a causal sequence into an analytical explanation couched in theoretical variables that have been identified in the research design. Some historians object that converting a rich historical explanation into an analytical one may lose important characteristics or the "uniqueness" of the case. This is true, and information loss does occur when this is done, and the investigator should be aware of this and consider the implications for his or her study of the fact that some of the richness and uniqueness of the case is thereby lost. But ultimately we justify the practice of converting historical explanations into analytical theoretical ones by emphasizing that the task of the political scientist who engages in historical case studies for theory development is not the same as the task of the historian.

Nonetheless, understanding of the nature and logic of historical explanation is essential for making effective use of the process-tracing method. The requirements, standards, and indeed the logic of historical explanation have long been discussed and debated by philosophers of history, and the important disagreements and controversies of this literature are pertinent to process-tracing, even though we cannot and need not resolve them.

We have found Clayton Roberts' book, *The Logic of Historical Explanation*, particularly useful.[42] Roberts offers a detailed statement of his own position that is, on the whole, remarkably consistent with our concept of process-tracing. Roberts rejects, as do we, the view advanced in the past by some commentators that historical explanation is no more than—and requires no more than—a description of a sequence of events. In principle, he holds, each step or link of a causal process should be supported by an appropriate "law," defined for historical explanation by Carl Hempel as a statement of a regularity between a set of events. Roberts distinguishes, however, between universalistic and probabilistic laws. While the Hempelian "covering law" model is deductive in form, it is clear that no explanation using probabilistic laws can be strictly deductive. Moreover, the covering law model cannot explain, Ernest Nagel observed, "collective events that are appreciably complex."[43] Given this problem, Roberts observes, "historians rarely seek to explain the occurrence of a

42.   Clayton Roberts, *The Logic of Historical Explanation* (University Park: Pennsylvania State University Press, 1996).

43.   Ernest Nagel, *The Structure of Science: Problems in the Logic of Scientific Explanation* (New York: Harcourt, Brace and World, 1961), p. 574.

complex event by subsuming it solely under a covering law," a process that he calls "macrocorrelation." Attempts to rely on macrocorrelation to explain complex events have failed: "The vast majority of historians do not use macrocorrelation to explain the occurrence of events they are studying, and those who do have met with little success."[44]

How, then, Roberts asks, do historians explain the occurrence of complex historical events if not by subsuming them under covering laws? Roberts argues that they do so "by tracing the sequence of events that brought them about." The similarity to what we call "process-tracing" is clear. Roberts notes that a number of earlier writers have made the same point, referring to process-tracing variously as "a genetic explanation" (Ernest Nagel), "a sequential explanation" (Louis Mink), "the model of the continuous series" (William Dray), "a chain of causal explanations" (Michael Scriven), "narrative explanations" (R. F. Atkinson), and "the structure of a narrative explanation" (Arthur Danto). Roberts chooses to call this explanatory process "colligation," drawing on earlier usages of this term and clarifying its meaning.[45]

Roberts' contribution is to explicate better than earlier writers the logic of such historical explanations. Laws that embody but are no more than "regularities" and "correlations," he argues, are not adequate explanations. A mere statement of a correlation, such as that between smoking and cancer, may have some explanatory power, but it is incomplete and unsatisfactory unless the causal relation or connection between the two terms is specified. He notes that historians and philosophers have given many names to such causal connections. (Later, Roberts refers approvingly to the recent philosophy of scientific realism and its emphasis on the need to identify causal mechanisms.)

Given that a correlation is not a substitute for investigating causation, how then can one determine whether some correlations are causal and others are not? Roberts asserts (as others, including ourselves, do) that it is only through colligation (process-tracing) that this can be done. He notes that historians, like geologists, often rely on process explanations to answer the question, "What has happened [to bring this about]?"

Roberts regards efforts to explain *complex* events solely by invoking a

---

44. Roberts, *The Logic of Historical Explanation,* pp. 9, 15.

45. Ibid., p. 20. Roberts notes that "colligation" has also been used by some writers to refer to "the grouping of events under appropriate conceptions." By this he evidently means subsuming single instances of a given type of phenomenon (e.g., revolution, deterrence) under a class of such events. Roberts prefers to refer to this second meaning of colligation as "classification" and drops it from his preferred definition of colligation. This point is worth noting here since use of case studies for theory development, as in structured, focused comparison, is based on studying one or several cases, each of which is an instance of a class of events.

covering law insupportable for two reasons: it is rarely possible to formulate general covering laws for this purpose, and reliance solely on them foregoes the necessary process-tracing of the sequence in the causal chain. Each step in such a causal sequence, Roberts holds, should be supported with an appropriate, though necessarily circumscribed, covering law. He labels this the practice of "microcorrelation" to distinguish it from efforts at "macrocorrelation" to explain complex events. As Roberts puts it, microcorrelation "is the minute tracing of the explanatory narrative to the point where the events to be explained are microscopic and the covering laws correspondingly more certain."[46]

We offer an example that illustrates the difference between "macrocorrelation" and "microcorrelation" and depicts reliance on microcorrelation for explaining a complex phenomenon. In *States and Social Revolutions,* Theda Skocpol wanted to provide a causal explanation for three social revolutions (the French, Russian, and Chinese revolutions). She identified and worked with two independent variables: international pressures on the state and peasant rebellion. To show how these two variables were causally related to the revolutionary social transformation in each of these countries, Skocpol employed a complex form of microcorrelation.[47] She used the process-tracing procedure to identify a complex sequence of events to depict how each of the two independent variables set into motion a complex causal chain. She also showed how the two causal sequences came together to trigger a revolutionary social transformation in each country. The procedure she employed for tracing each step (or link) in the causal chain was supported by combining Mill's methods with micro process-tracing. That is, Skocpol did not attempt to support the causal relationship between the two independent variables and the outcome of the dependent variable by means of macrotype covering laws; she identified a sequence of several steps or links between each independent variable and the outcome, supporting each by a form of micro process-tracing.[48]

---

46.   Ibid., p. 66. Roberts' discussion of microcorrelation is less clear than in the statement quoted here.

47.   This type of complex theory is referred to by Abraham Kaplan as "concatenated theory." See Kaplan, *Conduct of Inquiry* (San Francisco, Calif.: Chandler, 1964), p. 298: "A *concatenated* theory is one whose component laws enter into a network of relations so as to constitute an identifiable configuration or pattern. Most typically, they converge on some central point, each specifying one of the factors which okays a part in the phenomenon which the theory is to explain."

48.   Our construction of Skocpol's analysis is provisional and subject to reconsideration. A somewhat different construction of the analytical structure of Skocpol's study is suggested by James Mahoney (personal communication). Skocpol's study has generated a great deal of critical comment, much of it questioning her reliance on Mill's

Roberts recognizes that some explanations—particularly those supported by probabilistic laws—will be weak, and he discusses various strategies historians employ to develop stronger explanations. Of particular interest is "redescription," which describes the event to be explained in a less concrete, more abstract manner. Doing so may enable the investigator to use a credible covering law. This is similar to the practice in political science research of moving up the ladder of generality in formulating concepts.[49] A similar practice is frequently employed in statistical studies—"cell reduction" being a way of obtaining enough cases in a broader cell to permit statistical analysis. The new, larger cell necessarily requires a less concrete, more abstract label than the concepts attached to the old, smaller cells.

Roberts is particularly supportive of another strategy for strengthening weak explanations. "Microcorrelation," to which he referred earlier as noted above, strengthens an explanation via "the minute tracing of the explanatory narrative to the point where the events to be explained are microscopic and the covering laws correspondingly more certain." At the same time, Roberts recognizes that "the more microscopic the event to be explained, the more likely that the covering law will be a platitude . . . or a truism."[50]

Implicit in Roberts' disquisition is a rejection of the widespread belief that historians do *not* make use of covering laws. He attributes this misconception to the fact that most of the laws historians make use of are not only "parochial" but also are not generally visible in their historical narratives. Such laws are not visible because they are generally implicit in the explanatory accounts historians provide. Roberts defends this practice on the ground that many of the covering laws are "platitudinous," and therefore it would be tedious continually to list them and to assert their validity. Besides, these covering laws are so numerous in historical narratives that to list and justify them "would hopelessly clog the narrative."

Roberts recognizes that historians have an obligation to make sure

---

methods. However, as Jack Goldstone has pointed out in one of the most discerning and balanced of the evaluations of her study, Skocpol supplemented use of Mill's methods with considerable use of process-tracing, a fact that she did not clearly convey. Compare Jack Goldstone, "Methodological Issues in Comparative Macrosociology" (forthcoming); see also Goldstone, "Revolution, War, and Security" (manuscript, 1997).

49. This calls to mind, of course, Giovanni Sartori's well-known metaphor of "moving up and down a ladder of generality." See Sartori's seminal article, "Concept Misformation in Comparative Politics."

50. Roberts, *The Logic of Historical Explanation*, pp. 66–67.

that the implicit covering laws they employ are true. But he does not address the question of how this can be or is done, contenting himself with the observation that "reviewers and perceptive readers" can readily tell the difference between histories based on sound covering laws and those that are naïve and superficial." He adds that historians will occasionally make their supportive generalizations explicit, particularly when a controversy arises among historians over the truth of an explanation.[51]

In theory-based process-tracing, on the other hand, it is not desirable to rest explanations on implicit laws. Besides, the method of structured, focused comparison and process-tracing are employed not only in studies that attempt to provide explanations for specific cases but also to test and refine available theories and hypotheses, to develop new theories, and to produce generic knowledge of a given phenomenon. Given this theory development objective, it is all the more necessary to couch explanations in terms of theoretical variables and causal hypotheses.

In Chapter 6 on "The Logic of Colligation," Roberts distinguishes eight different forms that process-tracing may take. Several of these are of interest for the present study. The simplest form of process-tracing, linear colligation, depicts "a straightforward chain of events," which is often a naïve simplification of a complex phenomenon. Convergent colligation, on the other hand, depicts the outcome to be explained as flowing from the convergence of several conditions, independent variables, or causal chains. Skocpol's study, discussed above, is an example of convergent colligation, showing how two processes set into motion, one by international pressures causing state breakdown and the other by peasant rebellions, converged to cause revolutionary social movements.

Another type of process-tracing, repetitive colligation, provides the basis for Roberts' consideration of the relation of history to theory and science.[52] Whereas history often limits itself to searching for the cause of a single event, "the purpose of science is to discover the laws governing the behavior of a phenomenon," although laws of a correlational nature are used in the covering-law model of explanation. "To explain why a law exists, why a correlation occurs, one needs a theory," one which contains "a model that shows how the system works, the system that gives rise to the uniformities observed." It appears, here, that Roberts is alluding to what others have referred to as "causal mechanisms."

Roberts notes that the corpus of historical writing contains few theories, the reason being that historians have been unable to find any general laws that stood the test of time. The implicit assumption he makes here,

---

51. Ibid., pp. 87–88.

52. Ibid., pp. 145–159.

which may be questioned, is that absent "general laws," formulation of theory is not possible. In fact, as we emphasize throughout the book, researchers can develop middle-range theories comprising conditional generalizations and typological theories. The general failure of the social sciences (with the partial exception of economics) to find meaningful laws, Roberts observed, has led Jon Elster to conclude that "the basic concept in the social sciences should be that of a mechanism rather than of a theory." Roberts takes Elster's observations as consistent with his own concept of historical explanation as being "a marriage of colligation [process-tracing] and correlation."[53]

THE ROLE OF COUNTERFACTUAL ANALYSIS IN HISTORICAL EXPLANATION
We discussed some important requirements of effective use of counterfactuals in Chapter 8. Resort to counterfactual analysis is indeed a common practice in many different types of research. Mental experiments in the service of theory development have a long and often distinguished history.[54] Some writers have argued that, implicitly if not explicitly, all explanation and hypothesis testing require employment of counterfactual analysis or would benefit from it.

Here we add to the earlier discussion of counterfactuals by considering whether the within-case method employing process-tracing must be supported with counterfactual analysis. If it does, then the question arises whether the within-case method can be regarded as an alternative to controlled comparison and its use of experimental logic.

One may recognize that in principle any historical explanation implies a counterfactual in the sense that the historical outcome would not have occurred had the causal variables adduced in support of the explanation been different. Such a counterfactual can be said to serve the purpose of a second case and, if so, the real and counterfactual cases together might constitute a controlled comparison. However, such a claim rests on the supposition that the causal variable in question was a necessary condition for the occurrences of that outcome, at least in the particular case in question. It also assumes that the causal variable identified operated

---

53. Ibid., p. 155.

54. The uses and limitations of counterfactual analysis are also discussed in Chapter 8. See also Kaplan, *Conduct of Inquiry*, pp. 21, 91, 160; and James D. Fearon, "Counterfactuals and Hypothesis Testing in Political Science," *World Politics*, Vol. 43, No. 2 (January 1991), pp. 169–195. However frequently counterfactual analysis is employed, it lacks explicit criteria and standards for distinguishing good practice from often highly speculative, less disciplined uses. An important effort to explicate standards for counterfactual analysis is Philip E. Tetlock and Aaron Belkin, eds., *Counterfactual Thought Experiments in World Politics* (Princeton, N.J.: Princeton University Press, 1996).

independently of other causal variables. Such assumptions are often difficult to substantiate, a fact that makes the use of a counterfactual problematic.

Thus, one must recognize that a plausible, useful counterfactual case is often not possible and, if attempted, does not add much, if anything, in support of a within-case historical explanation. It is very difficult if not impossible to conduct a plausible, useful counterfactual when the explanation for a historical event is *very complex*. "Complexity" can take several different forms, for example:

When many variables, though independent of each other, are part of the historical explanation (as is often the case), it is difficult to formulate a plausible counterfactual.

When the historical explanation is in the form of *a sequential development over time,* and not a single variable or cluster of variables at a given point in time—i.e., when the explanation is not derived from a simple "before-after" comparison—then it is very difficult to formulate a plausible counterfactual case.

When the causal variables in the historical explanation are not independent of each other but *interdependent,* then formulation of a plausible counterfactual case is exceedingly difficult, since it requires varying a number of causal variables and runs into the difficulty of weighing the precise weight of each variable.

For these reasons, we believe that the burden of supporting a historical explanation must be met not by using a counterfactual but by employing the process-tracing method in order to infer and construct a causal chain account of how various conditions and variables interacted over time to produce the historical outcome. In any case, counterfactual support for the explanation of a historical outcome is not needed if that explanation is supported by a strong theory or generalization; or if the causal chain is highly plausible, consistent with the evidence, and survives comparison with alternative explanations.

This is not to discourage investigators from trying to develop plausible, useful counterfactual cases but to alert them to the difficulties that stand in the way. While we believe that in principle a counterfactual is not needed to support any historical explanation, we recognize that opinions on this question differ and are content to rest our argument on the ground that plausible counterfactuals are generally infeasible, for the reason indicated here and in Chapter 8. This is not to deny the possibility that forcing oneself to attempt counterfactual analysis—even under such adverse conditions—may be useful in clarifying the process-tracing basis for the explanation.

There is another, quite different question that needs to be recognized and discussed. The preceding discussion focused on getting a good explanation for a given historical outcome. But the investigator may want to undertake a different task—namely, to address the question of whether an outcome other than the historical outcome would have been possible if some of its causes could have been different. This question is often raised when observers are dissatisfied with the historical outcome and argue that policymakers could have achieved a better outcome if they had acted differently. For this type of exercise, a robust counterfactual is required—one that purports to identify the critical variable(s) and the alternatives actually available (considered and rejected) that might have produced a better outcome if they had been adopted. This type of reasoning often accompanies or underlies the assertion that in a given situation there was a "missed opportunity" to accomplish a desirable or better outcome.[55]

In this chapter we have discussed varieties of process-tracing and the different forms of causal processes to which process-tracing can be applied. In addition, we have discussed the various uses of this method in the formation, development, and the testing of theories, as well as the limitations of process-tracing. Finally, we have added a detailed discussion of historical explanation and indicated how it differs from process-tracing.

---

55.   See, for example, Alexander L. George and Jane Holl, "The Warning and Response Problem and Missed Opportunities for Preventive Diplomacy," a Report to the Carnegie Commission on Preventing Deadly Conflict (May 1997); Bruce W. Jentleson, ed., *Opportunities Missed, Opportunities Seized: Preventive Diplomacy in the Post–Cold War World* (Lanham, Md.: Rowman and Littlefield, 1999); and Deborah Welch Larson, *Anatomy of Distrust: U.S.-Soviet Relations During the Cold War* (Ithaca, N.Y.: Cornell University Press, 1997).

Chapter 11

Integrating Comparative and Within-Case Analysis: Typological Theory

Typological theorizing, or the development of contingent generalizations about combinations or configurations of variables that constitute theoretical types, has a long history in the social sciences. Significant developments date back to Max Weber's discussion of "ideal types" early in the twentieth century and Paul Lazarsfeld's analysis of "property spaces" in the 1930s.[1] Its advantages include its ability to address complex phenomena without oversimplifying, clarify similarities and differences among cases to facilitate comparisons, provide a comprehensive inventory of all possible kinds of cases, incorporate interactions effects, and draw attention to "empty cells" or kinds of cases that have not occurred and perhaps cannot occur.[2]

---

1. Max Weber, *The Methodology of the Social Sciences,* trans. Edward A. Shils and Henry A. Finch (Glencoe, Ill.: Free Press, 1949); Paul Lazarsfeld, "Some Remarks on the Typological Procedures in Social Research," *Zeitschrift fur Sozialforschung,* Vol. 6 (1937), pp. 119–139. This chapter also draws upon discussions of typological theory in Alexander L. George, "Case Studies and Theory Development: The Method of Structured, Focused Comparison," in Paul Gordon Lauren, ed., *Diplomacy: New Approaches in History, Theory, and Policy* (New York: Free Press, 1979), pp. 58–60; and Alexander L. George and Timothy J. McKeown, "Case Studies and Theories of Organizational Decision Making," in Robert F. Coulam and Richard A. Smith, eds., *Advances in Information Processing in Organizations,* Vol. 2 (Greenwich, Conn.: JAI Press, 1985), pp. 28–29. For an excellent review of typological theorizing and its application to the study of international relations, see Colin Elman, "Explanatory Typologies in the Qualitative Study of International Politics," in *International Organization* (Spring 2005).

2. Kenneth Bailey identifies most of these advantages in *Typologies and Taxonomies: An Introduction to Classification Techniques* (Thousand Oaks, Calif.: Sage Publications, 1994), pp. 11–14. Bailey also notes (and in most instances debunks) common critiques

In this chapter, we add to earlier discussions of typological theorizing in several ways. We show how typological theorizing and the cross-case comparisons it facilitates can be integrated with within-case methods of analysis to allow structured iterations between theories and cases. This combination of cross-case and within-case analysis greatly reduces the risks of inferential errors that can arise from using either method alone. We also demonstrate how typological theories can help identify which cases might best be selected for the research designs and theory-building purposes discussed by Harry Eckstein and other scholars. Case selection is arguably the most difficult step in developing a case study research design. It is an opportunistic process of seeking the intersection between the extant cases that history provides and the kind of cases and comparisons that are likely to best test or develop theories. Typological theorizing greatly clarifies which case comparisons and research designs are possible in view of the extant population of cases and which cases the researcher should select to carry out the research design she chooses. Finally, we discuss means of developing manageable typological theories of a half-dozen or more variables, despite the combinatorial complexity of such theories.

The chapter proceeds as follows. In the next sections we define typological theory and contrast typologies, which characterize variants of a phenomenon, with typological theories, which seek to identify the various causal mechanisms and pathways that link the independent variables of each "type," or cell in a typology, with its outcome. In the third section, we discuss inductive and deductive approaches to specifying typological theories: in the former, the researcher studies cases to see what causal pathways might operate in them; and in the latter, the researcher creates a logical structure of possibilities before studying cases. Fourth, we turn to the frequent need to reduce the property space; this practice can help a researcher decide which of the types specified in the theory are the best candidates for detailed study. Fifth, we discuss how to select specific cases from the reduced property space in order to construct each of the research designs discussed in Chapter 4. The sixth section discusses how process-tracing can be integrated with typological theorizing, and in the seventh section we offer an extended example of such work. The eighth section mentions some limitations of typological theory and possible remedies.

---

of typological theorizing (pp. 14–16); the most important critique, which we address, is that such theorizing can become unmanageably complex.

What Is Typological Theory?

In contrast to a general explanatory theory of a given phenomenon, typological theory provides a rich and differentiated depiction of a phenomenon and can generate discriminating and contingent explanations and policy recommendations.

We define a typological theory as a theory that specifies independent variables, delineates them into the categories for which the researcher will measure the cases and their outcomes, and provides not only hypotheses on how these variables operate individually, but also contingent generalizations on how and under what conditions they behave in specified conjunctions or configurations to produce effects on specified dependent variables.[3] We call specified conjunctions or configurations of the variables "types." A fully specified typological theory provides hypotheses on all of the mathematically possible types relating to a phenomenon, or on the full "property space," to use Lazarsfeld's term. Typological theories are rarely fully specified, however, because researchers are usually interested only in the types that are relatively common or that have the greatest implications for theory building or policymaking.

Typological theories specify the pathways through which particular types relate to specified outcomes. Such pathways are analogous to syndromes in pathology. A disease may arise through different causal paths, and it may exhibit varying symptoms and degrees of severity, so pathologists speak of syndromes—clusters of causes and outcomes—rather than a single manifestation of a particular disease. Typological theory is similarly open to the possibility of equifinality—the same outcome can arise through different pathways.[4] For example, one typological theory on de-

---

3. For similar notions, see Paul Diesing, *Patterns of Discovery in the Social Sciences* (Chicago: Aldine-Atherton, 1971); Charles C. Ragin, *The Comparative Method: Moving Beyond Qualitative and Quantitative Strategies* (Berkeley: University of California Press, 1987); and Daniel Little, "Causal Explanation in the Social Sciences," *Southern Journal of Philosophy*, Vol. 34 Supplement (1995), pp. 31–56.

Note that the categories of the variables for which the cases are to be measured could be nominal (such as democracy or nondemocracy), ordinal (such as high, medium, or low ranking of states in their protection of human rights), or interval (such as ranking percentiles of states by GNP per capita). One trade-off here is that simplifying continuous variables into nominal or other categories reduces the complexity of the theory, but also decreases the precision when placing cases in summary tables. The actual measurement of the variables in the case studies and narrative write-up of each case can convey a particular case's measurements on the continuous variables with greater precision.

4. Conversely, the researcher may be interested in how a particular manipulable

terrence, instead of simply addressing "deterrence failure," specifies different kinds of deterrence failure: failure through *fait accompli,* limited probes, or controlled pressure.[5]

Typological theories differ from historical explanations of a particular event. A historical explanation refers to a series of specific connections in an extant historical case, often supported by relevant theories. In contrast, typological theory identifies both actual and potential conjunctions of variables, or sequences of events and linkages between causes and effects that may recur. In other words, it specifies generalized pathways, whether the path has occurred only once, a thousand times, or is merely hypothesized as a potential path that has not yet occurred. A pathway is characterized in terms of variables, often with nominal cut off points distinguishing among types but sometimes with ordinal or interval cut off points, rather than by the values of these variables associated with a historical case. For example, instead of focusing on the Russian Revolution per se, a typological theory might explain this revolution as one example of the type of revolution that follows an international war; replaces weak state institutions; and takes place amidst an economic crisis. Even if there is only one revolution fitting this type, identifying the conjunctive effects of its underlying causal mechanisms allows us to generalize in a limited way to possible future revolutions that fit the same type.[6]

Such generalized pathways are what is distinctive about typological theory. They are abstract and theoretical even though they are closer to concrete historical explanations than are claims about causal mechanisms.[7] Specific pathways, in turn, can be supported by extant hypotheses on causal mechanisms. Cognitive dissonance theory and prospect theory, for example, provide causal mechanisms that support explanations of recurring patterns of behavior under certain conditions.

Typological theories are often constructed and refined through case

---

variable, such as a specified change in interest rates, can lead to different outcomes depending on the values of other variables.

5. Alexander L. George and Richard Smoke, *Deterrence in American Foreign Policy: Theory and Practice* (New York: Columbia University Press, 1974).

6. Indeed, as discussed below, deductive theorizing about the conjunctive effects of variables can provide some basis for predicting the dynamics of a type of case even if no historical case has yet occurred that fits this type.

7. In this regard, there is much confusion over Weber's notion of an "ideal type." Weber described an ideal type as one that accentuates the elements that constitute the type. He notes that "in its conceptual purity . . . [it] cannot be found empirically anywhere in reality." Weber, *Methodology of the Social Sciences,* p. 90. Bailey persuasively reads this to mean that cases close to an ideal type can be found, but these are simply not perfect or pure exemplars of the type. Bailey, *Typologies and Taxonomies,* pp. 17–20.

study methods; they can also benefit from quantitative methods and formal models. The hallmark of a fruitful and cumulative typological theory is the refinement of contingent generalizations that differentiate both independent and dependent variables in ways that produce increasingly close similarity of cases within each type, as well as sharper distinctions between types. Examples of such theories are evident in the literatures on coercive diplomacy, the security dilemma, political revolutions, alliance burden-sharing, and many other issues.[8]

Such differentiated theories not only allow for more discriminating explanations; they are also of greater practical value for policymakers, who can use them to make more discriminating diagnoses of emerging situations. Contrast, for example, a general explanatory theory such as "war is often the result of miscalculation" with a typological theory that distinguishes the conditions under which different types of miscalculations—misapprehensions about the changing balance of power, misinterpretations of an adversary's motives, failure to understand the bureaucratic or domestic constraints on the adversary, and so on—may lead to war. As another example, policymakers who are aware of different types of surprise may be better able to avoid being surprised by an adversary.

From Typologies to Typological Theories

The relationships among types, typologies, typological theories, and their usefulness in case study methods for theory development are important but underdeveloped topics. Some researchers have noted that typologies can control for specified variables and help establish similar cases for purposes of comparison.[9] Others have downplayed the role of typologies, without distinguishing them clearly from typological theories. We argue that typologies and especially typological theories can serve more ambitious purposes in case study research and social sciences than is generally acknowledged.

The formulation of typologies is a familiar activity in social science research. Analysts often partition events into types that share specified

8. See, respectively, Alexander L. George and William E. Simons, eds., *The Limits of Coercive Diplomacy*, 2nd ed. (Boulder, Colo.: Westview Press, 1994); Jack Snyder and Thomas Christensen, "Chain Gangs and Passed Bucks: Predicting Alliance Patterns in Multipolarity," *International Organization*, Vol. 44, No. 2 (Spring 1990), pp. 137–168; and Theda Skocpol, *States and Social Revolutions: A Comparative Analysis of France, Russia, and China* (Cambridge: Cambridge University Press, 1979). The burden-sharing example is discussed below.

9. Diesing, *Patterns of Discovery in the Social Sciences.*

combinations of factors.[10] Ideally, these types are mutually exclusive and exhaustive—that is, every case of the phenomenon fits into a type, and only into one type, and types are designed to minimize within-type variation and maximize variation between types.[11] Investigators are often interested in making a complex phenomenon, such as revolutions or military interventions, more manageable by dividing it into variants or types. They do so by identifying clusters of characteristics that differentiate instances of the phenomenon. Depending on the investigator's research objectives, identification of a single type may suffice, or the investigator may need to develop a differentiated typology of many types.

Typologies may thus take many different forms and have different uses, some more ambitious than others. Among the less ambitious uses, a typology may do little more than identify the qualitative types of a single multidimensional dependent or independent variable. For example, a differentiated dependent variable could be types of deterrence failure, and a differentiated independent variable could be types of coercive diplomacy employed to change the behavior of an adversary. Typologies can also characterize variants of a given phenomenon in terms of conjunctions of variables, such as types of social unrest that may or may not lead to revolutions. In their most complex form, typologies can include conjunctions of multidimensional independent variables together with types of a multidimensional dependent variable. For example, a typology might include types of military interventions that vary by regional context, domestic politics in the target state, scale, scope, goals, and instruments employed.[12]

In a typology, in contrast to a typological theory, the constituent characteristics or combinations of factors are not necessarily theoretical variables. This is likely to be the case when the typology has not been devel-

---

10.   Arthur Stinchcombe, *Constructing Social Theories* (New York: Harcourt, Brace, 1968), pp. 43–45.

11.   In practice, unless types are so finely grained that each case is its own type, some qualitative, ordinal, or interval variation will remain within types. Some approaches, including fuzzy-set theories, also explicitly allow for variance within type, and use degrees of membership rather than exclusive nominal categories. Types in which cases are nearly or exactly the same on the attributes measured are termed "monothetic," while those with varying degrees of membership are called "polythetic." Bailey, *Typologies and Taxonomies*, pp. 7–8.

12.   Andrew Bennett, *Condemned to Repetition? The Rise, Fall, and Reprise of Soviet-Russian Military Interventionism, 1973–1996* (Cambridge, Mass.: MIT Press, 1999). For an example of such a complex typology on the comparative politics of labor movements, see Ruth Berins Collier and David Collier, *Shaping the Political Arena: Critical Junctures, the Labor Movement, and Regime Dynamics in Latin America* (Princeton, N.J.: Princeton University Press, 1991).

oped within a theoretical framework. Nor does a typology itself link independent and dependent variables in a causal relationship. While the less ambitious uses of typologies may facilitate the development of theory, they do not in themselves constitute theory. As Paul Diesing has noted, types and typologies are at best only implicit theories or starting points for theory construction; hence "typologies must eventually be controlled by [explicit] theory of some sort to be reliable."[13] Even if it exhibits a perfect correlation among a set of factors, a typology alone cannot separate causal from spurious factors, or possible from unlikely or impossible combinations of variables.

However, the finding of a typological regularity can spur the search for underlying theoretical explanations or typological theories, which can then be tested through within-case analysis. For example, in research on the democratic peace, the findings of correlations among types of states and wars preceded the development of satisfying theoretical explanations for these correlations. The types of states and wars have become more refined at each stage of this process, including a shift from a general democratic peace to an interdemocratic peace, from democracies in general to transitional, parliamentary, and presidential democracies, and from wars to various levels and kinds of militarized interstate disputes. Our focus is on this more ambitious use of case studies to move from typologies to the development of typological theories, and on the use of typological theories for the design of case study research and the selection of cases to study.

Inductive and Deductive Means of Developing Typological Theories

Typological theories may be constructed through either inductive or deductive modes of inquiry. In many research projects and research programs, a combination of induction and deduction is useful or even necessary, depending upon the research objective, state of development of the research program in question, and availability of relevant cases to study. Case studies can contribute to the inductive development of typological theories in the early stages of a research program by identifying an initial list of possible theoretical variables. In the later stages of a research program's development, when theories have already been established and tested to some extent, the inductive study of deviant cases that do not fit

---

13. Diesing, *Patterns of Discovery in the Social Sciences*, p. 189. See also Christopher Achen and Duncan Snidal, "Rational Deterrence Theory and Comparative Case Studies" *World Politics*, Vol. 41, No. 2 (January 1989), p. 157; and Stinchcombe, *Constructing Social Theories*, pp. 44–45.

the existing theory may refine the typological theory and perhaps add new variables or a new causal path to it.[14] Theoretical arguments derived through these inductive processes must of course be subjected to further testing to prevent "overfitting" and forestall the introduction of spurious variables.[15]

The construction of deductive typological theories can suggest an initial list of variables and point out the cases whose study is most likely to provide theoretical insights. Often, a single researcher or a succession of researchers will move back and forth between induction and deduction, depending on the needs of a research program as it develops.

THE INDUCTIVE DEVELOPMENT OF TYPOLOGICAL THEORIES

In the early stages of reflection and research on a complex problem, an investigator may hesitate to build a research design and select cases based on a full, logically complete typology, or a typology that includes all of the logically possible types of a phenomenon. While the investigator may aim to develop a typological theory eventually, he or she may hope to develop such a theory through a series of individual case studies. Research at this stage may be of an exploratory nature, relying on feedback from the initial case studies to assess, refine, or alter the theoretical framework in which explanation of individual cases will be couched and to identify components of a useful typology. That is, the investigator seeks to gradually build a typology and a typological theory via empirical analysis of cases within a theoretical framework. This reduces the risk that a well-defined, comprehensive typology may prove inadequate after much research on a set of cases selected for that typology. While this strategy relies on induction, it is analytical, theory-driven induction. The use of ana-

---

14.   We use here the standard definition of deviant cases as those whose outcomes depart substantially from the predictions of all leading theories. This is different from what might be called extreme cases, where one variable is at such an extreme value that it far outweighs other variables in determining the outcome, which may also be at an extreme value. An extreme case may allow a researcher to attribute the outcome to the extreme variable and further study that variable's effects. In still other cases where all the variables reinforce one another's effects and overdetermine the outcome, the outcome may be at an extreme but not unexpected level.

15.   One standard for judging whether to include inductively derived variables in a theory is that such variables should not only explain the events or anomalies that spawned them, but offer insights into new cases, or into previously unexamined evidence from the cases from which they were derived. See Imre Lakatos, "Falsification and the Growth of Scientific Research Programs," in Imre Lakatos and Alan Musgrave, eds., *Criticism and the Growth of Knowledge* (London: Cambridge University Press, 1976), pp. 91–180. For clarification and critiques of this aspect of Lakatos' thought, see Colin Elman and Miriam Fendius Elman, eds., *Progress in International Relations Theory: Appraising the Field* (Cambridge, Mass.: MIT Press, 2003).

lytical induction does not exclude making use of deductive or quasi-deductive theoretical ideas, particularly theories on discrete causal mechanisms that may form the building blocks for more ambitious or integrative theories, to help guide the empirical approach.

An example may clarify why an empirical approach to the development of typologies and associated typological theories is useful. In the literature on deterrence, an *a priori* "logical" approach to typologizing outcomes of efforts to achieve deterrence often makes a simple distinction between "success" and "failure." (This characterization of deterrence outcomes continues to be used, particularly in large-N statistical studies.) An empirical approach relying on explanations for different cases of failure enables the investigator to discover different types of failures and to pinpoint specific explanations for each type of failure.[16] The different causal patterns of deterrence failure become part of a typological theory of deterrence. Such a differentiated theory of failures is significantly different from, and often more useful than, a theory that attempts to provide a single explanation for all deterrence failures.

Empirically derived, theory-oriented case studies are particularly suited for discovering equifinality and developing typological theory for the phenomenon in question. Each case may turn out to be useful if it permits the investigator to identify a different causal pattern. Differentiated explanations of the outcomes of the cases which are all instances of the class of events that is being investigated becomes a part of a cumulative typological theory, or what David Dessler has called a "repertoire of causal mechanisms."[17]

The investigator should avoid a premature, *a priori* characterization of variance of the dependent and independent variables. Instead, the variance should emerge via differences discovered in the explanation of the cases. In addition, the investigator should avoid overly general ways of characterizing variance that limit the variance to a few alternatives. For example, using the Alexander George and Richard Smoke deterrence study again, the variance in outcomes of deterrence attempts should not be limited to "success" and "failure"; rather, the case studies and their cumulation into a theory should be sensitive to the presence of equifinality. Hence, the possibility that each case of failure may have a some-

---

16. Most efforts to do systematic empirical research on the efficacy of deterrence have recognized the difficulty of making a valid determination of instances of successful deterrence. George and Smoke, *Deterrence in American Foreign Policy*, pp. 516–517.

17. David Dessler, "Beyond Correlations: Toward a Causal Theory of War," *International Studies Quarterly*, Vol. 35, No. 3 (September 1991), p. 343, citing Richard Miller, *Fact and Method: Explanation, Confirmation, and Reality in the Natural and the Social Sciences* (Princeton, N.J.: Princeton University Press, 1987).

what different explanation can lead to a typology of failures; similarly with cases of deterrence "success" (if it were possible to make a valid determination of "successful" deterrence).

The causal relationship between arms races and war provides another example of the need for more discriminating conditional generalizations. One comprehensive assessment of the voluminous literature on this problem concludes that "there is still no well-developed theory that describes the conditions under which arms races will or will not lead to war. Nor is there a theory that provides a reliable guide for policymakers."[18] What available scholarship does tell us is that arms races are neither a necessary condition for the occurrence of war nor a sufficient condition for war. Additional assessment of relevant cases should allow investigators to develop a typological theory of how and under what conditions an arms race will lead to war. Comparative analysis of different cases of a phenomenon may also enable the investigator to identify a number of conditions which, if present in an arms race, increase the likelihood of war. Such a finding would identify ways in which policymakers might act to reduce or control the likelihood that an ongoing arms race might result in war.

There is a danger that such a procedure will lead to an infinite number of types, as it can always be argued that each case is idiosyncratic enough to warrant creation of a new type to encompass it. The investigator can and should exercise judgment as to the extent to which to construct from the cases more and more refined, narrowly circumscribed types (and subtypes of a type). In the George and Smoke deterrence study, three major types of deterrence failure emerged from the cases studied; the possibility of introducing subtypes of the three types was recognized but not pursued, since the objectives of the investigation did not require it.

The typological theory that emerges obviously depends on what cases are selected for examination. Therefore, at the outset of the research, the development of a typology and its associated theory must be open-ended. For example, new cases of deterrence encounters that are studied may lead to identification of new types of "success" or "failure." Of course, new cases may turn out to be similar in type to one or another of those already studied.

This research method achieves a cumulation of findings via a "building-block" approach. That is, each case potentially provides a new component in the construction of a comprehensive typological theory. The

18. George Downs, "Arms Races and War," in Philip E. Tetlock et al., eds., *Behavior, Society, and Nuclear War*, Vol. 2 (New York: Oxford University Press, 1975), p. 75.

number of types that will eventually be identified remains indeterminate (although as stated above, not infinite) until more cases are examined.

This approach to theory development strongly differs with large-N statistical methods in its view of cell reduction—i.e., enlarging the scope of types in order to get more cases in each type so that statistical analysis becomes possible. This approach corresponds to what Giovanni Sartori has called moving up the "ladder of abstraction," or generality.[19] Such a shift to a higher level of generality eliminates the possibility of a more differentiated analysis and reduces the richness of empirical studies. In other words, moving up the ladder of generality reduces the probability of observed correlations that apply to the defined concept. For example, we can make only low probability observations on the relationship of parties and electoral laws in democracies, but we can observe higher probability correlations among specific types of parties (ruling, opposition, swing-voting, etc.) in states with specific types of electoral laws (winner-take-all, proportional, mixed, etc.) in specific types of democracies (presidential, parliamentary, etc.). While moving down the ladder of generality increases richness and raises observed correlations, it comes at the cost of parsimony and generalizability.

To be sure, cell reduction may be undertaken not only to permit statistical analysis but also for theoretical reasons. Investigators may use it in to identify and explain general characteristics that a large number of cases may have in common. Even when cell reduction is undertaken largely to satisfy the requirements of statistical analysis it may still generate new concepts for the wider and broader types it creates. Cell reduction is unwarranted, however, when it is not guided by theoretical hypotheses and instead constitutes an ad hoc opportunistic search for some findings of a general character to which new conceptual labels can be attached. This approach to theory development may produce findings or nonfindings that are artifacts of the push for cell reduction in order to make statistical analysis possible. An investigator employing an open-ended approach to developing typological theory can always engage in cell reduction at a later stage in the inquiry to formulate more general findings, so there is no need to resort to cell reduction prematurely.

The inductive development of typological theories has important limitations. One cannot infer from case findings how frequently each type of causal pattern appears in the universe of cases of that phenomenon.

---

19.   Giovanni Sartori, "Concept Misformation in Comparative Politics," *American Political Science Review,* Vol. 64, No. 4 (December 1970), pp. 1033–1053. See also David Collier and Steven Levitsky, "Democracy With Adjectives: Conceptual Innovation in Comparative Research," *World Politics,* Vol. 49, No. 3 (April 1997), pp. 430–451.

This limitation arises from the fact that typological theories can be constructed without identifying a representative sample of cases. The goal of typological theorizing is to identify the variety of causal patterns that can lead to the outcome of interest and determine the conditions under which these patterns occur. Observations on the frequency with which particular patterns occur are usually a secondary concern. In fact, investigators engaged in developing typological theory often explicitly disavow any effort to project frequency distributions from the cases they study. Sometimes, investigators deliberately select the least representative cases—deviant cases—to see if they embody previously unexamined causal paths. Thus, the value of typological theory does not rest upon any ability to project the expected frequency distribution of types in the total universe of cases of a given phenomenon. However, a representative sample of the theory's universe can be drawn, which is not always possible, and a large-N study can be undertaken to determine how frequently each type is likely to occur.[20]

THE CONSTRUCTION AND USE OF DEDUCTIVE TYPOLOGICAL THEORIES

In contrast to the inductive method, the deductive approach requires that the investigator first construct a theory-based map of the property space by defining variables and the types these variables constitute through all their mathematically possible configurations.[21] Such a framework can then be reduced to the most useful types for the purposes of research design, case selection, and theory development.

Of course, an investigator undertaking such a deductive exercise

---

20.   In fact, deductive typological theories of the kind described in the next section may alert researchers to the ways in which extant cases, whether few or numerous, are not a representative sample of the likely frequency distribution of such cases over a longer history. Such deductive typological frameworks encourage consideration of whether some kinds of cases are logically and socially possible but have simply not yet occurred. To take a simple physical example, a researcher could use a sample of ten rolls of two dice to represent the population of possible rolls, or they could construct population estimates by looking at all possible combinations of two dice, together with estimates of their probability. Of course, this example illustrates the principle but overstates the point, as probability estimates and causal mechanisms in social phenomena are almost never as precise as those for dice.

21.   In logic, what Lazarsfeld termed a property space is known as a "truth table." Lazarsfeld used the term "substruction" for the process of developing a comprehensive property space, but as this term is not intuitive and has not become common we simply talk in terms of "constructing" the property space to refer to the comprehensive delineation of all possible combinations of the variables. Lazarsfeld's use of the term "reduction" for narrowing a property space is more intuitive and hence we retain it. For a fuller discussion of property spaces and typologies that parallels our analysis, see Charles Ragin's insightful chapter, "Studying Cases as Configurations," in Charles Ragin, *Fuzzy-Set Social Science* (Chicago: University of Chicago Press, 2000).

must first designate the research objective of the investigation. The purpose may be to focus inquiry on the causal powers of particular factors or on the explanation of a particular type of outcome (or class of outcomes). When the research objective is to assess the causal properties or powers of particular factors, the investigator attempts to specify relevant theories, causal mechanisms, and variables that help provide such an assessment.[22] A similar procedure applies when the research objective is to explain a particular type of outcome (or class of outcomes). In assembling relevant theories and variables, it is important to focus on the predicted effects of interactions among combinations of variables.

An important advantage of typological theorizing is that it can move beyond earlier debates between structural and agent-centered theories by including within a single typological framework hypotheses on mechanisms leading from agents to structures and those leading from structures to agents.[23] This allows the theorist to address questions of how different kinds of agents (individuals, organizations, or states, depending on the level of analysis) behave in and change various kinds of structures. For example, Randall Schweller's work on alliance and alignment behavior essentially provides a typological theory on how different kinds of agents (status quo versus revisionist states) behave depending on their structural positions, or their military power and geographic circumstances relative to other states.[24] Many opportunities exist for fruitful typological theorizing that combines agents and structures into unified theories, such as theories of personality types and their interactions with different types of organizational designs, theories of types of states and their interactions with different types of international systems, or theories of types of economic systems and their interactions with types of economic sectors or other economic actors.[25]

---

22. When relevant theories are in short supply, the investigator should resort to the inductive approach. It may also be useful to draw upon the explanatory "theories in use" of participants and of regional or functional experts, rendered into theoretical form.

23. Of course, theories need not be modeled as typological theories to include both agency and structures. Also, it is not possible to causally model relationships in which there is simultaneous mutual constitution between agents and structures down to the finest level of analysis observable. If relationships between agents and structures can be separated into temporal stages or different levels of analysis, however, they can be modeled in typological theories.

24. Randall Schweller, "Bandwagoning for Profit: Bringing the Revisionist State Back In," *International Security*, Vol. 19, No. 1 (Summer 1994), pp. 72–107. Schweller does not explicitly style his theory as a typological one, but it fits this kind of theory as we have defined it.

25. For examples, see, respectively, Alexander L. George, *Presidential Decisionmaking*

As with the inductive development of typological theory, a key set of issues concerns how many independent variables to use, whether to partition these variables into two or more types, and how finely to differentiate the dependent variable. As new variables are added, the number of types multiplies. For example, a typology with n dichotomous variables has 2^n possible types. Thus, a theory with four independent variables and one dependent variable, all dichotomous, would have 2^5, or thirty-two types. It quickly becomes difficult for the researcher to remember, use, and articulate more than a few of the most important types of a typology of five or more variables. As discussed below, the researcher might respond by reducing substantially the number of types to be investigated.[26] Alternatively, the researcher can focus on a few variables that are hypothesized to have the greatest causal weight and construct a less complex property space (but one that risks violating the assumption of unit homogeneity within types because of the variables excluded from the analysis).[27]

The trade-offs involved in adding variables to a typology are different from those involved in adding an independent variable to a statistical research design. Statistical methods require positive degrees of freedom for a meaningful result. In such methods, each additional independent

---

in *Foreign Policy: The Effective Use of Information and Advice* (Boulder, Colo.: Westview Press, 1980); Stephen M. Walt, *Revolution and War* (Ithaca, N.Y.: Cornell University Press 1996); and Helen Milner, *Interests, Institutions, and Information: Domestic Politics and International Relations* (Princeton, N.J.: Princeton University Press, 1997).

26. Another important issue in the conversion of variables into typological theories is the question of where to put the partitions between typological categories. In other words, typologies often use categorical variables, such as "high," "medium," and "low," rather than continuous variables like those used in quantitative studies. The case studies themselves can give a nuanced analysis of what the variables actually were in a given case, but the typological theory must necessarily be more approximate and general. The partitions between typological categories should be placed so that the underlying theories predict the greatest difference between the probabilities of the specified outcomes on either side of the partition. This may be difficult to do in practice, and the researcher must be alert to whether the underlying theories or their expected interactions produce "threshold effects," or discontinuous jumps in the relationship between the magnitudes of the independent and dependent variables, and/or "inflection points," values at which the relationship between independent and dependent variables may reverse in direction, from a direct relationship to an inverse relationship, or vice versa.

27. Intervening variables—or variables temporally or spatially between independent and dependent variables that do not have any independent causal effects of their own—should not be included in constructing a typological theory. Intervening variables are often important sources of data for process-tracing, as they can indicate whether a specified process took place, but as they lack causal weight, they are not part of the theory.

variable requires a corresponding increase in the number of cases to be included in order to estimate the likelihood of a nonrandom relationship. This creates considerable pressure to keep the number of independent variables low unless data is extremely abundant, particularly if interaction effects (which also require a larger sample size to estimate) are to be taken into account.

This reasoning is appropriate to statistical methods, but it can be misleading on the issue of whether additional variables or types should be included in a typological theory that is to be explored through case studies. For the case study researcher, the exclusion of potentially relevant variables can be a greater threat to valid inferences than the inclusion of additional variables that may or may not be spurious. The exclusion of a relevant variable interferes with both within-case analyses and cross-case comparisons. Inclusion of an additional variable, on the other hand, is rather unlikely to lead to spurious inferences as long as sufficient process-tracing evidence is available to test whether the variable plays a causal role.

Adding variables increases the complexity of the research design, and each new variable requires additional observations if it is to be tested, but new variables do not raise an inherent problem of indeterminacy as long as they generate additional independent observable implications on causal processes and outcomes. This is true whether these independent observable implications are in the same case or in a separate case. The number of independent observations, not the number of cases, sets the upper limit on the number of independent variables that can be tested. Thus, the investigator should start with a broad range of variables that are potentially relevant to the phenomenon under study.

The more general trade-off for the case study researcher is whether the problem at hand requires added theoretical complexity, whether process-tracing evidence is available to deal with this complexity, and whether the problem is important enough to merit a complex theory—political scientists will create many subtypes of war, while the Inuit differentiate among many types of snow. Parsimony and simplicity are always preferable, but they should be sacrificed when complexity is necessary for adequate explanatory theory.[28]

As in the inductive development of typological theories, researchers should give as much thought to differentiation of the dependent variable in deductive theories as they do to that of the independent variables. Far too many research designs provide detailed attention to the independent

---

28. Gary King, Robert O. Keohane, and Sidney Verba, *Designing Social Inquiry: Scientific Inference in Qualitative Research* (Princeton, N.J.: Princeton University Press, 1994).

variables while lumping the dependent variable into a few vaguely defined categories. As emphasized in Chapter 4 on research design, the careful characterization of the dependent variable and its variance is often one of the most important and lasting contributions to research.

Once the specification of variables is complete, it defines the property space—the relevant universe of all possible combinations of variables, or types.[29] This is the point at which Ph.D. students often veer toward a nervous breakdown. Having specified their independent and dependent variables, and explored the theoretical literature on the causal mechanisms associated with each variable when it acts alone, thesis students are often dismayed to find, for example, that when five independent variables are assembled together with one dependent variable, there are sixty-four possible types. Moreover, with only a preliminary knowledge of the values that the variables assume in different cases, the researcher can only tentatively classify cases by type. In fact, a preliminary deductive effort at typological theorizing on how the variables might interact, together with preliminary research on a number of cases, can greatly reduce and simplify the property space and contribute to systematic procedures for case selection and specification of the research design. Often, the process of visually putting together combinations of variables and placing cases into types spurs useful preliminary theorizing on how combinations of variables interact.[30] In particular, we discuss three criteria for reducing the property space to the types for which intensive case studies are likely to have the greatest value, and three research designs that may flow from the preliminary placement of cases into types.[31]

---

29.   A well-specified type provides an answer to the important question, "What is this a case of?" Howard Becker and Charles C. Ragin, eds., *What is a Case? Exploring the Foundations of Social Inquiry* (Cambridge: Cambridge University Press, 1992), p. 6.

30.   Two points are worth noting here from our experience in urging students and colleagues to construct typological theories. First, the process of visually arraying variables into types shifts theorizing from univariate thinking on causal mechanisms and a focus on the explanatory weight of individual variables and "alternative hypotheses," to typological thinking and a focus on combinations of variables and their effects. Second, when graduate students construct a typological theory for the first time, they often discuss variables in their text that do not appear in their typological table, or include variables in the table that they do not discuss in their text. This suggests that by fostering more systematic thinking about theories and the contexts in which they apply, typological theorizing can quickly reveal inconsistencies in a theorist's views.

31.   This discussion assumes that cases may be selected on the basis of preliminary knowledge of the values of their variables. Of course, the values of the variables may turn out to be different once the researcher undertakes the actual case study, and finding that a case has commonly been misclassified is an important contribution. This is one reason that the selection of cases based on preliminary knowledge of the values of the variables is not necessarily vulnerable to confirmation bias.

Reducing the Property Space

The first criterion for reducing the property space is to remove types that are not socially possible.[32] A good theory may be able—in time, if not immediately—to specify hypothetical cases or combinations of variables that should not exist or should at least be highly unlikely.[33] In other words, a particular outcome may be impossible when the independent variables overdetermine a different outcome. For example, we do not expect deterrence to fail when the deterrer has overwhelming and usable instruments of force, is far more committed to success than the opponent, communicates its intentions clearly, and faces a rational, unified, and attentive opponent. If we do find a failure under such circumstances, it may be treated as a deviant case, which may suggest new variables that need to be added to our typological theory.[34]

Delineating types within the property space and developing a preliminary typological theory enables researchers to check whether they have been premature in deciding whether some types should not, according to the theory, exist in the social world. In other words, rather than merely assuming that the types which the theory predicts to be empty are in fact empty, the researcher should carefully consider whether there might be historical cases that fit these types, or whether such cases could occur in the future.[35] One constraint on typological theorizing, like that

---

32. Daniel Little, "Causal Explanation in the Social Sciences."

33. In some circumstances, statistical tests may be misleading if particular combinations of variables are impossible but the researcher is not aware of this. For example, a 2x2 table in which one square is not possible gives misleading results when a chi-squared test is applied. We thank Bear Braumoeller for providing this insight in private correspondence.

34. It is useful to distinguish between cases that are not logically possible and those that are not socially possible or at least highly unlikely in the social world. A logically impossible case would be a case of deterrence "success" when either no deterrent threat was issued or no action was contemplated by the state that was supposedly challenging the status quo. By definition, such cases do not constitute successful deterrence. A case that is socially impossible, or at least highly unlikely, is one in which all of the relevant variables, both singly and conjunctively, point in the same direction in overdetermining an outcome, yet that outcome does not occur. Except for measurement error or the existence of a strong but probabilistic causal mechanism, if such a case exists it indicates the presence of a left-out variable. We thank Bear Braumoeller for clarifying this distinction.

35. Bailey, following Lazarsfeld, suggests eliminating all empty cells. See *Typologies and Taxonomies*, p. 27. Lazarsfeld termed this process "functional reduction." In our view, such reduction should not be automatic, as the researcher must first consider whether the theory dictates that the cell should be empty, and whether an overlooked historical or a possible future case might fit it.

on John Stuart Mill's methods as discussed in Chapter 8, is that the social world has not necessarily produced cases of all the types of a phenomenon that are socially possible, and we cannot be certain whether a type of case cannot occur or merely has not yet occurred. The disciplined use of counterfactual inquiries is one way to fill in empty types for the purposes of comparison to actual cases. Fortunately, not all research designs require a fully inhabited property space. Single cases, if they are most-likely, least-likely, or especially crucial cases, can be quite revealing about the strength of a theory. Comparisons of a few cases, if they are most similar or least similar, can also be revealing.

Still, although single-case research designs and no-variance designs involving only the study of cases that are positive on the outcome of interest are valid, researchers sometimes make the basic mistake of over-generalizing from cases where the hypothesized cause and the hypothesized effect are both present. While there are valid research designs that use only one case study, or that focus on all the possible paths to a given effect or all the possible effects from a given cause, ideally the researcher should examine or at least invite others to propose and study cases where the hypothesized cause or effect are absent. More generally, when working with any given property space, the investigator's causal inferences will be strongest if she or he attempts to study (or at least contemplates) cases of various types.

Consider, for example, a simple version of the democratic peace hypothesis, in which states are either democracies or nondemocracies, and in which dyads have either engaged in war or maintained a peace. With these three dichotomous variables (democracy or nondemocracy for the first state, the same for the second, and either war or peace for the outcome) there are six possible types. (There are not eight types because the order of cases in the mixed dyads does not matter.) Most of the research on the democratic peace has focused on one type of case: dyads that are by some measures democratic but nonetheless go to war against one another (or the close cousins of these cases, near-democracies that go to war, and near-wars between democracies). The focus on these cases at the early stages of the research program is appropriate, but depending on the nature of the hypothesized causal mechanisms, it may also be important

---

Lazarsfeld's other modes of reduction are "pragmatic," which collapses contiguous types, and "arbitrary numerical," which, similar to Boolean algebra and QCA, collapses types into those sharing certain combinations that might be considered sufficient for the outcome. For example, we might code the habitability of a house with plumbing and no heat or refrigerator as the same as that of a house with heat and a refrigerator but no plumbing. Bailey, *Typologies and Taxonomies*, pp. 27–28. For our purposes, we find principles of reduction that focus on the suitability of specified types and extant cases for alternative case study research designs more useful.

to make comparisons to other kinds of cases. For example, do conflict resolution mechanisms between democracies differ from those between other kinds of dyads, including democracy/nondemocracy dyads and nondemocracy/nondemocracy dyads?[36]

This example suggests a second criterion for reducing the property space and choosing the specific cases to study from among the types that remain. When an outcome is overdetermined by existing theories and it turns out as expected, it is less likely to be theoretically informative—although process-tracing might show that causal mechanisms did not operate exactly as expected. Such most-likely cases are usually useful only when a theory unexpectedly fails to explain them, although process-tracing of most-likely cases with variables at extreme values can allow the researcher to see in stark relief how the underlying causal mechanisms operate.[37]

A third criterion for reducing the property space is the identification of which types and cases are suited to the research objective. This is true whether this objective is to test existing theories, compare typologically similar cases, identify and study deviant cases, or conduct a plausibility probe. The research objective and the case study research design should be devised with a view toward a research program's stage of development. For example, new and relatively untested research programs are more likely to be advanced by plausibility probes and inductive studies of deviant cases. More advanced research programs may offer few or no clear deviant cases, but may be amenable to theory-testing case studies and studies of typologically similar cases with slightly different outcomes that might yield new subtypes or more finely differentiated variables.

From Property Space to Research Design

There are four different research designs that can reconcile a scholar's research objective, the alternative research designs available, and the actual historical cases available for study. These include comparing similar or

---

36. For this reason, Miriam Fendius Elman's edited volume, *Paths to Peace: Is Democracy the Answer?* (Cambridge, Mass.: MIT Press, 1997), rightly includes case studies of mixed and nondemocratic dyads.

37. A researcher can also examine a "typical" case (as identified by a statistical distribution or more crudely by the most populated type in a typology) to see how causal processes unfold in such a case. The most-likely or extreme case corresponds with Weber's notion of an "ideal type" case, while the typical case corresponds with John McKinney's notion of a "constructed type." John McKinney, *Constructive Typology and Social Theory* (New York: Appleton-Century-Crofts, 1966). Both are examples of a "criterion" type, or a type against which other cases can be measured. Bailey, *Typologies and Taxonomies*, pp. 17–24.

differing cases in the same type; comparing most similar cases in adjacent types with differing outcomes; studying most-likely, least-likely, and crucial cases; and comparing least similar cases.

CASES IN THE SAME TYPE: CASES THAT VALIDATE THE TYPE VS. DEVIANT CASES

In the first research design, if two cases fit into the same type according to their independent variables, our working assumption is that they should have similar outcomes. This offers the most basic test of the validity of the specification of the type. If a preliminary classification of cases into their respective types indicates that cases in the same type have different outcomes, then the researcher can perform full studies of these cases to assess whether and why one of them deviates from the expected outcome. This can uncover errors in the preliminary measurement and classification of one or both cases, or it may point to additional variables that deserve attention.[38] Even if a change in the measurement of one of the cases or the addition of a new variable resolves the anomaly in the type in question, it may create another anomaly in another type, which then requires investigation.

MOST SIMILAR CASES: ADJACENT TYPES WITH DIFFERING OUTCOMES

A second potential research design arises when the preliminary classification of the cases indicates that two cases differ in only one independent variable and also in the dependent variable. This allows a most-similar cases research design. If exogenous variables can be ruled out as a source of variation in the outcome (admittedly not a simple matter), then there is some basis for inferring that differences in the outcome can be attributed to the one variable in the typology on which the cases differ. This basis for inference can be strengthened by using process-tracing to establish that the variation in the outcome was indeed due to the single independent variable that differed between the cases. Process-tracing can also test whether factors left out of the typological framework and that differed between the two cases were causally related to the variation in the outcome.

---

38.   If for the sake of simplicity the types are delineated into nominal or ordinal approximations of interval variables, the variance that remains in the levels of the independent variables within the same type may account for differences in the outcomes among cases in the type. In this instance, the researcher must decide whether to redraw the partitions between the types, which complicates the theory, or explain the discrepancy in the narrative explanations of the cases and in a footnote to any tables presenting the typological theory.

MOST-LIKELY, LEAST-LIKELY, AND CRUCIAL CASES

In a third research design, the preliminary analysis of the property space can point to single cases that may be particularly informative for theory development. Such analysis can facilitate the construction of tough tests by identifying which types might constitute most-likely, least-likely, and crucial cases. In a most-likely case, a single variable is at such an extreme value that its underlying causal mechanism, even when considered alone, should strongly determine a particular outcome. If at the same time the other independent variables, considered singly and together, point toward the same outcome as the extreme variable, then this is a crucial case. If the predicted outcome does not occur, then the hypothesized causal mechanism underlying the extreme variable is strongly impugned. The failure of this mechanism cannot be blamed on the operation of the other variables in the framework. Conversely, if a case is weakly determined or least likely for a single causal mechanism, and alternative hypotheses offer different predictions, but the causal mechanism still correctly predicts the outcome, then this constitutes a crucial case that offers the strongest possible support for the mechanism.[39]

LEAST SIMILAR CASE COMPARISONS

Finally, cases that are similar in their outcomes but differ on all but one independent variable constitute least similar cases. The typological space helps identify such cases, and a researcher who chooses to study such cases can use process-tracing to test whether these cases' similar outcomes are due to the one independent variable that they have in common.

Integrating Typological Theorizing and Process-Tracing

Once the research design is set and the cases are selected, the researcher can begin the case studies using methods of within-case analysis. This can lead to more accurate measurements of independent variables, which may lead to reclassification of some cases. The case studies may also lead the researcher to refine the cutoff points between types and to add new variables. Such changes to the preliminary typological theory may re-

---

39. This treatment of "crucial" cases is somewhat different from that of Harry Eckstein, who devised the term. See Harry Eckstein, "Case Studies and Theory in Political Science," in Fred Greenstein and Nelson Polsby, eds., *Handbook of Political Science*, Vol. 7 (Reading, Mass.: Addison-Wesley, 1975), pp. 118–120. Our formulation is more precise on whether a case is most- or least-likely for a particular theory, *and* whether alternative theories make complementary or contradictory predictions.

solve anomalies, but they may also create new ones. They can also lead to changes in the research design and in the cases selected for study.

This iteration between theory and data and between within-case analysis and cross-case comparisons is a key advantage of typological theorizing as compared to comparative methods used alone. The aspects of typological theorizing that rely on cross-case comparisons are in some respects vulnerable to inferential problems like those that beset Mill's methods. Although typological theorizing does not require that a single variable be necessary or sufficient for outcomes, as Mill's methods do, such theorizing, like all methods, remains vulnerable to erroneous inferences if relevant variables are omitted. Moreover, the most-similar and least-similar case comparisons facilitated by typological theorizing are based on the same logic as Mill's methods of difference and agreement, respectively. The key difference between typological theorizing and Mill's methods is that by relying on within-case methods as well as comparative methods, typological theorizing reduces the risks of mistaken inferences.

Process-tracing provides a check on whether the explanations developed from typological comparisons are spurious. While typological theorizing can help identify which cases are suitable for a most similar case comparison, for example, process-tracing is necessary to help determine whether the one independent variable that differs between two most similar cases is indeed causally related to the differences between these cases' outcomes. Process-tracing can also help identify variables and interactions among them that have been previously overlooked.[40] The inductive side of typological theorizing and process-tracing provides opportunities for researchers to identify variables they have not already thought to include. This does not guarantee that all relevant variables will be identified, but typological theorizing provides a technique for identifying deviant cases that are likely to provide clues on omitted variables, and process-tracing provides a means for exploring where those clues lead. Process-tracing on typical cases can also point to overlooked variables. Indeed, one of the most visible and important contributions of case study methods has been to identify causal variables left out of earlier analyses. This is evident in the literature on deterrence, for example, where case studies have added variables on psychological dynamics and domestic

---

40. Daniel Little, while more pessimistic than we are on the possibilities for typological theorizing, concurs that such theorizing can be strengthened by process-tracing. As an example, Little notes that Theda Skocpol's work on social revolutions, in addition to using traditional comparative analysis based on Mill's methods, uses established social theories in this manner. Little, "Causal Explanation in the Social Sciences," p. 54.

politics to spare deductive theories that included only interests, capabilities, and simple cost-benefit calculations.[41]

Similarly, the combination of typological theory and process-tracing can incorporate and help identify interactions effects. If a researcher has deductively outlined the interactions he or she expects in a type of case, process-tracing can test for their presence. If the researcher has only identified the configuration of variables that defines the type but has not specified the interactions among them, process-tracing can help identify inductively the interactions that took place in cases of the specified type.[42]

An Extended Example: Burden Sharing in Contemporary Security Coalitions

The above criteria for first delineating and then reducing the property space, specifying the research design, and selecting cases make it possible to reduce significantly the number of typological categories and cases to be studied. The use of a preliminary typological theory for case selection is in fact one of typological theory's most important functions. An example, involving two related studies of alliance burden-sharing in the 1990–1991 Persian Gulf conflict by Andrew Bennett, Joseph Lepgold, and Danny Unger, illustrates this process. The first study used existing theories to identify five variables that should affect alliance contributions: "a state's ability to contribute (from collective action theory); the specific threats Iraq presented to the potential contributor (balance of threat theory); the potential contributor's security dependence on the United States (alliance security dilemma theory); the issue-specific strength of the state vis-à-vis that of the society (strong state/weak state theory); and the power and interests of top government officials (bureaucratic politics theory)."[43]

This study used a preliminary assessment of interactions among these variables to help guide case selection, and then used the resulting

---

41.   Alexander L. George and Richard Smoke, "Deterrence and Foreign Policy, "*World Politics,* Vol. 41, No. 2 (January 1989), pp. 170–182; and Robert Jervis, "Rational Deterrence: Theories and Evidence," *World Politics,* Vol. 41, No. 2 (January 1989), pp. 183–207.

42.   We therefore disagree with the criticism that case study methods do not account for interaction effects. Stanley Lieberson makes this critique in "Small N's and Big Conclusions," in Ragin and Becker, eds., *What is a Case?* pp. 109–113. For a view that concurs with our emphasis on the ability of case study methods to incorporate interactions, see Ragin, *The Comparative Method.*

43.   Andrew Bennett, Joseph Lepgold, and Danny Unger, "Burden-Sharing in the Persian Gulf War," *International Organization,* Vol. 48, No.1 (Winter 1994), pp. 39–75.

cases to inductively refine and codify a better-specified typological theory. The second study added a sixth variable, "lessons that leaders drew from previous alliance experiences" (learning theory), and it tested the typological theory from the first study against additional cases.[44]

The dependent variable in both studies was differentiated into three kinds of alliance contributions: military, political, and economic. The resulting property space in the first study was complex, with thirty-two possible types of different combinations of independent variables, and three dichotomous outcome variables (or eight possible outcomes), yielding 256 possible types if all variables are treated as dichotomous (the second study involved an even more complex space of 512 possible types due to the added independent variable). Table 11.1 presents a version of the typological theory from the first study, simplified for purposes of illustration by collapsing the two domestic politics variables into one variable, displaying only the predicted outcomes rather than all possible outcomes, and presenting outcomes as only contribution/no contribution rather than breaking them into kinds of contributions. The variables for each of the constituent theories in the table are coded Yes or No as follows:

- Collective Action: Would a contribution from the country in question (including the use of military bases) be important to achieving the public good of expelling Iraqi forces from Kuwait?
- Balance of Threat: Did the country face a potential military threat from Iraq?
- Alliance Dilemma: Was the country dependent on the United States for its security?
- Domestic Politics: Did the public, legislature, and national security organizations generally favor a contribution?

The table also shows the placement of cases from both the first and second studies into their respective types. The coding of the cases is greatly simplified from the measures in the actual case studies, particularly for cases of France, Syria, and the Soviet Union, each of which contributed politically, militarily, or both to the Gulf coalition in part to "share the spoils" as part of the winning side and to maintain or establish good relations with the United States, even though none was greatly reliant on the United States for its security. Syria and the Soviet Union thus constituted deviant cases to some degree, drawing attention to "share the

---

44.   Andrew Bennett, Joseph Lepgold, and Danny Unger, eds., *Friends in Need: Burden-Sharing in the Persian Gulf War* (New York: St. Martin's Press, 1997).

Table 11.1. A Typological Theory on Burden-Sharing in the 1991 Gulf War.

Cases	Collective Action	Balance of Threat	Alliance Dilemma	Domestic Politics	Expected Outcome
Saudi Arabia	Y	Y	Y	Y	Contribute
Turkey	Y	Y	Y	N	Contribute*
	Y	Y	N	Y	Contribute
	Y	N	Y	Y	Contribute
	N	Y	Y	Y	Contribute
	Y	Y	N	N	Contribute*
United States	Y	N	N	Y	Contribute
	Y	N	Y	N	Contribute*
Britain	N	N	Y	Y	Contribute
Egypt	N	Y	Y	N	Contribute*
	N	Y	N	Y	Contribute
France, Canada, Australia	N	N	N	Y	Contribute
Germany, Japan	N	N	Y	N	Contribute*
Iran, Syria	N	Y	N	N	No Contrib.
	Y	N	N	N	No Contrib.
China, USSR	N	N	N	N	No Contrib.

* In types marked with an asterisk, countries are expected to contribute only if strong state leaders override domestic opposition, as happened in Egypt and Turkey. In Japan and Germany, security dependence on the United States was so high that domestic opposition was muted.

spoils" or "offensive bandwagoning" motives as an important factor omitted from the typological theory.

The typological table shows how it was possible to reduce substantially the number of types of interest and select which cases to study. Cases that were overdetermined by a mix of variables or by a few variables at extreme values, such as the Kuwaiti and Saudi contributions to the Desert Storm coalition, were deemed unlikely to be theoretically informative. (If such states had failed to contribute, they would have constituted potentially useful deviant cases.) The same was true of overdetermined noncontributors—distant states not threatened by Iraq, not dependent on oil or the world economy, and not reliant on the United States for their security.

The first study thus conducted case studies of the leading contributors: the United States, Great Britain, France, Germany, Japan, and Egypt. These states varied substantially in the kind of contributions they made, and provided most-likely cases for all but one of the theories whose variables contributed to the typological theory. (The exception was the balance of threat theory, with its overdetermined most-likely cases of Saudi

Arabia and Kuwait). However, as the authors noted, this first study relaxed the ideal criteria for case selection; it did not include studies of states that might have contributed but did not do so. The second study, which included additional case studies by regional experts, included a noncontributing "free-rider," Iran. This second study also included an abbreviated examination (or "mini–case study") of China, a state whose failure to make a substantial or costly contribution appeared to be (and upon closer study indeed was) overdetermined. This illustrates how abbreviated case studies can be used to fill in types that are unlikely to be surprising.

Finally, the second study included a brief examination of countries' contributions to the United Nations peacekeeping mission in Bosnia (UNPROFOR) and the NATO Implementation Force (IFOR) peacekeeping mission that succeeded it. This allowed a further test of the theoretical framework in a separate coalition. It also provided a before-after comparison of the effects of the alliance security dilemma variable, since the United States largely stayed out of the UNPROFOR mission but then joined the IFOR coalition and pushed others to do the same. Of course, this comparison is imperfect, as the 1995 Dayton Accords changed the context in Bosnia greatly.

The case selection in these burden-sharing studies allowed for a test of the key assertion that cases in the same type should have similar outcomes. Germany and Japan fit the same type, as they were both dependent on the United States for security, relatively distant from the Middle East, dependent on foreign oil, and domestically constrained on the use of force. The typological framework passed this test of its viability, as these similar cases had very similar outcomes—both states provided over $8 billion each but sent no combat troops. Other states, such as Syria and Iran, had similar values on many of their independent variables but very different outcomes, pointing to Syria as a deviant case that allowed a test of which independent variables accounted for the differences in outcomes (in this instance, differing domestic politics, relations with the United States, and offensive bandwagoning motivations). This illustrates how case study researchers, after constructing a property space, should be alert to "targets of opportunity," identifying potential case studies that might fit various research designs, including most similar cases, least similar cases, deviant cases, crucial cases, and so on. It is also often possible to carry out more than one of these kinds of case study or case comparison within a single study—cases that are most similar with respect to one another, for example, may be least similar to a third case, or a case may be most-likely for one hypothesis and least-likely for another.

Table 11.1 also draws attention to the empty types. Most of the empty types in this instance seem socially possible, and readers may be able to think of examples from the Gulf War or other security crises. Indeed, some of the cases studied were of types that seemed least plausible according to the theory. For example, it seems unlikely that a country whose contribution would be useful or even necessary for defeating Iraq, whose security was threatened by Iraq, and whose security depended on the United States would face significant domestic opposition to contributing to the coalition—yet this domestic opposition was strong in Turkey, so unusual domestic political circumstances may have been omitted from the theory. (Indeed, in 2003, a newly elected Turkish government, facing intense public opposition to assisting the imminent U.S. invasion of Iraq, chose not to allow the United States to use Turkish territory to launch the invasion.) Thus, even though the outcome in this case fit that predicted by the theory, the process was rather surprising. Similarly, we might expect few instances in which a country had no international incentives to contribute but domestic audiences favored a contribution, yet there were many such countries (most of which made symbolic contributions). These cases point to altruistic "share the spoils" motives left out of the theory.

Subsequent opportunities for alliance burden-sharing, while not yet studied in full, appear upon initial examination to fit this typological theory fairly well and offer opportunities to further refine it. These more recent cases include NATO's participation in air strikes against Serbia over the issue of the status of Kosovo, the U.S.-led coalition in the war against the Taliban government of Afghanistan, and the U.S.-led coalition in the 2003 invasion of Iraq.[45] The war against the Taliban, in particular, provides a good example of a potential building-block addition of a new type to the theory. In the study of the 1990–1991 Gulf War, the authors set aside the case of Israel as too idiosyncratic to include in the general theoretical framework. In effect, Israel contributed to the 1991 anti-Iraq coalition by not contributing—it heeded U.S. requests not to take military action against Iraq, even while under attack from Iraqi Scud missiles, because action by Israel would have made it difficult politically for Arab states to continue to contribute to the coalition. Although this provided a clear historical explanation for the case of Israel, the phenomenon of "contribution by inaction" seemed insufficiently common to merit in-

---

45. In brief, the theory's explanation for why the coalition for the 2003 War against Iraq was much narrower than that of the 1990–1991 Persian Gulf War was that, in 2003, there was a much weaker consensus that removing the Iraqi regime was a public good; states were tempted to ride free and reduce the terrorist threat to themselves by not contributing; security dependence on the United States was much lower by 2003 because a resurgent Russian threat was less likely than in 1991; Iraq posed less of a conventional military threat to the region than in 1991; and the domestic politics in many countries made contributions less likely due to rising anti-Americanism.

cluding in and thereby complicating the theory. The coalition against the Taliban, however, also included a country that contributed by inaction. India offered assistance to the coalition, but it was clear that Indian participation would reduce Pakistan's willingness to assist the United States, so the United States demurred at India's offer. The Israeli and Indian cases also appear similar in that each country arguably used the U.S. desire to keep them on the sidelines as a source of leverage over U.S. policies of interest to each country (respectively, Middle East peace talks and the status of Kashmir). An opportunity may thus exist to add a new type to the theory by including a variable for "relations among potential contributors" and studying these and other cases of contribution by inaction.

Finally, these burden-sharing studies demonstrate how a complex typological theory can be presented as a causal diagram, albeit a complex one. The causal diagram in Figure 11.1, from the first study, corresponds with the typological theory in Table 11.1 (the correspondence is inexact because Table 11.1 collapses the two domestic variables into one for presentational simplicity). Figure 11.1 groups together similar outcomes while still allowing for alternative paths to these outcomes (i.e., equifinality). Moving from the left to the right of the figure, the five boxes on the left represent the independent variables, the three "outcome" boxes represent the dependent variable, and the boxes on the right represent path-dependent interpretations of cases that might have arrived at the same outcome through different routes. Each possible path through the five boxes on the left corresponds with one of the types in Table 11.1 (except that the table has one fewer variable and hence 16 fewer possible paths). For example, Iran and China both arrived at Outcome 1, but through very different processes. Iran greatly valued the goal of an Iraqi defeat, but did not depend on the United States; it "rode free" on the efforts of the U.S.-led coalition that fought Iraq. China did not greatly value the goal of an Iraqi defeat, so it kept its distance by making only the minimal political contribution of not exercising its veto on the UN Security Council.

More generally, the four path-dependent interpretations in the figure turn on whether a state's contribution, or lack thereof, matched the value it placed on the public good of reversing the Iraqi invasion. First, a state "rides free" if, like Iran, it values the good but does not contribute. Second, a state "keeps its distance" if, like China, it does not value the good and does not contribute. Third, a state "reveals its preferences and pays up" if it values the good and contributes. This could arise through various contributions of perceived threat, alliance dependence, and domestic politics, as in the cases of Britain and Egypt. Fourth, a state is "entrapped" if it does not value the good but contributes anyway due to alliance dependence, as in the cases of Japan and Germany.

Figure 11.1. Decision-Making Model of Security Coalition Contributions based on Perceptions of Public Good.

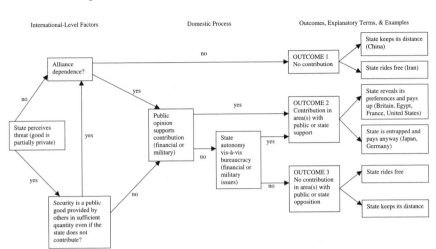

Limitations of Typological Theory and Potential Remedies

Despite the strengths and flexibility of typological theories, the development of typological theory suffers from important limitations.[46] Researchers are liable to miss some possible causal relationships and to face indeterminacy in assessing others. The main reason for this is that extant historical cases may represent only a few of the combinations of variables that are possible in the social world. In addition, left-out variables and probabilistic causal mechanisms can further weaken causal inferences from case studies and the development of typological theories.

In practice, the severity of these limitations may be reduced through rigorous case study methods. First, as noted above, not all cases are equally theoretically informing, and a single crucial or nearly crucial case can strongly support or undermine a theory. Second, good case study researchers should be careful to avoid overgeneralizing their conclusions or claiming to have uncovered all possible causal paths. Finding cases that represent previously undocumented causal paths has always been a priority for case study researchers. Third, as our example of alliance burden-sharing indicates, much of the property space in a given study can be set aside as unlikely or uninformative, allowing relatively strong inferences from even a small number of cases if they fall into the types of greatest interest. Fourth, the use of previously validated causal mechanisms or social theories to build typological frameworks, together with

---

46. Little, "Causal Explanation in the Social Sciences."

the use of process-tracing and other methods of within-case analysis, can strengthen the inferences that would otherwise have to be made on the basis of comparative methods alone. Fifth, it is important to distinguish between instances where the range of extant historical cases is insufficient for strong causal inferences and instances in which the researcher does not have the resources to study all of the potentially informative cases. In the former instance, case study methods will be weak but may be the only methods available. In the latter, researchers may focus their efforts on a subset of the property space, where even a few cases may exhaust the causal paths of most interest, they may add mini–case studies of otherwise unexamined types to test and strengthen their inferences.

Conclusion

The use of case studies for the development of typological theories, and the use of these theories to design case study research and select cases, are iterative processes that involve both inductive study and deductive theorizing. An inductive, building-block approach to developing typological theories can identify causal paths and variables relevant to a given outcome. Such an approach is particularly useful in new or emerging research programs and in the study of deviant cases. Ultimately, as additional cases are examined, this building-block process can outline an increasingly comprehensive map of all of the causal paths to an outcome. A deductive approach to typological theorizing can help test established theories when they are available and propose integrative theories that incorporate interaction effects and address the problem of equifinality. Combining these modes of inductive and deductive development of typological theories with methods of within-case analysis, particularly process-tracing, can substantially reduce the limitations of Mill's methods and other methods of comparison.

A greater awareness of the strengths and uses of typological theories and case studies, however, also provides a sharper understanding of their limits. Typological theories, case studies, process-tracing, and congruence tests can only reduce the inferential limits that are similar to those that afflict Mill's methods of agreement and difference. Left-out variables and measurement errors can undermine causal inferences no matter what methods are used. Case study researchers should be sensitive to interaction effects, but there is no guarantee that they will incorporate and explain such effects adequately. Finally, when low-probability causal relations hold and there are only a few cases, no methods of causal inference work well.

Chapter 12

Case Studies and Policy-Relevant Theory

Political scientists generally agree that research in their field should address important real-world problems.[1] This view is expressed not only by international relations scholars but also by scholars in the American and comparative politics fields and adherents of the rational choice approach.

---

1.   A detailed assessment of early efforts to use case studies for developing policy-relevant materials was published over thirty years ago by Hugh Heclo, who noted "the great untapped potential in the use of case studies for policy analysis." He pointed to important steps in this direction with publication of Robert Dahl, ed., *Who Governs? Democracy and Power in an American City* (New Haven, Conn.: Yale University Press, 1961), Edward Banfield, *Political Influence* (Glencoe, Ill.: Free Press, 1962), and Glenn Paige, *The Korean Decision* (New York: Free Press, 1968). He also praised Raymond Bauer, Ithiel de Sola Pool, and Lewis Dexter, *American Business and Public Policy: The Politics of Foreign Trade* (New York: Atherton Press, 1963). See Hugh Heclo, "Review Article: Policy Analysis," *British Journal of Political Science*, Vol. 2, No. 1 (January 1972), pp. 83–108. Meanwhile, research specialists within and outside the government have produced a great deal of policy evaluation research. We have not reviewed this work; much of it is highly specific, in the nature of applied policy research with little effort to contribute to the development of theory. An important example of rigorous policy evaluation research is the work of Robert Yin's COSMOS organization. He has discussed methods for this type of research in Robert Yin, *Case Study Research: Design and Methods*, Second Edition (Thousand Oaks, Calif.: Sage, 1994).
   The present chapter focuses on the development of theory on substantive policy problems. Another objective of policy research, not addressed in this chapter, is to illuminate and improve the policymaking process. The distinction between substantive theory and process theory is discussed in Alexander L. George, *Bridging the Gap* (Washington, D.C.: United States Institute of Peace, 1993), pp. xxi–xxiii. A quite critical survey of efforts to develop policy process theory via large-N studies is provided by William Blomquist, "The Policy Process and Large-N Comparative Studies" in Paul A. Sabatier, ed., *Theories of the Policy Process* (Boulder, Colo.: Westview Press, 1999), pp. 201–230.

Participants in a symposium on "The Role of Theory in Comparative Politics," for example, agreed that "comparative politics is very much a problem-driven field of study. What motivates the best comparative politics research are puzzles of real world significance. . . . This problem orientation distinguishes comparative politics from other social science fields that tend to be driven primarily by theoretical and/or methodological ends. Given a strong interest in real-world puzzles, comparative politics scholars tend to treat theories, approaches, and methods mainly as tools to help frame and explain empirical puzzles."[2]

Although many other scholars also subscribe in principle to the view that theory and methodology are mainly tools for the study of real-world problems, social scientists differ in their view on the extent to which research on such problems should take precedence over emphasis on good methodology and theory. Yet few would disagree that priority should also be given to the development of theories and methodology needed for a better understanding of real-world problems. Some would argue that it will be only through the development of better methods and theory that research will produce solid knowledge about real-world problems. While social scientists disagree on what these better theories and methods are, few would reject policy relevance as a legitimate objective—though not the only one—of scholarly research.

On the other hand, many supervisors of Ph.D. dissertations enjoin their students to give priority to sound methodology and making contributions to theory. The choice of real-world problems for dissertation research is often deemed of secondary importance, and problems are framed to permit adherence and contributions to sound methodology and theory.[3] As a result, even when important real-world problems are singled out for study, the ways in which requirements of method and theory are pursued can reduce the significance of research results for policy.

---

2.   Atul Kohli in "Conclusion" to the symposium, "The Role of Theory in Comparative Politics: A Symposium," *World Politics*, Vol. 48, No. 1 (October 1995), pp. 1–49. The other participants in the symposium were Peter Evans, Peter Katzenstein, Adam Przeworski, Susanne H. Rudolph, James C. Scott, and Theda Skocpol.

3.   This point is also made by Stephen Walt, who decries the fact that much research is "'method-driven'" rather than "'problem-driven' . . . on topics chosen not because they are important, but because they are amenable to analysis by the reigning *méthode du jour.*" Stephen M. Walt, "Rigor or Rigor Mortis? Rational Choice and Security Studies," *International Security*, Vol. 23, No. 4 (Spring 1999), pp. 5ff. Walt's article triggered a spirited debate in *International Security*, Vol. 24, No. 2 (Fall 1999), pp. 5–114, with contributions by Bruce Bueno de Mesquita and James Morrow; Lisa Martin; Emerson Niou and Peter C. Ordeshook; Robert Powell; and Frank Zagare. Walt also offers a reply in the same issue (pp. 115–130).

A problem-oriented approach in research, therefore, does not necessarily lead to knowledge with appreciable policy relevance or significance. Furthermore, many scholars are reluctant to engage in policy-applicable research. Among the reasons for this is that they wish to avoid producing narrow applied policy research of an essentially atheoretical nature which is, indeed, not a proper goal for academic scholarship.

In the next section, we discuss the gap between the needs of policy specialists and decision-makers in government and those of academic political scientists. The highly general theories favored by many political scientists offer little insight into how decision-makers can choose policy instruments to influence outcomes. In contrast, middle-range theories, which aim to explain various subclasses of general phenomena, provide better guidance about when various strategies will be effective. We then detail what types and kinds of knowledge are useful to policymakers; touch on how such knowledge can be developed through theory-oriented case studies, within-case analysis, and process-tracing, and the development of middle-range theory; and detail how much policymakers, who must weigh numerous trade-offs, use scholarly knowledge as an aid to decision-making. Next, we identify six points that can guide scholars who seek to produce theoretically oriented knowledge that is useful to practitioners, and finally we mention a number of other contributions that scholarly research can make to policymaking.

Bridging the Gap Between Theory and Practice

Certainly a "gap" exists between much of the theory produced by political scientists in academic settings and the knowledge needs of policy specialists. This gap, which reflects important differences between the two worlds of academia and policy, can be bridged though not eliminated. In fact, important scholarly contributions to policy are being made, though much more is possible. Better two-way communication between scholars and policy specialists can further bridge the gap between theory and policy.[4]

Scholarly research can make a greater contribution to policymaking

---

4. Important contributions have been made by David D. Newsom, "Foreign Policy and Academia," *Foreign Policy*, No. 101 (Winter 1995), pp. 52–67; Philip Zelikow, "Foreign Policy Engineering: From Theory To Practice and Back Again," *International Security*, Vol. 18, No. 4 (Spring 1994), pp. 143–171; Joseph Lepgold and Miroslav Nincic, *Beyond the Ivory Tower: International Relations Theory and the Issues of Policy Relevance* (New York: Columbia University Press, 2001); and Joseph Lepgold and Miroslav Nincic, eds., *Being Useful: Policy Relevance and International Relations Theory* (Ann Arbor: University of Michigan Press, 2000).

by emphasizing the development of middle-range theories that are narrower in scope but closer to types and forms of knowledge needed in policymaking.[5] We question the higher value some political scientists place on developing general theory rather than, as we have done in this study, on middle-range theory.[6] Highly general theories that attempt to formulate broad covering laws tend to have quite limited explanatory and predictive power. These broad generalizations often end up as probabilistic in character, with little indication of the conditions under which they hold. They are pitched at a level of abstraction that fails to give insightful explanation of foreign policy decisions or of interactions between states that lead to specific outcomes. Middle-range theories, on the other hand, are deliberately limited in their scope; they attempt to explain different subclasses of general phenomena. Middle-range theories attempt to formulate well-specified conditional generalizations of more limited scope. These features make them more useful for policymaking.[7] For example, recent work has focused on the conditions under which power-sharing, peacekeeping, or partition are most effective in resolving ethnic conflicts.[8]

---

5.   A similar point is made by Robert Keohane in his commentary on structural realism: "Even if a large-scale theory can be developed and appropriately tested, its predictions will be rather gross. To achieve a more finely tuned understanding of how resources affect behavior in particular situations, one needs to specify the policy-contingency framework more precisely. The domain of theory is narrowed to achieve greater precision." Robert O. Keohane, ed., *Neorealism and Its Critics* (New York: Columbia University Press, 1986), p. 188.

6.   The need for middle-range theory is emphasized also by George R. Boynton, who argues that the "right type of law" for social science is highly specific and relates a limited number of variables to each other under stated conditions. These conditions should state the values of other variables that are necessary for the theoretical relations in question to hold among the explanatory variables. George R. Boynton, "On Getting From Here to There," in Eleanor Ostrom, ed., *Strategies of Political Inquiry* (Beverly Hills, Calif.: Sage, 1982), pp. 29–68.

7.   Bruce Jentleson discusses in detail why middle-range theory serves the needs of policymaking better than general theory. See Jentleson, "In Pursuit Praxis: Applying International Relations Theory to Foreign Policy-Making," in Lepgold and Miroslav, eds., *Being Useful*, pp. 133–135. Jentleson discusses his personal experience in the Department of State's Policy Planning Staff and presents two cases studies that illustrate the utility of middle-range theory. See also Bruce Jentleson, "The Need for Praxis: Bringing Policy Relevance Back In," *International Security*, Vol. 26, No. 3 (Spring 2002), pp. 169–183.

    The importance of conditional generalizations is emphasized also by John Lewis Gaddis, "In Defense of Particular Generalizations," in Colin Elman and Miriam Fendius Elman, eds., *Bridges and Boundaries: Historians, Political Scientists, and the Study of International Relations* (Cambridge, Mass.: MIT Press, 2001), pp. 301–326.

8.   See, for example, Timothy D. Sisk, *Power Sharing and International Mediation in Ethnic Conflicts* (Washington, D.C.: Carnegie Commission on Preventing Deadly Conflicts

In our view, research that aims to produce policy-applicable knowledge and theory is not at all inconsistent with efforts to develop international relations theory. Rather, efforts to develop policy-relevant knowledge are indispensable for the further development and refinement of international relations theory. A similar position has been expressed for the development of political science as a whole by a number of scholars. Peter Ordeshook, a proponent of formal theory, has called on his colleagues to take more seriously the need to make their research more policy-relevant: "Until the 'engineering' component of the discipline assumes a central role, research—whether theoretical, empirical, or any combination of the two—will continue to generate an incoherent accumulation of theories, lemmas, correlations, and 'facts.'"[9] Similarly, in several unpublished papers, David Dessler has made similar observations regarding the need to infuse a "pragmatic dimension" into international relations theory.[10]

One example of the limited policy relevance of covering-law type generalizations is structural-realist theory, the dominant theory of international relations in American political science. These limitations have become increasingly evident in recent years and have triggered lively debates.[11] While structural-realist theory is certainly necessary, it remains insufficient by itself either for *explaining* foreign policy decisions and out-

---

and U.S. Institute of Peace Press, 1996); see also Paul C. Stern and Daniel Druckman, eds., *International Conflict Resolution After the Cold War* (Washington, D.C.: National Academy Press, 2000).

9. Peter Ordeshook, "Engineering or Science: What is the Study of Politics?" in Jeffrey Friedman, ed., *The Rational Choice Controversy* (New Haven, Conn.: Yale University Press, 1995), pp. 175–188.

10. David Dessler, "Talking Across Disciplines in the Study of Peace and Security: Epistemology and Pragmatics as Sources of Division in the Social Sciences," Center for International Security and Arms Control, Stanford University, June 1996.

11. See, for example, the selection of essays, "Formal Models, Formal Complaints," *International Security*, Vol. 24, No. 2 (Fall 1999). A lucid analysis of two major shortcomings of international relations systems theories—their low levels of explanatory determinism and policy relevance—is provided in Jack Snyder and Robert Jervis, eds., *Coping With Complexity in the International System* (Boulder, Colo.: Westview Press, 1993). They urge that systems theories such as Kenneth N. Waltz's structural realism theory be broadened to consider how structural variables interact with nonstructural variables such as military technology, actor preferences, and domestic politics. In addition, they emphasize the need to focus on variables that are more manipulable by policymakers. Many other writers have also criticized ultraparsimonious systems theories that fail to capture the dynamics of international relations. See also the detailed analysis in Robert Jervis, *Systems Effects: Complexity in Political and Social Life* (Princeton, N.J.: Princeton University Press, 1997), and his article, "Complexity and the Analysis of Political and Social Life," *Political Science Quarterly*, Vol. 12, No. 4 (Winter 1997/1998), pp. 569–593.

comes or for *conducting* foreign policy. Indeed, Kenneth Waltz himself has emphasized that his structural-realist theory is *not* a theory of foreign policy. He warned against expecting his theory to "explain the particular policies of states" and regarded it as an error "to mistake a theory of international politics for a theory of foreign policy." Waltz regards structural realism as a theory of constraints on foreign policy rather than a theory of foreign policy: ". . . what it does explain are the constraints that confine all states."[12] In this important (though limited) sense, structural realist theory is indeed policy-relevant.

We are left, therefore, with a large vacuum in international relations theory that must be addressed if one wishes to develop better knowledge that will help explain and inform foreign policy. We believe it would be of limited value to try to develop a very general theory of foreign policy, or "statecraft," as historians used to call it. More useful contributions are made by focusing specifically on each of the many *generic problems* encountered in the conduct of foreign policy—problems such as deterrence, coercive diplomacy, crisis management, war termination, preventive diplomacy, mediation, conciliation, cooperation, and so on. Theories that focus on such generic problems are examples of middle-range theory. Examples of middle-range structural-realist theories are present in the works of Thomas Christensen, Jack Snyder, and Randall Schweller, who formulate more contingent generalizations than does Kenneth Waltz about circumstances under which states balance, bandwagon, or buck-pass. These generalizations include not only structural or material characteristics, but also statespersons' foreign policy goals and their expectations of whether offensive or defensive forces will predominate in battle.[13]

Quite early in pursuing the research program that has led to the publication of this book, we became aware of the need to move beyond structural-realist, rational-choice, and game theories. These deductive ap-

12. Kenneth N. Waltz, *Theory of International Politics* (New York: McGraw-Hill, 1979), pp. 121–122. Waltz reemphasized this point in "International Politics is Not Foreign Policy," *Security Studies*, Vol. 6, No. 1 (Autumn 1996), pp. 54–57. See, however, Colin Elman's observation that Waltz seems to want it both ways, i.e., that structural-realism is and is not a theory of foreign policy, in "Horses for Courses: Why NOT Neorealist Theories of Foreign Policy?" *Security Studies*, Vol. 6, No. 1 (Autumn 1996), pp. 7–53.

13. Thomas Christensen and Jack Snyder, "Chain Gangs and Passed Bucks: Predicting Alliance Patterns in Multipolarity," *International Organization*, Vol. 44, No. 2 (Spring 1990), pp. 137–168; and Randall L. Schweller, "Bandwagoning for Profit: Bringing the Revisionist State Back In," *International Security*, Vol. 19, No. 1 (Summer 1994), pp. 72–107.

proaches "black-box" around both the process of policymaking and the strategic interaction between states that leads to foreign policy outcomes; they deal with these two processes by assumption and by refinement of assumptions. In our view, it is necessary to engage in the direct (and admittedly difficult) empirical study of decision-making processes and strategic interaction. However, deductive and empirical ways of developing knowledge and theory of international relations are hardly antithetical; as emphasized in Chapter 11 and elsewhere, it is desirable to link deductive and empirical approaches more closely together.[14]

Development of generic knowledge is not the only type of middle-range theory and knowledge that is relevant for policymakers. We shall note other types of scholarly research at the end of this chapter after discussing ways of developing generic knowledge of the tasks policymakers faced repeatedly (though in different contexts). (Throughout the chapter, we use the term "usable knowledge" as a synonym for policy-applicable theory and will comment later on the relationship of usable knowledge to scientific knowledge.[15])

What is Usable Knowledge?

We find it useful to address the challenge of developing usable knowledge by posing three more specific questions for discussion:[16]

1. What kinds of knowledge do practitioners need for dealing with different generic problems?
2. How can such knowledge be developed?
3. How can generic knowledge be used by policy specialists?

The answers to these three questions are interrelated. Scholars who acquire a realistic understanding of how generic knowledge can enter into the policy analysis that precedes and contributes to decision-making can better identify and develop the forms of knowledge that practitioners

---

14. This position is similar to that expressed by some leading proponents of rational choice and game theories. See, for example, the study by Robert Bates et al., *Analytic Narratives* (Princeton, N.J.: Princeton University Press, 1998).

15. We have taken the phrase "usable knowledge" from Charles E. Lindblom and David K. Cohen, *Usable Knowledge: Social Science and Social Problem Solving* (New Haven, Conn.: Yale University Press, 1979).

16. This section draws on George, *Bridging the Gap*, and Alexander L. George, "The Role of Force in Diplomacy: A Continuing Dilemma for U.S. Foreign Policy," in Horst W. Brands, ed., *The Use of Force After the Cold War* (College Station: Texas A&M University Press, 2000).

need. Policy specialists and decision-makers need much more specific information about particular situations they face than outside scholars possess. We must recognize, therefore, the limited usefulness of generic knowledge—but appreciate at the same time why it is indispensable for policymaking and how it should be used in policy analysis.

What Types of Knowledge Do Practitioners Need?

Turning to the first of the three questions posed above, policy specialists need a *general conceptual model* of every particular strategy or policy instrument that identifies the general logic associated with successful use of a policy tool. A discussion of the relatively simple concept of deterrence will illustrate this point. A threat to respond to actions an adversary may be contemplating is a critical component of general deterrence theory. The actions threatened for purposes of deterrence may or may not be ambiguous. In any event, the general logic of deterrence requires that threats to respond to possible provocations should be sufficiently credible and sufficiently potent to the adversary to persuade him or her that the costs and risks of the contemplated actions are likely to outweigh the expected gains. The logic of this abstract deterrence model, therefore, rests on a general assumption that one is dealing with a rational opponent who is able to calculate correctly the benefits, costs, and risks of actions he or she contemplates taking.

Two limitations of the usefulness of such abstract models for both theory development and policymaking should be noted. First, a general conceptual model is *not* itself a strategy but merely the starting point for constructing a strategy that fits a specific situation and is likely to influence a specific actor. The conceptual model identifies only the general logic—that is, the desired impact of a deterrent threat on an adversary's calculations and the behavior needed for the chosen strategy to be effective. But the abstract model itself does not indicate what the policymaker must do to introduce that logic into the adversary's calculations. The policymaker has to convert the abstract model into a specific strategy that fits a particular situation, taking into account those behavioral characteristics of the particular adversary that are likely to influence his or her response to the deterrent threat.

One example will suffice to indicate what a policymaker must do to move from an abstract conceptual model to a specific strategy tailored to a particular situation. Coercive diplomacy relies on threats to induce an adversary to stop or undo a hostile action in which he or she is already engaged. To convert the abstract concept of coercive diplomacy into a specific strategy, the policymaker has to make a specific determination for each of the following four variable components of the general model:

1. What demand to make on the opponent
2. Whether and how to create a sense of urgency for compliance with the demand
3. How to create and convey a threat of punishment for noncompliance that will be sufficiently credible and sufficiently potent to persuade the adversary that compliance is in his or her best interest;
4. Whether to couple the threat with a positive inducement (i.e., a "carrot") to make compliance easier for the adversary and, if so, what kind and how much of an inducement to offer and how best to make the positive incentive sufficiently credible and sufficiently potent

These variable components of the abstract model of coercive diplomacy may be likened to blank lines that the policymaker must fill in when designing a specific strategy of coercive diplomacy.

The strongest strategy of coercive diplomacy is the ultimatum— either explicit or tacit—in which the demand on the opponent is accompanied by a deadline (or a sense of urgency about compliance) and is backed by a sufficiently potent and sufficiently credible threat of punishment for noncompliance.[17] A weaker variant of coercive diplomacy is the "gradual turning of the screw," in which the sense of urgency about compliance is diluted, though not altogether absent, and the punishment threatened is not a single potent action but an incremental progression of severe pressure. Even weaker is the "try-and-see" variant of coercive diplomacy, in which the demand is not accompanied by a sense of urgency for compliance and may be backed only by a modest coercive threat or action, which, if ineffective, may or may not be followed by another modest action or threat.

Therefore, a general concept is not itself a strategy; rather, it needs to be converted into a particular strategy. There is only one concept of deterrence and one concept of coercive diplomacy, but there are quite a few different deterrence and coercive diplomacy strategies.

This distinction between concepts and strategies, and the relation between them, is of considerable contemporary significance. Consider the debate as to whether U.S. policy toward China should be one of containment or engagement. In simplistic versions of this debate, these terms serve as little more than rhetorical slogans. Theory and policy both require recognition that there are different strategies of containment and different variants of engagement.[18]

---

17. There are a number of important risks associated with giving opponents an ultimatum of which policymakers must be aware and to which appropriate attention must be given in any situation. See George, *Bridging the Gap*, pp. 81–82.

18. Recall in this connection that John Lewis Gaddis emphasized that over time U.S. administrations pursued significantly different strategies of containment toward the

CONDITIONS THAT FAVOR SUCCESS

In addition to conceptual models that lead to formulation of strategies, practitioners need *generic knowledge* about the conditions that favor the success of specific strategies they may employ. Much of this knowledge takes the form, as emphasized in this book, of conditional generalizations—statements that indicate the conditions under which a strategy is likely to be effective or ineffective.

Generic knowledge is a useful label for a form of theory that is of recognizable interest to policy specialists. This can be illustrated by recalling the experience one of the authors had some years ago in interviewing policy specialists. Their eyes would glaze over as soon as he used the word "theory." But they nodded approvingly when he spoke instead of the need for "generic knowledge." It is not difficult to understand why they responded favorably to this phrase. Policy specialists recognize that many generic problems arise in the conduct of foreign policy—for example, the task of deterrence emerges repeatedly over time with different adversaries and in different contexts. Therefore, policy experts readily understand and agree that generic knowledge about the uses and limitations of every particular strategy or policy instrument can be helpful when one considers possible uses of that strategy in a new situation.[19]

Generic knowledge is not sufficient to determine what action to take, but it is useful to policy specialists who must first diagnose a new situation to see whether or not favorable conditions exist or can be created for employing a particular strategy. Good generic knowledge enables a practitioner to increase the chances of making the right decision about whether and how to employ a particular strategy. Generic knowledge is most useful when it identifies conditions, processes, and causal mechanisms that link the use of each strategy to variance in its outcomes.

CORRECT IMAGE OF THE ADVERSARY

The policymaker needs a *correct image of the adversary* whose behavior the strategy is designed to influence. Policy specialists and academic scholars agree on this fundamental point: in conducting foreign policy one must try to see events—and even assess one's own behavior—from the per-

---

Soviet Union. See his *Strategies of Containment* (New York: Oxford University Press, 1982), a study that makes use of the method of structured, focused comparison. Two recent studies illustrate how a conceptual model is converted into strategies: Stephen R. Rock, *Appeasement in International Politics* (Lexington: University Press of Kentucky, 2000); and Bruce W. Jentleson, ed., *Opportunities Missed, Opportunities Seized* (Lanham, Md.: Rowman and Littlefield, 2000).

19.   George, *Bridging the Gap*.

spective of the adversary. Only by doing so can the practitioner diagnose a developing situation accurately and select appropriate ways to communicate with and influence the other actor. Faulty images of an adversary often lead to major errors in policy, avoidable catastrophes, and missed opportunities.

Scholars and policymakers often assume that adversaries are rational, unitary actors. Both components of this assumption seriously oversimplify the task of understanding and influencing other actors. More discriminating "actor-specific" behavioral models are needed that recognize that an adversary is not a unitary actor, but often includes a number of individuals who may differ in important ways in their analysis of challenges and opportunities to be considered in deciding policy. Similarly, the particular rationality of an opponent may reflect values, beliefs, perceptions, and judgments of acceptable risk that differ from those of the side that is attempting to influence its behavior. Simple assumptions that one is dealing with a rational or unitary actor may be particularly dangerous when one is trying to deal with *non-state actors*, such as warlords, terrorists, or rivals in civil wars.[20]

We have identified three types of knowledge practitioners need for dealing with generic problems: general conceptual models, generic knowledge, and correct images of adversaries. We turn now to a discussion of the *forms* of knowledge most useful for policymaking.

What Forms of Knowledge Do Practitioners Need?

Much scholarly theory and knowledge is cast in the form of probabilistic generalizations of a broad character. These are not without value for policymaking, but leave the policymaker with the difficult task of deciding whether the probabilistic relationship in question applies to the particular case at hand. Political scientists should therefore make a move from theory and knowledge cast in probabilistic terms to conditional generalizations of more limited scope. For example, additional research is needed to transform the general probabilistic proposition that arms races are likely to lead to war into more specific contingent generalizations that will identify the conditions under which arms races are likely to lead to war.[21] Conditional generalizations are more useful when they identify

---

20.   A more detailed discussion is provided in Alexander L. George, "The Need for Influence Theory and Actor-Specific Models of Adversaries," in Barry R. Schneider and Jerrold M. Post, eds., *Know Thy Enemy* (Maxwell Air Force Base, Ala.: U.S. Air Force Counterproliferation Center, November 2002), pp. 211–230.

21.   This was the major conclusion drawn by George Downs in his survey of research

variables over which policymakers can exercise some leverage. Conditional generalizations may also be couched in probabilistic terms, but are more specific and more limited in scope than general probabilistic ones.

Similarly, statistical-correlational findings about different aspects of international relations are not without some value for policymaking, but their usefulness is often sharply reduced because such studies often do not include causal variables that the decision-maker can influence. Policymakers need knowledge that identifies the causal processes and causal mechanisms that explain how an antecedent condition or variable is linked in well-defined contexts to variance in the outcome variable. Thus, policy-relevant research tries to go beyond statistical-correlational findings in order to identify causal processes.

The science of microbiology and its relation to medical practice offers a highly relevant model. Consider the relationship of smoking cigarettes (and exposure to other carcinogens) to cancer. Statistical-correlational studies have long since convinced most of us that some kind of causal relationship does indeed exist. These studies were thus policy-relevant even though the underlying mechanism was not known. It is better, however, to understand the causal mechanism and process that links exposure to carcinogens to cancer, and use them to develop policy interventions. To use an analogy, a person stranded on a desert island has more use for a barometer than for a theory of weather. Observing the barometer would soon lead to a rough prediction of incoming storms. However, the combination of a barometer and a theory of weather would lead to far more precise predictions on how air pressure, temperature, prevailing wind patterns, and other factors will shape the weather. Similarly, microbiologists have been working for years—lately with considerable success—to identify the intervening causal processes between smoking and cancer. Finding causal links between smoking and cancer creates opportunities for developing intervention techniques to halt the development of cancer.

In the same way, a knowledge of causal mechanisms and patterns offers foreign policy practitioners opportunities to identify possibilities for using leverage to influence outcomes of interaction with other actors. Of course, the success of microbiology in identifying causal mechanisms may not be easily duplicated in the study of international relations or in other branches of political science. Nonetheless, it is heartening that in recent years political scientists have increasingly recognized the importance of studying causal processes and causal mechanisms.

---

on "Arms Races and War," in Philip S. Tetlock et al., eds., *Behavior, Society, and Nuclear War*, Vol. 2 (New York: Oxford University Press, 1991), p. 75.

Developing Policy-Relevant Knowledge

How can scholars develop the knowledge that practitioners need in order to deal with different problems that arise in the implementation of foreign policy? This, indeed, is the subject of the preceding chapters. In brief:

- Theory-oriented case studies of past historical experience with different problems and different strategies are needed to identify and cumulate the lessons of experience into usable knowledge for policymaking.
- Within-case analysis and process-tracing are important alternatives to reliance on variable-oriented approaches that attempt to replicate the experimental method.
- Individual case studies can contribute to all phases of theory development.
- The method of structured, focused comparison provides a research strategy for single as well as comparative case studies. In this alternative research approach, a "case" should be considered to be an instance of a class of events (rather than simply as a single measure of a key variable).
- Middle-range theories are more likely to constitute usable knowledge for policy than broad, general theories.
- Middle-range theory is produced by identifying sub-classes of a major phenomenon and by selecting instances of each particular sub-class for study. This is one of the major conclusions we have drawn from many efforts in the past thirty years to use case studies for theory development.
- Finally, development of usable knowledge derived from historical experience is enhanced if scholars are attentive to the phenomenon of equifinality (multiple causation) and to the desirability of developing typological theory.

We turn now to the third question posed above—regarding how generic knowledge is used by policy specialists. An understanding by scholars of the nature and scope of usable knowledge, we believe, will be enhanced if they understand how it can enter into policy analysis and decision-making.

How Can Scholarly Knowledge Be Used by Policymakers?

To move toward bridging the *gap between theory and practice,* both scholars and policy specialists need a realistic understanding of the limited and (often indirect, but still important) impact that scholarly knowledge, theory, and generic knowledge can have on policymaking.[22] Academics need to understand how policymakers arrive at their decisions.

Theory and generic knowledge are best understood as a source of inputs to policy analysis of specific problems within the government. They are an *aid, not a substitute for policy analysis and for judgments that decision-makers make when choosing a policy.* Even the best theoretical conceptualization of a problem and the most highly developed generic knowledge of a strategy cannot substitute for competent analysis by governmental specialists who must consider whether some version of a strategy is likely to be viable in the particular situation at hand. In addition, for policymakers to judge which action to take, they must take into account a number of considerations that cannot be anticipated or addressed in generic articulations of strategies.

One or another of seven different types of judgments, most of which involve trade-offs, must be made by top-level decision-makers. Such judgments can be aided only to a limited extent by theory and generic knowledge—or even by policy analysis within the government. These include:

- trade-offs between the quality of decisions, the need for political and bureaucratic support for policies adopted, and the prudent management of time and political and policymaking resources;
- judgments of political side effects and opportunity costs of given courses of action;
- judgments of the utility and acceptable risks of different options;
- trade-offs between short-term versus long-term payoffs;
- judgments as to whether to satisfice or optimize;
- judgments as to how best to deal with the value complexity imbedded in decisional choice; and
- judgments as to when to make a decision.[23]

22. George, *Bridging the Gap.* See also the important observations by Newsom, "Foreign Policy and Academia," which notes that prominent faculty specialists are often recruited for high policy positions. Newsom notes that five national security advisers since the administration of John F. Kennedy were professors before becoming special assistant for national security affairs: McGeorge Bundy, Walter Rostow, Henry Kissinger, Zbigniew Brzezinski, and Anthony Lake. Since Newsom called attention to this, another professor, Condoleezza Rice, has served in the same position. Newsom also calls attention to the fact that many academic scholars offered policy critiques and suggestions that were proven right in the long run.

23. For a discussion of these types of judgment and the importance of developing a better understanding of the relationship of analysis to judgment, see George, *Bridging*

The critical role of judgment in policymaking was emphasized by George Ball, undersecretary of state during the Cuban Missile Crisis. He described the complexity of the problem faced by policymakers during the crisis: "We were presented . . . with an equation of compound variables and multiple unknowns. No one has yet devised a computer that will digest such raw data as was available to us and promptly print out a recommended course of action."[24]

No theory or systematic generic knowledge can provide policy specialists with detailed, high-confidence prescriptions for action in each contingency that arises. Such policy-relevant theory and knowledge does not exist and is not feasible. Rather, we must think in terms of an analogy with traditional medical practice, which calls for a correct diagnosis of the problem before prescribing a treatment. Policy-applicable theory and knowledge facilitate two essential tasks of policymaking: the *diagnostic* task and the *prescriptive* one. We emphasize their contribution to the diagnosis of new situations rather than their ability to prescribe sound choices of policy, largely because top-level decision-makers must take into account factual information about the situation and trade-off judgments that are not covered by theory and generic knowledge. Various theories of rational decision-making have been designed to help policy specialists to make decisions of high analytic quality, but as yet no theory of *effective* decision-making guides policymakers in making the seven important judgments noted above. The policymaker, like the physician, acts as a clinician in striving to make a correct diagnosis of the problem before determining the best choice of a treatment.

It is often assumed that policymakers do not make use of generalizations in diagnosing and prescribing. This view is mistaken. Indeed, one of the major tasks of policy-oriented scholars is to discourage the decision-maker from applying *oversimplified* generalizations for purposes of policymaking. It is not only academic researchers with a passion for correlating only two variables who can be charged with engaging in "crude empiricism;" the policymaker, too, is often a crude empiricist. He or she can make highly dubious use of univariate propositions of the form: "if A, then B"—for example: "If appeasement, then World War III." However, the decision-maker does not always operate as a crude empiricist.

the Gap, chap. 2. See also the detailed innovative study, Stanley Renshon and Deborah Welch Larson, eds., *Good Judgment in Foreign Policy: Theory and Application* (Lanham, Md.: Rowman and Littlefield, 2003).

24.   George Ball, "Lawyers and Diplomats," address before the New York Lawyers' Association, New York City, December 13, 1962; reprinted in Department of State, *Bulletin,* December 31, 1962, pp. 987–991.

Figure 12.1. Knowledge and Judgments for Policymakers.

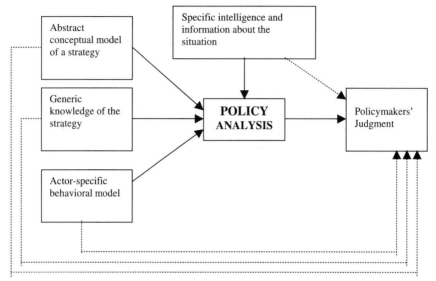

Ways in which the three types of knowledge together with specific information about the situation contribute to the policy analysis that precedes the various judgments policymakers must make.

He or she often goes beyond available generalizations to note, in addition, what is special about the case at hand. We need to study and learn more about what a person does when he or she "goes beyond" available generalizations to deal with a single case. Evidently, he or she is trying to assess other relevant variables—not included in the generalizations—and the possible interactions among these many variables to make a judgment about the present case that goes beyond a crude probabilistic treatment.

Figure 12.1 indicates how the three types of knowledge that policymakers need—abstract conceptual models of strategies, generic knowledge of strategies, and actor-specific behavioral models of adversaries—enter into policy analysis within the government.[25] The diagram also reflects the fact that policy analysis requires specific intelligence and information about the situation, and that the decision finally taken by the top policymaker is influenced by one or more of the seven types of judgment that need to be made in choosing among available options.

---

25.   The diagram is adapted from the one that appears in George, *Bridging the Gap,* p. 133.

Implications for Scholarly Research and Policymaking

The preceding analysis has the following six implications for researchers. First, however desirable in its own right, theory and knowledge that fully meet scientific standards are not essential for the sensible conduct of foreign policy.[26] As early as thirty years ago the distinguished psychologist Donald Campbell noted that "we must not suppose that scientific knowing replaces common-sense knowing." Similarly, James March has endorsed "a perception of theory as contributing marginally to ordinary knowledge rather than summarizing all knowledge."[27]

Just as intelligent people generally manage the many chores of everyday life reasonably well without benefit of fully developed scientific knowledge, so too can intelligent policymakers use the best available knowledge of different aspects of international affairs. To be useful in policymaking, conditional generalizations about the efficacy of a strategy need not satisfy the high degree of verification associated with scientific knowledge. Of course, policymakers would like the general knowledge on which they base decisions to be as valid as possible, but in practice they will settle for more modest levels of precision. When verification of conditional generalizations is limited, policymakers can still make use of them, even though the generalizations have limited empirical support and therefore are only plausible.[28] By drawing on available information about a particular case, policymakers can often judge whether the plausible generalization is likely to hold for that situation.

Second, academic scholars should include manipulable variables, variables over which policymakers have some leverage, in their research design. Strategy is just such a variable. We noted earlier the limited relevance for policymaking of quantitative correlational research on international relations that deals only with non-decision-making variables in attempting to account for variance in foreign policy outcomes.

The importance of "leverage variables" is noted by sophisticated policymakers, who are at times explicit about their need for information

---

26. This discussion draws directly from ibid., pp. 139–143.

27. Donald T. Campbell, "Qualitative Knowing in Action Research," paper given at the American Psychological Association meetings in New Orleans, La., September 1974, p. 4; and James March, "Decision Making Perspective," in Andrew H. Vandeven, ed., *Perspectives in Organizational Design and Behavior* (New York: Wiley, 1981).

28. A conditional generalization is plausible if it is not contradicted by available evidence and if at least some evidence supports it. For a detailed discussion of the limits of scientific verification in social science and the need to settle for "acceptable" verification, see Charles E. Lindblom, *Inquiry and Change* (New Haven, Conn.: Yale University Press, 1990), chap. 10.

about the critical variables in a situation. Dean Acheson, for example, advanced a theory of the "missing component" in describing how he adapted the problem-solving approach to policymaking. He believed that many problems could be solved if the statesman discovers the missing component, the introduction of which would make a difficult situation manageable. The art of finding the missing component lies in mastering a knowledge of all the present and potential elements in a situation and determining what new element, if added by U.S. policy, would make the difficult situation more manageable. Acheson tried to apply this theory to the perennial question of whether to give economic and military aid to underdeveloped countries. He recommended against it when U.S. aid could not provide the local governments in question with the other necessary elements they lacked—the loyalty of their people and honest and efficient administration.[29]

Third, taking note of a concern often expressed by policymakers, scholars should not define concepts and variables at too high a level of abstraction. The more abstract a concept, the more remote it is from its referent in the real world, and the more difficult the intellectual demand on the practitioner to make that linkage and to benefit from it.

Fourth, scholars should recognize that too strict a pursuit of the scientific criterion of parsimony in their efforts to theorize is inappropriate for developing useful policy-relevant theory and knowledge. A rich theory—one that encompasses a relatively large number of the variables that can influence the outcome of a policy—is often more useful in policymaking than a simpler theory of narrow scope, such as structural-realist theory, that encompasses only a few causal variables. The policymaker who must deal with complex situations that embrace many variables gets more help from a rich theory (even though it may enjoy less verification) than from a simple, parsimonious theory that establishes a firm linkage of some kind among only a few of the operative variables. This does not mean that the policymaker is reduced to making highly speculative judgments. Thorough verification of rich theories is not usually a major issue for policymakers; they can try to assess the validity of a theory or generalizations for at least the particular case at hand by using the detailed information available on that case.

A rich theory is useful to policymakers if it meets two criteria: its contents must be at least plausible, and it must indicate the special conditions under which its propositions are likely to be true or false. Such a

---

29. David S. McLellan, "Comparative 'Operational Codes' of Recent U.S. Secretaries of State: Dean Acheson," paper delivered at the Annual Meeting of the American Political Science Association, September 1969, pp. 18, 28.

rich, differentiated theory serves at the very least as a sophisticated checklist to remind policy analysts and policymakers of the numerous conditions and variables that can influence their ability to achieve desired outcomes and to avoid undesired ones in any given foreign policy activity. When more fully developed, a rich, differentiated theory about a particular type of foreign policy activity identifies those conditions that favor the policy's success. Such conditions have causal relevance even when, as is often the case, they cannot be regarded as being either necessary or sufficient for a given outcome to occur.

Fifth, the production of such relatively specific conditional generalizations should be an important objective in developing policy-applicable theory. These are more useful in policymaking than broad generalizations that merely assert a probabilistic relationship between two variables without identifying the conditions under which the relationship does and does not hold. Conditional generalizations of more limited scope are also more useful than deductive theories and universal generalizations that can claim no more than perhaps to have identified a necessary condition for the success of a particular policy instrument or undertaking (without assessing the extent of its causal importance), but say little or nothing about what else must also be present for that favorable outcome to occur.

This is not to say, however, that producing conditional generalizations is a relatively simple research task. For example, despite the considerable research effort of many scholars over the years on the question "Do arms races lead to war?" a recent review of this literature tells us that "there is still no well-developed theory that provides a reliable guide for policymakers."[30] However, research on this question does show that arms races are neither a necessary condition for the occurrence of war (since wars do sometimes occur in the absence of a prior arms race) nor a sufficient condition (since an arms race is not always followed by war). Additional study should attempt at least to identify a number of conditions that can be said to favor the likelihood of war and perhaps to identify ways in which policymakers can reduce or control the likelihood of an arms race resulting in war.

Sixth, but by no means least in importance, in attempting to develop conditional generalizations, scholars should consider whether the phenomenon in question is characterized by equifinality (or "multiple causation"); that is, the possibility or fact that similar outcomes in different cases of a phenomenon can have different causal explanations. An example of equifinality was the discovery that deterrence can fail in several

---

30. George Downs, "Arms Races and War," p. 75.

different ways, leading to the identification of three different causal patterns leading to deterrence failure.[31] Another example of equifinality emerged in the identification of several different paths to "inadvertent war" (a war that occurs even though neither side wanted or expected it at the beginning of the crisis).[32]

The phenomenon of equifinality pervades much of international relations and many other areas of life, as John Stuart Mill recognized so many years ago in his *System of Logic*. Mill warned that the methods of agreement and difference he outlined were not applicable to many social phenomena, because their occurrence was subject to "plurality of causes."[33] Equifinality has important implications not only for the form that causal knowledge of foreign policy outcomes often must take but also for research strategies aimed at developing causal theory. For example, the fact that the phenomenon being studied is subject to equifinality and that alternative causal paths may lead to similar outcomes directly contradicts the familiar insistence of some scholars that the researcher *must* vary the dependent variable. Scholars should not assume, as they often do, that the task of developing theory and causal knowledge consists in finding a single causal generalization or pattern for all instances of an undertaking that have resulted in a similar outcome. Rather, the research task will be better pursued and be more fruitful if the investigator is alert to discovering different causal patterns that lead to a similar outcome.

Other Types of Scholarly Contributions to Policymaking

As noted earlier in this chapter, although we focus discussion on one important type of knowledge that scholarly research can contribute to policymaking, there are also other types of contributions.[34] For example, well-informed, objective analyses of problems such as the impact of conflicts of a nationalistic, ethnic, and religious character on intrastate and

---

31. See Alexander L. George and Richard Smoke, *Deterrence in American Foreign Policy: Theory and Practice* (New York: Columbia University Press, 1974), chap. 18, "Patterns of Deterrence Failure: A Typology." For a detailed discussion of this study, see the Appendix, "Studies That Illustrate Research Design."

32. Alexander L. George, ed., *Avoiding War: Problems of Crisis Management* (Boulder, Colo.: Westview Press, 1991), pp. 545–553.

33. Amitai Etzioni and Frederick Dubow, eds., *Comparative Perspectives: Theories and Methods* (Boston: Little, Brown, 1970), pp. 207–208.

34. For a more comprehensive listing of social science research that contributes to policy, see, for example, *Fostering Human Progress: Social Science and Behavioral Science Research Contributions to Public Policy* (Washington, D.C.: Consortium of Social Science Associations, 2001).

interstate relations, problems of nuclear proliferation, environmental and ecological problems, population and demographic trends, problems of food production and distribution, water scarcities, health and sanitation problems—all these and other analyses improve the knowledge base required for management of challenges to national, regional, and worldwide well-being.

In addition, scholars can—and indeed do—make a variety of other types of contributions. Among these are the development of better concepts and conceptual frameworks that can assist policy specialists to orient themselves to the phenomena and problems with which they must deal.[35] Similarly, scholars can make an important contribution by challenging simplistic concepts being employed by policymakers. A recent example of such a contribution is Robert Litwak's criticism of policymakers' use of the concept of "rogue states" and his outline of a number of different strategies of engagement.[36]

Although scholars may not be able to advise policymakers how best to deal with a specific instance of a problem that requires timely action, they can often provide a useful broader discussion of how to think about and understand that general phenomenon—such as, for example, the problem of ethnicity and nationalism. Predictions about such matters should not be regarded as the most important goal of academic scholarship. As David Newsom notes, a more suitable goal is the identification of underlying social forces, mismatches between regimes and peoples, and current policies that may be doomed to failure.[37]

In recent years scholars have devoted a great deal of attention and research to problems of intrastate conflicts. Much of the knowledge base for avoidance and management of *inter*state conflict that was acquired during the long years of the Cold War is not relevant or very useful for addressing the many *intra*state conflicts that have emerged since the end of that era. An impressive contribution is being made by many scholars to

---

35. The importance of conceptual clarification and refinement has been persuasively emphasized by David Collier in several recent publications, including: David Collier and James Mahoney, "Conceptual Stretching Revisited: Adapting Categories in Comparative Analysis," *American Political Science Review,* Vol. 87, No. 4 (December 1993), pp. 845–855; and David Collier and Steven Levitsky, "Democracy with Adjectives: Conceptual Innovation in Comparative Research," *World Politics,* Vol. 49, No. 3 (April 1997), pp. 430–451. Also see David Laitin, "Disciplining Political Science," *American Political Science Review,* Vol. 89, No. 2 (June 1995), pp. 454–456.

36. Robert S. Litwak, *Rogue States and U.S. Foreign Policy: Containment After the Cold War* (Washington, D.C.: Woodrow Wilson Center Press, distributed by Johns Hopkins University Press, 2000).

37. Newsom, "Foreign Policy and Academia."

building knowledge for a better understanding of such conflicts and ways of preventing or dealing with them. For example, in 1997 the Carnegie Corporation of New York completed a three-year study of the problems of preventing deadly conflicts. This study drew on available scholarly knowledge and stimulated important new research efforts to fill the gaps in such knowledge. It is a fine example of a collaborative effort of high-level policymakers and scholars to analyze the sources of violent conflicts and to evaluate tools for preventing or limiting them.[38] In parallel with the work of the Carnegie Commission on Preventing Deadly Conflict, the National Academy of Sciences established a Committee on International Conflict Resolution, which has published monographic studies of a number of problems in this issue area.[39]

Another example of research undertaken by academic scholars at the behest of government officials focuses on improving knowledge of circumstances that lead to "state failure." In 1994, at the behest of Vice President Albert Gore, the U.S. government established the "State Failure Task Force." Over a period of years, the task force collected and undertook quantitative analysis of a large body of data comprising many variables and issued several useful reports.[40]

Conclusion: Bridging the Gap

To further bridge the gap between theory and practice, scholars must take a realistic view of the limited, indirect, and yet important impact that scholarly knowledge about foreign policy can have on policymaking. In addressing this question, we advanced three central themes. First, three types of policy-relevant knowledge—conceptual models, generic knowledge, actor-specific behavior models—can indeed help bridge the gap,

---

38. Carnegie Commission on Preventing Deadly Conflict, *Preventing Deadly Conflict* (New York: Carnegie Corporation of New York, December 1997). This report includes an appendix that lists all of the monographic studies that were commissioned, which are available on request.

39. Stern and Druckman, eds., *International Conflict Resolution After the Cold War.*

40. See, for example, Daniel C. Esty et al., *Working Papers: State Failure Task Force Report* (McLean, Va.: Science Applications International Corporation, 1995); Daniel C. Esty et al., *The State Failure Task Force Report: Phase II Findings* (McLean, Va.: Science Applications International Corporation, 1998); Daniel C. Esty, Jack Goldstone, and Ted Robert Gurr, eds., *Preventive Measures: Building Risk Assessment and Crisis Early Warning Systems* (Lanham, Md.: Rowman and Littlefield, 1998); and Daniel C. Esty et al., "The State Failure Report: Phase II Findings," *Environmental Change and Security Project Report,* Vol. 5, (Summer 1999). A detailed analytical summary and evaluation of the Task Force's work was published by Gary King and Langche Zeng, "Improving Forecasts of State Failure," *World Politics,* Vol. 53, No. 4 (July 2001), pp. 623–658.

but they cannot eliminate it. Rather, scholarly knowledge is best conceptualized as an input to policy analysis of specific issues within the government and as an aid to, not a substitute for, the judgments that policymakers must exercise when choosing policies. Indeed, policymakers sometimes have good reasons not to choose the policy option that best meets the criterion of analytic rationality.

Second, although scholarly knowledge can generally be expected to make only an indirect, limited contribution to policymaking, its contribution will nevertheless often be critical for the development and choice of sound policies.

Third, in thinking about the kind of policy-relevant knowledge that needs to be developed, we should give more emphasis to its contribution to the *diagnosis* of problem situations than focusing on its ability to prescribe sound choices of policy. The three types of knowledge identified are particularly helpful in diagnosing situations for which a policy response must be designed. The same cannot be said for theories that ignore the need for actor-specific behavior models and that bypass the task of situational analysis or deal with it by assumption and instead proceed directly to offering prescriptive advice on policy choices.

Appendix
Studies That Illustrate Research Design

We have emphasized that phase one of theory-oriented case studies is of critical importance. Inadequate research design is likely to lead researchers to undertake the case studies in ways that will make it difficult to draw robust implications from case study findings and achieve the objectives of the study. Of course, even a well-developed design cannot ensure a successful study, since that also depends on the quality of the individual case studies (phase two) and on effective use of the findings of the case studies to achieve the objective of the study in phase three.[1]

In this Appendix we review a large number of studies to demonstrate the variety of research designs that have been employed in the past. The selection of these studies for presentation here is intended to illustrate the flexibility and variety of methods for case research.

These studies are not representative of all case studies, which number, no doubt, in the hundreds. Many other studies could be cited, but space limitations require that we restrict the number described here. We use these studies to illustrate how case research has either made explicit use of the method of structured, focused comparison or has approximated it. Our commentary on the design of these studies is selective; to give a full description of the research strategies these studies employ would require much more space. If our brief account of a study is of particular interest to a reader, he or she will want to turn to the book in question.

The studies we review use the within-case approach to causal analysis and employ process-tracing for this purpose. A few of these books make use of the congruence method as well as process-tracing.[2] In almost all of these studies,[3] the author

---

1.   Problems that affect the quality of phases two and three are discussed in Chapters 5 and 6.

2.   Specifically, Jeffrey M. Paige, *Agrarian Revolution: Social Movements and Export Agriculture in the Underdeveloped World* (New York: Free Press, 1975); D. Michael Shafer, *Deadly Paradigms: The Failure of U.S. Counterinsurgency Policy* (Princeton, N.J.: Princeton University Press, 1988); and the study by Khong referred to in Chapter 9.

3.   An exception is the study by Evans, Putnam, and Jacobson, whose research objective required selecting widely different cases. Peter B. Evans, Harold K. Jacobson, and

chose a research objective that focused on a particular subclass of a broader phenomenon and contributes to the development of middle-range theory.[4] Choosing to focus on a particular subclass has two important implications: it determines the type of case to be selected for study and it circumscribes and delimits the scope of the findings and theory. This can be depicted as follows:

Figure A.1. Implications of Subclass Selection for Middle-Range Theory.

In most of the studies reviewed, it should be noted that the author or authors carefully specified a subclass and justified it with reference to the research objective of the study. A number of authors called attention to the limited scope of their findings and cautioned against generalizing them to the entire class of the phenomenon (e.g., all revolutions, all interventions).[5] Others implied as much and avoided overgeneralization of their findings.

In these commentaries, we focus largely on research design; we do not attempt to evaluate the overall merit of the studies. The commentaries focus on research design because of its importance. Inadequate research design is likely to make it more difficult to select appropriate cases and to study them in ways that will produce case findings that will enable the investigator to draw robust implications for the study's research objectives. Three of the studies report research in the field of American politics, eleven are in comparative politics, and nineteen are from the field of international relations.[6] In addition to the cases reviewed here, a large number of case studies in international political economy are briefly noted by John S. Odell, a former editor of *International Studies Quarterly* (which published many articles in the field of international political economy) in his article, "Case Study Methods in International Political Economy." He states that "research on the world political economy relies heavily on qualitative methods" and urges greater use of "thoughtfully designed case studies."[7]

Robert D. Putnam, eds., *Double-Edged Diplomacy: International Bargaining and Domestic Politics* (Berkeley: University of California Press, 1993).

4. The importance of developing sub-classes of a more general phenomenon in order to produce middle-range theories and conditional generalizations is noted in several of Charles Ragin's publications. See his discussion of "casing" in Charles Ragin and Howard Becker, *What Is A Case?* (New York: Cambridge University Press, 1992), and *Fuzzy-Set Social Science* (Chicago: University of Chicago Press, 2000), pp. 36, 61.

Robert Keohane also emphasizes that it is useful to focus research on smaller subclasses of a phenomenon: "the larger the domain of a theory, the less accuracy of detail. . . . Even if a large-scale theory can be developed and appropriately tested, its predictions will be rather gross. To achieve a more finely-tuned [theory] . . . one needs to specify the policy contingency framework more precisely." Robert O. Keohane, ed., *Neorealism and Its Critics* (New York: Columbia University Press, 1986), p. 188. For additional discussion of the utility of middle-range theories, see Chapter 12.

5. These include Fenno, Levite, et al., Walt, Goldstone, Vertzberger, and Owen.

6. Additional case studies in American politics are referred to in Hugh Heclo, "Review Article: Policy Analysis," *British Journal of Political Science*, Vol. 2, No. 1 (January 1972), pp. 83–108.

7. John S. Odell, "Case Study Methods in International Political Economy," *International Studies Perspectives*, Vol. 2 (2001), pp. 161–176; quoted material from p. 161.

Studies From American Politics

RICHARD F. FENNO, *CONGRESSMEN IN COMMITTEES*. BOSTON: LITTLE, BROWN, 1973.

Fenno undertook this study to more systematically document the strong impression gained from recent studies of individual congressional committees that there are marked differences among them. Rejecting the widespread tendency to settle for empirical generalizations that attribute similarity to committees, Fenno emphasized the need for more discriminating research that would produce a new set of differentiated, middle-range generalizations. He enjoined political scientists "not to eschew the possibility of making limited comparisons."[8] In this and other respects, Fenno's book is in accord with the research experience we discuss in the present book.

To achieve his objective, Fenno employed a theoretical framework that enabled him to pinpoint the similarities and differences between committees. Five variables were employed for this purpose: member goals, environmental constraints, strategic premises, decision-making processes, and decisions.[9] Six committees of the House of Representatives, as they functioned from 1955 to 1966, were singled out for study; Fenno explicitly disclaimed that these committees were a representative sample of all committees. In other words, the study makes heuristic use of case studies, and the author limits his claim to its being what Harry Eckstein calls a plausibility probe: "sufficient to support an initial foray into comparative analysis."[10]

The findings of the study are clearly stated and carefully circumscribed. Only a brief indication of the results can be given here: "A committee's decisions are explainable in terms of its members' goals, the constraints of its environment, its decision strategies, and—to a lesser, refining degree, perhaps—by its decision-making processes. . . . We have not, of course, *proven* anything, for we have not tried very determinedly to muster a contrary body of evidence."[11] The study makes considerable use of what we refer to as process-tracing but, as this quotation suggests, process-tracing is not fully used to assess the hypotheses developed.

MORRIS P. FIORINA, CONGRESS: *KEYSTONE OF THE WASHINGTON ESTABLISHMENT*. NEW HAVEN: YALE UNIVERSITY PRESS, 1977.

This study is an interesting example of how specialists in American politics can use comparative case studies as a component of a more complex research strategy. The author's objective was to ascertain whether a Washington "establishment" exists, and, if it exists, to discern its nature and workings. In Eckstein's terms, the study is best characterized as a plausibility probe.

Fiorina develops the thesis that the Washington establishment is a hydra-headed phenomenon, whose three parts are congressional representatives, government bureaucracies, and organized subgroups of the citizenry, each seeking to achieve its own goals. Further, he regards Congress as "the key" to the establishment.[12]

The author's research strategy evolves from an analysis of the reasons for the marked decline in "marginal" (or "swing") congressional districts, defined by political

8. Fenno, *Congressmen in Committees*, p. xiv.

9. Ibid., p. xv.

10. Ibid., p. xvi.

11. Ibid., p. 276.

12. Fiorina, *Congress*, p. 3.

scientists as those districts not firmly in the camp of one party or the other. Fiorina reviews various explanations for the decline of marginal districts that provide some clues for this trend, but then considers it useful to undertake a carefully constructed case comparison of two congressional districts, one a "vanishing" marginal and the other what might be regarded as a robust marginal in which highly competitive elections had occurred since the end of World War II.

The two districts were chosen to resemble each other closely in every other important respect. In effect, therefore, Fiorina's study approximates Mill's method of difference. The two districts were from the same region and from the same state and had reasonably similar demographic profiles. Each district contained a medium-sized city and an important agricultural sector. Their occupational, educational, and income profiles were quite similar. Neither district contained a large minority population. The religious breakdowns were also similar. "In short," Fiorina concludes, "a gross look at the characteristics of the two districts does not reveal any striking differences that might correspond to the dramatic disparity in their congressional election results."[13]

In addition to employing standard methods for analysis of electoral returns, Fiorina visited both districts and talked to constituents of the congressmen. The field trips proved quite useful in developing and supporting explanatory hypotheses as to the different paths taken by the two districts.

"Clearly," Fiorina wrote, "our two districts indicate that major changes in their congressional election patterns go hand in hand with behavioral changes on the part of the congressmen they elected." This led the author to search for what might have produced the kind of behavioral differences observed.[14]

Fiorina postulated that over time, congressmen shift from functioning principally "as national policymakers," which led to reasonably close elections resulting in marginal districts, to a heavy emphasis on "nonpartisan, nonprogrammatic constituency service"—a demand that grows as government expands, and which resulted in a shift of a district out of the marginal camp.[15]

JOHN W. KINGDON, *AGENDAS, ALTERNATIVES, AND PUBLIC POLICIES.* BOSTON: LITTLE, BROWN, 1984.

Kingdon identified twenty-three cases to serve as units of analysis. He addresses the possibility of case selection bias as follows: "I make no claim that twenty-three cases somehow represent all possible cases of initiative over the last three decades in health and transportation."[16] However, he also holds that these cases do constitute major instances of policy initiation and that they were coded similarly in his interviews.

Although Kingdon's use of case studies does not address all of the requirements of the structured, focused method, they do play an important role in the analysis by providing some degree of process-tracing. These case studies "proved to be quite useful since they provided concrete instances of the process under study and since they had a dynamic quality which would not be explored using static methods of observation that concentrate on one point in time. . . . I used them to obtain a better understanding of the processes involved, to develop some theories of agenda setting by aggregate models based on individual cases, and to illustrate the agendas."[17]

13.   Ibid., pp. 29–30.

14.   Ibid., p. 35.

15.   Ibid., p. 37.

16.   Kingdon, *Agendas, Alternatives, and Public Policies,* Figure A-3, p. 230.

17.   Ibid., p. 230.

Studies From Comparative Politics

MAX WEBER (TALCOTT PARSONS, TRANS.), *THE PROTESTANT ETHIC AND THE SPIRIT OF CAPITALISM*. LOS ANGELES: ROXBURY, 1996.
We review this classic work to illustrate two basic problems that frequently afflict comparative studies: the need to specify carefully the subclass of a more general phenomenon that is the focus of investigation; and the need to avoid case selection bias. Weber's failure to avoid these two problems is noted by Clayton Roberts:

Weber posited a correlation between the appearance of Protestantism and the rise of capitalism. Historians, among them Henri Pirenne, promptly disputed this thesis. By tracing the growth of capitalism [via process-tracing] in late medieval Venice, Florence, Genoa, Augsburg, Nuremberg, Cadiz, Lisbon, Rouen, Antwerp, and Lubeck, all Catholic cities, they cast serious doubt on the validity of the thesis.[18]

Yet, as Roberts observes, "the curious correlation between Protestantism and commercial wealth in modern Europe" intrigued other historians. Roberts cites an article by Hugh Trevor-Roper, who showed through process-tracing "that the explanation lay in the hostility of Counter-reformation Catholicism to capitalism," a hostility that drove capitalists from a number of Catholic cities to Protestant lands.[19]

From this account one may assume that Weber inadvertently engaged in case selection bias and overgeneralized the findings of his study. One may also see the value, as Roberts does, of process-tracing as employed both by Weber's critics and by Trevor-Roper in his circumscribed, delimited support for Weber's thesis.

ROBERT PUTNAM, *MAKING DEMOCRACY WORK: CIVIC TRADITIONS IN MODERN ITALY*. PRINCETON, N.J.: PRINCETON UNIVERSITY PRESS, 1993.
This study addresses both a general problem and a more specific one. The general problem is "what are the conditions for creating strong, responsive, effective political institutions?" The specific problem, a subclass of the general one, is to explain the divergence in the performance of the Italian regional governments that were established in 1970.[20] To answer this specific question, the study develops through several distinct phases. First, Putnam attempts to explain the variation in performance of the newly established regional governments. He finds that differences in the development of civic community among the regional governments account for the differences in

---

18.   Clayton Roberts, *The Logic of Historical Explanation* (University Park: Pennsylvania State University, 1996), pp. 31–32.

19.   Max Weber's study is cited as an example of the "endogenity problem" and attention is called to David Laitin's critical commentary on Weber's study in Gary King, Robert Keohane, and Sidney Verba, *Designing Social Inquiry: Scientific Inference in Qualitative Research* (Princeton, N.J.: Princeton University Press, 1994), pp. 186–187. John Odell, too, calls attention to critiques of Weber's thesis in "Case Study Methods in International Political Economy," p. 168.

20.   This brief review draws on a more detailed commentary prepared for this project by Daniel Kelemen. The Putnam study is referred to briefly by King, Keohane, and Verba, *Designing Social Inquiry*, as a good example of combining quantitative methods (p. 5) and one which utilizes one of the approaches they recommend for increasing the number of observable implications of his exploration of the sources of effective democratic performance (pp. 223–224).

their performance. Then he asks, "where do [these] differences in civic community originate?"

The research strategy chosen to meet these research objectives is multi-layered. First, he notes, the 1970 reform that established regional governments for the first time provides a before-after type of quasi-experiment. Existing socioeconomic and cultural variables that differed among the regions remained fairly constant in the before and after periods, while the structure of political institutions was abruptly altered. This provides an opportunity for a systematic comparative analysis and an explanation for the differences in the impact of the reform on the performance of its region.

Putnam chose six of the twenty regions for this analysis. They were "selected to represent the vast diversities" in Italy and provided an opportunity to study what accounted for differences in performance of the regional governments over time. Although not a "representative" sample, the case selection suited Putnam's research agenda and the types of analytical conclusions he wished to draw. In a later part of the study that drew on more easily obtainable material, Putnam gathered data on all twenty regions, thus reducing a case selection problem.

In a second part of the study, Putnam addressed the question of how to explain the diversity in "performance" of the regions (which was based on an array of measures). Two major independent variables were considered: socioeconomic modernity and development of civic community (measured by an index based on four indicators). A number of other possible explanatory variables were also briefly considered, perhaps insufficiently to convincingly refute them.

In a later stage of the study, Putnam considers the historical source of civic community and offers some support for hypotheses that early medieval patterns account for the differences in performances of the northern and southern regions of Italy. After finding a difference between medieval regions that were rich in associations and other horizontal ties and other regions that were based on hierarchical ties (centralization, paternalism, and lack of trust), he engages in a form of process-tracing to support the inference of a causal link between the horizontal ties and the phenomenon of civic community. Covering a huge span of history in a cursory fashion, he tracks the persistence of traces of civic community in northern Italy from the late Middle Ages until the nineteenth century, and its absence in southern Italy. He supplements this with an effort, drawing on rational choice and game theory, to posit that it is rational for people to cooperate in networks to overcome collective problems in the political culture of the trustful, associational, and horizontally organized North and to be less inclined to do so in the distrustful, nonassociational, and hierarchically organized South. Such traits of a community develop slowly and cannot be simply changed overnight. Therefore, they constitute what Putnam refers to as "social capital," which allows people to cooperate in ways that make government and economy stronger.[21]

AREND LIJPHART, *THE POLITICS OF ACCOMMODATION: PLURALISM AND DEMOCRACY IN THE NETHERLANDS*. BERKELEY: UNIVERSITY OF CALIFORNIA PRESS, 1968. This well-known study exemplifies the usefulness of a deviant case analysis for theory refinement.[22] Lijphart's research objective is to ascertain why stable democracy was possible in the Netherlands between 1917 and 1967 despite the absence of preconditions for democracy postulated in previous pluralist theories.

---

21.   Putnam, *Making Democracy Work,* p. 176.

22.   This commentary on Lijphart's study draws on a paper prepared by Donald Share for Alexander George's seminar in 1980.

Lijphart argues that the three main propositions of pluralist theory held that: extreme pluralism tends to be detrimental to stable democratic government; stable democracy requires the presence of secondary groups that help to disperse power, check the government, protect freedom and so on; and stable democracy requires cross-cutting applications.

Lijphart focuses on the third proposition, but recognizes that the three conditions are interrelated. His examination of the Netherlands case challenges and requires reassessment of all three propositions. He demonstrates how stable, effective democracy was possible in the highly segmented society of the Netherlands, despite the absence of these three conditions. His analysis shows that Dutch society was in fact extremely pluralistic, highly segmented, and not cross-affiliated. Stable democracy in the Netherlands is best explained by what he calls the politics of accommodation. Lijphart traces the development of the politics of accommodation through the history of the Netherlands. The plausibility of his thesis is enhanced by demonstrating that five alternative hypotheses do not provide valid explanations for the viability of Dutch democracy.

Lijphart recognizes the limits as well as the advantages of the methodology he has employed. His statement is worth quoting in full:

The usual disclaimer about the conclusions to be drawn from a case study are in order here. A case study may be able to disprove a generalization, but only if the generalization is stated in absolute terms and most of the general propositions in the social sciences are not universal but probabilistic in nature. A single case study can obviously not be the sole basis for a valid generalization. Case studies have a more modest function. In particular, deviant case analysis can lead to the identification of additional variables and to the refinement of concepts and indicators.[23]

In this spirit, Lijphart offers a number of amendments to enrich pluralist theory, making it more differentiated and more complete. He places emphasis on the development of an elite political culture that defined rules for accommodation that were able to overcome mass level societal divisions.[24]

GABRIEL A. ALMOND, SCOTT C. FLANAGAN, AND ROBERT J. MUNDT, *CRISIS, CHOICE, AND CHANGE: HISTORICAL STUDIES OF POLITICAL DEVELOPMENT.* **BOSTON:** LITTLE, BROWN, 1973.

This project, completed thirty years ago, is a remarkably interesting and unique effort to address a serious impasse that had developed in the previous fifteen years in comparative politics. The four major theories employed by comparative politics scholars to understand emerging crises in political development in many societies—how some had been avoided and why others had resulted in severe crisis and breakdown—had not produced satisfactory explanations. Moreover, the methodologies employed had failed to produce hoped-for results.

---

23.   Lijphart, *The Politics of Accommodation*, p. 181.

24.   A detailed critical commentary on the evolution of Lijphart's theory of consociational democracy from the standpoint of Imre Lakatos' writings is advanced by Ian S. Lustick, "Lijphart, Lakatos, and Consociationalism: Almond and Lijphart: Competing Research Programs in an Early-Lakatosian Mode," *World Politics*, Vol. 50, No. 1 (October 1997), pp. 88–117.

In this situation, the authors of *Crisis, Choice, and Change* turn to history. "The logic of our inquiry was simple. Since the development we are seeking to explain occurred in history, why not select historical episodes, examine them in great detail, try out our [four] varieties of developmental explanation, and see how they fit?"[25] The four extant theories were system functional theory, social mobilization theory, rational choice and coalition theory, and leadership theory.

Having decided to engage in in-depth historical case studies, the authors state, "we gave up any prospects of coming out with a good research design."[26] The historical cases—from the histories of Britain, France, Germany, Mexico, Japan, and India—were chosen because "they were interesting and important" in and of themselves, "not because they represented a systematic typology of developmental causation. We lacked the theory to enable us to choose that at the outset."[27]

Each of the historical case analyses attempted in a systematic way to provide a critical, balanced assessment of how each of the four theories may have contributed at one or another point in each developmental crisis. For this purpose, the authors developed a sequential model of development which approximated a complex before-after research procedure.[28]

The project, therefore, was clearly an exploratory study. Its detailed findings offered many hypotheses and pointed to how systematic analysis of history from a multitheoretical perspective suggested a new methodological approach. A codification of the study's methodology (not attempted here) would suggest that it was an important precursor of the method of structured, focused comparison that made considerable use of analytical process-tracing.

Also noteworthy was that the authors decided that purely idiographic, detailed historical explanations would not serve their purposes, and that the seven historical episodes had to be transformed into "analytical episodes."[29] In this respect, the authors anticipated by almost thirty years the research by Robert Bates and his co-authors, reported in *Analytic Narratives*.[30] Indeed, the Almond project went much further in articulating explicit methods for evaluating seemingly competing explanations and theories.

HUGH HECLO, *MODERN SOCIAL POLITICS IN BRITAIN AND SWEDEN*. NEW HAVEN: YALE UNIVERSITY PRESS, 1974.

This book is an example of careful specification of a research problem and a research objective. The general problem that interested Heclo was the relationship of the political process in democratic societies to the choices made in welfare policy. Recognizing that this general problem arises in many democratic states with respect to a variety of welfare policies, Heclo decided that to make the study more manageable he would focus on fewer countries and on one set of welfare policies. Accordingly, he designated a subclass of income maintenance policies that were undertaken during the last century

---

25. Almond, Flanagan, and Mundt, *Crisis, Choice, and Change*, p. 22.

26. Ibid., p. 619.

27. Ibid.

28. Ibid., pp. 618–620.

29. Ibid., pp. 24–28.

30. Robert Bates et. al., *Analytic Narratives* (Princeton, N.J.: Princeton University Press, 1998).

and limited the study to a comparison of Britain and Sweden, which he regarded as well suited to comparative analysis. A further delimitation of the study concentrated on three important income maintenance policies: unemployment insurance; old age pensions; and superannuation (earnings-related occupational insurance).

Heclo's research objective was to assess the explanatory power of four general theories bearing on the problem and demonstrate the need for a more differentiated in-depth analysis of how democratic political processes operate to affect social policy choices. Accordingly, he focused on a few detailed cases rather than undertaking a large-N statistical analysis. Heclo seems to have recognized that a "controlled comparison" would not be possible since the two cases did not match in every respect but one, and therefore did not provide the functional equivalent of an experiment. Accordingly, he relied heavily on historical explanation (process-tracing) of developments in social welfare policy in each country. His developmental analysis approximated a complex before-after type of assessment to explain changes in welfare policy over time. Each developmental case for Britain and Sweden is broken into a series of subcases that unfold over time. The subcases are, of course, not independent of each other, a fact which Heclo recognizes and makes use of in emphasizing the critical role of "policy learning" in both countries.

PETER B. EVANS, HAROLD K. JACOBSON, AND ROBERT D. PUTNAM, EDS.,
DOUBLE-EDGED DIPLOMACY: INTERNATIONAL BARGAINING AND DOMESTIC POLITICS.
BERKELEY: UNIVERSITY OF CALIFORNIA PRESS, 1993.

This study provides a useful counterpoint to those to which we have already referred. In this study, the authors defined their research objective very broadly: they wished to examine the interrelationship between international bargaining and domestic politics in a variety of issue-areas and settings. The class of events, accordingly, included case studies of security issues, economic disputes, and North-South tensions. This study also illustrated the need for a close correspondence or fit between the research objective and the class or subclass of events chosen for study.

The authors had a very good reason for not delimiting the study to a narrowly circumscribed subclass. Their research objective addressed two basic questions: first, whether the insights and hypotheses that Robert Putnam had advanced in an earlier study applied also to non-Western countries; and second, whether they were applicable to negotiations other than the economic ones that had been the focus of the earlier study. A related objective was "to explore the extent to which Putnam's [two-level bargaining] metaphor or model could be developed, enhanced, and expanded."

The selection of case studies covered an appropriately wide spectrum. Altogether, eleven cases were taken from the diplomacy of dictators, democracies, developed countries, and developing countries. The case selection was *not* intended to constitute a representative sample of what is surely an enormous number and variety of negotiations. The question of possible selection bias in choosing cases may arise in some readers' view. But it should be noted that a conscientious effort was made to include cases that constitute tough tests for the Putnam model. For example, the cases included instances of highly conflictual negotiations, whereas Putnam's theory had looked largely at negotiations aimed at producing cooperative results.

The research was designed along the lines of a structured, focused comparison—one that was clearly theory-driven, made use of a set of general questions to ask of each case, and relied heavily on process-tracing. At the same time, the authors recognized that they were not engaged in formal hypothesis testing, but were conducting a plausibility probe.

DIETRICH RUESCHEMEYER, EVELYNE HUBER STEPHENS, AND JOHN D.
STEPHENS, *CAPITALIST DEVELOPMENT AND DEMOCRACY.* CAMBRIDGE, MASS:
POLITY PRESS, 1992.

This book reexamines the relationship between capitalism and democracy, a question that has engaged the interest of many scholars. The authors review past research and offer a new theoretical framework that they believe "can account for the apparent contradictions of earlier findings."[31] Their theoretical framework is tested in three sets of broad historical comparisons of countries in the advanced stages of capitalist development in Central and South America and in the Caribbean Islands.

They note that quantitative cross-national comparisons of many countries have consistently found a positive general correlation between development and democracy. On the other hand, comparative historical studies that examine complex sequences of development trace the rise of democracy to the presence of a favorable historical constellation of conditions in early phases of capitalism. Therefore, the conclusions of these small-n studies are more pessimistic about today's developing countries than the large-N correlational studies, which are relatively optimistic about the chances for democracy in the developing countries of today.

The authors regard the task of reconciling these contradictory results as a difficult one, precisely because they derive from different methodologies. Their own study builds on both research approaches and seeks to reconcile their methodological and substantive differences. The authors do not challenge the main findings of the large-N cross-national work, but they emphasize that such a correlation does not constitute an explanation: "It does not identify the causal sequences accounting for this persistent relation, not to mention the reasons why many cases are at odds with it."

As we do in the present work, the authors emphasize that the statistical-correlational mode of analysis is not sufficiently sensitive to the possibility that the phenomenon in question is subject to equifinality: that is, it cannot account "for how the same end can be reached by different historical routes. The repeated statistical finding has a peculiar 'black box' character that can be overcome only by theoretically well grounded empirical analysis."[32] The authors argue that "causal analysis is inherently sequence analysis," and they make considerable use of process-tracing.

Emphasis is given to the need to ground empirical analysis in small-n research conducted within a well-developed theoretical framework. This is an essential requirement for coping with the limitations of studying a small number of cases.[33] These authors' methodological strategy makes use of analytical induction, a strategy that must be grounded in a cogent theoretical framework.[34]

The critical importance of case selection in small-n comparative studies is recognized; indeed, it is regarded as a more important concern in comparative historical research than in quantitative cross-national studies "because the latter typically reach for the largest number of cases for which relevant information is available."[35]

Three types of case comparisons were analyzed. A chapter on advanced capitalist societies "takes as its central problems a comparative review of the democratization processes and the question of which democracies broke down in the interwar period

---

31.   Rueschemeyer, Stephens, and Stephens, *Capitalist Development and Democracy*, p. 1.

32.   Ibid., p. 4.

33.   Ibid., pp. 4–5.

34.   Ibid., pp. 36–39.

35.   Ibid., p. 34.

and which did not." The chapter on South American cases is of special interest "because political independence here came earlier than in other parts of the Third World and liberal ideas had a strong political appeal in this area during the nineteenth century, in which the fate of democracies was very different from the liberal centers of Europe." This provides an opportunity to explore the relevance of factors that could not be studied in the more limited comparisons of advanced capitalist societies.

The chapter on Central America and the Caribbean "analyzes a startling contrast between the Spanish- and the English-speaking countries," but "comes to conclusions quite different from a simplistic explanation in terms of the difference in cultural heritage."[36]

JACK A. GOLDSTONE, *REVOLUTION AND REBELLION IN THE EARLY MODERN WORLD*.
BERKELEY: UNIVERSITY OF CALIFORNIA PRESS, 1991.

This prize-winning book is notable for formulating a detailed general explication of the nature and requirements of comparative history and for illustrating it in a study of revolution.[37]

This is not a study of all revolutions and rebellions, but like other books summarized in this section, it focuses on a subclass of such events, in this case revolutions and rebellions in the early modern period beginning in 1600. Goldstone notes that the English Revolution of 1640 was part of a wave of revolts from 1600 to 1660 that stretched across Portugal, Italy, Spain, France, and Ming China. From 1789 to 1848, "governments again shook and fell, not only in France, but all across Europe and in the Middle East and China."[38]

The central question Goldstone addresses is "why these waves of crisis occurred on such a broad scale."[39] His theoretical framework consists of two interrelated parts. First, "an analysis of how world-wide population trends affected early modern societies"; and second, the use of a "conjunctural model" of state breakdown that addresses "how changes in economic, political, social, and cultural relations affect states *and* elites *and* different popular groups."[40] Goldstone emphasizes that these two features have been neglected in most previous studies by historians and political scientists who have underestimated the role of demography in political crises and have tended to develop one-sided social theory instead of recognizing that social order is maintained on a multiplicity of levels.

Recognizing that his focus on a subclass of revolutions limits the scope of his findings, the author emphasizes that the details of the causal model apply only to the early modern period. At the same time, he suggests that the basic principles of his model may be useful for understanding such crises in the more modern period.[41]

In order not to overwhelm the reader with an enormous mass of historical detail for so many cases, Goldstone adopts a research strategy that focuses first on a detailed treatment of the English Revolution of 1640, "building a full mathematical model of it, testing it, and engaging current debates among specialists in English his-

---

36.   Ibid., pp. 38–39.

37.   Goldstone, *Revolution and Rebellion in the Early Modern World*; see especially pp. 39–62.

38.   Ibid.

39.   Ibid., p. xxii.

40.   Ibid., pp. xxvii–xxviii; emphasis in original.

41.   Ibid., p. xxii.

tory."[42] A somewhat more modest treatment is accorded the French Revolution of 1789. Other cases of revolution are treated briefly, examining how they resembled or differed from the revolutions in Europe. Considerable use is made of process-tracing, which Goldstone regards as essential for developing explanations.[43]

The author explains that he does not attempt to compose a full case history of each crisis, but emphasizes common elements across cases.[44] As with the method of structured, focused comparison, Goldstone is interested in selective aspects of the cases rather than in a complete description of each case. He recognizes that his characterization of the cases will be regarded as incomplete by historians who are specialists on each case.

Goldstone develops "a simple theory" which posits that revolution "is likely to occur only when a society *simultaneously* experiences three kinds of difficulties." These are a state financial crisis; severe elite divisions; and a high potential for mobilizing popular groups. He adds that the conjunction of these three conditions "generally produces a fourth difficulty: an increase in the salience of heterodox cultural and religious ideas; heterodox groups then provide both leadership and an organizational focus for opposition to the state."[45]

We do not discuss how these findings are developed, except to note that Goldstone alerts the reader to two major disadvantages of his approach—the complexity and unfamiliarity of the mathematical models implemented, and the danger that readers will mistakenly assume that the study espouses demographic determinism—as well as its major advantage, which is that since it deals with measurable quantities (unlike so many other theories), it can be tested and hence is falsifiable.[46]

JEFFREY M. PAIGE, *AGRARIAN REVOLUTION: SOCIAL MOVEMENTS AND EXPORT AGRICULTURE IN THE UNDERDEVELOPED WORLD.* **NEW YORK: FREE PRESS,** 1975.

This study exemplifies a complex research design and strategy that has been employed by other investigators. Paige, a sociologist, starts with a deductive theory, undertakes a large-N statistical analysis, and adds a small number of intensive case studies that employ process-tracing.[47]

Paige's research objective is to determine the effect of the agricultural export economy on social movements of cultivators in plantations and farms in the developing world. His research strategy begins with the formulation of a deductive theory of rural class conflict designed to show how and why different modes of production in export agriculture generate different rural social movements. He then attempts to test this deductive theory with a large-N study of the world population of export agricultural sectors and their accompanying rural social movements. Finally, he assesses the deductive theory a second time, and elaborates and refines it with several detailed studies of cases in Peru, Angola, and Vietnam. The study raises fundamental questions about U.S. involvement in the developing world, where it generally has sided with

---

42.   Ibid., p. xxvi.

43.   Ibid., pp. 59–61.

44.   Ibid., pp. xxi–xxvii.

45.   Ibid., pp. xxiii–xxvi; emphasis in the original.

46.   Ibid., p. xxvi.

47.   The commentary on this study draws on a paper prepared by Mark Peceny for Alexander George's seminar in 1985.

landlords and plantation owners against the peasants, sharecroppers, and agricultural laborers who took up arms against them.

Paige is critical of a number of existing theories drawn from political sociology and formulates a complex theory of his own. The large-N study and the case studies use fundamentally the same kind of data in a similar format. The three case studies are well chosen to enable Paige to demonstrate the workings of his theory via the congruence method and some process-tracing that looks for a direct causal relationship between agrarian structures and social movements.

The three case studies are not used to create an analytic inductive theory through controlled comparison. Nor are they used as crucial or tough tests to provide a rigorous assessment of his deductive theory. Rather, Paige uses the three cases as a tool of the "parallel demonstration of theory," described earlier by Somers and Skocpol.[48] That is, the three cases are used to demonstrate in some detail the usefulness and applicability of Paige's deductive theory. Further, the three cases provide some new insights into changes or refinements that theory may need.

STEPHEN M. WALT, *REVOLUTION AND WAR*. ITHACA: CORNELL UNIVERSITY PRESS, 1996.

The central question addressed by the author is "whether revolutions encourage states to view the external environment in ways that intensify their security competition and make war appear to be a more attractive option."[49]

The research design includes two interrelated components: the choice of what type of revolution to study influences the selection of historical cases. Walt distinguishes two basic types of revolution: mass revolutions (or "revolutions from below") and elite revolutions (or "revolutions from above"). He chooses to focus principally on mass revolutions, because such revolutions are "more common and because their international effects are usually more worrisome." This excludes not only elite revolutions but also "most civil wars, unless the victorious faction eventually imposes a new political order in its society."[50] He also notes but puts aside a definition employed in statistical studies of the general phenomenon of revolutions as including any violent regime change, of which there are well over a hundred cases.

Walt chose to focus on a well-specified subclass, a certain type of revolution of which there exists a smaller number of historical cases. Nonetheless, Walt recognizes that there are more such cases than he chooses to include in his study, but he believes that the seven cases he singles out are "sufficiently representative" so that "the inclusion of other cases would not undermine my fundamental results."[51] These seven are the French, Russian, and Iranian revolutions, which he examines in detail, and shorter studies of the American, Mexican, Turkish, and Chinese revolutions.[52] Walt recognizes

---

48. Theda Skocpol and Margaret Somers, "The Uses of Comparative History in Macrosocial Inquiry," *Comparative Studies in Society and History*, Vol. 22, No. 2 (April 1980), pp. 174–197.

49. Walt, *Revolution and War*, p. 3.

50. Ibid.

51. Ibid., pp. 12–14.

52. Stephen Walt recognizes that the Turkish revolution was an elite revolution and that the American one falls somewhere in between an elite and a mass revolution. These are included for purposes of comparison with the five that he regards as being clear examples of mass revolution. Picking these five relatively uncontroversial exam-

that the precise nature of the revolutionary process differs in these cases but that all are widely recognized as revolutionary events.

Walt notes that although each of these seven revolutions "led to greater security competition between the new regime and several other powers . . . open warfare occurred in only four of them." He contrasts these four cases with the three in which war was avoided in an effort "to discern why war follows some revolutions but not others."[53]

The research design and the procedures followed include several different types of comparisons. First, a before-after comparison is made for each country, using "the old regime as a control case in order to isolate the independent impact of the revolution on [its] foreign policy."[54]

Second, to test his theory that explains why revolutions increased the level of security competition, Walt undertakes to process-trace the relationship between each revolutionary state and its main foreign interlocutors for at least ten years after the revolution.[55] Walt explains that process-tracing "is especially appropriate because the universe of cases is too small for a statistical analysis and the number of independent variables too large for a rigorous application of John Stuart Mill's 'method of difference.'"[56] Process-tracing is appropriate also "because my theory focuses on the way revolutions shape the perceptions of the relevant actors. Process-tracing allows the analyst to 'get inside' the case (where one may find multiple opportunities to test the theory's predictions) and to evaluate the separate causal links that connect the explanatory variables with the predicted outcomes."[57]

A third type of comparison is undertaken to explain why some revolutions lead to war. For this purpose, the French, Russian, Iranian, and Chinese revolutions are compared to the American, Mexican, and Turkish cases. This comparison does not lead to definitive results but enables the author to advance several possible explanations worthy of additional consideration.[58]

At various points Walt notes some limitations of the study, and interesting questions he does not address.[59] His main argument regarding the impact of revolutions on the balance of threats between states that leads to more intense security competition is tested and refined by examining the French, Russian, and Iranian revolutions in detail. In the four other cases, "the fit between theory and reality was less obvious."[60]

The study does not make explicit use of the five design tasks of the structured, focused method. For example, the research design does not include a statement of the questions to be asked of each case in order to obtain the data necessary for assessing the author's theory. The reader must infer from a reading of the case studies which

---

ples of mass revolution, he suggests, "may reduce controversy over whether the cases chosen were appropriate for testing the theory," p. 14.

53. Ibid., p. 14.

54. Ibid., p. 15.

55. Ibid.

56. Ibid.

57. Ibid., pp. 15–16.

58. Ibid., p. 16.

59. See, for example, ibid., pp. 16–17.

60. Ibid., p. 331.

questions were asked, not a difficult task since the author has stated the components of the theory in considerable detail.

ERIC STERN AND FREDERIK BYNANDER, EDS., *CRISIS AND INTERNATIONALIZATION: EIGHT CRISIS STUDIES FROM A COGNITIVE-INSTITUTIONAL PERSPECTIVE*. STOCKHOLM: THE SWEDISH AGENCY FOR CIVIL EMERGENCY PLANNING, 1998.

This book is one in a series under the supervision of Bengt Sundelius in a project aimed at building case banks drawn from several countries and from different types of crises in areas such as the military, financial, environmental, and health sectors.

In this unusually broad-spanning study, coherence and systematic comparison are achieved by employing a three-step approach. First, each crisis is described in considerable detail. Second, critical decision points in the crisis are identified, and a path-dependency analysis is undertaken that focuses on the crisis as experienced and managed by decision-makers. Third, causal analysis of each crisis addresses a number of specific questions, such as, "In which decision unit were crisis decisions made?" "To what extent was decision-making centralized?" "What were the group dynamics in the decision-making units?" "How and by whom were decisional problems framed?" "How was the flow and analysis of information managed?" "How did decision-makers deal with the media?" "What kind of leadership occurred within the decisional unit?" "What sequencing of decision points occurred during the crisis, and to what extent and how were responses to the crisis influenced by other issues, problems, and developments?"

This project aims to develop a variety of lessons from the study of past crises that may be helpful to crisis managers. To this end, the authors identify the kinds of problems that can be expected to emerge in crisis. In the concluding chapter, the editors of the volume discuss six themes that emerge from cross-case comparison of the crises analyzed. These themes are crisis prevention and mitigation, problem-framing and information processing, problems of value-complexity, the role of bureaucratic politics, the influence of the particular sequencing during a crisis, and how decisions were influenced by other developments.

Studies from International Relations

JOHN LEWIS GADDIS, *STRATEGIES OF CONTAINMENT*. NEW YORK: OXFORD UNIVERSITY PRESS, 1982.

This book, written by a leading diplomatic historian and specialist in American foreign policy, is a study of several variants of containment strategy employed by the United States since the beginning of the Cold War. It employs structured, focused comparison and makes use of process-tracing to elaborate the five distinct types of containment that were employed. It also makes an important general point that characterizes not only the concept of containment but all other strategies that states employ in the conduct of foreign policy.

Containment—like all other "strategies" such as deterrence, coercive diplomacy, détente, conciliation, etc.—is a general, abstract concept. Such general concepts do little more than to identify, as best one can, the critical variables embraced by a concept, and some identify the general logic associated with successful uses of that instrument of policy. Several characteristics of such strategic concepts limit their immediate usefulness for policymaking. The concept itself is not a strategy but merely the starting point for converting the concept into a strategy. The concept identifies only the general logic—that is, the desired impact that certain means can have on the adversary's calculations and behavior—that needs to be achieved if a strategy is to be successful. But it does not indicate precisely what the policymaker must do to induce that reasoning into the adversary's behavior. To achieve the goal of containment, deterrence, coercive diplomacy, or détente, etc., the policymaker must convert the abstract concept into a specific strategy for the particular situation at hand, carefully taking into account the behavioral characteristics of the particular adversary.[61]

Gaddis' study is an effort to show how the general concept of containment was converted into five distinctive types of containment strategy during the course of American foreign policy. An important objective of his study is to explain "the successive mutations, incarnations, and transformations that concept [containment] has undergone through the years."[62]

Gaddis identifies "five distinct geopolitical codes" among American foreign policy specialists since the beginning of the Cold War. He uses these codes (beliefs) to explain the choice of particular containment strategies over time by different U.S. leaders. The choice of a new containment strategy was influenced also by lessons drawn from the experience with preceding versions of containment, by efforts to adapt the strategy to new geopolitical developments, and by constraints of domestic and international politics.

The analytical and methodological issues embedded in this study of containment strategies has broad relevance for the study of the other strategic concepts already mentioned and also for the contemporary discussions of engagement as an alternative to containment. Engagement, too, is a general concept that must be developed into one or another specific strategy of engagement. We are not aware of any systematic study of various ways in which the general concept of engagement can be converted into alternative strategies of engagement.

JACK SNYDER, *THE IDEOLOGY OF THE OFFENSIVE: MILITARY DECISION MAKING AND THE DISASTERS OF 1914*. ITHACA: CORNELL UNIVERSITY PRESS, 1984.
Snyder foregoes an effort to study offensive military strategies in all times and places. He restricts his inquiry to a quite circumscribed but important subclass: the offensive strategic doctrines of France, Germany, and Russia, and the role they played in World War I. He addresses an important historical puzzle: "why did the military strategists of Europe's major continental powers choose to defy the inexorable constraints of time, space, and technology, which so heavily favored the defensive?"[63] A secondary research objective addresses the question whether these offensive strategies, and not some other factors, caused the offensive disasters of 1914.[64]

We do not attempt a full description of Snyder's rather complex research strategy, but note that Snyder makes explicit use of the method of structured, focused compari-

---

61.   Another limiting characteristic of abstract concepts such as containment or deterrence is that they are typically not full-fledged deductive theories that can be used to predict whether a strategy will succeed in particular situations. For a more detailed discussion of the relationship between concepts and strategies that uses deterrence and coercive diplomacy as examples, see Alexander L. George, *Bridging the Gap* (Washington, D.C.: United States Institute of Peace Press, 1993), pp. 117–120.

62.   Gaddis, *Strategies of Containment*, p. viii.

63.   Snyder, *The Ideology of the Offensive*, p. 9.

64.   Ibid., p. 34.

son and relies heavily on process-tracing. He found that an effort at controlled comparison of the three countries occasionally proved useful, "but it provides a generally inferior method of testing causal relationships because so many variables are left uncontrolled."[65] For this reason, Snyder concluded that the method of controlled comparison, which attempts to achieve the functional equivalent of an experiment, was not serviceable and that it was necessary to engage in what we have called within-case analysis that makes use of process-tracing. Snyder is not at all apologetic about using this alternative method: "Methodologists tend to denigrate single case studies, because they allegedly provide no controls on the operation of the variables. This claim is false. Given the difficulty of finding two cases that are similar in all respects except the variable to be tested, comparisons within cases are likely to be better controlled than comparisons between cases."[66]

ARIEL E. LEVITE, BRUCE W. JENTLESON, AND LARRY BERMAN, EDS.,

FOREIGN MILITARY INTERVENTION: THE DYNAMICS OF PROTRACTED CONFLICT. NEW

YORK: COLUMBIA UNIVERSITY PRESS, 1992.

Rather than study all varieties of military intervention, the authors chose to study the very specific subclass of "protracted interventions." These are interventions that proved longer, more costly, and less successful than had been anticipated when undertaken.

The designation of the subclass was determined by the research problem. Their objective was to understand better how states entered into such interventions and why they became prolonged and costly. The authors provide a detailed statement regarding the importance of prolonged military interventions. These tend to be "seminal events" due to their domestic and international consequences. They are a persistent phenomenon. Ideology plays a role that exacerbates the phenomenon, particularly during the Cold War, but there are alternative explanations as well.

Three explicit criteria were employed for selecting appropriate cases. The cases chosen cover a spectrum of protracted interventions. The authors do not hold these cases to be a representative sample of all protracted wars and, quite appropriately, the findings are not extrapolated to characterize the entire universe of protracted interventions.

The study was explicitly designed in accordance with the procedures of the structured, focused type of comparative case study; it utilized a set of standard questions to ask of each case and also employed process-tracing.

LISA L. MARTIN, *COERCIVE COOPERATION: EXPLAINING MULTILATERAL ECONOMIC*

SANCTIONS. PRINCETON, N.J.: PRINCETON UNIVERSITY PRESS, 1992.

The author focuses on a well-defined, quite circumscribed subclass of instances in the post–World War II period of efforts by states to cooperate in imposing economic sanctions.[67] She contrasts cases in which states did or did not cooperate in imposing economic sanctions. Several research objectives were formulated: (1) Under what conditions do states cooperate to impose economic sanctions? (2) What are the ways in

---

65. Ibid., p. 35.

66. Ibid.

67. This statement draws from a more detailed analysis prepared for this project by Daniel Drezner.

which institutions can contribute to and facilitate such cooperation—what are the underlying causal mechanisms? (3) What different types of cooperation problems can be identified and differentiated?

The dependent variable in the study is the level of cooperation given by other states to the initiator of sanctions; this is determined by the number of countries that also invoke sanctions. The author proposes the additional question of whether such cooperative efforts prove to be successful.

Martin effectively uses existing theories from the neorealist and neoliberal schools to identify five relevant independent variables. She argues that these two schools can be combined to explain a greater class of events. A multi-method research strategy is employed that combines and skillfully coordinates game theory, a large-N statistical study of some ninety-nine instances of attempts at sanctions cooperation, and four well-chosen case studies. These cases were selected to highlight the effects of three factors: motivation, costs, and bipolarity. They included U.S. unilateral sanctions on behalf of human rights in Latin America, European Community sanctions against Argentina in the Falkland Islands war, Western technology export sanctions against the Soviet Union following the invasion of Afghanistan, and the attempted gas-pipeline sanctions during the Polish crisis in 1982. Two of the cases involved bipolarity and two did not; two of the cases involved international institutional support and two did not; two of the cases had significant costs to the sanctions initiator, two did not.

The author uses the four case studies to assess the hypotheses generated by the large-N study and also, she emphasizes, to establish causal relationships. Of particular interest for the present study's emphasis on the importance of process-tracing is the author's argument on behalf of her multi-method research strategy:

I cannot, however, fully address many of the most interesting questions about cooperation through statistical analysis alone. For example, we can understand the role of international institutions only through careful process-tracing, focusing on how institutions constrain and influence states' decision-making processes. Thus, while looking at the statistics gives us some confidence about generalizations, explanation of how and why certain results appear requires careful case studies.[68]

Martin recognizes that the strong relationship in the statistical study between institutions and cooperation can be challenged by arguing that "states make their decisions on sanctions without regard to any organization constraints and then turn to institutions to ratify those decisions. In the cases, I show [via process-tracing] that institutional calls for sanctions actually have an impact on state behavior."[69]

It should be noted, finally, that Martin recognizes that equifinality operated; different causal processes produced cooperation. Only through close inspection of the decision-making chain through process-tracing in the case studies, Martin suggests, would it be possible to distinguish one causal process from the other.

---

68. Martin, *Coercive Cooperation*, p. 10. King, Keohane, and Verba do not adequately characterize the purpose and function of Martin's four case studies. They state that she carried out case studies simply "in an attempt to gather more evidence relevant to her causal inference." They do not refer to her statement, quoted here, that she felt it necessary to engage in process-tracing. King, Keohane, and Verba, *Designing Social Inquiry*, p. 5.

69. Martin, *Coercive Cooperation*, p. 96.

STEVEN WEBER, *COOPERATION AND DISCORD IN U.S.-SOVIET ARMS CONTROL.*
PRINCETON, N.J.: PRINCETON UNIVERSITY PRESS, 1991.
Weber's research objective emerged from his identification of a theoretical puzzle. Commenting on Robert Axelrod's formal deductive theory, which holds that cooperation in a prisoner's dilemma situation is possible under certain conditions, Weber posits that even when Axelrod's conditions are present cooperation does not always occur. The puzzle is to explain such anomalous outcomes as well as successes.

This research objective is pursued by delimiting the total universe of arms control cases to a well-defined subclass: major U.S.-Soviet strategic arms limitations. The research strategy extends Axelrod's theory in an empirical direction; process-tracing is employed to force the theory to confront a set of historical cases in which Weber identifies the "processes or causal paths through which strategies influence outcomes."[70] Weber feels that it is necessary to go beyond Axelrod's formal deductive theory and go into the black boxes of U.S. and Soviet decision-making and strategic interaction between them. For this purpose Weber adds independent variables—in particular, those specifying variants of strategy employed by the United States in these cases.

Weber's research strategy is implemented in an ingenious way—he selects three cases that fulfill Axelrod's structural conditions for cooperation, only one of which resulted in cooperation. Hence, the case selection captures the paradox that motivated the study and offers an opportunity, indeed a need, to explain the variance in outcomes. The research objective and research strategy required Weber to select cases based on variation in the outcome of the dependent variable (thus departing from the general injunction of some methodologists not to do so).

The three cases are the Antiballistic Missile Treaty (ABM) negotiation, which ended in U.S.-Soviet cooperation; the Anti-Satellite Missile (ASAT) in which the two sides achieved a partially cooperative arrangement that deteriorated over time; and the Multiple Independently-targetable Reentry Vehicle (MIRV) negotiation, in which despite the presence of Axelrod's conditions, the two sides failed to achieve a cooperative outcome.

Put simply, Weber selected cases in which the independent variables highlighted by Axelrod's conditions for cooperation were present—and are held constant for the three cases—while the outcome of the dependent variable (cooperation or lack of it) varies. Thus, the three cases present a challenge to Axelrod's theory, and Weber attempts to show how that theory might benefit from elaboration and refinement. Weber's chief addition to the theory is to introduce three variants of strategy employed by the United States in an effort to achieve an acceptable cooperative outcome. Weber employs process-tracing to identify the causal paths through which variations in strategy influenced the variation in outcomes.

The goal of the study was summarized by Weber as follows: "to force a formal model of cooperation to confront a set of historical cases . . . [and thereby] to expand [Axelrod's formal] model" so that one can explain anomalous outcomes.

RICHARD NED LEBOW, *BETWEEN PEACE AND WAR: THE NATURE OF INTERNATIONAL CRISES.* BALTIMORE: JOHNS HOPKINS UNIVERSITY PRESS, 1981.
This comparative case study examines the relationship between crisis and war. The author examines the origins of crises, the outcome of crises, and circumstances in which crises intensify or ameliorate the conflict between antagonists.[71]

---

70. Weber, *Cooperation and Discord in U.S.-Soviet Arms Control*, p. 16.

71. Lebow, *Between Peace and War*, pp. 4–5.

The author's research strategy consists of three parts. First, three types of crises are identified and analyzed: (1) "justification of hostility" crises in which the decision for war is made *before* the crisis commences, the purpose of which is to justify war; (2) "spin off" crises with third parties, which "are secondary confrontations arising from a nation's preparations for or prosecution of a primary conflict" with a different party; and (3) "brinkmanship" crises, which one side initiates in the expectation that the adversary will back down rather than fight.

These types are derived empirically from the examination of a large number of crises.[72] The author does not claim that this typology encompasses all crises—for example, it does not include crises that occur "accidentally" when a provocation triggers a crisis that was "both undesired and unsanctioned by central decision makers."[73]

The typology of crises fits the author's research strategy in that it is used to show that each type is "associated with very different international and domestic conditions."[74]

Part Two analyzes crises outcomes, asking why some crises are resolved while others lead to war. Part Three addresses "the relationship between crisis and the broader pattern of international relations. That is, whether and why some crises intensify and others diminish the underlying causes of tension and hostility."[75]

The author draws on a variety of theories and concepts to address the questions raised in the three parts of the study. These include theories of affect and cognition, communication theory, organizational theory, models of governmental politics, and psychodynamics.

Twenty-six historical cases of international crisis spanning a period of seventy years were selected for the study. Case selection was made by compiling a list of twentieth-century crises in which at least one of the protagonists was a great power. The list was then limited to crises that the author regarded as "acute . . . in which war was perceived as a fairly distinct possibility by policy-makers of at least one of the protagonists."[76] A few crises were eliminated for lack of source material, but the roster of cases "includes most of the major crises of the last seventy-five years."[77]

Accordingly, these cases are not a sample of all instances comprising the subclass of crises singled out; they include virtually the entire universe of such crises.

The methodology of the study approximates that of a structured, focused comparison and employs a great deal of process-tracing. The author states that the crises were examined "in terms of a prepared set of explicitly formulated questions," but these are not set forth and would need to be gleaned from the study itself.[78] This is not an easy task, however, because the author decided to structure the book not by presenting a separate analysis of each crisis, but rather "in terms of a conceptual framework" in which "particular cases are described only so far as they are useful or necessary to document theoretical propositions."[79]

---

72. Ibid., p. 18.

73. Ibid., p. 23.

74. Ibid., p. 18.

75. Ibid., p. 19.

76. Ibid., p. 9.

77. Ibid., p. 13.

78. Ibid., p. 6.

79. Ibid., p. 5.

The study combines hypothesis formation and plausibility probes, and is intended to draw lessons about crises from examination of historical experience.

YAACOV Y.I. VERTZBERGER, *RISK TAKING AND DECISIONMAKING: FOREIGN MILITARY INTERVENTION DECISIONS*. STANFORD: STANFORD UNIVERSITY PRESS, 1998.

Vertzberger develops an alternative—the sociocognitive approach—to the rational choice way of accounting for risk-taking and choice behavior. Vertzberger develops a complex, multisided theoretical approach to decision-making.

In this book, Vertzberger builds on his previous work to develop a sociocognitive approach to decision-making as an alternative to the parsimonious way in which rational choice theory attempts to deal with risk behavior and choice. His approach integrates individual-level variables (e.g., belief system, operational code, personality attributes), social-level variables (e.g., group dynamics and organizational structure), and cultural-level variables (e.g., cultural-societal attributes and norms). He argues that to provide "a comprehensive explanation of the multiple causal influences on risk judgment and preferences, the theoretical analysis has to be multivariate and interdisciplinary." He also emphasizes that because decisions to accept risk or to avoid it are subject to equifinality—that is, similar choices can result from different causal paths—a credible theoretical analysis of risk taking should map the spectrum of alternative patterns rather than unrealistically invoking the principles of parsimony and attempting to identify a single path.[80]

The major objective of the study is to examine how risk perceptions and risk-taking preferences evolve in the decision-making process and affect choice. Following the format of the structured, focused method, Vertzberger maps out three sets of questions to address in developing a deductive model and then employing process-tracing in a detailed analysis of five cases "in order to test, expand, and modify the [initial] deductive theoretical analyses of risk taking and intervention."[81]

Five cases were chosen to provide "a quasi-controlled experiment with history that allows for careful manipulation and observation of the main dependent and independent variables—intervention and risk."[82] To this end, the author chose three cases that represent low-to-moderate-risk decisions (the U.S. interventions in Grenada in 1983 and in Panama in 1989 and Soviet intervention in Czechoslovakia in 1968), and two cases that represent high-risk decisions (U.S. intervention in Vietnam in 1964–1968 and Israeli intervention in Lebanon in 1982–1983). The labeling of these cases is based on the decision-makers' perceptions as inferred from an analysis of historical facts and counterfactuals.[83]

Varying the levels of perceived risk enables the author to observe the effect of changing levels of risk on the process and quality of intervention decisions.[84] The author addresses the question of the generalizability of the study's findings and offers several qualifying comments. He believes that the study findings are "plausible rather than definitive" in effect, characterizing his study as a plausibility probe.

---

80.   Vertzberger, *Risk Taking and Decisionmaking*, p. 8.

81.   Ibid., p. 9.

82.   Ibid.

83.   Ibid.

84.   Ibid.

Vertzberger emphasizes that this book "is first and foremost about how *judgment* of risk is formed and how *choice* among risk-taking preferences is made."[85] He provides a quite useful discussion of previous research on military intervention, which leaves a gap that his study attempts to fill.[86]

JACK S. LEVY, "THE ROLE OF CRISIS MISMANAGEMENT IN THE OUTBREAK OF WORLD WAR I," IN ALEXANDER L. GEORGE, ED., AVOIDING WAR: PROBLEMS OF CRISIS MANAGEMENT. BOULDER: WESTVIEW PRESS, 1991, PP. 62–117.

This study illustrates how elements of a rational choice approach can be used with other theories to develop a rounded, more comprehensive explanation of complex events.[87] Complexity in this case took the form of interactions among six major actors at a number of key "decision points" during the six weeks leading up to World War I. Additional complexity stemmed from the fact that during this period political leaders in the six states had to consider the relative desirability of a peaceful settlement and different kinds of war, based on their assessment of the likely outcomes of each. These were a *negotiated peace* (NP), based on significant but not unconditional Serbian concessions; a *localized war* (LW) in the Balkans between Austria-Hungary and Serbia; a *continental war* (CW) involving Germany on the side of Austria, and Russia and France on the side of Serbia; and a general European *world war* (WW) with Britain joining the war against Germany and Austria.

Levy attempted to empirically identify the six actors' preferences for these four possible outcomes of the crisis, and to do so independently of the behavior he was trying to explain. He assumed that these preferences were stable over the course of the crisis (and found no evidence to the contrary). This enabled him to infer that any changes in behavior were due to changes in international and domestic constraints or changes in information available to decision-makers—not to changes in preference at different points in the diplomatic crisis. An analysis of available historical materials enabled Levy to identify the actors' preferences as follows. (The symbol ">" means preferred to, and "?" indicates that a definitive preference could not be established.)

Figure A.2. Actors' Preferences for Particular Outcomes.

Austria-Hungary	LW	>	CW	>	NP	>	WW
Germany	LW	>	CW	>	NP	>	WW
Russia	NP	>	WW	>	CW	>	LW
France	NP	>	LW	>	WW	>	CW
Britain	NP	>	LW	>	WW	?	CW
Serbia	NP	>	WW	>	CW	>	LW

---

85. Ibid., p. 12.

86. Ibid., pp. 1–7.

87. A slightly different version was published by Jack Levy in *International Security*, Vol. 15, No. 3 (Winter 1990/91), pp. 151–186.

Thus, all five European great powers and Serbia preferred a negotiated peace settlement (NP) to a world war (WW), yet they ended up in a world war. In this sense World War I may qualify as an "inadvertent war"—one that neither side expects or wants at the beginning of the crisis, but that occurs as a result of interactions and decisions as the crisis develops.

To examine how these countries' interactions led to World War I, Levy employed a path dependency research design that identified critical decision points during the six-week diplomatic crisis. He emphasizes that political leaders were not confronted by a single decision whether or not to go to war, but instead faced a series of decisions at a succession of critical decision points as the crisis unfolded. Their preferences over final outcomes were relatively stable over time, Levy finds, "but their policy options, strategic constraints, available information, and policy dilemmas were often different at these successive decision points. Moreover, each decision altered the constraints that decision makers faced at the next critical juncture and further narrowed their freedom of maneuver."[88]

Levy observed that the theoretical literature fails to recognize that not all international crises—even those that end up as "inadvertent" wars—are equally amenable to crisis management. "Some crises are structured in such a way—in terms of the preferences of the actors and the diplomatic, geographical, technological, and organizational constraints on their freedom of action—that they are likely to escalate to war in spite of the desires of statesmen to avoid it."[89] To avoid overstating the importance of crisis mismanagement in war outbreaks, such studies "must begin by specifying the underlying preferences of each of the actors and the structural constraints on their actions."[90] Even so, Levy notes, there were several critical points in this prolonged crisis "at which political leaders could have behaved differently without seriously threatening their vital interests." However, the windows of opportunity for more effective crisis management were "not only narrow but were constantly changing, and at different times for each of the great powers."[91]

JEFFREY W. KNOPF, *DOMESTIC SOCIETY AND INTERNATIONAL COOPERATION: THE IMPACT OF PROTEST ON U.S. ARMS CONTROL POLICY*. **CAMBRIDGE: CAMBRIDGE UNIVERSITY PRESS,** 1998.

The research objective of this study is to show that citizen activism can be an important source of state preferences in foreign policy, especially on decisions to seek international cooperation. The subclass of this phenomenon singled out for empirical and theoretical analysis is the impact under certain conditions that peace movements in the United States have had on decisions to seek arms control with the Soviet Union.

The book contributes to international relations theory by significantly expanding our understanding of the impact that domestic society can have on foreign policy. Domestic society is generally treated as a source of incentives that lead policymakers to diverge from the national interest. Knopf shows that the opposite is also possible: social activism triggers foreign policy initiatives that most analysts would regard as con-

---

88.   Jack S. Levy, "The Role of Crisis Mismanagement in the Outbreak of World War I," in Alexander L. George, ed., *Avoiding War: Problems of Crisis Management* (Boulder: Westview Press, 1991).

89.   Ibid.

90.   Levy, "The Role of Crisis Mismanagement in the Outbreak of World War I," p. 63.

91.   Ibid., p. 87.

sistent with state interests.[92] He notes that "so far, the possibility that a state's interest in cooperation could arise in a bottom-up manner, from public pressure, has not been given much consideration by international relations theory."[93]

The empirical research developed in this study constitutes a tough test for demonstrating the impact of social activism, because a key national security issue is involved. "Superpower arms control is one of the least likely areas for finding that citizen activism can foster cooperation."[94]

The research design of the study combines statistics and case study methods. A quantitative analysis of the U.S. decision to enter arms talks assesses whether protest activity was significant when the most relevant system-level variables are controlled for. But, Knopf maintains, "statistical correlations by themselves . . . often do not make clear the causal connections involved." Therefore, he employs case studies as a second mode of analysis, employing the method of structured, focused comparison, "to corroborate the statistical results" and particularly to identify causal mechanisms by which citizen activism could have brought about the observed results.[95]

Knopf developed a theoretical framework to assess and identify causal connections between protest and policy. A key insight that emerged from the study was that more than one potential pathway exists for activist influence in the United States; this is an example of equifinality.[96] Three specific processes, or causal mechanisms, by which domestic groups might exert influence on arms control were identified: electoral pressure, shifting congressional coalitions, and the publicizing of ideas that are utilized by bureaucratic actors. Knopf offers this as a new technique for assessing the impact of citizen activism on policymaking. He carefully circumscribes the contribution his study makes,[97] but suggests that the theoretical framework and research techniques used in the study are potentially generalizable: with suitable changes to take account of . . . different issues or different countries, the basic technique utilized by this book could be used to evaluate the foreign policy impact of citizen activism in a variety of other cases."[98]

The criteria and rationale for selecting four cases for the qualitative component of the study are clearly described. The universe of possible cases was limited to those where U.S.-Soviet arms talks were not already taking place, so that Knopf could focus on explaining the initial development of a preference for cooperation. He excluded negotiations in the early Cold War period because the negotiators did not appear to have a genuine interest in or realistic opportunity for achieving cooperation. "From the remaining candidate cases, in order to avoid biasing the results, I selected cases that vary in the independent variable of interest (activism)."[99] The four case studies exemplify the within-case mode of causal analysis via process-tracing.[100]

---

92.   Knopf, *Domestic Society and International Cooperation*, p. ix.

93.   Ibid., p. 6.

94.   Ibid., p. 2.

95.   Ibid., p. 9.

96.   Ibid., pp. 251–252.

97.   Ibid., pp. 6–8.

98.   Ibid., p. 4.

99.   Ibid., pp. 9–10.

100.   Ibid., p. 250.

DEBORAH WELCH LARSON, *ANATOMY OF MISTRUST: U.S.-SOVIET RELATIONS DURING THE COLD WAR*. ITHACA: CORNELL UNIVERSITY PRESS, 1997.

Larson addresses the question of whether the United States and the Soviet Union missed important opportunities to reduce Cold War tensions and better manage the arms race. This historical problem is addressed within a broad theoretical framework of international cooperation, and Larson presents her study as the first systematic study of missed opportunities for international cooperation. The focus on U.S.-Soviet relations is a subclass of this general phenomenon.[101] The author regards the Cold War era as a least-likely case for U.S.-Soviet cooperation and a good test of cooperation theory in international relations.[102]

Larson focuses on the importance of trust as a central variable in her research strategy, a factor inadequately developed in international relations research. She discusses and synthesizes what various social science literatures have to say about the nature of trust and distrust, how they emerge, and what role they play in interpersonal and interstate relations. Her study also incorporates disciplined counterfactual analysis to make the case that opportunities existed but were "missed."

Trust is usually regarded as being a necessary condition, though not a sufficient one, for states to cooperate.[103] However, trust should not be viewed as a dichotomous attribute with complete trust being a necessary condition; rather, the amount of trust required for an agreement varies greatly.[104] For example, states "must [also] have a shared interest in controlling their competition, adequate domestic support, and the ability to verify an agreement."[105]

A "missed opportunity" for an agreement is defined as "a situation in which there was at least one alternative that parties to a conflict preferred or would have preferred to nonagreement."[106] To make the case that a missed opportunity existed "entails showing that both sides wanted an agreement, that history need not be completely rewritten to end up with a different outcome—in other words, that a plausible sequence of events could have led to an agreement."[107] This analytical standard is employed to guide the study of a variety of available data.

Larson examines five periods in which there was a major policy shift by one or both of the superpowers—a change she regards as being of critical importance for creating the possibility of a significant cooperative agreement. These were periods that had the potential for being "branching points" at which U.S.-Soviet relations could have taken or did take a different path. Although Larson compares cases of successful and ineffective cooperation, she makes it clear that they should not be viewed as independent of each other. Each leader's efforts to improve relations drew on earlier experience.[108]

Citing David Collier's statement that "causal inferences about the impact of dis-

---

101.   Larson, *Anatomy of Mistrust*, p. x.

102.   Ibid., pp. 35–36. For a broader treatment of this question, see Alexander L. George, Philip J. Farley, and Alexander Dallin, eds., *U.S.-Soviet Security Cooperation: Achievements, Failures, Lessons* (New York: Oxford University Press, 1988).

103.   Larson, *Anatomy of Mistrust*, p. 6.

104.   Ibid., pp. 12, 243.

105.   Ibid., p. 32.

106.   Ibid., p. 12.

107.   Ibid., p. 3.

108.   Ibid., p. 36.

crete events can be risky if one does not have an extended time series of observations," Larson engages in extensive process-tracing of developments in each period.[109] "Process-tracing," she maintains, "is essential for uncovering the causal mechanism—in this case, cognitive processes [by the actors] of interpretation and inference."[110]

Her case studies lead to an important finding: "Where the superpowers successfully reached cooperative agreements—the Limited Test Ban Treaty, the first Strategic Arms Limitations Treaty (SALT I), the Intermediate-Range Nuclear Forces (INF) Treaty—one side demonstrated its good intentions through several conciliatory actions, and it is difficult to envision how a cooperative outcome could have been achieved otherwise."[111] Here and elsewhere she documents the role of trust-building measures.

In cases of missed opportunities, she notes, "one must study non-events—things that did not happen. . . . To explain the causes of non-events, the analyst will have to vary initial conditions mentally . . . one should identify the critical turning points and consider whether alternative actions might have made a difference."[112]

JOHN M. OWEN IV, *LIBERAL PEACE, LIBERAL WAR: AMERICAN POLITICS AND INTERNATIONAL SECURITY.* ITHACA: CORNELL UNIVERSITY PRESS, 1997. The author cites a suggestion made by Joseph Nye that the democratic peace thesis needs "exploration via detailed case studies to look at what actually happened in particular instances."[113] This is, indeed, what Owen does in this study. He examines ten war-threatening crises involving the United States between the 1790s and the close of the nineteenth century "to see precisely what keeps liberal states at peace with one another and what leads them to war with illiberal states."[114]

The need for small-n studies, Owen maintains, "stems from the requirements of establishing causality." Large-N quantitative methods can establish correlations, and in such studies one can control for other variables "to see whether other possible causes can wholly account for the effect." But even so, "there remains a black box between cause and effect" and it is within the black box that in-depth case studies attempt to make observations.[115] Owen also discusses the limitations of using a rational choice framework to suggest what occurs in the black boxes of decision-making and strategic interaction.[116]

Owen prefers to employ liberalism rather than democracy as providing the main impetus leading to the absence of war between liberal states. He stresses the importance of the adversary states' perceptions of each other and employs developmental

---

109.   David Collier, "The Comparative Method: Two Decades of Change," in Dankwart A. Rustow and Kenneth Erickson, eds., *Comparative Political Dynamics* (New York: Harper Collins, 1991), p. 19.

110.   Larson, *Anatomy of Mistrust,* p. 37.

111.   Ibid., p. 241.

112.   Ibid., p. 244.

113.   Joseph S. Nye, Jr., *Understanding International Conflicts* (New York: Harper Collins, 1993), p. 40.

114.   Owen, *Liberal Peace, Liberal War,* p. 5.

115.   Ibid., pp. 10–11. In this context Owen cites the emphasis on the need to go "beyond correlations"; see David Dessler, "Beyond Correlations: Toward a Causal Theory of War," *International Studies Quarterly,* Vol. 35, No. 3 (September 1991), pp. 337–355.

116.   Owen, *Liberal Peace, Liberal War,* p. 11–12.

analysis within each case to show liberalism at work in three types of cases. In the first group of cases he employs a before-after type of research design in which "liberals in state A sometimes shifted from a belligerent to a cooperative attitude with state B when B liberalized internally."[117]

In other cases he notes that subjects in state A advocated policies toward B "in violation of their immediate material interest." In a third group of cases, subjects in state A disagreed over whether B was a threat, and their disagreement reflected judgments about whether B was a liberal state.

In all three types of cases, Owen maintains, one cannot understand state A's perceptions of state B and the strategies A employed (and thus the crisis outcomes) without understanding the role of ideology.[118]

Owen places emphasis on how liberalism gives rise to both a foreign policy ideology and political institutions that translate that ideology into policy. He also illustrates the validity of this argument via ten historical cases. In each case, a liberal state, the United States, was in immediate danger of war. Sometimes the war crisis would be with a state that U.S. elites and citizens considered a fellow liberal state. Sometimes the crisis was with a state thought to be despotic, and at other times with a state on which U.S. opinion was deeply divided.

Owen also addresses an important counterargument, which holds that liberal perceptions may be the consequences of other variables, a position taken in recent works by Stephen Walt and Jack Snyder.[119] He also takes issue with ideas expressed in early works by Kenneth Waltz and Theodore Lowi.[120]

This leads Owen to use process-tracing and structured, focused comparison in order to identify causal pathways. Finally, Owen avoids making simplistic or unqualified claims for his theory.[121]

MICHAEL KREPON AND DAN CALDWELL, EDS., *THE POLITICS OF ARMS CONTROL TREATY RATIFICATION.* NEW YORK: ST. MARTIN'S PRESS, 1991.

This collaborative study adheres strictly to the procedural requirements of the structured, focused method. The authors note that the politics of treaty ratification of arms control agreements in the United States is a relatively unexplored area compared to the voluminous research and memoirs concerning negotiations of such agreements with other states. They also point out that there have been few theoretically informed analyses of treaty ratification and call attention to Robert Putnam's observation in his seminal essay on two-level games that a more adequate account of the domestic determinants of foreign policy and international relations must stress domestic as well as political factors.[122]

The subclass of treaty ratifications chosen for study was limited in several ways. During the past two hundred years, the Senate has approved more than 1,500 treaties, approximately 90 percent of those submitted to it by the president; many others failed because they were withdrawn by the president or because the Senate's leadership

117.   Ibid.

118.   Ibid., p. 20.

119.   Ibid., pp. 51–55.

120.   Ibid., pp. 55–56.

121.   Ibid., pp. 9, 10, 63, 229.

122.   Robert D. Putnam, "Diplomacy and Domestic Politics: The Logic of Two-Level Games," *International Organization*, Vol. 42, No. 3 (Summer 1988), pp. 427–460.

chose not to bring them to a vote when it appeared unlikely they could achieve the two-thirds majority required for approval. Only seventeen treaties were actually rejected by the Senate.[123]

In selecting cases for the study, the authors decided to focus on treaties that limited weapons in some way and were negotiated in the twentieth century. This still left quite a few candidate cases. To winnow down the list, two additional selection criteria were employed; the cases must be considered particularly important by both the academic and policymaking communities and they must provide a mix of ratification successes and failures. Based on these criteria, seven cases were selected for analysis: the Versailles Treaty, the Washington Naval Treaties, the Geneva Protocol, the Limited Test Ban Treaty, the Antiballistic Missile (ABM) Treaty, the Second Strategic Arms Limitations (SALT II) Treaty, and the Intermediate-Range Nuclear Forces (INF) Treaty.

To ensure systematic comparison of the cases, the two project leaders formulated a set of questions to be asked of each case in order to obtain the data required to satisfy the research objective of the study. To assess the adequacy of the questions, an iterative procedure was followed. After initial case study drafts were written, the questions were reformulated and used as the basis for the final analysis of the seven cases.

The project leaders asked writers of each case analysis to answer a common set of questions and to structure the organization and presentation of each case according to the framework the questions provided. "As a result," the coeditors note, "the case studies . . . have been written on the basis of a common analytical and organizational framework, and comparison across cases has thereby been facilitated."[124]

The set of standardized questions fell into five substantive areas: the international political context of the treaty; the domestic political context; the role of the president; executive-congressional relations; and public opinion and the role of interest groups.

Given the deliberately limited selection of cases, the coeditors appropriately note that attempts to extrapolate the findings of the study to other types of treaties would "require the utmost caution."[125] This was a hypothesis-forming exercise that relied exclusively on process-tracing.

Finally, the project leaders selected a mix of historians, political scientists, and former policymakers to do the case studies in the expectation that this would contribute to the intellectual vitality of the project.[126]

DANIEL W. DREZNER, *THE SANCTIONS PARADOX: ECONOMIC STATECRAFT AND INTERNATIONAL RELATIONS.* CAMBRIDGE: CAMBRIDGE UNIVERSITY PRESS, 1999. This book effectively employs the research strategy of "triangulation." Drezner employs game theory to develop a "conflict expectations model." He then tests the model against alternative explanations employing a variety of quantitative and qualitative methodologies.

A "robust model," he writes, "should find empirical support using different methodologies. Statistics, comparative analysis, and case studies," he maintains, "all have their advantages in hypothesis testing." Statistics can demonstrate "significant

---

123.   Krepon and Caldwell, eds., *The Politics of Arms Control Treaty Ratification,* p. 7.

124.   Ibid., p. 8.

125.   Ibid., p. 13.

126.   Ibid., p. 113. We are indebted to Michael Krepon, one of the project leaders, for providing us with a detailed account of the problems encountered in following strictly the requirements of the structured, focused method.

correlations across a large number of events. Usually, however, the data are too coarse to permit any serious examination of the causal mechanisms."[127] Drezner uses Charles Ragin's comparative method that employs the logic of Boolean algebra to test for combinations of causes and assess causal complexity. Drezner also notes its limitations.

The author endorses the utility of the method of structured, focused comparison, noting that it has "the singular advantage of identifying causal mechanisms with a smaller chance of producing spurious results." But the small number of cases employed in this method "inherently limits the generalizability of the results."[128]

Awareness that each of these methodologies has limitations leads the author also to use "triangulation." That is, used in concert these methodologies "can offer compelling support to bolster or reject a hypothesis. . . . Large-N and small-n approaches can complement each other in the testing of international relations theory."[129]

Drezner first outlines the testable implications of his "conflict expectations" model. Then he tests them by using a combination of statistical, comparative, and process-tracing methods. The statistical tests support the model, but he undertakes comparative case studies and process-tracing of instances of Russia's use of economic coercion against the newly independent states of the former Soviet Union to see whether the causal mechanisms postulated by the model are actually present.[130] Process-tracing is also employed to assess a major hypothesis he develops in examining the role of sanctions and positive inducements in economic statecraft.[131] In one chapter, Drezner supplements process-tracing, for which historical data are limited, with the congruence method and finds that both methods support the model's hypothesis as applied to U.S. efforts to deal with South Korea and North Korea's nuclear aspirations.[132] The author concludes with a useful discussion of the theoretical and methodological limits to his work.[133]

In his brief summation of this rich study, Drezner states that its main contribution is a demonstration that "the range and utility of economic coercion is more varied than previously thought. . . . Economic coercion between adversaries is likely to be . . . less successful at forcing concessions "than economic coercion between allies," for reasons consistent with the expectations of his model and supported by the various methodologies he has employed.[134]

PAUL K. HUTH, *EXTENDED DETERRENCE AND THE PREVENTION OF WAR.* NEW HAVEN: YALE UNIVERSITY PRESS, 1988.
The objective of this study is to identify political and military conditions that affect the success or failure of a deterrence commitment by a strong power in support of an ally. Huth's research strategy combines large-N statistical analysis with a more detailed examination of a smaller number of cases. He regards the integration of these two meth-

---

127. Drezner, *The Sanctions Paradox: Economic Statecraft and International Relations,* pp. 21–22.

128. Ibid., p. 22.

129. Ibid., pp. 21–22.

130. Ibid., chaps. 5, 6, and 7.

131. Ibid., chap. 8.

132. Ibid., p. 303.

133. Ibid., pp. 311–321.

134. Ibid., p. 321.

ods as "the most productive method for deriving generalizations about political behavior. The two approaches are essential to the development and verification of theories in social science research."[135]

His procedure is to formulate and then empirically test a set of hypotheses about factors that influence deterrence outcomes. The theoretical focus of the study is on how the balance of military capabilities, alternative strategies of bargaining, past behavior, and issues at stake affect the credibility and/or stability of the defender's deterrent posture and actions.[136]

Huth identified fifty-eight cases of attempted extended deterrence between 1885 and 1984. He believes this comprises the entire universe of cases during the period, thereby avoiding questions of case selection bias for the large-N component of the study. Twenty-four of these cases were coded as deterrence failures; thirty-four as successes.[137]

The research objective and the statistical analysis of this study require cases that provide variance in the outcome of deterrence efforts—cases of both deterrence success and deterrence failure. Huth broadly defines successful deterrence as instances "in which the potential attacker [either] refrains from using military force or engages in small-scale combat with the protégé (fewer than 200 combined fatalities among the regular armed forces of both sides) and fails to force the defender to capitulate to its demands under the threat of force." Huth recognized that it can be difficult to identify cases of successful deterrence, and he closely surveyed secondary sources and consulted with country experts and diplomatic historians in coding the cases. The counterpart to the definition of successful deterrence was used to code cases of deterrence failure.[138]

Ten cases were examined in more detail in order to evaluate generalizations suggested by the statistical analysis of the fifty-six overall cases. Several criteria were employed for choosing cases for more detailed analysis: cases must be recognized by experts as the most important; cases must provide diversity in geographic regions and time periods; and perhaps more interestingly, cases must "deviate from the expected results to illustrate some possible limitations and necessary refinements in the generalizations" that were suggested by the statistical analysis.[139]

The qualitative analysis of the ten cases distinguishes between those in which military calculations were particularly important in influencing outcomes and those in which more broadly defined political reputational variables played a more important role in determining outcomes.

D. MICHAEL SHAFER, *DEADLY PARADIGMS: THE FAILURE OF U.S. COUNTERINSURGENCY POLICY.* **PRINCETON, N.J.: PRINCETON UNIVERSITY PRESS,** 1988.

The puzzle that motivated this study was Shafer's observation that "despite changes in the international distribution of power, presidential administrations, bureaucratic coalitions and capabilities, the locale of the conflict and nature of the insurgencies, and the governments they threaten," there existed a continuity in U.S. policymakers' assessments of the sources of insurgency and prescriptions for assisting governments

---

135. Huth, *Extended Deterrence and the Prevention of War*, pp. 13–14.

136. Ibid., p. 13.

137. Ibid., pp. 23–26.

138. Ibid., pp. 26–27.

139. Ibid., p. 85.

threatened by it during the period from 1945 to 1965. Explaining this continuity is the major research objective of this study.[140] Accordingly, the subclass of all counterinsurgency efforts singled out for the study is appropriately limited to U.S. efforts during the period; this, of course, limits the scope of the findings, though it generates important hypotheses for consideration in other studies.

A complex research strategy is developed that makes explicit use of the method of structured, focused comparison and relies on process-tracing in the case studies to supplement use of the congruence method.

Shafer assesses the contribution of four theories—realism, presidential politics, bureaucratic politics, and "American exceptionalism"—to the explanation of the puzzle. The argument he develops is that while these approaches indeed contribute to understanding the problem, they are insufficient for explaining the puzzle. This makes necessary a fifth approach that focuses on cognitive variables—U.S. policymakers' strategic codes, assumptions about American interests in the world, perceptions of political threats, and feasible responses.

To test and support his argument for the fifth approach, Shafer selects several cases that provide tough tests. The cases chosen "had to be 'critical cases,' those in which my explanation was either least or most likely to hold. By this logic, if the explanation applied where [it was] least likely, then it had promise; conversely, if it could be disproved where most likely to fit, then it offered little [promise]."[141]

Two cases of U.S.-supported counterinsurgency efforts, in Greece and the Philippines, constitute the most-likely "type of tough test in that since they constitute counterinsurgency successes they were most likely to give support to the reliance and effectiveness of American counterinsurgency doctrine."[142] Thus, to be able to claim, as Shafer does, that U.S. counterinsurgency policy was "irrelevant or counterproductive [in these cases] . . . constitutes the strongest possible test of my explanation" and supports it.[143]

The Vietnam case does not serve as a tough test and has a different purpose. Shafer's argument is that because the failure of U.S. counterinsurgency in Vietnam is so often attributed to the cognitive model he advances, "it is essential to demonstrate that other models do not offer better explanations and that mine applies."[144]

Shafer's book is marked by an unusual degree of methodological self-consciousness. He remarks on why reliance on Mill's methods is unsatisfactory, which makes it necessary to undertake process-tracing in each case.

Also interesting is the similarity of his research design in some respects to Graham Allison's three accounts of the Cuban Missile Crisis in *Essence of Decision*. Shafer presents "three very different, equally plausible accounts . . . by asking different questions of different kinds of evidence" that allow analysts to reach very different conclu-

---

140. The author also undertook two secondary research objectives that address the question why U.S. counterinsurgency beliefs were incorrect and what their effects were.

141. Shafer, *Deadly Paradigms*, p. 14. Two other criteria for case selection were that the cases should be "manifestly important and of some duration," and that they should differ on critical variables. With respect to the latter criterion, Shafer indicates that his aim was to show that explanations based on the other four theories "do not explain continuity across cases, while my focus on policymakers' insensitivity to variation across cases does."

142. Ibid., p. 14.

143. Ibid.

144. Ibid., p. 15.

sions.[145] Also noteworthy is Shafer's methodology, which combines the congruence method with process-tracing.

DAN CALDWELL, *AMERICAN-SOVIET RELATIONS: FROM 1947 TO THE NIXON-KISSINGER GRAND DESIGN.* WESTPORT, CONN.: GREENWOOD PRESS, 1981.

A major objective of this study was to analyze U.S.-Soviet interactions from 1947 through 1976. Caldwell divided this era into three periods: the acute Cold War (1947–1962), the limited détente (1963–1968), and the détente period (1969–1976). This division facilitates an assessment of the effect of variance in the overall U.S.-Soviet relationship on interactions between them.

The author chose to focus on interactions in three issue areas: crisis management, economic relations, and arms control. These issue areas were chosen for several reasons, among them their high degree of salience in the overall relationship.

Part Two of the study employed structured, focused comparison to assess the ways in which U.S.-Soviet interactions in these three issue areas varied under different systemic conditions. To highlight the comparison, Caldwell selected cases from the first and third periods. This enabled the author to make a sharper assessment of the importance of the shift from acute Cold War to détente on their interaction in the three issue areas. (A number of other criteria also entered into case selection). After identifying all significant U.S.-Soviet interactions during these two periods, Caldwell selected one major case in each issue area for each of the two periods:

The comparison of matched cases enabled Caldwell to identify the extent to which U.S. and Soviet interaction differed in each issue area in each period and to develop plausible explanations for the contrasting outcomes. A variety of factors were considered in explaining outcomes.[146] Caldwell gave particular attention to the development of procedures, rules, and new U.S.-Soviet institutions over the course of the entire period that led to at least a partial regime for each issue-area.[147] A number of reasons for differences in U.S.-Soviet crisis management behavior in the Cuban Missile Crisis and October War cases are discussed.[148] Following the onset of the Cold War, several important norms were developed for managing crises to prevent unwanted escalation.

Figure A.3. U.S.-Soviet Interactions Under Different Systemic Conditions

ISSUE AREA	PERIOD 1947-1962	PERIOD 1969-1976
Economic	Trade Negotiation 1958-1961	Trade Agreement 1972
Arms Control	London Subcommittee Negotiations, 1955-1957	Strategic Arms Limitations Treaty 1969-1972
Crisis Management	Cuban Missile Crisis, 1962	Middle East October War, 1973

---

145.   Ibid., pp. 25ff.

146.   Caldwell, *American-Soviet Relations*, pp. 170ff.

147.   Ibid., cf. e.g., pp. 181, 200.

148.   Ibid., pp. 228ff.

Since Caldwell was writing on recent, often controversial aspects of superpower relations, very little classified data was available. Therefore, he worked with a range of readily available sources and he interviewed former U.S. policymakers.[149]

THOMAS F. HOMER-DIXON, *ENVIRONMENT, SCARCITY, AND VIOLENCE.*
PRINCETON, N.J.: PRINCETON UNIVERSITY PRESS, 1999.
This book synthesizes the findings of a large number of research projects Homer-Dixon has directed since 1989 that involved more than one hundred experts from fifteen countries. These studies, together with research by other groups, reveal a clearer picture of the links between "environmental stress" and "violence" that the author presents in this most recent of his many publications. Homer-Dixon emphasizes the difficulty of identifying the causal role that environmental scarcity plays in social breakdown and violence. The picture he provides in this book is "still, in some ways, only a preliminary sketch," though useful observations are presented in detail.

Homer-Dixon stresses that the research program did not aim to identify all the factors that cause violent conflict around the world; "rather it sought to determine whether a specific factor—environmental scarcity—can be an important cause of conflict."[150] This required careful clarification of key concepts and a focus on the possible causal roles of environmental scarcity. The author also found it advisable to narrow the scope of the problem in several ways. First, he moved from the very broad class of events identified as "environmental security," which "encompasses an almost unmanageable array of sub-issues," to a narrower focus on how environmental stress affects conflict rather than security. But this, he finds, still leaves the problem "too vast," and he narrows it further by focusing only on "how environmental stress affects violent national and international conflict."[151] Therefore, Homer-Dixon follows the procedure of defining an important subclass of a larger phenomenon in order to undertake useful research.

Homer-Dixon relies on process-tracing "to identify general patterns of environment-conflict linkages across multiple cases."[152] Researchers in the project "used an exacting, step-by-step analysis of the causal processes operating in each of our regional and country cases." He identifies seven variables that affect the causal relationship between political-economic factors, environmental scarcity, social stress, and violent conflict.[153] He also provides an unusually detailed discussion and defense of his approach to "hypothesis testing and case selection."[154]

Homer-Dixon notes that a number of methods are available for testing hypotheses in environment-conflict research. Two are conventional quasi-experimental methods (correlational analysis of a large number of cases, and controlled case comparison). The third is process-tracing of the kind described by Alexander George and Timothy McKeown.[155] Homer-Dixon defends his reliance on process-tracing by noting that "the stage of research strongly influences the method of hypothesis testing a researcher can use to best advantage."[156] He believes that process-tracing is advanta-

---

149. Ibid., p. xii.

150. Homer-Dixon, *Environment, Scarcity, and Violence*, p. 6.

151. Ibid., p. 3.

152. Ibid., p. 9.

153. Ibid., Appendix to chap. 5, pp. 104–106.

154. Ibid., Appendix to chap. 7, pp. 169–176.

155. Alexander L. George and Timothy J. McKeown, "Case Studies and Theories of

geous particularly in the early stages of research on highly complex subjects. In these circumstances "hypotheses are liable to be too crude to support testing that involves quantitative analysis of a large number of cases." Research resources are used to best advantage "by examining cases that appear, *prima facie*, to demonstrate the causal relations hypothesized."[157]

It is in this context that Homer-Dixon provides a detailed argument for selecting on the dependent as well as the independent variables. He recognizes that this could lead to criticisms of biased case selection, but defends the procedure by noting that process-tracing was used mainly on cases characterized as having both environmental scarcity and violent conflict (rather than cases in which environmental scarcity was neither a necessary nor sufficient cause of violent conflict). In response to criticism of his focus on cases embracing both environmental scarcity and violent conflict, Homer-Dixon argues that in the early stages of research, such a procedure is often the best and sometimes the only way to begin. For particular cases it can show whether or not the proposed independent variable is a cause of the dependent variable. That is, by making use of process-tracing, it answers the question of whether there are "any cases in which the independent variable is causally linked, in a significant and important way, to the dependent variable."[158]

Homer-Dixon notes that in highly complex systems, such as the ecological-political systems he has studied, it is not likely that the proposed independent variable (environmental scarcity) will be a sufficient cause of the dependent variable (violent conflict). Rather, it will be necessary to identify and add "numerous and detailed scope conditions"—i.e., conditional generalizations. Without including adequate scope conditions, "a statistical analysis of the distribution of cases . . . will probably reveal little correlation, even though there might be important and interesting causal links between environmental scarcity and conflict" (i.e., a false negative).[159]

Homer-Dixon notes that in such circumstances "careful process-tracing, involving close examination of the causal process" operating in the cases in which both the independent variable and the dependent variable were present "will help identify the relevant scope conditions."[160] The author notes that researchers can then ask whether the scope conditions and intermediate variables identified via process-tracing were present, and why in other cases in which environmental scarcity existed violent conflict did not ensue. If these factors were present in a case, researchers could attempt to determine what other factors prevented environmental scarcity from causing violent conflict.[161] Thus, Homer-Dixon suggests, researchers can develop from the findings presented more sophisticated hypotheses, and can test them using a broader range of methodologies, including cross-national statistical analysis, counterfactual analysis, and carefully controlled comparisons of cases varied on both the dependent and independent variable. Of particular interest are cases that exhibit all the condi-

Organizational Decision Making," in Robert F. Coulam and Richard A. Smith, eds., *Advances in Information Processing in Organizations,* Vol. 2 (Greenwich, Conn.: JAI Press, 1985), pp. 31–32.

156.   Homer-Dixon, *Environment, Scarcity, and Violence,* p. 171.

157.   Ibid.

158.   Ibid., pp. 172–173.

159.   Ibid.

160.   Ibid., pp. 173–174.

161.   Ibid., p. 174.

tions hypothesized to produce violence (including environmental scarcity) that do not result in violence.[162]

In summarizing the findings of this research program, Homer-Dixon emphasizes that "environmental scarcity by itself is neither a necessary nor a sufficient cause of violent conflict . . . when it does play a role, it always interacts with other contextual factors—be they physical or social—to generate violence." To gauge the relative causal contribution of environmental scarcity "is especially intractable. . . . I therefore try to avoid entangling myself in the metaphysical debate about the relative importance of causes." But Homer-Dixon is able to show that for many conflicts around the world, violence "cannot be properly understood or explained without taking account of the causal role of environmental scarcity."[163]

Homer-Dixon subscribes to the emphasis we have given to the diagnostic rather than the prescriptive contribution that policy-relevant research can make. Each case of environmentally induced conflict "is complex and unique. . . . Policy tools available in one case will not be available in another. . . . Successful policy intervention thus requires customization based on a careful analysis of the character of the specific case and of the policy tools available in that case." In this book, Homer-Dixon emphasizes, "I can do no more than give policymakers a rough understanding of key causal processes and of useful intervention points in these processes."[164]

ALEXANDER L. GEORGE AND RICHARD SMOKE, *DETERRENCE IN AMERICAN FOREIGN POLICY: THEORY AND PRACTICE.* NEW YORK: COLUMBIA UNIVERSITY PRESS, 1974.

This was the first study to make explicit use of the three phases of structured, focused comparison. The research objectives were, first, to subject the then-dominant abstract, deductive theory of deterrence to critical examination; second, to question its suitability as a prescriptive model for policymaking; and third, to call attention to the fact that deterrence theory does not adequately define its own scope or relevance as an instrument of foreign policy and must be absorbed into a broader influence theory for dealing with the conflict potential in interstate relations.[165]

The authors studied a particular subclass of efforts to employ extended deterrence; they focused on eleven U.S. efforts during the Cold War to employ this strategy on behalf of weaker allies and friendly neutrals. The authors explicitly forego efforts to

---

162.   Ibid., p. 182.

163.   Ibid., p. 7.

164.   Ibid., p. 10. Homer-Dixon's research program was critically assessed by Nils Petter Gleditsch, "Armed Conflict and the Environment: A Critique of the Literature," *Journal of Peace Research,* Vol. 35, No. 3 (May 1998), pp. 381–400. A detailed reply was published by Daniel M. Schwartz, Tom Deligiannis, and Thomas Homer-Dixon, "The Environment and Violent Conflict: A Response to Gleditsch's Critique and Some Suggestions for Future Research," *Environmental Report: Change and Security Project,* Issue No. 6 (Washington, D.C.: The Woodrow Wilson Center, Summer 2000), pp. 77–94. The authors indicate that their reply "makes use of our work in preparation and highlights misunderstandings of ways in which case studies and process-tracing contribute to theory development." The exchange also appears in Paul F. Diehl and Nils Petter Gleditsch, eds., *Environmental Conflict* (Boulder, Colo.: Westview Press, 2000).

165.   Seven questionable assumptions and simplifications of the early abstract, deductive theory of deterrence were identified and subjected to critical examination. See George and Smoke, *Deterrence in American Foreign Policy,* pp. 71–82, 503–508.

generalize from this subclass to the total universe of deterrence efforts. The scope of the findings is appropriately delimited.[166]

A standard list of general questions was developed and employed in each of the case studies to ensure comparability and cumulation.

The third phase of the study ("Toward a Reformulation of Deterrence Theory") draws on the case findings to develop a more refined, empirically grounded, and differentiated theory of deterrence than the abstract deductive theory. The case studies examined made use of process-tracing to derive explanations of the outcomes of deterrence efforts. Since valid identification of cases of deterrence success is extremely difficult, no cases of this kind were included in the study.[167] However, some instances of deterrence failure that were studied could also be regarded as partial successes, since the adversary chose limited options for challenging deterrence rather than all-out attacks. In reformulating deterrence theory, the authors presented propositions and hypotheses (derived indirectly from analysis of deterrence failures) regarding conditions that would "favor" deterrence success, though not necessarily serving as necessary or sufficient conditions for success.

The authors noted that the defender's strategy and tactics for achieving extended deterrence had received the most attention in early deterrence theory. Several criticisms were offered: early deterrence theory contained an oversimplified conceptualization of the defender's "commitment" to weaker allies. This theory took too narrow of an approach in discussing how credibility of commitments might be achieved. These limitations of early deterrence theory stemmed from its apolitical treatment of deterrence strategy and a narrow technocratic conceptualization of the task of establishing and maintaining deterrence.

George and Smoke also noted that the decision of states on whether to and how to challenge a defender's deterrence effort had received much less attention and insufficiently detailed analysis in early deterrence theory. Accordingly, they presented a formulation of "initiation theory."[168] In addition, their study of deterrence outcomes focused on how the initiator's choice of a strategy for challenging a deterrence commitment was guided by its perception of the nature of the defender's commitment.

Eight variables having to do with the initiator's utility calculations were drawn from the case analyses. Two of them were singled out as of major significance: the initiator's estimate of whether he or she could calculate and control the risks of each of the several options available for challenging deterrence; and the initiator's view of the defender's commitment, which could take one of three forms: (1) the initiator's belief (correct or incorrect) that the defender had not made a commitment to forcefully oppose an attack on a weak ally or friendly neutral; (2) the initiator's uncertainty

---

166.   That George and Smoke delimit the scope of these findings is overlooked in the critique by Christopher Achen and Duncan Snidal, "Rational Deterrence Theory and Comparative Case Studies," *World Politics*, Vol. 41, No. 2 (January 1989), p. 162. These two authors correctly emphasize that the findings of a nonrandom sample cannot be projected to the entire universe of deterrence cases, something which, in fact, George and Smoke do not do.

Achen and Snidal are often quoted by other writers only for their criticism of case selection bias in small-n research on deterrence. It is important to note their favorable assessment of key aspects of the George-Smoke study (see below, endnote 171) and their emphasis in the conclusion of their article on the indispensable role that case studies play in the development of theory, and in the rational deterrence type theory they favor (p. 161).

167.   George and Smoke, *Deterrence in American Foreign Policy*, pp. 516–517.

168.   Ibid., chap. 17.

Figure A.4. Typology of Deterrence Failure (causal patterns of the different ways deterrence can fail).

Variable: Initiator (I) challenges deterrence when he believes the risks of doing so are sufficiently calculable and/or controllable. This determines whether I challenges deterrence.

Variable: But how the Initiator will challenge deterrence -- i.e., what type of option he will utilize -- will be influenced by I's view of the Defender's commitment

These two variables interact to produce three types of deterrence failure:

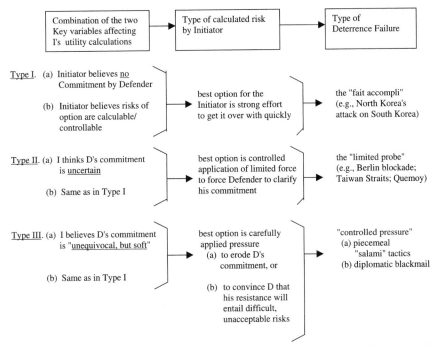

whether the defender had made a commitment to defend an ally; or (3) the initiator's belief that the defender's commitment was "soft" and subject to erosion by tactics for challenging it.[169]

Case findings suggested that a relatively parsimonious theory for explaining dif-

---

169. In addition to these two conditions (variables), which played a critical role in the initiator's decision whether and how to challenge deterrence, six other conditions or variables affecting the initiator's response to a possible commitment were identified. These had to do with the initiator's evaluation of (a) the adequacy and appropriateness of the defender's military capabilities for dealing with different options available to the initiator for challenging deterrence; (b) the evaluation of the strength of the defender's motivation to respond to the initiator's options; (c) the belief whether only force or the threat of force by the initiator could bring about a change in the status quo it desired; (d) whether the initiator was willing to consider the possibility of some kind of compensation in return for foregoing a challenge to deterrence; (e) the strength of the initiator's desire to change the status quo by challenging deterrence; and (f) the time pressure felt by the initiator to secure the desired change. These six conditions influenced the initiator's two major utility calculations identified above.

Figure A.5. Three Interrelated Components of Deterrence Theory.

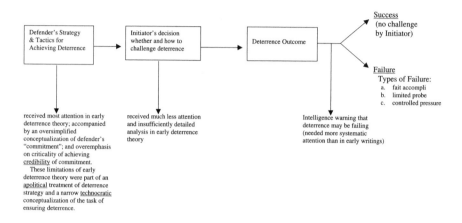

ferent types of deterrence failures could be formulated by focusing on the interaction of these two major conditions. In this way, a typology of deterrence failures was identified that noted three different ways in which the two conditions interacted. These three patterns of deterrence failure and their explanations are summarized in Figure A.4, "Typology of Deterrence Failures." In all three types of deterrence failure, the initiator believed that the risks of deterrence by means of a particular method were calculable and controllable. However, the initiator's view of the defender's commitment varied and led to a different type of challenge to deterrence. The three types of deterrence failure were the "fait accompli" attack, the "limited probe," and the "controlled pressure" tactic (which entailed resort by the initiator either to piecemeal "salami tactics," "diplomatic blackmail," or "blockade.") The historical cases of deterrence failure studied were examples of either one or another of these three types.

An interesting—and unanticipated—result of the study was the development of a concatenated theory of deterrence, one that formulated subtheories for important components of the deterrence process. Two of its components have already been discussed—the authors' reformulation of "commitment" theory and of "initiation" theory. The third component of the concatenated theory was arrived at by noting that in a number of the historical cases, deterrence failed in stages. This gave the defender an opportunity to respond in some fashion as the crisis developed before deterrence failed entirely. This led the authors to formulate another component of deterrence theory, "Response Theory," which identified various options for responding to warnings that deterrence might be failing. The three components of the concatenated theory are depicted in Figure A.5.

The authors claim that their concatenated theory should help policy analysts and policymakers to make better diagnoses of new situations that arise.[170] Awareness that extended deterrence can fail in three different ways should contribute to a better ca-

---

170. At many points in the study, the authors emphasize that the chief contribution of an investigation of this kind is to enhance the ability to diagnose new cases correctly (pp. 3, 97, 505, 509–512, 622–624, 631, 635). On the importance of the diagnostic value of case study research, see also Chapter 12.

pacity for identifying and evaluating warning indicators that deterrence may be failing and, more generally, to facilitate the all-important situation analysis needed for fine-tuning policy.[171]

171.　Despite their criticism of comparative case study research on deterrence, Achen and Snidal acknowledge the important contributions of the George-Smoke study, labeling it "a sophisticated version of `middle-range theory'" which presents a "major reformulation of deterrence theory. . . . The discovery of empirical generalizations . . . is a considerable achievement, and a success that only comparative case studies are likely to achieve." Continuing, "in the hands of George and Smoke, the case-study approach helps to generate theory in a very direct way. Indeed generalizations like theirs are a necessary condition for building relevant theory. . . . George and Smoke argue correctly that the deterrence failures of the second and third patterns are not those envisaged by the conventional rational deterrence theory. . . . They are clearly of major importance for policy, and in theory as well. The discovery of empirical generalizations like these . . . is a considerable achievement, and a success that only comparative case studies are likely to achieve." Achen and Snidal, "Rational Deterrence Theory and Comparative Case Studies," pp. 155–156; see also pp. 161, 167–168.

　For a more recent statement summarizing the state of deterrence theory and practice, see Alexander L. George, "The Role of Force in Diplomacy: A Continuing Dilemma for U.S. Foreign Policy," in Horst W. Brands, ed., *The Use of Force After the Cold War* (College Station: Texas A&M University Press, 2000), especially pp. 73–80.

Index

BCSIA Studies in International Security

Published by The MIT Press

Sean M. Lynn-Jones and Steven E. Miller, series editors
Karen Motley, executive editor
Belfer Center for Science and International Affairs (BCSIA)
John F. Kennedy School of Government, Harvard University

Agha, Hussein, Shai Feldman, Ahmad Khalidi, and Zeev Schiff, *Track-II Diplomacy: Lessons from the Middle East* (2003)

Allison, Graham T., Owen R. Coté, Jr., Richard A. Falkenrath, and Steven E. Miller, *Avoiding Nuclear Anarchy: Containing the Threat of Loose Russian Nuclear Weapons and Fissile Material* (1996)

Allison, Graham T., and Kalypso Nicolaïdis, eds., *The Greek Paradox: Promise vs. Performance* (1996)

Arbatov, Alexei, Abram Chayes, Antonia Handler Chayes, and Lara Olson, eds., *Managing Conflict in the Former Soviet Union: Russian and American Perspectives* (1997)

Bennett, Andrew, *Condemned to Repetition? The Rise, Fall, and Reprise of Soviet-Russian Military Interventionism, 1973–1996* (1999)

Blackwill, Robert D., and Michael Stürmer, eds., *Allies Divided: Transatlantic Policies for the Greater Middle East* (1997)

Blackwill, Robert D., and Paul Dibb, eds., *America's Asian Alliances* (2000)

Brom, Shlomo, and Yiftah Shapir, eds., *The Middle East Military Balance 1999–2000* (1999)

Brom, Shlomo, and Yiftah Shapir, eds., *The Middle East Military Balance 1999–2000* (2000)

Brown, Michael E., ed., *The International Dimensions of Internal Conflict* (1996)

Brown, Michael E., and Šumit Ganguly, eds., *Fighting Words: Language Policy and Ethnic Relations in Asia* (2003)

Brown, Michael E., and Šumit Ganguly, eds., *Government Policies and Ethnic Relations in Asia and the Pacific* (1997)

Carter, Ashton B., and John P. White, eds., *Keeping the Edge: Managing Defense for the Future* (2001)

de Nevers, Renée, *Comrades No More: The Seeds of Political Change in Eastern Europe* (2003)

Elman, Colin, and Miriam Fendius Elman, eds., *Bridges and Boundaries: Historians, Political Scientists, and the Study of International Relations* (2001)

Elman, Colin, and Miriam Fendius Elman, eds., *Progress in International Relations Theory: Appraising the Field* (2003)

Elman, Miriam Fendius, ed., *Paths to Peace: Is Democracy the Answer?* (1997)

Falkenrath, Richard A., *Shaping Europe's Military Order: The Origins and Consequences of the CFE Treaty* (1994)

Falkenrath, Richard A., Robert D. Newman, and Bradley A. Thayer, *America's Achilles' Heel: Nuclear, Biological, and Chemical Terrorism and Covert Attack* (1998)

Feaver, Peter D., and Richard H. Kohn, eds., *Soldiers and Civilians: The Civil-Military Gap and American National Security* (2001)

Feldman, Shai, *Nuclear Weapons and Arms Control in the Middle East* (1996)

Feldman, Shai, and Yiftah Shapir, eds., *The Middle East Military Balance 2000–2001* (2001)

Forsberg, Randall, ed., *The Arms Production Dilemma: Contraction and Restraint in the World Combat Aircraft Industry* (1994)

Hagerty, Devin T., *The Consequences of Nuclear Proliferation: Lessons from South Asia* (1998)

Heymann, Philip B., *Terrorism and America: A Commonsense Strategy for a Democratic Society* (1998)

Heymann, Philip B., *Terrorism, Freedom, and Security: Winning without War* (2003)

Howitt, Arnold M. and Robyn L. Pangi, eds., *Countering Terrorism: Dimensions of Preparedness* (2003)

Hudson, Valerie M., and Andrea M. den Boer, *Bare Branches: The Security Implications of Asia's Surplus Male Population* (2004)

Kayyem, Juliette N., and Robyn L. Pangi, eds., *First to Arrive: State and Local Responses to Terrorism* (2003)

Kokoshin, Andrei A., *Soviet Strategic Thought, 1917–91* (1998)

Lederberg, Joshua, *Biological Weapons: Limiting the Threat* (1999)

Martin, Lenore G., and Dimitris Keridis, eds., *The Future of Turkish Foreign Policy* (2004)

Shaffer, Brenda, Borders and Brethren: *Iran and the Challenge of Azerbaijani Identity* (2002)

Shields, John M., and William C. Potter, eds., *Dismantling the Cold War: U.S. and NIS Perspectives on the Nunn-Lugar Cooperative Threat Reduction Program* (1997)

Tucker, Jonathan B., ed., *Toxic Terror: Assessing Terrorist Use of Chemical and Biological Weapons* (2000)

Utgoff, Victor A., ed., *The Coming Crisis: Nuclear Proliferation, U.S. Interests, and World Order* (2000)

Williams, Cindy, ed., *Holding the Line: U.S. Defense Alternatives for the Early 21st Century* (2001)

Williams, Cindy, ed., *Filling the Ranks: Transforming the U.S. Military Personnel System* (2004)

The Robert and Renée Belfer Center for Science and International Affairs

Graham T. Allison, Director
John F. Kennedy School of Government
Harvard University
79 JFK Street, Cambridge MA 02138
Tel: (617) 495–1400; Fax: (617) 495–8963
http://www.ksg.harvard.edu/bcsia   bcsia_ksg@harvard.edu

The Belfer Center for Science and International Affairs (BCSIA) is the hub of research, teaching and training in international security affairs, environmental and resource issues, science and technology policy, human rights, and conflict studies at Harvard's John F. Kennedy School of Government. The Center's mission is to provide leadership in advancing policy-relevant knowledge about the most important challenges of international security and other critical issues where science, technology and international affairs intersect.

BCSIA's leadership begins with the recognition of science and technology as driving forces transforming international affairs. The Center integrates insights of social scientists, natural scientists, technologists, and practitioners with experience in government, diplomacy, the military, and business to address these challenges. The Center pursues its mission in four complementary research programs:

- The **International Security Program** (ISP) addresses the most pressing threats to U.S. national interests and international security.

- The **Environment and Natural Resources Program** (ENRP) is the locus of Harvard's interdisciplinary research on resource and environmental problems and policy responses.

- The **Science, Technology and Public Policy Program** (STPP) analyzes ways in which science and technology policy influence international security, resources, environment, and development, and such cross-cutting issues as technological innovation and information infrastructure.

- The **WPF Program on Intrastate Conflict, Conflict Prevention and Conflict Resolution** analyzes the causes of ethnic, religious, and other conflicts, and seeks to identify practical ways to prevent and limit such conflicts.

The heart of the Center is its resident research community of more than 140 scholars: Harvard faculty, analysts, practitioners, and each year a new, interdisciplinary group of research fellows. BCSIA sponsors frequent seminars, workshops and conferences, maintains a substantial specialized library, and publishes books, monographs, and discussion papers.

The Center's International Security Program, directed by Steven E. Miller, publishes the BCSIA Studies in International Security, and sponsors and edits the quarterly journal *International Security*.

The Center is supported by an endowment established with funds from Robert and Renée Belfer, the Ford Foundation and Harvard University, by foundation grants, by individual gifts, and by occasional government contracts.